D0618221

WARNING

READER BEWARE

MANY OF THESE SKILLS

Are to be used specifically in the extended-care setting
- Wilderness
- Disaster
- Remote
- Military
- Extreme / austere environments
- Beyond the Golden Hour

SOME OF THESE SKILLS

Require specific training, practice, and certifications

Are not commonly taught or practiced by pre-hospital personnel in the United States

Are beyond the normal scope of practice for EMS providers

Need the approval of your State Bureau of EMS

WILDCARE™

Working In Less than Desirable Conditions And Remote Environments

By Dr. Frank Hubbell, DO

Published by
Stonehearth Open Learning Opportunities, Inc.
621 Tasker Hill Rd., Conway, NH 03818
www.soloschools.com

All rights reserved. No part of this book may be reproduced or transmitted in any form or by any means, electronic or mechanical, including photocopying, recording, or by any information storage or retrieval system without written permission from the publisher, except for the inclusion of brief quotations in a review.

© 2014 by Franklin R. Hubbell, DO

ISBN: 9780-615-98516-9

Printed in Canada by Friesens Corporation, Altona, Manitoba

DISCLAIMER: Emergency medicine is an ever-changing field, and although the author and publisher have made every effort to ensure that the information in this book was correct at press time, the author and publisher do not assume and hereby disclaim any liability to any party for loss, damage, injury, or disruption caused by errors or omissions, whether such errors or omissions result from negligence, accident, or any other cause. This book has been designed as a companion resource to specific SOLO Wilderness First Responder and Wilderness Emergency Medical Technician courses, and the possession of this book in no way implies or confers upon the owner or user any level of expertise whatsoever. The author and publisher advise readers to take full responsibility for their safety and know their limits—do not take risks beyond your level of experience, aptitude, training, standard of care, licensure, and comfort level.

NOTE: SOLO students appear in some of the photographs and images in this book, and they have granted permission for this use as part of their agreement to take a SOLO course. And while we stress the use of personal BSI protection equipment (e.g., latex gloves) when working on patients, we do not always require its use during mock teaching scenarios—so some people may appear without gloves in some images.

WILDCARE™ is dedicated to the team that made it happen. A book, such as this, is not the accomplishment of an individual, but, rather, the collective work of a highly dedicated and skilled group of individuals who gave a tremendous amount of time and effort to its creation. WILDCARE took several years to complete, and I greatly appreciate all of their contributions, their determination, and belief in this project. Their work on this book, often after hours or on days off, also speaks to their commitment to SOLO, to all of our students, our sponsors, and to one another.

THE WILDCARE TEAM

Frank Hubbell

Frank, the author. As the co-founder and Medical Director of SOLO, I had a vision of wanting to write a book that would be worthy of the spirit of excellence that has been at the heart of SOLO since its inception. SOLO courses have always been a little "different," and WILDCARE is no exception. The purpose of writing this text was to draw upon four decades of my own experiences in outdoor recreation, as well as the knowledge I gained from experts like Murray Hamlet, DVM; in EMS, from EMT to Paramedic; mountain rescues in all conditions using both wilderness and remote medical skills; teaching in urban and austere environments; and practicing as a physician in an urgent care setting. The desire was not simply to organize a lot of words into sentences and paragraphs for a reference manual, but, instead, to create an interactive, exciting teaching text for all SOLO students around the world. For me, this is a dream come true, and I could not have done it without this WILDCARE team. Thanks to all of you and all the staff who believed in and supported this endeavor.

S. Peter Lewis

Peter, the architect. He is the inspiration and creativity behind the layout, design, and overall beauty of the book. He also read, reread, edited, and fretted over every word, diagram, photo, and illustration, insisting on accuracy, consistency, readability, and beauty. His injection of humor throughout the text sets WILDCARE apart from other medical resources.

Ted Walsh

Ted, the illustrator. His incredible ability to combine his artistic talents with his education experience to produce images that are not only beautiful, but teach, is remarkable. His dedication to this book is equaled by his willingness to rethink, redraw, and do whatever had to be done to make it happen and be the best it could be.

Lee Frizzell

Lee, the grammarian. She is the co-founder, Executive Director of SOLO , and my wife. Through her proofreading and editing, Lee "tried" to make me look smart. She applied her skills as a longtime, former English teacher to the words that I put on paper. She not only utilized the rules of grammar, making concessions when she had to, but she also applied her knowledge as both a thirty-five year-long practicing National Registry EMT and NH EMT instructor/coordinator.

Jill MacMillan
Jill, truly a "Jill of All Trades." The Executive Director at SOLO, Jill has been with us from the beginning. She is involved in every aspect of what is going on at SOLO, and she applied that same dedication to this book as well. From her former teacher's perspective and her daily exposure to SOLO's training, she read WILDCARE and noted comments or sections that needed to be clearer or more accessible to the layperson while not oversimplifying those sections for anyone with prior medical knowledge. On occasion, she borrowed Lee's red pen to strike out errant commas or typographical errors.

Josh MacMillan
Josh, the EMS teacher. Assistant Director of Education and Senior Instructor, Josh combined his experience in EMS, ambulance service, mountain rescue, ski patrol, and remote medicine to help to build, rebuild, and design different sections of the book, always keeping in mind his students and their needs.

Paul MacMillan
Paul, the consummate educator. The Director of Education at SOLO, he is an educator's educator. Applying his many years in education as well as EMS, he took the time to read the text for accuracy and teachability to make sure that the book read and taught as well as it possibly could.

THANKS TO THE GREATER SOLO FAMILY

This book is both a team effort and a family affair, and we would like to acknowledge all the people who have worked and volunteered their time, energy, creativity, and skills over the almost 40 years that we have been teaching wilderness medicine and developing curricula—you may not be named here, but we couldn't have done it without you. And to the over 350,000 students who have passed through our doors to date, thank you for the chance to help you develop the skills to save lives.

Dr. Frank Hubbell and Lee Frizzell—the founders of SOLO

CONTENTS

FOREWORD

YOU ARE ABOUT TO EXPERIENCE a significant upgrade from all previous books on wilderness medicine. By significant, I mean more sequentially and logically organized than similar volumes, filled with useful diagrams and photographs, and written with no superfluous text. It is the result of over 40 years of designing, teaching, and working in many remote environments by Dr. Frank Hubbell, who deserves credit for creating the foundation and first offerings for this field, and his team, who believed in his vision. While at the University of New Hampshire in the late 50s, I took the standard first aid courses that were available at the time. Our outing club was (and still is) very active, and we knew that we needed to have the skills to take care of each other, should it be necessary. Working for Outward Bound in the 60s and 70s resulted in supplementing the basic first aid training with training we designed ourselves. Many of us took EMT courses, but then had to figure out what to do when the ambulance didn't appear in ten minutes. Then, about 1980, I attended my first of many SOLO courses and refreshers. I remember thinking to myself, where was this kind of training when I needed it? Frank told us the story about bringing a patient to the ER with an angulated arm fracture and being asked by the doc, "Why didn't you straighten his arm before you splinted it?" Frank knew from that moment that we could be doing a lot more for folks injured when immediate transportation and definitive treatment were not available. Thousands of wilderness emergency medical courses at different levels have been taught on the SOLO campus and in many locations around the country and the world. Applications of this type of training are now being used in disaster situations and austere environments. This reference work raises the bar and provides all of us—those new to the field and seasoned instructors—with a guidebook we will immediately put to good use. Thank you, Frank, et al.

— **John E. (Jed) Williamson**
President Emeritus, *Sterling College*
Editor, *Accidents in North American Mountaineering, '74 – '14*
Co-author, *Manual of Accreditation Standards (AEE)*
Certified Alpine Guide, *American Mountain Guides Association*
Current board member: *Central Asia Institute, Heartbeet*
Former board member: *National Outdoor Leadership School, Student Conservation Association, American Alpine Club, Association for Experiential Education*

INTRODUCTION

WILDCARE: The birth of a dream

Dr. Hubbell, (center, in tan coat) teaches an early SOLO wilderness first aid course at the University of New Hampshire, in 1974. All SOLO staff either are, or have been, practicing in the field of EMS or wilderness education

You are holding in your hands the compilation of over 40 years of experience by the talented, skilled, and dedicated team of medical education professionals at Stonehearth Open Learning Opportunities (SOLO), led by Dr. Frank Hubbell. It was the vision of Frank and his wife Lee Frizzell in 1974, to create the premier and first wilderness medicine school in the United States. With little more than a dream and a piece of forest on a hilltop in New Hampshire, they built a campus, developed curricula, hired and trained staff, and began running courses—and during all this, Frank somehow found enough time to complete medical school. Since then (over 300,000⁺ students later), the dream keeps chugging along, helping people learn to make a difference when bad things happen.

The principles and practices in this book have been developed and refined during the life of SOLO, and they reflect the most up-to-date information in the ever-advancing world of wilderness medicine. Forming the core of this text is the material found in the handouts and support documents of SOLO's Wilderness First Aid (WFA), Wilderness First Responder (WFR), and Wilderness Emergency Technician (WEMT) courses, as well as the wealth of information found between the pages of the Wilderness Medicine Newsletter (a SOLO publication founded in 1988 and still going strong).

All in all, we have pored over more than 1,500 pages of teaching material to bring you this compilation (distillation, really), which represents the best information you will find on the fascinating (and life-changing) subject of wilderness medicine.

The SOLO campus sits on 300 acres at the top of a hill in the White Mountains of New Hampshire. At its heart is Kaila Hall, the main teaching facility, through which multiple thousands of students have passed since 1976.

WHAT THIS BOOK IS (AND WHAT IT IS NOT)

WILDCARE is designed as the companion teaching text for SOLO's courses, primarily the WFR and WEMT programs. Because we want to convey a vast amount of information as concisely as possible, the book has been written and designed using text-bites, captions, bullets and numbered lists, charts, tables, sidebars, illustrations, and photographs, along with traditional paragraphs—it is a blueprint rather than a novel. As such, it is intended primarily to be a tool used by a teacher who will give the background, illustrate with case-studies, flesh out between the lines, and answer the inevitable questions. It is also a good resource for anyone. Our philosophy is to teach principles and application, not medicine-by-numbers. After the course, for all students, regardless of their training level, the book will be an excellent follow-up resource.

HOW THIS BOOK IS STRUCTURED

The book is divided into five sections:

1. **Response, Patient Assessment, and Critical Care**—foundational to all wilderness medicine.

2. **Trauma**— soft tissue injuries, joint and bone trauma, bandaging.

3. **Medical Emergencies**— deteriorating LOC, poison, diabetes, seizures, stroke, behavioral emergencies, fever, shortness of breath, asthma and related disorders, chest pain, acute abdomen.

4. **Environmental Emergencies**— heat- and cold-related injuries, lightning, drowning, dive injuries, altitude issues, bites and stings.

5. **Appendices**—disaster response, survival, water purification, tropical disease, childbirth, plus other things of a back-of-the-book nature.

A note about wilderness

Wilderness medicine is any medical care that takes place far from definitive care (e.g., a hospital), and by "far" we mean a time frame: 60 minutes—the Golden Hour. In traditional emergency medicine, the definition is rather nebulous:

GOLDEN HOUR:

"[A] time period lasting from a few minutes to one hour following [a] traumatic injury being sustained by a casualty, during which there is the highest likelihood that prompt medical treatment will prevent death."

—*Wikipedia*

This is an example of the classic problem-based model where treatment decisions are based on the assumption that the patient will quickly be passed out of the hands of the first responders (EMTs and paramedics) and into the hands of the specialists (physicians and surgeons). It deals primarily with the ***cause*** of the problem and the appropriate immediate care that will stabilize the patient, rather than the ***time*** involved in getting the patient to the hospital.

For our purposes, the Golden Hour is clear—if either time or distance (or both) dictates that a sick or injured person can't be transported to the hospital in one hour or less, then this is a wilderness situation. It may be the traditional wilderness (six miles up some muddy trail), or in some hybrid "wilderness" caused by circumstance (working with a trauma victim in a collapsed building), or just about anywhere in the developing world. Whatever the circumstances, the traditional urban medicine problem-based model of ***response > assessment > treatment > transport to hospital***, all within the Golden Hour, is impossible. We must look beyond that.

So, we will teach the treatments of illnesses and injuries based on both the traditional problem-based model (e.g., with a broken leg, do immediate steps 1,

New Hampshire's Tuckerman Ravine on Mount Washington, a recreational playground whose harsh weather and treacherous terrain often puts careless or unfortunate adventurers way out beyond the Golden Hour.

In 2010, teams of SOLO staffers spent seven weeks in Haiti after a 7.0 magnitude earthquake turned an entire nation into a wilderness area. They spent their time working on the streets and in field hospitals dealing with the traumatic and infectious aftermath of the tragedy.

LEFT: Wilderness? Sure. How much more wildernessy could it get? It's obvious that without a helicopter there's no way you're going to get a hurt person out of here in under 60 minutes.

BELOW: Wilderness? Yup, this is wilderness, too. It just isn't as obvious because there's a hospital around the corner—oops, sorry, its been flattened by an earthquake.

2, 3, etc.), and also a time-based model that goes beyond the Golden Hour (how to continue treatment of that broken leg six hours later while carrying the patient down the trail in a litter that you built with sticks and rope). Here's how we break it down:

1. **First Response**—the first five minutes
2. **Emergency Care**—the first 60 minutes (the Golden Hour)
3. **Extended Care**—the first 24 hours—like it or not, we're in the wilderness now
4. **Remote Care**—days to weeks... you're all you've got

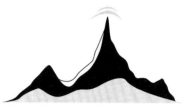

Urban versus Wilderness Medicine Distinctives

1. **We treat things** that in the urban world would be left for ER docs in the hospital:
   - Straightening angulated fractures
   - Reducing dislocations
   - Clearing the spine
   - Cleaning wounds

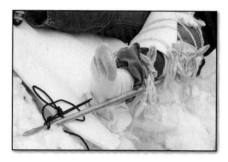

2. **We improvise equipment** typically found on ambulances and in hospitals:
   - Splints/bandages
   - Litters
   - Compression dressings
   - Cervical collars and spinal immobilization

3. **We provide extended care** (beyond the Golden Hour) not only for injuries and illness, but for day-to-day needs:
   - Food/water/pee/poop
   - Protection from the elements
   - Long-term injury/illness treatment
   - Emotional support

4. **We evacuate the patient**, which often requires improvisation:
   - Technical rescue/extrication
   - Litter carries
   - Survival skills (e.g., navigation, weather forecasting)

5. **Documentation**
   - Urban: run forms
   - Wilderness: SOAPnote

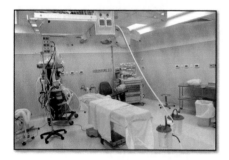

For a detailed look at WILDERNESS AND DISASTER MEDICINE, read the article that follows this introduction.

MANY OF US wander through our ordinary days walking, driving, and working without ever actually touching anything that wasn't made by the hand of man; yet then we close our eyes and our imagination blurs, and suddenly we're in one of those magical places which the hand of man has never touched.

YES, YOU SHOULD GO.

BUT GO PREPARED.

SECTION 1

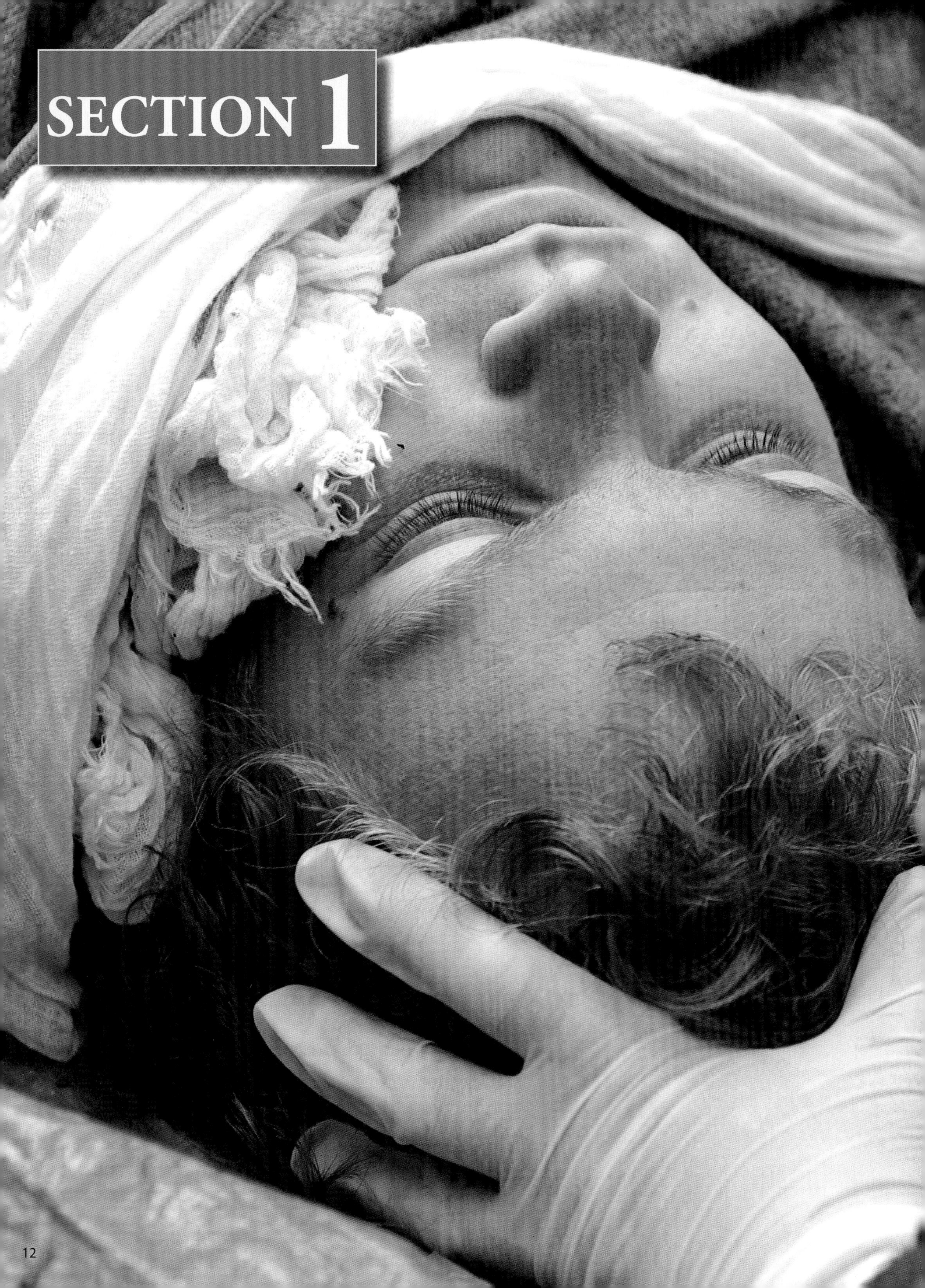

RESPONSE

PATIENT ASSESSMENT &

CRITICAL CARE

Let's go head to toe...

OVERVIEW: THE BIG PICTURE

RESPONSE

Wilderness medical emergencies, by definition,
happen fast—at least initially. Something bad happens, unexpectedly, without warning, just when things are going so well:

- A hiker slips and their ankle snaps.
- An ice fisherman falls through the ice, and their core temperature begins to plummet.
- A bird watcher is stung by a bee and in minutes is having trouble breathing.
- A camper cutting firewood cuts an artery instead.
- Response is simple: it's what you do, and when you do it. In wilderness medicine we break response down as follows:
  - **FIRST RESPONSE**—the first 5 minutes.
  - **EMERGENCY CARE**—the first 60 minutes (the Golden Hour).
  - **EXTENDED CARE**—the first day (the first 24 hours).
  - **REMOTE CARE**—the days and weeks that follow (think disaster or remote medicine).

PATIENT ASSESSMENT SYSTEM

The Patient Assessment System (PAS) is the initial step-by-step process that the responder to an emergency goes through in order to evaluate a patient's physical condition and identify the nature and extent of their injuries or illness. The principles of PAS are:

- **SCENE SAFETY**—ensure that no one, including responders and bystanders, are in danger.
- **BODY SUBSTANCE ISOLATION**—put on clothing or equipment (e.g., gloves, goggles) to protect responders from exposure and contamination.
- **GENERAL IMPRESSION**—your first reaction: is this really bad (obvious life-threatening trauma or medical emergency), not so bad (no one is going to die, but we still have to act quickly and decisively), or minor (just a sprained ankle)?
- **LEVEL OF CONSCIOUSNESS (LOC)**—Conscious or unconscious? Responsive or unresponsive?
- **PRIMARY ASSESSMENT**
  - **A—Airway**: Does the patient have an open, functioning airway?
  - **B—Breathing**: Are they breathing? If so, how well?
  - **C—Circulation**: Do they have a pulse? Is there any obvious bleeding?
  - **D—Deformity**: Are all the patient's limbs intact, and in proper anatomical alignment?
  - **E—Environment**: Are they in a safe place? Can they stay where they are?
- **SECONDARY ASSESSMENT**
  - **Vital signs**: How well is the patient doing?
  - **Patient exam:** What are the patient's specific injuries?
  - **AMPLE History**: What is their past medical history?
  - **SOAPnote**: How should we record their medical data?
- **RESCUE PLAN** How are we going to get help?

CRITICAL CARE ASSESSMENT

Critical care refers to the treatment of immediate life threats that are discovered in the first few minutes of Patient Assessment. These are conditions that must be addressed **NOW**, or the patient will likely get worse or die.

- **CHANGE IN LEVEL OF CONSCIOUSNESS**—can indicate traumatic brain injury, drug overdose, or other major medical emergencies.
- **A COMPROMISED AIRWAY**—you've got about six minutes.
- **SHORTNESS OF BREATH**—has many causes and can indicate a serious emergent[1] condition.
- **SEVERE BLEEDING**—must be controlled immediately or the patient will develop hypovolemic shock and die.
- **CHEST PAIN**—without a trauma mechanism, must be assumed to be a cardiac emergency; may lead to cardiac arrest.
- **ANAPHYLAXIS**—a severe allergic reaction (e.g., from a bee sting) that can cause death by asphyxia.
- **SHOCK**—a serious condition indicating an external or internal circulatory system compromise, which can kill in minutes.

---

1   Emergent: From a medical standpoint, this is any condition that needs immediate treatment. Federal law requires emergency rooms to treat emergent conditions (e.g., heart attack) immediately, regardless of the patient's ability to pay.

URBAN (SHORT-TERM)
VERSUS WILDERNESS CARE (LONG-TERM OR EXTENDED)

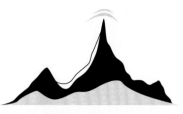

	Urban	*Wilderness*
TIME AND DISTANCE	Within the Golden Hour Rapid notification via technology—usually via 911 Rapid response and evacuation time, usually within minutes	Beyond the Golden Hour Very delayed notification—often via foot, which may take hours Very delayed response and evacuation time, usually hours
ENVIRONMENTAL CONCERNS	Short-term exposure; minimal weather concerns Little or no impact on patient care and rescuers Night/inclement weather/cold add few if any difficulties	Long-term exposure and weather concerns Potentially dramatic impact on patient care and rescuers Night/inclement weather/cold add problems

DIFFICULTY OF TERRAIN	Terrain risks are usually minimal and easily controlled (an exception would be disaster situations with collapsed structures)
	
	Scene safety is almost always easy to manage
	
	Abundant resources are typically available quickly
		Scene safety for rescuers may be difficult to manage
		
		Technical or semi-technical terrain adds risk
		
		Frequent, unavoidable, rough handling of patient (a jostling, uneven litter ride during evacuation is inevitable—especially on uneven terrain)
		
		Difficult footing for rescuers (dangerous)
		
		May require specialized equipment and technical skills
		
		    Climbing equipment
		
		    Specialized litters
		
		    Lowering/raising skills
		
		Semi-technical terrain may require litter passes—which will require more personnel (at least 12 people) than is typical for an evacuation

IMPROVISATION OF EQUIPMENT AND RESOURCES	Easy access to state-of-the art equipment; many other resources readily available	Have to carry emergency gear on your back; minimize weight to maximize efficiency Specialized rescue/medical equipment is typically unavailable The need to improvise equipment is common (splints, litters) Limited access to other resources

SPECIALIZED SKILLS	The need for specialized skills is rare
	
	If specialized skills are necessary (e.g., confined space/high-angle rescue), there are experts to call
	
	If unsure, call Medical Control
		Providing long-term patient care and team management
		
		Reducing angulated fractures and dislocations; clearing the spine
		
		Managing environmental emergencies
		
		Expert outdoor skills
		
		    Using map and compass
		
		    Search and rescue skills
		
		    Forecasting weather and surviving severe weather conditions
		
		    Bivouac and survival skills
		
		    Food and water

MEDICOLEGAL ISSUES AND TERMS

MEDICOLEGAL: "of or relating to both medicine and the law." Laws differ slightly from state to state, and certifications and licenses may not transfer. Some organizations have their own rules and regulations to follow, in addition to state laws. Laws vary greatly from country to country.

CERTIFICATION—Upon the successful completion of a training course, a certification is awarded for that specific level of training.
- Certification is not a license to practice medicine—each state regulates licensure and governs scope of practice for each level of training.

LICENSURE—A license to practice medicine is issued by each state's office of emergency medicine (or equivalent).
- A license gives permission to provide patient care; a certification from a course does not.

STANDARD OF CARE—Acceptable level of care based on level of certification.
- Duty to perform
- Duty to inform
- What is prudent and reasonable
- Helps determine negligence

PROTOCOLS—A set of standing orders produced by an authoritative body, e.g., a state, that establishes the levels of licensure and the standards of care.
- Protocols give permissions for various aspects of providing patient care.

GOOD SAMARITAN LAWS—Protect and grant immunity to anyone who has acted in good faith to provide care, within their level of training.
- These laws were created to protect either volunteers or professionals in situations where they do not have a "duty to act."
- They do not protect volunteers on an organized rescue team or ambulance corps (they have a team name and advertise their ability to help; therefore, they are considered professionals, not Good Samaritans).

INFORMED AND EXPRESSED CONSENT—is received from an adult (or emancipated minor) who is mentally competent to make a rational decision.
- You are obligated to get consent to provide patient care.
- You inform the patient about the care you intend to provide and why that care is appropriate; the patient then either agrees or refuses to receive your care (See Right to Refuse Care).

IMPLIED CONSENT—If the patient is unconscious or irrational, the law assumes that they would want appropriate care, and you do not need their permission to provide care.

CONSENT FOR MINORS—In situations of life-threatening injury or illness, consent becomes implied.
- Parents and guardians may give consent before an injury or illness occurs via a pre-activity form.
- These forms do not fully negate the child's rights.
- Parents can also sign an assumption of liability for any lawsuits brought on behalf of or by the child.

RIGHT TO REFUSE CARE—The patient must be legally able to refuse (they are either an adult or an emancipated minor).
- The patient must be mentally competent and rational.
- The patient must be fully informed.
- The patient should sign a release form.

ABANDONMENT—The premature abandonment of care.

NEGLIGENCE—The failure to act or provide care as a reasonably prudent person would in the same conditions and with the same knowledge, experience, and background as you. Elements of negligence include:
- Duty to act: You were required to help due to a prior relationship or an offer to render aid.
- Breach of duty or standard of care: You did not help, or you provided care below or above the standard to which you are trained.
- Proximate cause: Your breach caused a patient's condition to worsen.

MEDICAL RECORD—In wilderness medicine, a SOAPnote records the events and medical care provided.
- Patient Care Report (PCR)
- It is confidential and legal.
- It allows for continuity of care as the patient is passed on to other providers.
- It provides legal protection, a record of what happened, what problems were found, and how those problems were treated.
- A SOAPnote can be used by programs for quality improvement.

CONFIDENTIALITY—Any information you obtain about the patient must be kept confidential, and it can only be passed on to others directly involved in patient care.

ADVANCE DIRECTIVES—A legal document that allows a person to state their choices for medical treatment before they actually need such care (e.g., a Do Not Resuscitate order—see below).
- They are used by emergency medical personnel to delineate the care a patient wants to receive.

DNR (Do Not Resuscitate) ORDERS—A type of advance directive in which a person requests no cardiopulmonary resuscitation in the event their heart or breathing stops.
- Patients may have a legal form requesting no CPR or that no "heroic" measures be taken.
- Patients may wear a DNR tag or bracelet.
- Check for this (and for medical alert tags, e.g., a blood type or diabetes tag) during patient assessment.

REPORTABLE CASES—Some emergencies must be reported to the police or other authorities.
- Possible child, elder, or spouse abuse or neglect
- Apparent homicide or suicide
- Injuries sustained during a felony
- Animal attacks

INFECTIOUS DISEASE CONTROL

Like all living organisms, we engage in a constant battle against invading microorganisms. We have defense mechanisms to help protect us from these constant threats of invasion, but once our defenses are breeched and the offending organisms are living in us (and off us), we develop an infection. Our primary defense against infectious organisms is the integumentary system, our skin, a waterproof and pathogen-proof barrier. (For an in-depth look at skin, see the discussion at the front of the soft tissue injury section). Our second line of defense is the immune system, in particular, our white blood cells (WBCs). White blood cells are constantly scouring our body, seeking and destroying invading pathogens.

Illness

DISEASE—An interruption, alteration, or cessation of normal body system or organ function.

- It has a recognizable etiological or causative agent.
- It has an identifiable set of signs and symptoms.
- It has consistent anatomical alterations.

INFECTIOUS DISEASE—A disease caused by or resulting from the presence and activity of microbiological agents.

PATHOGEN—A disease-producing organism that causes infectious disease. (See details in the Appendix.)

BLOOD-BORNE PATHOGEN— Pathogenic (disease-causing) microorganisms present in infected human blood that can cause disease in another person.

COMMUNICABLE DISEASE—A disease that can be transmitted from one person to another by one of the modes of transmission (described later in this section).

Types of infectious organisms

PRION—A proteinaceous infectious particle (causes deadly brain diseases).

VIRUS—A small infectious agent that can replicate only inside the living cells of organisms.

- Genetic material, RNA or DNA, surrounded by a protective protein coat
- Obligate intracellular parasites
- Unable to reproduce on their own
- Examples: hepatitis A, B, C, HIV, common cold, rabies, viral meningitis

BACTERIA—A large group of single-celled microorganisms, typically a few millimeters in length, exhibiting a wide range of shapes, and which grow in every habitat on earth.

PROTOZOA—A unicellular heterotrophic protist, such as an amoeba. Like bacteria, they are unicellular, but protozoa have some form of locomotion.

MYCOSES—Fungal infections are single-celled organisms that reproduce by budding.

HELMINTHS—Multicellular intestinal worms that are usually parasitic.

Relationships

SYMBIOSIS—The biological association of two or more species for their mutual benefit

COMMENSALISM—A relationship where one organism benefits from another, but not at any cost to the other (e.g., a barnacle attached to a clam shell)

HOST—The organism in or on which an infectious agent lives and causes symptoms, and which the agent is dependent upon for its energy

PARASITE—An organism that lives on or in a host at the expense of that host

RESERVOIR—Living or nonliving material on which an infectious agent multiplies and develops and is dependent upon to survive in nature

VECTOR—The method or vehicle by which infectious disease is transmitted: e.g., water, food, insects, fomites (inanimate objects), coughs, sneezes, etc.)

Defenses

INTEGUMENTARY SYSTEM—Skin, a waterproof, pathogen-proof barrier.

IMMUNE SYSTEM—Responsible for recognizing self from non-self and destroying and eliminating anything that is non-self.

- Cellular immunity: the action of white blood cells to surround and kill any non-self entity
- Humeral immunity: the production of antibodies to help destroy invading pathogens and to create a memory of those microorganisms, thus preventing any future illness that could by caused by a re-infection with the same organisms

10 keys to prevention

1. **Immunizations**—keep up-to-date
2. **Hands**—wash them often
3. **Food**—know what it is and how it was prepared
4. **Antibiotics**—use exactly as prescribed
5. **Worsening infection**—report to a doctor immediately
6. **Wild/domestic animals**—keep away from those that you are unfamiliar with
7. **Insects**—use appropriate protection
8. **Sex and injected drugs**—protect the first with condoms; avoid the second
9. **Disease threats**—keep alert regarding threats in the area you travel to; get recommended immunizations and take protective medications (e.g., for malaria)
10. **If sick**—allow yourself time to get well; avoid contact with others while contagious

Modes of transmission of infectious disease

DIRECT CONTACT—Disease is spread by direct contact with the blood or other body substances (saliva, sputum, urine, feces, secretions) of an infected individual.

■ These include blood-borne pathogens and sexually transmitted diseases (STDs).

AIRBORNE—Disease is spread through the air by coughing and sneezing.

■ Minimize this by containing coughs and sneezes, and by washing hands frequently.

■ Do not allow contagious people to help with food preparation.

INDIRECT CONTACT—Disease is spread through indirect contact when someone touches a contaminated inanimate object (referred to as a fomite, e.g., clothing, a doorknob, stretcher, countertop, food, etc.) and then transfers the pathogen to their eyes or mouth with their hands. Alternately, indirect contact also includes airborne contamination, which occurs when someone inhales infected droplets of saliva or sputum expelled into the air by the coughing or sneezing of an infected person.

■ Sharps containers—Always dispose of sharps, such as needles, appropriately. To prevent accidental needle sticks, never re-cap a needle.

■ Surfaces—Clean surfaces appropriately after each patient contact to prevent the spread of pathogens by indirect contact.

■ Clothing and linen disinfection—Minimize handling to reduce the spread of pathogens by indirect contact. Launder appropriately.

■ Infected waste—Expendable materials that have become contaminated, such as gauze and dressings, must be disposed of properly (usually at the hospital) in a red bag labeled "Contaminated Human Waste." In the wilderness—double-bag infected waste and carry it out.

INSECT VECTOR—Disease is spread from one person to another by blood-sucking insects such as mosquitoes, fleas, black flies, or ticks. (See Bites and Stings in the Environmental Emergencies section.)

■ After the insect has had a blood meal from an infected person, the infectious agent migrates to the insect's salivary glands.

■ When the insect takes a subsequent blood meal from another person, it transfers the infectious agent to the bite site through its saliva.

WATERBORNE AND FOOD-BORNE—Disease is spread by the consumption of contaminated water or tainted food. When tainted by human waste, this is called oral-fecal contamination. Here are some basic guidelines for preventing this kind of contamination when traveling in the backcountry or in developing countries.

■ Don't take ice in your drinks (freezing doesn't kill all the bugs).

■ Purify your water.

■ Don't eat raw or undercooked meat or vegetables (just say no to salad).

■ Wash your hands frequently and follow that with chemical hand sanitizer.

Total Body Substance Isolation (BSI) and Universal Precautions

GLOVES

- To prevent **direct contact**, put gloves on before any potential exposure to body fluids.

HAND-WASHING

- To prevent patient-to-patient and hand-to-mouth transfer of pathogens by **indirect contact**, wash your hands frequently, especially after contact with any person, substance, or object that may be contaminated.
- Wash your hands before and after any patient contact.
- Use hand sanitizer frequently.

MASKS

- Masks prevent the **airborne** spread of disease by creating a barrier between you and droplets suspended in the air.
- Wear a surgical mask before any potential exposure to airborne pathogens, especially tuberculosis and influenza.

GOWNS

- Whenever it is appropriate to wear gloves, it is also appropriate to wear a waterproof gown to protect yourself from the splashing of potentially infected fluids, including bodily fluids.
- In the non-hospital setting, use turnout gear, rain gear, garbage bags, etc.
- Clean or dispose of all protective clothing after use.

RESUSCITATION EQUIPMENT

- Have resuscitation equipment, such as pocket masks and bag valve masks (BVM), available to prevent the need for direct-contact mouth-to-mouth resuscitation and to avoid possible exposure to saliva or blood.
- Clean or dispose of equipment after use.

EYE PROTECTION

- Protect your eyes—pathogens can be absorbed though the mucosa of the eyes.
- Wear eye protection or glasses to avoid splashing fluids into your eyes.
- Clean after use.

NETTING, CLOTHING, INSECT REPELLENTS

- Use mosquito netting while sleeping and bug head-nets while working outside.
- Wear long-sleeved shirts and pants (tuck pants into shoes) and avoid open-toed shoes, sandals, flip flops, etc.
- Use insect repellents. (See Bites and Stings in the Environmental Emergencies section.)
- Don't forget the palm of your hand (see smack, right).

In the "good mosquito" versus "bad mosquito" discussion, this is the good one. **Of course, it would have been better if you'd flattened it *before* it bit you...**

An ounce of prevention...
Vaccinations

A vaccine is used to pre-educate your immune system to recognize a pathogen before exposure. The vaccine contains killed or inactivated live pathogen which act as an antigen (from "antibody generator"). The immune system reacts to the antigen, producing antibodies against the disease-producing pathogen. If future exposure to that pathogen occurs, the immune system already has the antibodies needed to destroy the invading pathogenic organism before it can cause disease.

COMMON VACCINATIONS
- **DTap**: diphtheria, tetanus, and acellular pertussis (require boosters every 10 years)
- **MMR**: mumps, measles, and rubella (given during childhood)
- **OPV**: oral polio vaccine (given during childhood)
- **IPV**: injectable polio vaccine (given to adults and travelers)
- **HAV**: hepatitis A virus vaccine (2 shots, 6 – 12 months apart)—see sidebar, below
- **HBV**: hepatitis B virus vaccine (3 shots: day 1, at 1 month, and at 6 months)—see sidebar, below

OTHER VACCINATIONS
- Rabies: Both direct antibodies, Human Rabies Immunoglobulin (HRIG) for rabies exposure, and killed virus to develop antibodies over time (IMOVAX); rabies vaccines for both pre-exposure and post-exposure prophylaxis
- Varicella: Prevents chickenpox
- Typhoid: Prevents this tropical diarrheal disease
- Hib: Prevents haemophilus influenza B infections (which cause epiglottitis)
- Meningococcal vaccines: Prevents bacterial meningitis
- Yellow fever: Prevents the lethal viral yellow fever illness
- Influenza: Decreases the likelihood of contracting the flu

GLOBAL NUMBER OF POLIOMYELITIS (POLIO) CASES, 1980 – 2004
A GLOBAL VACCINE SUCCESS STORY
(priority funding by Rotary International and the Bill & Melinda Gates Foundation)

Number of cases (y-axis): 0, 10,000, 20,000, 30,000, 40,000, 50,000, 60,000, 70,000
Years (x-axis): 1980 1982 1984 1986 1988 1990 1992 1994 1996 1998 2000 2002 2004

When the U.S. Postal Service polled Americans about the most important science and technology advancements of the 1950s, the polio vaccine developed by Jonas Salk ranked first. On May 26, 1999, the Postal Service honored this achievement with a commemorative stamp. The stamp was unveiled at the Rackham Auditorium in Ann Arbor, Michigan—the same place where the vaccine announcement was made on April 12, 1955.

HEPATITIS—VITAL VACCINES

- The hepatitis vaccines are essential for all healthcare workers.
- Having hepatitis A virus will make you sick for several weeks with 100% recovery.
- Having hepatitis B virus will make you very sick for 2 – 3 months; it can kill you or leave you in a permanently weakened state.
- But, even with a 100% recovery from HBV, you will remain at risk for developing liver cancer.
- Hepatitis viruses have no treatment: vaccination equals prevention.
- Hepatitis C, another common form of the disease, currently has no vaccine.

BODY SYSTEMS OVERVIEW

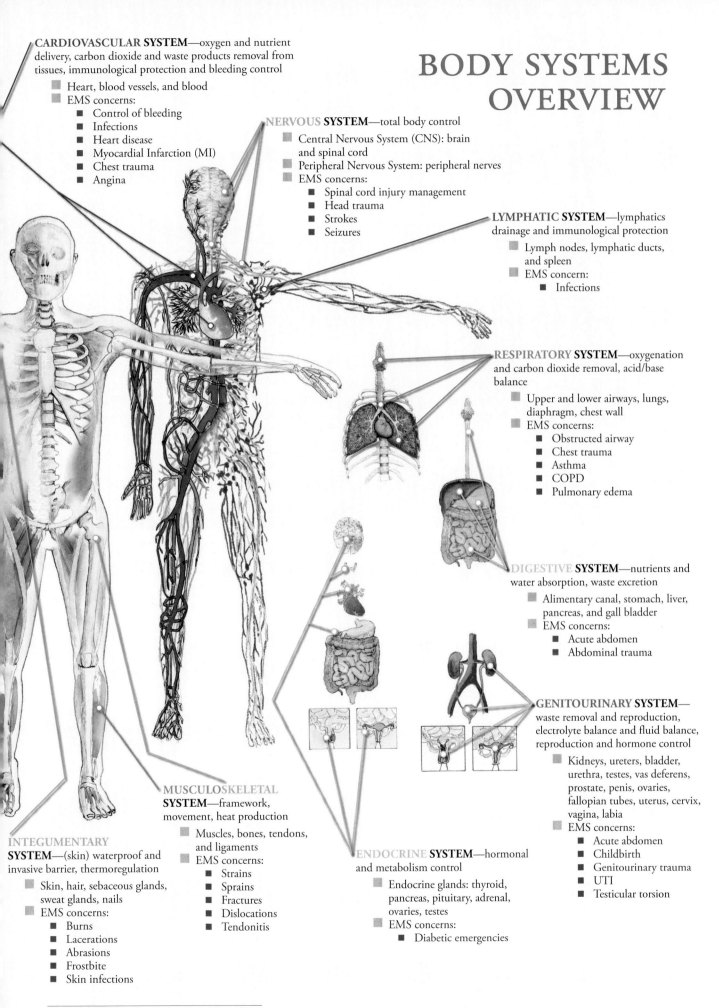

CARDIOVASCULAR SYSTEM—oxygen and nutrient delivery, carbon dioxide and waste products removal from tissues, immunological protection and bleeding control

- Heart, blood vessels, and blood
- EMS concerns:
    - Control of bleeding
    - Infections
    - Heart disease
    - Myocardial Infarction (MI)
    - Chest trauma
    - Angina

NERVOUS SYSTEM—total body control

- Central Nervous System (CNS): brain and spinal cord
- Peripheral Nervous System: peripheral nerves
- EMS concerns:
    - Spinal cord injury management
    - Head trauma
    - Strokes
    - Seizures

LYMPHATIC SYSTEM—lymphatics drainage and immunological protection

- Lymph nodes, lymphatic ducts, and spleen
- EMS concern:
    - Infections

RESPIRATORY SYSTEM—oxygenation and carbon dioxide removal, acid/base balance

- Upper and lower airways, lungs, diaphragm, chest wall
- EMS concerns:
    - Obstructed airway
    - Chest trauma
    - Asthma
    - COPD
    - Pulmonary edema

DIGESTIVE SYSTEM—nutrients and water absorption, waste excretion

- Alimentary canal, stomach, liver, pancreas, and gall bladder
- EMS concerns:
    - Acute abdomen
    - Abdominal trauma

GENITOURINARY SYSTEM—waste removal and reproduction, electrolyte balance and fluid balance, reproduction and hormone control

- Kidneys, ureters, bladder, urethra, testes, vas deferens, prostate, penis, ovaries, fallopian tubes, uterus, cervix, vagina, labia
- EMS concerns:
    - Acute abdomen
    - Childbirth
    - Genitourinary trauma
    - UTI
    - Testicular torsion

MUSCULOSKELETAL SYSTEM—framework, movement, heat production

- Muscles, bones, tendons, and ligaments
- EMS concerns:
    - Strains
    - Sprains
    - Fractures
    - Dislocations
    - Tendonitis

ENDOCRINE SYSTEM—hormonal and metabolism control

- Endocrine glands: thyroid, pancreas, pituitary, adrenal, ovaries, testes
- EMS concerns:
    - Diabetic emergencies

INTEGUMENTARY SYSTEM—(skin) waterproof and invasive barrier, thermoregulation

- Skin, hair, sebaceous glands, sweat glands, nails
- EMS concerns:
    - Burns
    - Lacerations
    - Abrasions
    - Frostbite
    - Skin infections

THE PATIENT

ASSESSMENT SYSTEM

IN THIS BOOK we are going to teach you how to care for injured and sick people from the moment you find them until the moment you deliver them to definitive care (a hospital). Sometimes you will do this within the Golden Hour; sometimes you will spend the night in the woods or be out for days; and sometimes you may be so far from help that you are the only definitive care the patient ever gets.

But, know this: lives are saved in the first 5 minutes

Nothing matters more than what you do in the first 5 minutes.

If a person's airway is blocked
or they stop breathing
or their heart stops beating
or they are bleeding profusely...

...we're going to teach you how to fix these things

While it's rewarding to learn how to build splints, or cobble a rescue litter together out of branches, or create a cozy bivouac site, or understand the ways to pull someone back from the edge of hypothermia, these and many other wilderness medical skills only matter *if your patient is alive*.

The way you handle the first five minutes of an emergency can make the difference between life and death. During these first fleeting moments you must discover all the potentially life-threatening problems and solve them as quickly as possible. The solution can be as simple as repositioning a patient's head to open their airway or applying direct pressure to control bleeding, or as complex and dramatic as rescue breathing, inserting an airway, or doing CPR.

To find and treat the most basic life-threats requires a logical approach to response and assessment—the Patient Assessment System (PAS), which consists of a list of questions that need to be answered and corresponding tasks that need to be performed, all during those first **precious** minutes.

We have arranged these questions and tasks by priority and they *must be done in order*. Short-cutting the system can make things worse—don't move on until you have successfully completed the task you're on.

This section deals with first response (the first five minutes) and emergency care (the Golden Hour), in order:

Survey the Scene
Assess overall site dangers.

Primary Assessment
Identify and treat immediate life threats.

Secondary Assessment
Identify other problems, take vital signs.

Rescue Plan
Implement the evacuation.

Survey the scene

Scene safety: The overall safety of an accident scene is of primary importance to the victim, the rescuers, and any bystanders. Ensuring the safety of the scene keeps bad things from getting worse.

The first priority at any scene is to minimize the number of casualties, and although it seems obvious that you should stop and look around, it's all too easy to focus immediately and intently on the hurt person and rush to their aid while potentially putting yourself or others at risk in the process. It doesn't matter what the crisis is or where it has occurred, as you approach an accident scene the first thing to do is to stop and get a handle on the *big picture*.

As you go down the scene safety question list,

STOP!!!

at each step, then analyze, decide, take action, and

GO!!!

Don't just rush in with your gloves off and your head spinning.

1. Am I safe and am I going to stay safe?

2. Is the group safe and will they stay safe?

3. Is the victim safe and will he or she stay safe?

- When you approach an accident scene, stop when you can see and communicate with the victim but before you are so close that you risk missing obvious dangers. The answers to these first three questions should be obvious, and they should come quickly—seconds count. Consider the following:
  - Look for obvious objective hazards: danger from falling rocks, avalanche, rushing water, and other terrain threats.
  - Consider environmental dangers: approaching severe weather, darkness, extreme cold or heat, etc.
  - Assess issues with the group: more than one hurt person, unattended children, uninjured people in obvious distress (e.g., cold and hungry), etc.
  - Make immediate decisions to minimize any risks identified.
- If you answer "No" to any of the three scene-safety questions, you must take action before continuing. Once you've assessed overall scene safety, made any critical immediate decisions and acted on them (e.g., someone will have to direct the uninjured people away from the edge of the cliff), swiftly continue with the next steps.

4. Take appropriate BSI precautions.

5. Form your general impression.

- How serious is this? What happened? What is the Mechanism of Injury[1] (MOI)—is it significant (see sidebar)? Will the victim have to be moved in order to be assessed? How will you safely approach the victim?

6. Attempt to communicate with the victim.

- Before you approach the victim[2], shout: "Are you okay?" Do you get a response? (By doing this from a distance you can help minimize risk to yourself—imagine this response: "Help! There are bees everywhere!")
- When you arrive, kneel and place a hand on the patient's forehead—this protects their cervical spine and provides the "human touch."
- Are their eyes open? What position are they in?
- If they are conscious, ask them what happened and where they hurt.

HOW DID THE PATIENT GET HERE?
SIGNIFICANT MOI

Mechanism of injury is considered *significant*—requiring head and spine immobilization or clearing the spine—if any of the following are true:

1. A fall greater than 3x body height
2. Rapid deceleration (e.g., mountain bike crash)
3. Direct impact to the head or spine
4. Twisting, tumbling falls (e.g., skiing)
5. Axial loading (e.g., head-first impact)
6. Unknown and/or unresponsive, but suspicious MOI (e.g., person unconscious at the base of a cliff)

---

1 MOI: The circumstances causing traumatic injury, e.g., sudden deceleration (falling, auto accident), wounding by a projectile, or crushing by a heavy object. See the sidebar at right for more information.

2 A victim is a person who has had an accident or is having a medical emergency. They become your patient as soon as you begin your physical examination.

Primary Assessment

The primary assessment is your initial physical exam. It takes just a few minutes and identifies any immediate life threats using a simple A, B, C, D, E system (*Airway*, *Breathing*, *Circulation*, *Deformity*, and *Environment*). Any compromise in the first three (the ABCs) can kill a person in just a few minutes; a significant deformity (femur or spine) that goes untreated can kill or paralyze a patient when they are moved; and the environment (freezing rain, avalanche) can be deadly.

The steps are straightforward and the tasks, simple—sure, the situation may be dramatic, even dire, but your work is uncomplicated: if the person isn't dead, your job is to keep them that way. As you do your lifesaving work, think about and practice the following principles. Your attentiveness to your patient, other people at the scene, the environment, and your own well-being is critically important.

 Be observant: **use your senses**
- Don't miss the forest for the trees: it's easy to get caught up in the drama and miss the big picture.
- What do your senses tell you about what's going on in your chaotic, perhaps even frantic world?

The primary assessment deals with the most basic life issues, and frequently begins with the most basic of human contacts: the touch of a hand.

 This is a step-by-step process: **be linear**
- Don't move on to the *next* thing until the *current* thing is done—stopping your patient's bleeding doesn't help if their airway is blocked and they're not breathing.
- Getting things out of order can put your patient at greater risk—be dogged and stick to the plan!

☑ Be aware of your surroundings: **be alert**
- Whenever you get a few seconds' break, step back mentally and take an inventory of the entire scene: are you missing anything?
- Has anything changed that you need to address?
- Don't get tunnel vision.

☑ Look, listen, and feel (LLF): **use all three**
- Be linear, but also learn to process things simultaneously using your eyes, ears, and hands.
  - What do you *see* right in front of you and all around?
  - What do you *hear* from the patient, from bystanders, from the environment (e.g., thunder)?
  - What do you *feel* with your hands? Are things cold, hot, wet, dry, sticky, gooey, crunchy, or out of place?

Primary Assessment: step by step

This is a quick, hands-on exam that seeks to answer the most basic questions about your patient's condition. You have arrived on the scene, made some basic safety decisions, attempted to communicate with the victim, and made initial physical contact—they are now your patient. And you probably did all this in about *30 seconds*. It's time to roll up your sleeves and get on with the ABCDEs.

Visually inspect the airway.

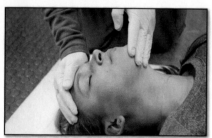
Perform a head-tilt/chin-lift.

Give rescue breaths (mouth-to-mask).

A

APPROACH AND ASSESS—Determine your patient's *level of consciousness*. Are they conscious and responsive or unconscious and unresponsive?
- **Look**: Are their eyes open, and do they track movement?
- **Listen**: Ask, "Hey, how are you doing?" Do they respond to you?
- **Feel**: Pinch the skin on the back of their hand or give them a sternum rub. Do you get a response?
- Talk to the patient—they may be able to hear even if they cannot respond.

AIRWAY—Assess the quality of your patient's airway. If they responded verbally during your initial contact or when you determined their LOC, then their airway is open and functioning. If they are unresponsive, your first job is to open their airway.
- **Look**: Open and visually inspect their airway. Is it clear? What color is it?
- **Listen**: Can you hear air moving in and out?
- **Feel**: Put your ear to their mouth—Can you feel air moving in and out?

If you answered YES to all of the airway questions, *move on to B.*
If you answered NO to any of the airway questions, *take airway actions.*

AIRWAY ACTIONS
1. To open the airway, perform a head-tilt/chin-lift (this moves the musculature of the tongue forward and opens the airway):
   - Move the head into proper anatomical position.
   - Tilt it slightly back (extension).
   - Gently pull the lower jaw (mandible) forward.
2. Is the airway clear? If not, log roll the patient into the recovery position. This allows any blood, fluid, or vomitus to drain.
3. Is the patient spontaneously breathing?

If the patient is breathing, *move on to B.*
If the patient is not breathing, *begin rescue breathing.*

RESCUE BREATHING
1. Give two rescue breaths and check for a pulse.
2. If they have a pulse, continue to give rescue breaths every 4 – 5 seconds until they begin breathing.
3. If the patient has no heartbeat, initiate CPR (see next spread).
4. If the patient does not respond within 30 minutes, stop all resuscitation efforts.

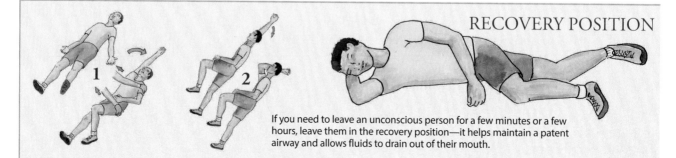

RECOVERY POSITION

1 2

If you need to leave an unconscious person for a few minutes or a few hours, leave them in the recovery position—it helps maintain a patent airway and allows fluids to drain out of their mouth.

B

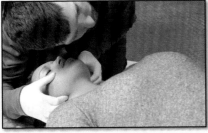

While holding the airway open, check for chest rise—which demonstrates that the patient is breathing.

Log roll the patient into the recovery position.

BVM

BREATHING—Assess the quality of your patient's breathing—are they breathing often enough and deeply enough to get an adequate supply of oxygen?

▧ **Look**: Do you see their chest rising and falling?

▧ **Listen**: Is their breathing clear and without adventitious breath sounds (wheezing, gurgling, or snoring)?

▧ **Feel**: Can you feel the patient's chest rise and fall as they breathe? Is the rate normal:10 – 30 breaths per minute (bpm)?

If you answered YES to all of the breathing questions, *move on to C.*
If you answered NO to any of the breathing questions, *take action.*

BREATHING ACTIONS

1. Log-roll your patient into the *recovery position* to help clear and maintain an open airway—gravity will help drain fluids and allow the tongue to fall forward and open the airway. Swipe their mouth, if necessary.

2. If their breathing does not improve sufficiently, or it is too fast (>30bpm) or too slow (<10bpm), control their respirations with a pocket mask using mouth-to-mask ventilation at a rate of 12 – 20bpm.

Now *move on to C.*

HOLD ON, WE'RE GETTING AHEAD OF OURSELVES—I'M ALL ALONE HERE

I'm only on B and I'm already in trouble. I'm by myself and I don't have any of that fancy equipment you keep talking about. BVMs? Nasopharen-whatever-airwhoosits? What should I do?

Do the best you can with what you have.

If you're alone in a remote setting without specialized gear (who carries a BVM on a backcountry ski trip, right?) and you come across a critical patient, start by opening their airway, and, well, that may be as far as you get.

Maybe all you will be able to do is rescue breathe for them for ten minutes; or control gross bleeding; or treat them for shock; or maybe just make them comfortable while you wait for help. Or a mixture of the above.

The unfortunate reality is that bad things happen to people when they're far away from definitive care, and sometimes you are all you've got. It's impossible to be prepared for every possible emergency situation. Learn the skills, practice them, bring the appropriate personal first aid and bivouac equipment, and be ready to help. ***That's all you can do.***

CIRCULATION (PULSE)—Assess your patient's circulatory system.
- **Look**: What is their skin color? Are they bleeding, and is it controlled?
- **Listen**: Put your ear to their chest—can you hear a heartbeat?
- **Feel**: Palpate their carotid artery—do you feel a pulse?

If the patient has a pulse, note quality (fast, slow, weak, strong) and *move on to bleeding.*

If the patient has no pulse, *perform CPR* **and continue until successful,** exhausted, or until 30 minutes have passed.

Check the carotid pulse.

CPR
1. 30 compressions to 2 ventilations
2. 5 cycles (about 2 minutes)
3. Compression rate of 100 per minute (about 1.5 compressions per second)

CIRCULATION (BLEEDING)—Assess for bleeding.
- **Look and feel**: Visually scan and use your hands to check for bleeding (make sure to check underneath the patient)—if you find any bleeding, is it under control (minor/clotted/ not pooling)?

If the patient is not bleeding, or the bleeding is controlled, *move on to D.*
If the patient has uncontrolled bleeding, *take action.*

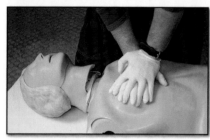

Perform CPR.

BLEEDING ACTIONS
1. Find the source(s) of the bleeding by scanning down the body and reaching under the torso and limbs. If there is significant mechanism of injury (MOI)—e.g. a fall greater than three times body height, consider the possibility of spinal injury and do not compromise the spine while searching for bleed(s).
2. Apply direct pressure until the bleeding stops.
3. Apply pressure dressing(s) as necessary.
4. When the bleeding has been controlled, move on to D (or get someone else to control the bleeding while you move on with the exam).
5. Hemostatic clotting agents and tourniquets are generally not available in remote settings.

Once bleeding is controlled, *move on to D.*

Control bleeding.

AFTER THE ABCs

You have a good idea of how injured or sick your patient is. If this is a life-threatening situation, then you may be breathing for your patient and/or performing CPR; get whatever information you can about the patient from bystanders, and call 911, or send someone for help. If your patient is not critically injured or ill, move on to D.

STOP!
When is enough CPR enough?
The 30-minute CPR guideline is well-established in wilderness settings where defibrillation is not available. Pulseless, normothermic (normal body temperature) people in full cardiac arrest simply do not recover after 30 minutes of continuous CPR. Continuing may put rescuers at risk for exhaustion—sadly, it's time to move on.

Check for deformity.

Splint unstable fractures right away.

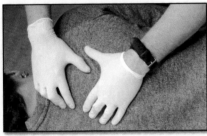
Assess the spine from neck to sacrum.

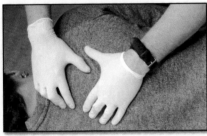
An improvised C-collar.

DEFORMITY—Assess your patient, checking for deformation, alignment, symmetry, and impaled objects.

■ **Look:** Scan your patient's body—is it free from obvious deformities—angulated fractures (bone fragments out of alignment), compound fractures (bone ends poking through the skin), dislocations (joint deformities), or impaled objects?

■ **Listen:** Is the patient pain-free?

■ **Feel:** Do a "chunk check" by palpating major body parts: is your patient still pain-free? Are there signs of deformity or crepitus (bone fragments grating)?

If no major deformities are found, *move on to disability.*
If major deformities are found, *take action.*

DEFORMITY ACTIONS

1. If you find any skeletal injuries, inspect them to determine if there is anything you need to treat immediately.
2. Femur fractures are the most dangerous because they can pose grave internal bleeding risks. If found, traction must be applied as soon as possible. Bilateral femur fractures (both femurs broken) are considered life-threatening.

Once stabilized, *move on to disability.*

DISABILITY—Assess your patient for head and/or spinal injuries.

■ **Look:** Was the MOI insignificant (see previous spread)? Is the patient able to move their extremities with ease? Do they appear free from injury or deformity?

■ **Listen:** Is the patient free from neck or back pain?

■ **Feel:** Does everything feel right? Does your palpation elicit no additional pain? Does the patient have normal sensations in their extremities?

If you answer yes to all of these questions, *move on to E.*
If you answer no to any question, *take action.*

DISABILITY ACTIONS

■ Neck and spine fractures pose a risk of paralysis and death.

1. If the patient is unconscious and the MOI is significant, assume a risk of spine injury; if possible, have someone hold the patient's head still.
2. If the patient is conscious and the MOI is significant, keep them lying still.

Once stabilized, *move on to E.*

Assess the scene—is it safe? It's easy to get tunnel vision and focus on the patient while losing sight of obvious hazards (e.g., the overhanging and potentially unstable dead snag).

Moving a patient onto a foam pad.

ENVIRONMENT (THE PATIENT)—Assess the terrain, weather conditions, and the condition of your patient.

- **Look**: Consider where your patient is lying: are they safe and comfortable where they are (e.g., they're not lying in water)? Are they protected from cold, heat, sun, or objective hazards? Is the weather good and is darkness far off?
- **Listen**: Are they telling you that they are comfortable—not too hot, cold, or wet?
- **Feel**: Do they feel normal (not hot, cold, or wet)?

If you answered yes to all the above questions, *move on to everyone else.*
If you answered no to any question, *take action.*

ENVIRONMENTAL (THE PATIENT) ACTIONS

1. Whenever possible, keep the patient lying still where you found them until you complete the entire patient assessment.
2. If you must move the patient, decide where and how they can be relocated (see the lifting and moving section).
3. At a minimum, as soon as you can, get them on a foam pad to protect them from the ground.
4. You may need to surround them with insulating material (see hypo-wrap) and move them into a shelter (e.g., a tent).

Once the patient's environment is stable, *move on to everyone else.*

This isn't just an alphabet lesson— the ABCDEs really matter...

ENVIRONMENT (EVERYONE ELSE)—Assess the terrain, weather conditions, and the condition of the rest of the group.

- **Look**: Does everyone else look okay? Are they going to stay okay?
- **Listen**: Is everyone verbalizing that they are okay, with no complaints about being cold, wet, hungry, or scared?
- **Feel**: Is your general impression that the group doesn't need any immediate attention?

If you answered yes to all the above questions, *your Primary Assessment is complete.*

If you answered no to any question, *take action.*

ENVIRONMENTAL (EVERYONE ELSE) ACTIONS

1. Take whatever actions are necessary to protect yourself, your patient, and the group from environmental challenges and hazards.
2. Ensure everyone's safety and comfort and see to their basic needs (food, shelter, warmth, emotional support).
3. Direct someone in the group to take charge and keep everyone safe, fed, hydrated, sheltered, warm, and busy.

Once the group's environment is stable, *your Primary Assessment is complete.*

Don't get tunnel vision—there may be others in the group who need help (perhaps just reassurance and direction).

Sometimes the best shelter for your group is the one you bring with you.

...in fact, if this is all you ever learn, you'll be able to save lives!

Secondary Assessment

At this point—assuming things are either not critical or that others are taking over any necessary life-saving procedures (e.g., ventilations or CPR), you have likely spent less than five minutes at your patient's side, and your physical examination of them has been limited to the basics—finding and treating major problems. You have an overall understanding of their condition (ABCDs), are aware of the group dynamics (the patient, anyone with the patient, and you and your group) and any environmental (E) challenges (terrain, weather, darkness) that must be dealt with. You now have the luxury of time.

Once the primary assessment has been completed, it's time to take a much closer look at your patient. During the Secondary Assessment, you will explore your patient's body with your eyes and hands, palpating virtually every inch of them, uncovering, identifying, and diagnosing their injuries and/or illnesses. You will measure data about their basic body systems and collect information about their past and present medical history. You will make specific treatment decisions and begin to take (or direct) specific treatment actions. The secondary survey consists of four parts.

1 Vital Signs

Measurements of basic body functions:
- Level of Consciousness (beyond merely responsive/unresponsive)
- Respiratory rate and effort (RR)
- Heart rate (HR—pulse)
- Heart effort (BP—blood pressure)
- Skin color, temperature, and moisture (SCTM)
- Pupil size and reaction to light (PERRL)

2 Patient Exam

A detailed physical examination that helps you locate and determine the extent of injuries and make treatment decisions

3 AMPLE History

Information about the patient's medical history gathered using a simple mnemonic:
- **A**: Allergies
- **M**: Medications
- **P**: Past medical history
- **L**: Last in (food) and last out (poop and pee)
- **E**. Events leading up to the accident/crisis (the short history of what happened)

4 SOAPnote

The wilderness medicine equivalent of a patient's medical chart

1 VITAL SIGNS

The collection of data that forms a patient's vital signs (you will often hear EMS personnel talk about "getting a set of vitals") tells you how the patient is doing *right now*. And, when the "vitals" are updated regularly (every 5 – 15 minutes, depending on the circumstances) they tell you how your patient is doing *over time*. Knowing which way your patient is headed (improving or deteriorating) helps you adjust your treatment and evacuation plans on the fly. Vital signs don't tell you what the specific injuries or illnesses are—the patient exam does this—but they do tell you how your patient is responding to their injuries and illnesses, as well as to your treatment.

LEVEL OF CONSCIOUSNESS (LOC)

Level of consciousness is a measure of a person's arousability and responsiveness to stimuli. You made a basic determination of their alertness when you called to the victim—if they answered you coherently, then you know three things:

- They are conscious.
- They have an open airway.
- They are breathing.

In wilderness medicine, we differentiate a person's level of consciousness by using the **AVPU** scale.

AWAKE: This person is spontaneously responsive and completely aware of their surroundings. They shouted back when you first hailed them, and now that you are by their side they are talking freely. If they answer the following diagnostic questions correctly, they are said to be Alert and Oriented Times Three (AOx3): alert as to person, place, and time.

1. What is your name?
2. Where are you?
3. What is the date?

If they respond appropriately to those three questions, then ask them what happened.

VERBAL: This person is not spontaneously responsive, but does respond to verbal stimuli. They are lethargic. They likely did not give you a hearty reply to your shout—although they may have groaned in response. When you talk to them, they do answer (which confirms an open airway), but they may not make complete sense. Ask them the same three diagnostic questions to determine how altered their mental status is.

PAINFUL: This person does not respond to verbal stimuli. They are stuporous and will likely appear to be asleep. Even shouting right in their ear elicits no response. Pinch the skin on the back of their hand or give them a sternum rub. If this arouses them, then they are deemed to be painfully responsive (if they groan, this also confirms at least a partially open airway).

UNRESPONSIVE: This person appears comatose and they make no purposeful response to any stimuli: you speak, shout, and pinch to no avail. Unresponsive people are often in serious trouble, but they still may be able to hear and comprehend—talk to them, encourage them; don't pretend they're not there.

RESPIRATORY RATE AND EFFORT (RR)

The respiratory rate and effort shows you how well the respiratory system (the airway and lungs) is exchanging oxygen, in particular, in supplying the brain with oxygen. Look, listen, and feel air move in and out of the lungs.

- **RESPIRATORY RATE:** Count the number of breaths per minute (breaths in 15 seconds x 4).
  - The typical rate is 10 – 30 breaths/minute (BPM).
  - If the rate is slower than 10 or faster than 30, the patient needs assisted ventilations via mouth-to-mouth, mouth-to-mask, or a bag valve mask (BVM) at a rate of one breath every 4 – 5 seconds (12 – 15 breaths per minute) to make sure they are getting enough oxygen into their lungs.

*Painful stimulus may be the only way to get your patient to respond—but it's got to **hurt**—so go ahead, tweak that skin, yank on those wrist hairs, grind into that sternum. You won't injure them, but you may get their attention.*

BREATHING IS REALLY IMPORTANT
Perhaps we're stating the obvious, but if your patient's breathing is labored, or shallow, or rapid, or if they are complaining of shortness of breath, their brain is telling the respiratory system that it is not getting enough oxygen—this is a serious situation, and you must find the cause for this and fix it, if you can.

- **RESPIRATORY EFFORT**: In addition to how many breaths per minute your patient is taking, you also need to assess how hard they are working.
  - **Look:** Do they look like they are having difficulty breathing? Are they complaining of shortness of breath or difficulty breathing?
  - **Listen:** Are the patient's breath sounds normal and quiet?
  - **Feel:** Is the patient's chest moving normally as they breathe? Breathing should be easy and effortless. It should not take any noticeable effort to breathe or take a deep breath.

HEART RATE/PULSE (HR)

The heart rate (pulse) and effort (blood pressure—see next) tell you how well the circulatory system (heart and blood vessels) is doing.
- **RATE**: Palpate the pulse at the wrist and count the beats per minute (beats in 15 seconds x 4).
- **QUALITY**: based on palpation, determine if the pulse is normal, weak, strong, pounding, or thready (eg., weak, hard to palpate, often rapid—characteristic of hypovolemia, such as occurs with severe hemorrhage).
  - **Look:** What is the skin color? It should be normal for their race.
  - **Listen:** Does your patient have normal heart sounds ("lub-dub:)?
  - **Feel:** Do they have a radial pulse?

Taking radial pulse.

Checking blood pressure with a BP cuff (sphygmomanometer) and stethoscope.

BLOOD PRESSURE (BP)

Blood pressure tells you how hard the heart is working—the effort it takes to pump blood around the body. There are two measurements of arterial pressure, systolic and diastolic, and they are both typically taken via a blood pressure cuff with an accompanying pressure gauge (called a sphygmomanometer) and a stethoscope. The measurement units are millimeters of mercury (mmHg).
- **SYSTOLIC**: This is the pressure in the arteries while the left ventricle of the heart is contracting. The acceptable systolic pressure range is 90 – 140mmHg.
- **DIASTOLIC**: This is the residual arterial pressure when the heart is relaxed and the left ventricle is refilling. The acceptable diastolic pressure range is 60 – 90mmHg.

MEASURING BLOOD PRESSURE VIA AUSCULTATION (LISTENING)

The traditional method used in a doctor's office or hospital, this requires a sphygmomanometer (BP cuff) and a stethoscope.
1. Remove the clothing from one arm, if possible.
2. Locate the brachial artery at the elbow.
3. Place the cuff with the "artery" tag pointing at the brachial artery above the elbow and position the pressure gauge so that you can read it easily.
4. Place the diaphragm of the stethoscope over the brachial artery distal to the cuff—you will not hear any pulse yet.
5. Tighten the valve on the cuff and inflate it to 200mmHg.
6. Slowly deflate the cuff while listening carefully.

  - When you first hear a pulse through the stethoscope, it means that the blood pressure has overcome the constricting power of the cuff and is forcing blood through the artery—this is the systolic pressure.

  - When the sound of the pulse disappears, it means that the cuff is no longer restricting the blood flow at all—this is the diastolic pressure.
8. Remove the cuff and record your findings.

MEASURING BLOOD PRESSURE VIA PALPATION (FEELING)

With only a BP cuff but no stethoscope, you can still determine the systolic pressure.
1. Do steps 1 – 4, and 6, above.
2. Deflate the cuff slowly and note the pressure at the point where you feel a pulse—this is the systolic pressure.
3. Record this finding as "systolic by palpation."

GOING CUFF-LESS IN THE WILDERNESS

If you do not have a BP cuff, the presence or absence of pulses at different locations on the body can be used to estimate the minimum systolic pressure, and can help determine if the patient's blood pressure is changing over time.

- If a pulse is present in the carotid artery in the neck, the minimum systolic pressure is 60mmHg—which is only enough to perfuse the brain, but not the other vital organs.

- If a pulse is present in the radial artery at the wrist, the minimum systolic pressure is 90mmHg—enough to perfuse the entire body.

- If a pulse is present in the femoral artery in the leg, the minimum systolic pressure is 80mmHg—enough to perfuse the vital organs and the brain.

Normal Caucasian skin: pink, warm, and dry

Pale, cool, and clammy skin: gray to bluish (cyanotic), abnormally cool, and damp

SKIN COLOR, TEMPERATURE, AND MOISTURE (SCTM)

The skin (the integumentary system) is the largest organ in the human body, accounting for about 10% of a person's total body weight. It is durable, self-repairing, and very sensitive to internal changes. A healthy person at rest in a benign environment (neither hot nor cold) will have skin that is normal in color, warm, and dry. Any deviation in any of the three characteristics indicates some compromise in health. When you are looking at a patient's skin, keep two points in mind:

1. Skin color varies by race. For Caucasians, the normal skin color is pink. For darker races, non-pigmented areas such as the fingernail beds, under the eyelids, or inside the mouth should be checked—these areas are non-pigmented and should be pink.

2. When evaluating your patient's skin, consider their recent physical activity—vigorous exercise will cause skin to become reddish, warm, and sweaty.

SKIN COLOR AND CAPILLARY REFILL

▪ Loss of color (pallor) or cyanosis (bluish or purplish coloration) of the skin or mucous membranes indicates that the person's brain has perceived that there is a crisis and is shunting blood away from the skin to the vital organs: the brain, heart, lungs, liver, and kidneys.

▪ How quickly the capillaries refill is easy to test by looking at a person's fingernails.

 ▪ Squeeze the blood out of a fingertip by pinching it until the skin underneath the fingernail turns white—then release it.

 ▪ In a healthy person, the capillary bed beneath the nail should refill and turn pink within two seconds—a delay indicates a compromise in circulation.

 ▪ This test works in people of all races because there is no pigment in the skin beneath the fingernails.

SKIN TEMPERATURE AND MOISTURE

▪ Touch the patient's abdomen—are they hot or cold to the touch? Temperature gives you a good indication of whether a person is hyperthermic or hypothermic, and to what degree.

▪ Is their skin dry or sweaty (clammy)? Excessive moisture can indicate sweating associated with exercise or a fever, and can be associated with anxiety, shock, or an acute myocardial infarction (heart attack).

PUPIL SIZE AND REACTION TO LIGHT

Our pupils are extremely sensitive to changes in light and their reaction to these changes are good indicators of how well a person's brain is functioning. In a healthy person, their pupils should be PERRL: Pupils Equal, Round, and Reactive to Light.

▪ Look at both of your patient's pupils—are they equal in size?

▪ Are they both round?

▪ Use a light source such as a penlight or headlamp and swipe it past your patient's eyes—do both pupils contract immediately and equally?

▪ If your patient is awake and alert, ask them to keep their head still and track your finger with their eyes as you move the light back and forth and up and down—do both eyes track smoothly and in unison?

 ▪ Unequal pupil size, sluggish or unequal reaction to changing light intensity, and tracking problems can indicate increased intracranial pressure (ICP), nerve damage, drug interference, or other problems.

Note: If your patient's pupils are fixed (they do not react to light at all) and fully dilated (as big as they can get), the situation is extremely serious—brain injury is likely. Evacuate as quickly as possible.

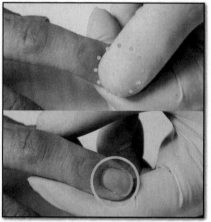

Testing for capillary refill: (top) squeeze the blood out from under a fingernail for five seconds (top), then quickly release the finger and observe how long it takes for the nail bed to pink-up again (bottom)—it should take two seconds or less in an adult and three seconds or less in an infant. (Note: colored nail polish will make this test impossible.)

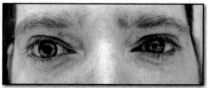

Unequal pupil size means something bad is going on inside your patient's head—even if there are no obvious injuries, unequal pupil size indicates a true emergency and evacuation should begin immediately.

PATIENT EXAM

In the Primary Survey you examined your patient, you touched them, albeit briefly and superficially. You held their head still, especially if you suspected significant MOI. You may have performed a jaw thrust, done a quick chunk check to look for deformity and disability, logrolled them to clear their airway, or even moved them out of the way of an environmental hazard. You were looking for life-threats, and you were in a hurry. Now it's time to settle down and go over things an inch at a time.

The detailed physical exam outlined here is designed to help you determine everything that is wrong with your patient, to identify both surface injuries (e.g., contusions, lacerations) as well as underlying musculoskeletal and soft tissue injuries (fractures, tenderness). It is done *efficiently*, *deliberately*, and *systematically*.

The critical first five minutes have passed and your patient is still alive (and, if you're fortunate, stable). What you do in the next 5 – 10 minutes will determine what you need to treat, how you need to treat it, and how (and how quickly) to evacuate your patient. In the numbered list that follows, when we write "examine," we mean with your eyes and your hands.

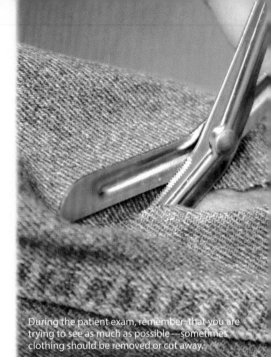

During the patient exam, remember that you are trying to see as much as possible—sometimes clothing should be removed or cut away.

PRINCIPLES OF THE PATIENT EXAM

- **LOOK**
  - Inspection: Be observant—look for bleeding, impaled objects, and deformities.
  - Comparison: compare the symmetry of body parts (arms to arms, legs to legs); if symmetry is compromised, determine why.
- **LISTEN**
  - Is the patient complaining of pain or tenderness? What are their symptoms[1]?
- **FEEL**
  - **Palpation**: palpate the muscles, bones, and joints—is there deformity, crepitation (the sound of grating bone ends and fragments) or tenderness? (See palpation sidebar on the next page for tips on doing this.)
  - **Circulation (C)**: are there pulses in all four extremities?
  - **Sensation (S)**: is there normal sensation (pressure, temperature, pain) in all four extremities?
  - **Movement (M)**: is there normal range of motion in all four extremities?

    Note: These last three points are referred to as a patient's CSMs—get used to hearing the term; you will be checking CSMs regularly.

- **THINGS TO REMEMBER**
  - Talk to your patient; explain what you are doing.
  - If you elicit pain, ask the patient to describe it.
    1. Precisely where does it hurt?
    2. What kind of pain is it (dull, sharp, etc.)?
    3. How much does it hurt (0 – 10 scale with 0 being no pain and 10 being the worst pain they have ever experienced)?
  - Move the patient only as much as is necessary to complete the exam —needless movement of the head, neck, spine, or limbs can cause further injury.
  - Conduct the patient exam in the order described.

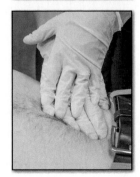

---

1 **Symptoms** are things the patient communicates to you (e.g., "My arm hurts"), while **signs** are things you observe (e.g., skin color, respiratory rate, etc.).

THE NOT-SO-GENTLE ART OF PALPATION

- Use light-to-firm pressure (like a good massage).
- Assess everything from soft tissue to bony structures.
- If unconscious, monitor for pain response.
- Evaluating levels of pain is part of the assessment.
- Hands, fingers, and finger tips are three different tools to use during assessment.

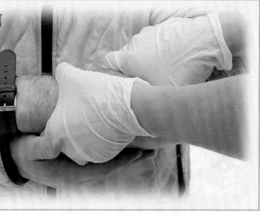

Good palpation is not difficult, but it is as much an art as a science. Use enough pressure—remember, you are trying to identify broken bones. Squeezing hard is necessary, and causing momentary pain is diagnostically useful. If working on an appendage, squeeze circumferentially so you do not risk additional deformity.

HEAD

1
- Examine the entire scalp.
- Examine the face, including the facial bones: cheeks, jaw, and the area around the eyes.
- Examine the ears, nose, and mouth (including teeth). If you know or suspect significant MOI for trauma, look for bruising behind the ears (Battle's Sign) and around the eyes (raccoon eyes), and for clear fluid (cerebral spinal fluid—CFS) coming from the ears or nose—any of these things indicate serious head injury (and a life-threatening emergency).

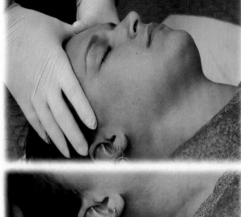

NECK

2
- Examine the cervical spine and trachea.
    - With your fingers, walk the spine from the base of the skull to between the shoulder blades, palpating for tenderness—if you find it, you must immobilize your patient's C-spine with a cervical collar.
    - When you examine the trachea, look for two things: 1) Note if the trachea has shifted from its normal, center-line position (called tracheal shift) and, 2) look to see if either jugular vein is swollen, called jugular vein distension (JVD)—either or both of these signs often point to lung damage.

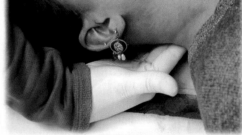

SHOULDER

3
- Examine the shoulders by compressing each one in your hands—palpate for tenderness and deformity.

CHEST

4
- Examine the clavicles.
- Examine and gently compress the rib cage.
    - Severely broken ribs (e.g., a flail chest), puncture wounds involving the lungs, holes with air moving in and out, and other major injuries will need immediate attention.

ABDOMEN

5 ▦ Compress the abdomen in all four quadrants.
- ■ Push hard enough to determine if there is any rigidity (which can indicate internal bleeding).
- ■ If your palpation elicits pain, note its type (e.g., sharp, dull, etc.) and position—there may be severe internal damage or a problem such as appendicitis.

PELVIS

6 ▦ Compress the pelvis both front-to-back (like opening a book) and outside-to-inside (like closing a book).
- ■ If you find instability during either of these tests, it indicates a pelvic fracture, which is potentially extremely serious—the pelvic girdle is laced with major blood vessels and severe internal bleeding is a real risk. The pelvis will have to be immobilized.

  Note: An unstable pelvis should be moved only once; otherwise you risk damage to its vast vasculature.

LEGS

7 ▦ Palpate both legs from hip to ankle (there is a lot of muscle here, so squeeze hard).
  ▦ Check for Circulation, Sensation, and Movement (CSMs).
- ■ Check for a pedal (on the foot) pulse and capillary refill (toes).
- ■ If the patient is conscious, grab a toe and ask the patient to identify it.
- ■ Flex the knees and ankles, looking and feeling for abnormal movement or crepitation—stop if you elicit pain.

ARMS

8 ▦ Palpate both arms from shoulder to wrist.
  ▦ Check for Circulation, Sensation, and Movement (CSMs).
- ■ Check for a radial pulse (at the wrist) and capillary refill (fingers).
- ■ Flex the elbows and wrists.

BACK

9 ▦ Palpate the spine along the length of the back from the base of the skull to the coccyx (tail bone), walking your fingers, feeling for tenderness and deformity .
  ▦ You may need to logroll your patient to gain access to their back.
- ■ If there is significant MOI, you must keep the entire spine in line and immobilized while you perform the log roll—this may take more than one person.
- ■ If you find any injuries, logroll the patient onto their uninjured side to avoid further injury and pain.

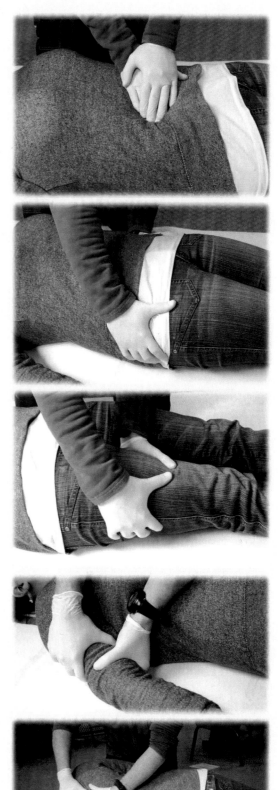

AMPLE HISTORY

For anyone having a medical emergency, their past medical history—both the distant past and the recent past—as well as their recent behavior and actions, can have great bearing on the situation and help you make both diagnostic and treatment decisions. To remind us of the appropriate questions to ask our patients, we use the simple mnemonic *AMPLE*. Talk to your patient, or others in the group, to gather the following information.

A: ALLERGIES

- Is your patient allergic to any medications or foods?
- Do they have any environmental allergies (e.g., bee stings)?
- If they have any allergies, find out what happens when they have a reaction, and what treatment should take place (Do they have an EpiPen?).

M: MEDICATIONS

- Is your patient taking any prescription or over-the-counter (OTC) medications? It's easy to forget these.
- If so, what, how much, how often, and when did they take it last?
- What happens if they don't take their med?

P: PAST MEDICAL HISTORY

- Has your patient ever had any previous major medical problems or surgeries? If so, what and when?
- Have they ever been hospitalized overnight? If so, for what and when?
- Is there any recent or past injury or illness that could contribute to the current problem? If so, what and when?

L: LAST IN, LAST OUT

- When did your patient last eat and drink? What did they last eat and drink? And how much?
- When did they last have a bowel movement and void their bladder?

E: EVENTS LEADING UP TO THE ACCIDENT/ILLNESS

- What led up to the accident or illness? (What was the specific trigger?)
- What occurred prior to the event? (This may give you valuable insight into peripheral things—e.g., a 15-mile hike in a cold rain without much to eat may account for someone seeming "out of it" and point to hypothermia).

PATIENT INTERVIEWING SKILLS

The purpose of the patient interview is to gather information to aid in diagnosis and treatment. Here are some guidelines to make it most effective.

- Get informed consent (see the medicolegal section).
- Tell the patient what you are doing—it will help them relax.
- Use the patient's name—it demonstrates empathy and sensitivity.
- Don't make promises you can't keep—"Everything will be okay."
- Never lie (but show restraint—too much truthful information can add stress).
- Be respectful (the patient exam may make some people feel vulnerable).
- Make eye contact and try to speak to patients on their own physical level; kneel if necessary.
- Be confident and comforting—be tender, it's okay to touch them.
- Use good observation and listening skills—there is a difference between hearing and listening, and sometimes responding to a seeming insignificant request (e.g., "Can I have a sip of water?") will really help.
- Avoid leading questions—begin broadly and gradually become more specific.
- Remember follow-up questions. For example, if your patient tells you they are allergic to something, ask them what happens when they are exposed to it.
- Take advantage of all sources of information—look around, ask members of the group, family members, friends, and bystanders; look for medical forms and medical alert tags.
- Avoid medical jargon: "Whoa, how long have your toes been blue?" not, "When did these phalanges become cyanotic?"

DETERMINE THE CHIEF COMPLAINT

Ask your patient to name the thing that is bothering them the most.

- ▦ Sometimes it's obvious—that broken femur really hurts.
- ▦ Sometimes it's not obvious; in fact, it may take you by surprise—your patient may have a dramatic injury (e.g., a compound fracture), but when asked, they say, "I have the worst headache that I've ever experienced." Pay attention to this—it may be the most medically relevant thing going on!

EXPLORE THE HISTORY OF PRESENT ILLNESS (HPI)

The next set of questions seeks to gather all the information about the patient's current illness or injury, specifically as it relates to the pain they are feeling.

- ▦ **TIMING**
  - ■ **Onset: *When did the pain begin?*** The timing of the onset of pain gives you an idea of how serious the problem may be.
  - ■ **Duration: *How long have you had the pain?*** Someone with an acute onset of pain or a sudden worsening of pain is much more concerning than someone who has had pain for the past several days or weeks and is just not getting any better.
  - ■ **Frequency: *How often does it occur and how long does it last?*** The nature of the pain's frequency can give you valuable clues regarding its cause—especially if the chief complaint is vague or the injury/illness isn't obvious.

- ▦ **LOCATION**
  - ■ ***Where does it hurt?*** Have them verbalize this and point to the location (or locations) if possible.
  - ■ Sometimes the places the patient tells you they feel pain are not obvious or consistent with their apparent injuries.

- ▦ **DESCRIPTION and SEVERITY**
  - ■ **Quality: *What does the pain feel like?*** Let the patient describe it in words—you're looking for adjectives like sharp, dull, throbbing, etc. If they have trouble, ask the question in different ways (but don't lead them).
  - ■ **Quantity: *How bad is the pain?*** Ask them to rate the pain on a 0 – 10 scale, with 0 being no pain at all and 10 being the worst pain they have ever felt.

- ▦ **EXACERBATION and RELIEF**
  - ■ ***What makes the pain feel worse?***
  - ■ ***What makes the pain feel better?***

Yes, you get extra points for stuff like this.

SOAPNOTE

Subjective:
S: (age, sex, mechanism of injury(MOI), chief complain
on a wet, icy trail and is now complaining
and right knee.

Objective:
O: (vital signs(VS), patient exam(PE), AMPLE history)
Vital signs:

time:	3:30	3:45	4:00
LOC:	A+Ox2	A+Ox2	A+Ox2
RR:	20	16	12
HR:	88	72	60
SKIN:	P/c/c	P/c/c	P/c/c

Patient exam: Describe locations of pain, tender
22 y.o. male who appears cold. Skin is
He answers questions accurately but s
Shivering slightly. Positive for pain on
Abrasion of the right palm. full ROM & C
AMPLE:
allergies: _Penicillin; Sulfa; Codeine_
medications: _Sudafed; Albuterol Inhaler_
past pertinent medical history: _Seasonal Alle_
last oral intake: _had lunch at 12:30 ; Chees_
events leading up to accident: _Hikin in rain &_

Assessment:
A: (problem list)
1. _Fractured right ankle_
2. _Pain in right knee_
3. _Abrasion right hand_
4. _Hypothermia_

Plan:
P: (plan for each problem on the problem list)
1. _R. ankle splinted w/ensolite splint_
2. _R. knee splinted in position of comfort_
3. _Abrasion cleaned & bandaged_
4. _Wet clothing removed, hypothermia wrap_
5. MONITOR - How often do you plan to monitor the
   improvement of hypothermia, will contin

SOAPnote

At this point in the patient assessment system, you have obtained a fair amount of information that needs to be organized and recorded—it's time for the wilderness version of the ubiquitous medical chart. But unlike on TV, where a clipboard dangles from the foot of every hospital bed, out here in the howling wilderness we may need to improvise by scribbling on a scrap of paper, the back of a map, or even a bandanna. So, what's a SOAPnote? It's a simple record of the following info—and it always travels with the patient.

SUBJECTIVE INFORMATION

- This is the information you get from the patient or others in the group.
  - The age and gender of the patient
  - The Mechanism of Injury (MOI)—what happened? "I was running from a bee and tripped over that log"
  - The Chief Complaint (CC—what hurts?) "My forearm hurts bad"
  - The History of Present Illness (HPI, see previous page): e.g., (**O**) it began when she fell and has been steady since; (**P**) support makes it feel better; motion makes it worse; (**Q**) it is described as "sharp"; (**R**) it does not radiate; (**S**) on the pain scale it is 4/10; (**T**) it hurts pretty much all the time

OBJECTIVE INFORMATION

- The baseline vital signs (first set), and subsequent sets (every 5 – 15[1] minutes depending on circumstances)
  - Level of Consciousness (LOC)
  - Respiratory Rate and effort (RR)
  - Blood Pressure (BP)—remember, without a BP cuff, you will have to estimate BP based on which pulses are present: carotid, radial, medial, or femoral
  - Skin color, temperature, and moisture (SCTM)
  - Pupils equal, round, and reactive to light (PERRL)
- The results of the Patient Exam (PE)
  - Locations of pain, tenderness, and injuries
- AMPLE History
  - Allergies
  - Medications
  - Past Medical History
  - Last oral intake, last bowel movement and bladder void
  - Events leading up to the accident/illness

ASSESSMENT

- This is where you write down what you think is wrong—your problem list. Using the example from the HPI (above):
  - The MOI and CC indicate a possible broken forearm
  - Possible dehydration
  - Possible allergy to bee sting

PATIENT CARE PLAN

- This is where you outline your treatment and evacuation plans.
  - Splint lower right arm; check CSMs distal[2] to splint
  - Hydrate and feed patient
  - Evacuate to definitive care by walking, if PT[3] is able
  - Continue to monitor vitals and CSMs every 15 minutes

---

1 Record vital signs every 5 minutes for critical patients, every 15 minutes for non-critical patients.
2 "Distal" means farther away from the heart; contrast with "proximal," which means closer to the heart.
3 "PT" is the standard abbreviation for "patient."

Rescue Plan

Rescue Algorithm

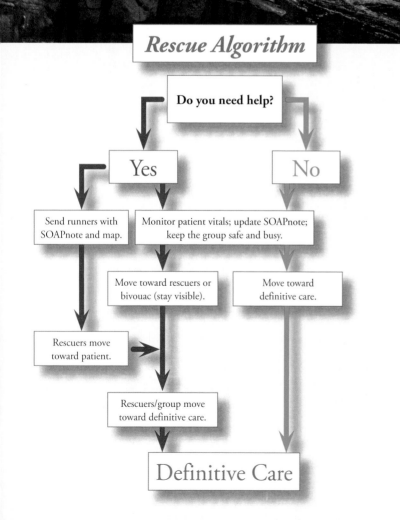

Do you need help?

Yes   No

Send runners with SOAPnote and map.

Monitor patient vitals; update SOAPnote; keep the group safe and busy.

Move toward rescuers or bivouac (stay visible).

Move toward definitive care.

Rescuers move toward patient.

Rescuers/group move toward definitive care.

Definitive Care

Congratulations!

1. The scene is safe.
2. The primary and secondary surveys are done.
3. You've checked on the group and ensured that they are comfortable, safe, and busy.
4. You've examined the patient from head to toe and taken their vital signs.
5. You've interviewed them, diagnosed and field-treated their injuries, and recorded everything on a SOAPnote.
6. Now you are ready to consider the rescue options.

Don't evacuate

Evacuate

Initiate rescue

Don't evacuate: go—green light

You don't need to evacuate your patient if their problem is minor enough that they will recover quickly and can continue on their own.

- Minor musculoskeletal injuries (e.g., ankle strain, jammed finger)
- Minor soft tissue injuries (e.g., contusions, minor burns, muscle strain)
- Minor environmental emergencies (e.g., mild hypothermia or heat exhaustion)
- Resolved medical issues (e.g., hypoglycemia, a bee sting that doesn't evolve into anaphylaxis)
- If you decide evacuation is not necessary, be sure that the patient and each person in the group will remain safe until the group can carry on.
  - Ensure that they have shelter, food, water, etc.
  - If a bivouac is necessary, make sure that the group knows how to do this, or that you help them (especially important if you are going to leave the group on their own for any length of time).

Evacuate: yield—what are your options?

If your patient's injury or illness is severe enough that they need further treatment by a physician, you must evacuate—which raises additional questions, including two big ones:

1. Can you perform a self-rescue?
2. Do you need help (see below)?

- If you decide to self-rescue, you must:
  - Know how to do it.
  - Know when you can start and how long it will take.
  - Have the necessary personnel, skills, and equipment. For instance, can the patient walk with assistance? Will you improvise a litter, and are there enough people to carry it?
  - Do you know how to lift and carry the patient, if necessary (see the lifting and moving section on the next page)?
  - Can you be certain that the patient and each person in the group will remain safe until you get everyone out?

Initiate rescue: stop—you need help

Your patient needs definitive care, and you don't have the personnel, skills, or equipment to effect a rescue on your own. Okay...

- How will you get help? Via runners (send two people, if possible), cell phone, radio, or a combination?
- If you send runners, what will they have with them?
  - SOAPnote (also, begin a new SOAPnote for your patient after the runners leave)
  - A list of the people in your group
  - A map with your location (GPS coordinates), landmarks and the time you left clearly marked
  - Bivouac equipment, and food, if necessary
  - Communication devices, if available
- Will you bivouac and wait for the rescuers or move toward the rescuers as they respond to the scene? (See algorithm at left).
- What will you do to keep your patient stabilized while you wait or move?
- What things can you do to keep the group safe—sheltered, fed, hydrated, and busy?

WHILE WAITING FOR HELP . . .

- **Keep track of people**—use the buddy system: no one wanders off alone.
- **Keep everyone busy** (e.g., gathering wood, making shelters, cooking, rubbing each other's feet, etc.).
- **Create shelter** for everyone in the best location (e.g., safe, access to water, fuel for fire, etc.).
- **Get water** or melt snow and make something warm to drink (purify the water first).
- If food is available, **make a meal** and eat.
- **Keep spirits up**, be positive, reassure, make sure everyone has something to do.
- **Create light and warmth**—build a fire; hypo-wrap if necessary.
- **Make yourselves big** and easy to find: fire (light and smoke), whistle (three blasts), survey tape (string it everywhere to lead rescuers to you).
- Continuously **monitor** your patient.
- Continuously **monitor** everyone else in the group.

Patient lifting and moving techniques

At some point during any backcountry rescue, the patient will have to move themselves or be moved by others. Unless scene safety or patient/rescuer safety is a concern, the patient should be kept lying still until the extent of their injuries is determined.

WHEN TO MOVE YOUR PATIENT FIRST

In situations when objective hazards pose an immediate danger, consider moving your patient before beginning your assessment. These hazards include, but are not limited to, the following:

- Cold water
- Rockfall
- Icefall
- Avalanche
- Proximity to a drop off

Other reasons to move the patient early may include:

- To assure and maintain a patent[1] airway
- To better splint injuries or stabilize the spine
- To get the patient off the cold ground or protect them from the environment

INDIVIDUAL AND GROUP CONSIDERATIONS

- Know your own strength and physical limitations—do not put yourself (or your back) in danger.
- Work together—many hands make light work.
- Plan your moves.
- The person at the patient's head always directs the team's movements (counting "one, two, three, lift" is the usual method).

SPECIFIC INSTRUCTIONS ON LIFTING AND MOVING

- It's always safe to move a patient from the position of injury to the position of function.
- Avoid flexion[2] of the head and neck—although it's always fine to gently move the head back to a neutral position.
- Avoid rotating the pelvis out of alignment with the shoulders.
- Use proper body mechanics.
    - Lift with your legs and keep your back straight.
    - Try not to overreach or twist.
    - Keep the weight as close to your body as possible.
    - Use assists, such as foam pads and tent flies, to help slide your patient.
- Logroll the patient to assess their spine or get them onto a pad.
    - Keep their head, shoulders, and pelvis in line while rolling them onto their side (avoid rolling them onto an injury, e.g., broken ribs).
    - Although one person can do it, two or three make it much easier.
- Lifting and moving over a distance.
    - If you drag the patient, drag them in line with their spine (not sideways).
    - Logroll them onto a pad or other device.
    - If there are not spinal concerns, consider carrying them.
- Body Elevation and Movement (BEAM).
    - Use many hands (5 – 7 people) to support the body and spine.
    - With good spinal immobilization, you can move the patient short distances (<30 feet).

KEYS TO SAFE LIFTING

- If possible, have help
- Lift in unison
- Lift with your legs
- Keep your back straight
- Don't twist as you lift
- Don't reach as you lift
- Use aids (e.g., drag pads)

When moving a patient as a group, the person at the head makes the call, "One, two, three...lift." Everyone lifts as one with the patient being supported evenly. If the person is crumpled, move them and place them on a pad in their original (crumpled) position. You will de-crumple and reposition them as the evaluation continues.

---

1 A patent airway is one that is open, functioning normally, and will likely stay functioning normally.
2 Flexion of the head is movement that brings the chin toward the chest.

PATIENT ASSESSMENT CHECKLIST

SCENE SURVEY
- ☐ IS THE SCENE SAFE?
- ☐ IS THE PATIENT SAFE?

PRIMARY ASSESSMENT
- ☐ IS THE PATIENT CONSCIOUS?
- ☐ DO THEY HAVE AN OPEN AIRWAY?
- ☐ ARE THEY BREATHING?
- ☐ DO THEY HAVE A PULSE?
- ☐ ARE THEY BLEEDING?
- ☐ ARE THERE ANY SERIOUS INJURIES ON THE CHUNK CHECK?
- ☐ DO THEY NEED TO BE MOVED?
- ☐ DO WE NEED TO PROTECT THEM FROM THE ENVIRONMENT?

SECONDARY ASSESSMENT — VITAL SIGNS
- ☐ WHAT IS THEIR RESPIRATORY RATE & EFFORT?
- ☐ WHAT IS THEIR HEART RATE & EFFORT?
- ☐ WHAT IS THEIR LEVEL OF CONSCIOUSNESS?
- ☐ WHAT IS THEIR SKIN COLOR, TEMPERATURE, & MOISTURE?

SECONDARY ASSESSMENT — PATIENT EXAM
- ☐ HEAD: SCALP, FACE, EYES, NOSE, MOUTH
- ☐ NECK: SPINE, TRACHEA
- ☐ CHEST: CLAVICLES, SHOULDERS, RIBS
- ☐ ABDOMEN: COMPRESS THE ABDOMEN
- ☐ PELVIS: COMPRESS THE PELVIS ANTERIOR/POSTERIOR, LATERAL
- ☐ LEGS: CIRCULATION, SENSATION, MOTION
- ☐ ARMS: CIRCULATION, SENSATION, MOTION
- ☐ BACK: LOG ROLL AND PALPATE THE LENGTH OF THE SPINE

SECONDARY ASSESSMENT — AMPLE HISTORY
- ☐ ALLERGY: ALLERGY TO DRUGS, FOODS, INSECTS, ETC.
- ☐ MEDS: PRESCRIPTION & NONPRESCRIPTION DRUGS
- ☐ PREVIOUS: SIGNIFICANT PAST MEDICAL HISTORY, SURGERIES
- ☐ LAST: INTAKE & OUTPUT
- ☐ EVENT: EVENTS LEADING UP TO THE CRISIS

SOAP NOTE
- ☐ PUTTING IT ALL TOGETHER & CREATING TREATMENT PLAN

RESCUE PLAN
- ☐ LOOKING AT ALL FACTORS & PLANNING EVAC-UATION

Really? Did you not see *PLAN* in the header?

Talking into a glove? Huh? It's called improvising. During a night whitewater rescue training exercise, the rescuers needed to waterproof their radios. Brilliant!

The first 5 minutes...
CRITICAL CARE
dealing with immediate life threats

There are certain medical emergencies that scream **NOW!**

These are the things you find during your primary and secondary

surveys that can **KILL** your patient, maybe in the next few minutes,

maybe in the next hour or two. This isn't the time to

boil Ramen Noodles or build an igloo—it's time to move,

and move fast! Diagnose > treat > and then

GET YOUR PATIENT OUT OF THERE!

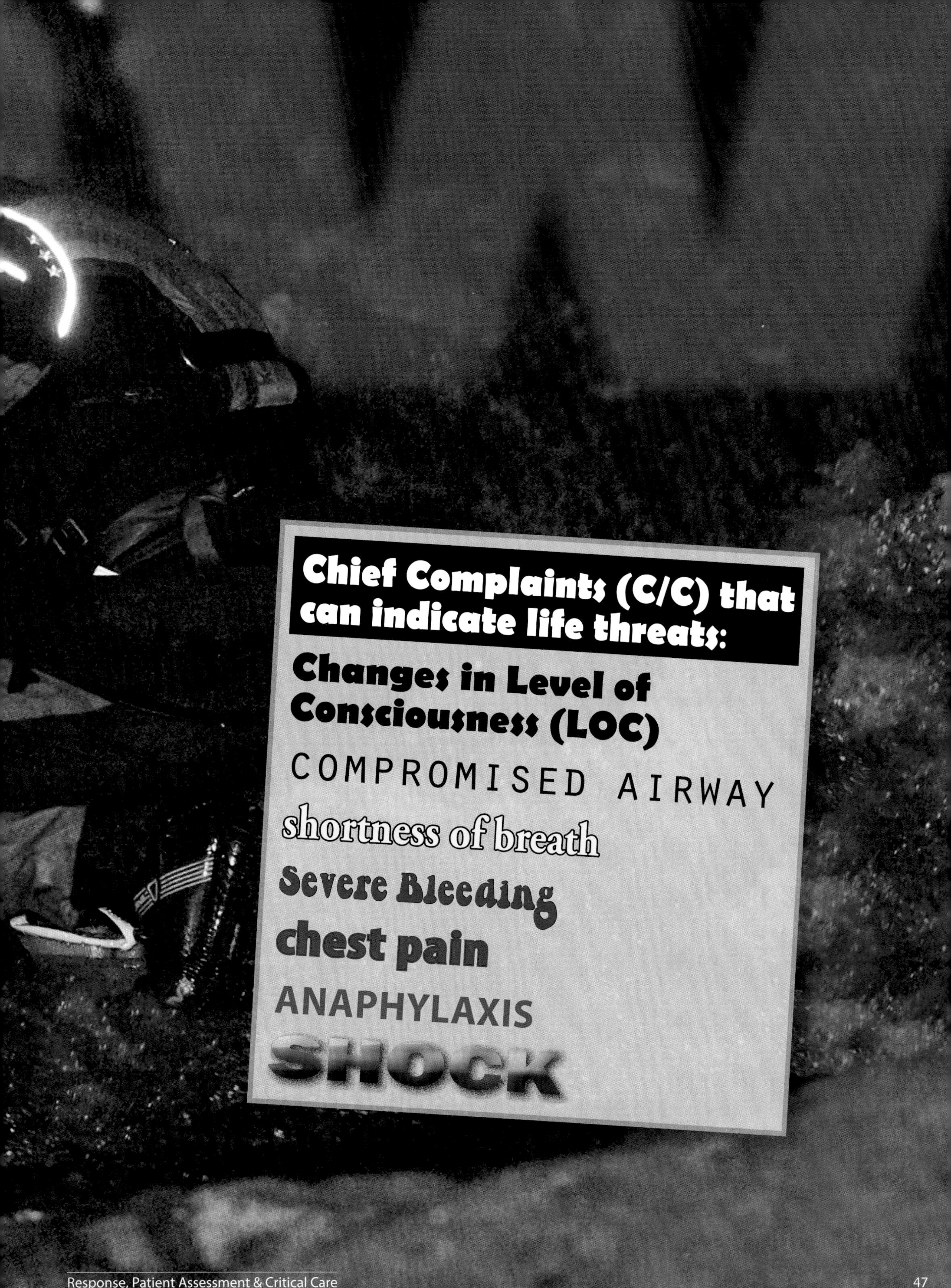

Chief Complaints (C/C) that can indicate life threats:

Changes in Level of Consciousness (LOC)

COMPROMISED AIRWAY

shortness of breath

Severe Bleeding

chest pain

ANAPHYLAXIS

SHOCK

Chief complaint: Change in Level of Consciousness

A change in level of consciousness indicates that there is something wrong with the brain—a potentially life-threatening problem. If the patient's LOC deteriorates over time, assume their condition is getting worse. To survive and thrive, the brain needs:

- oxygen
- glucose
- the ideal temperature
- proper intracranial pressure
- appropriate neuronal (electrical) activity

Etiology* of Changes in LOC

The **"H's"** of my aching **H**ead remind us of the various etiologies that can cause a change in level of consciousness. These etiologies can be divided into five groups based on their cause(s) and the differential diagnosis **(d/d)**. Keep these etiologies in mind so that when there is a change in level of consciousness, you will be prepared to determine the underlying cause, and treat it.

Hypoxia

Oxygen

Hypoxia is caused by too little O_2 in the air we breathe.
d/d: anoxic atmosphere (extremely low oxygen level: methane, carbon dioxide displace O_2)

Hypoxia is caused by too little O_2 in the blood.
d/d: CO poisoning, obstructed airway, pulmonary emboli, pulmonary edema

Hypoxia is caused by too little blood flow to the brain.
d/d: heart failure, cerebrovascular accident (CVA), shock

Hypoglycemia
Hyperglycemia

Glucose

Hypoglycemia occurs when there is plenty of insulin but not enough blood glucose.
d/d: insulin shock

Hyperglycemia occurs when there is too much blood glucose and not enough insulin.
d/d: diabetic coma, diabetic ketoacidosis (DKA)

Hypothermia
Hyperthermia

Temperature

Hypothermia: too cold to think
d/d: hypothermia, core temp <96°F

Hyperthermia: too hot to function
d/d: heat stroke, infectious disease—high fever, temperature >104°F

Head trauma

Pressure

Head trauma: too much Intracranial Pressure, ICP
d/d: traumatic brain injury with swelling, hemorrhagic CVA

Hypoactivity
Hyperactivity

Neuronal Activity

Hypoactivity: neuronal activity with slowed conduction
d/d: drugs, alcohol, toxins

Hyperactivity: too much neuronal activity
d/d: seizures, drugs, toxins

* The cause, set of causes, or manner of causation of a disease or condition

WILDCARE™

Changes in LOC
Physiology & Treatment

P Physiology

Oxygen & Glucose

The brain is a hypermetabolic organ with a constant demand for oxygen and glucose. Both are delivered to the brain via the circulation, therefore, there is a constant demand for cerebral blood flow. Anything that interferes with the amount of cerebral blood flow or the amount of O_2 or glucose in the blood will cause a deteriorating LOC.

Temperature

The brain is very temperature-sensitive, especially to the cold, and when the brain cools down, we get very stupid, very fast. As the core temperature goes down, the thought processes of the brain slow. Initial effects of cooling begin at a core temperature of around 96^0F and worsen as the temperature falls.

The brain is also affected by high core temperatures caused by a fever or heat stroke. As the temperature of the brain climbs past 104^0F, the neuronal activity increases and can cause hallucinations as well as seizures. The risk of a febrile seizure has more to do with how quickly the temperature goes up rather than how high the temperature goes.

Pressure

Within the cranium, intracranial pressure (ICP) should be constant. If that pressure increases, it will interfere with the blood flow to the brain. As the ICP increases, the systolic blood pressure must also increase to get the blood from the heart and lungs to the brain. The classic signs of increasing ICP are decreasing LOC, with increasing respirations, increasing systolic BP, widening pulse pressure (the systolic pressure goes up much faster than the diastolic pressure, widening the difference between the two, which equals increasing pulse pressure), and a slowing heart rate (bradycardia).

Neuronal Activity

The brain is made up of nerve cells and their supporting structure. The nerves are constantly working, chatting with one another using bursts of electrical activity to keep us functioning. These electrical impulses are known as neuronal activity. If the neuronal activity becomes too fast or chaotic, a seizure will occur.

T Critical treatment steps

Determine and monitor LOC with the AVPU scale

Conscious: *"The lights are on, but is anyone home?"*
 Awake: but are they alert and oriented times 3 (A&Ox3)?
  1. Person: Do they know who they are?
  2. Place: Do they know where they are?
  3. Time: Do they know the day, week, and year?
Unconscious: But are they responsive or unresponsive?
 Verbal stimuli: *"Hello, is anyone in there?"*
  ☑ Speak to them. Do they react to hearing your voice?
  ☑ Do they follow simple commands (e.g., give a thumb's up)?
 Painful stimuli: *"That's got to hurt."*
  ☑ No response to verbal stimuli, but is there response to painful stimuli?
  ☑ Gently pinch them or rub your knuckles on their sternum or pull the hairs on the back of their hand—is there an appropriate response to pain?
 Unresponsive: *"I'm not getting anything, here."*
  ☑ No response to verbal or painful stimuli? The patient is considered to be comatose.

Consider the causes by asking these questions

 ☑ Are they getting enough oxygen?
 ☑ Does the patient have an open airway and are they breathing?
 ☑ What is their skin color? Are they pale, cyanotic, and/or diaphoretic (sweaty)?
 ☑ How well are they breathing? Are they gurgling or making any snoring sounds when they breathe?
 ☑ How is their circulation?
 ☑ What is their heart rate and blood pressure?
 ☑ Do they have signs and symptoms of shock?
 ☑ What is their skin temperature? Is it warm or cool, wet or dry?
 ☑ Is there a change in personality?
 ☑ Do they have any signs of head trauma indicating a possible head injury with increasing intracranial pressure?
 ☑ Are they having any seizures indicating an increase in neuronal activity?

Principles of managing changes in LOC

 ☑ Neurological assessment is an ongoing process. Continuously monitor the patient's LOC, where they are on the AVPU scale, and their vital signs.
 ☑ Maintain and monitor the airway and breathing.
 ☑ If unconscious, place the patient in the recovery position to protect their airway.
 ☑ If the patient is seizing, protect them from further injury.
 ☑ If their respiratory rate is less than 10 or greater than 30 breaths per minute, assist-breathe, 1 breath every 5 seconds.
 ☑ If you suspect a diabetic emergency, give the patient sugar.
 ☑ If oxygen is available, give the patient 10 – 15lpm of oxygen by non-rebreather mask.
 ☑ Recognize changes in LOC early and evacuate the patient ASAP if deterioration occurs; these patients tend to worsen rapidly.
 ☑ Get help; a patient with a deteriorating LOC needs to be evacuated immediately.

COMPROMISED

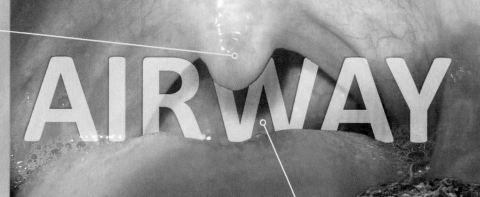

AIRWAY

Yeah, that's the "hangy-downy thing" in the back of your mouth that you asked your mom about when you were a kid—technically, it's your uvula, a still-mysterious appendage nearly unique to humans that aids in speech and provides a gag reflex.

Don't even think about asking us how we got this photo.

Yum. Mom's famous meatballs. But if one of them gets stuck in your trachea on the way to your gullet, then it becomes a Foreign Body Airway Obstruction (FBAO)—which is very bad and requires immediate action.

FBAO
FOREIGN BODY AIRWAY OBSTRUCTION

Assess for airway obstruction
1. Can they talk? Are they moving air? If yes, wait and let them cough and clear their own airway.
2. Is there poor or no air exchange, increased respiratory difficulty, possible cyanosis, or are they giving the universal choking sign?

Position them for abdominal thrusts
1. Stand or kneel behind the patient and wrap your arms around the victim's waist.
2. Place the thumb side of your fist against their abdomen, in the midline, slightly above the navel and well below the sternum.

Deliver abdominal thrusts
1. Grasp your fist with your other hand and press your fist into the patient's abdomen with a quick, forceful upward thrust.
2. Repeat thrusts.
3. Repeat thrusts until the object is expelled from the airway or the patient becomes unconscious.
4. Obese or pregnant: perform chest thrusts instead of abdominal thrusts.

If the patient becomes unresponsive
1. Activate the Emergency Response System—**call 911**.
2. Send someone to call for help, but do not leave the patient alone.
3. Begin CPR—30:2.
4. Lower the patient to the ground and begin chest compressions at a rate of 100 per minute.
5. Each time you go to give ventilations, open the victim's mouth wide and look inside for the object—if the object is visible and easily removed, do so.

Other causes of partial or complete airway obstruction
- Epiglottitis—acute swelling of the epiglottis seen mostly in children 2 – 6 years of age.
- Mucus plugs—commonly seen in patients with a stoma
- Airway Burns—Swelling caused by burns to the airway after the inhalation of super-heated gases from a fire or chemicals.
- Peritonsillar abscess—A pocket of infection around the tonsil causing swelling and significant trouble swallowing.
- Croup—tends to appear in children between 3 months and 5 years old and starts as what appears to be a mild cold but is typically identified as having a seal-like bark cough. It is most commonly caused by a virus.

For any patient with partial airway obstructions:
Follow the SOB guidelines on the next page.

8 MINUTES: THAT'S ABOUT ALL YOU'VE GOT

C/C
shortness of breath

The **SENSATION** of shortness of breath (SOB) occurs when the brain perceives that it is not getting enough oxygen (O_2). There is either not enough oxygen getting into the blood, or there is not enough oxygenated blood getting to the brain.

Sucking wind? Here's an asthma simulator—run hard and then try breathing through a straw.

CAUSES OF lack of O_2

ANOXIA—not enough oxygen in the air.

HYPOXIA—there is plenty of O_2 in the air, but it cannot get into the alveoli, and therefore into the blood.

HYPOPERFUSION—the blood is oxygenated, but it is not getting to the brain quickly enough.

ASTHMA—chronic airway inflammation.

ANAPHYLAXIS—allergic reaction, narrows the bronchi causing acute reduction of airflow.

PRINCIPLES OF MANAGEMENT OF shortness of breath

LOOK at your patient. ○ Are they struggling to breathe? ○ Is their mouth wide open? ○ Are they obviously working to breathe? ○ Are they using accessory muscles[1] to breathe? ○ Are they cyanotic or diaphoretic (sweaty)? ○ Watch them as they breathe. ○ Does the rib cage expand and contract normally? ○ Is there any obvious bruising, deformity, or a sucking chest wound?[2]

LISTEN to their breath sounds. ○ Is there wheezing, gurgling, and/or crepitation?[3] ○ Are there breath sounds on both sides of the rib cage?

FEEL their chest wall. ○ As they breathe, is their chest wall expanding and contracting normally? ○ Is there splinting[4] or paradoxical motion?[5]

TREATMENT OF shortness of breath

CHECK THE ABCS ○ Airway, Breathing, Circulation

SUPPORT THE PATIENT'S RESPIRATIONS ○ sitting them up may help.

ASSIST-BREATHE for them if they cannot move enough air on their own, or if their respiratory rate is less than 10 or greater than 30 breaths per minute. ○ 1 breath every 5 seconds.

IF OXYGEN IS AVAILABLE ○ give them 10 – 15lpm by non-rebreather mask.

IF MEDICATION IS AVAILABLE ○ assist/administer epinephrine, diphenhydramine, or inhalers, as prescribed.

GET HELP ○ **This patient needs to be evacuated ASAP!**

$<O_2$

---

1. **Accessory muscles**: The diaphragm and intercostal muscles do most of the work during normal breathing; when breathing is labored, many other muscles of the chest, abdomen, and back come into play—and it's obvious.
2. **Sucking chest wound**: A pneumothorax, typically resulting from trauma, where air collects in the pleural space, growing larger with each inhalation, and slowly collapsing the lung—this is a life-threatening emergency.
3. **Crepitation**: The grating sound and palpable sensation of broken bone ends rubbing against each other.
4. **Splinting** (as it relates to shortness of breath): A tensing and stiffening of the abdominal muscles to minimize pain during breathing.
5. **Paradoxical motion**: The lung deflates during inhalation and balloons out during expiration—the opposite of normal breathing.

severe bleeding

C/C

Severe bleeding can be both a Chief Complaint and a Sign—by definition, *severe bleeding* will be obvious, even if the patient doesn't complain about it!

For an in-depth look at bleeding, see the PAS and soft tissue injury sections.

CONTROLLING BLEEDING
This is a primary concern with any wound—try to keep as much of the "red stuff" in the vasculature as possible! And before you start treating any wound, **put on your BSI**.

Direct pressure—Because the vast majority of bleeding is venous, it is under low pressure, and can usually be controlled with direct pressure.

1. Apply pressure directly to the wound with your gloved hand.
2. If possible, place some absorbent material, such as gauze pads, on top of the wound before applying pressure—it will act as a sponge and help hold the blood in place.
3. Once the bleeding has stopped, maintain direct pressure for an additional ten minutes to allow blood clots to form—may replace direct pressure with a pressure dressing.

Pressure dressing

1. Wrap an elastic bandage or tie a cravat over a bulky dressing to hold it in place—wrap it tightly enough so that it stays in place and controls bleeding. This frees up the rescuer's hands for further assessment or treatment.
2. Leave the pressure dressing in place for *only* 20 minutes.
3. Check distal pulses after application—they should still be palpable (do not cut off circulation).

Hemostatic agents

- These are chemical substances that act by inhibiting fibrinolysis (the body's natural tendency to prevent blood clots from growing too large) and/or promoting coagulation (clotting).
- Several types of hemostatic agents are available, among them: QuikClot, HemCon, Woundstat, Celox, and Combat Gauze.
  - QuikClot and HemCon were the first two and were found to be effective but had the side effect of being exothermic (heat-causing) in their reaction to the bodily fluid (blood) and could cause cutaneous burns.
  - Woundstat, Celox, and Combat Gauze were found to be consistently more effective without causing exothermic reactions.
- Hemostatic agents should only be used for large bleeds or bleeds that cannot be controlled with direct pressure and pressure dressings.
- Most hemostatic agents are incorporated into gauze rather than being used granulated or as a powder—the loose agent could be blown into the rescuer's eyes, causing significant vision problems or reacting with other bodily fluids.
- To maximize effectiveness, Gauze-style hemostatic agents should be applied with 3 minutes of sustained direct pressure over the bleeding site, followed by the application of a pressure dressing for an additional 20 minutes.

The advantages of hemostatic agents

They are capable of stopping large arterial and venous bleeding within 2 minutes of application when applied to an actively bleeding wound through a pool of blood.

No pre-application preparation is needed.

They are simple for the rescuer or the injured person to apply.

They are lightweight and durable.

They have a long shelf-life, even in extreme environments.

They are safe to use with a very low risk of injury and transmission of disease or infection.

They are inexpensive.

TOURNIQUETS

THE LAST RESORT FOR SEVERE BLEEDING

6

Quarts/liters of blood in the average adult human—*exsanguination* (bleeding to death) can occur in mere minutes if a major artery is cut; lose 40% (2.4 quarts), and without immediate help you will die.

A **tourniquet** is the last option—a device used when extreme, life-threatening bleeding in an extremity cannot be controlled in any other way. Unlike direct pressure and pressure dressings, which are utilized immediately and with no reservations, a tourniquet is *resorted to*—there are inevitable complications that must be understood (e.g., extreme pain, losing the limb to save the patient). Fortunately, the majority of bleeding can be controlled with conventional measures, so tourniquets are rarely needed. But for uncontrolled bleeds in major limb arteries (femoral, brachial, or radial), this may be your only option to save a life.

- Tourniquets are used on extremities only.
- Because they compress the tissues overlying the artery with enough force to shut off that artery, tourniquets produce ischemia in the distal tissues, depriving those tissues of oxygen and increasing the risk of tissue death.
- There are a variety of tourniquets available on the market—every commercial tourniquet is designed for a single use.
- The two tourniquets identified as being 100% effective at stopping bleeding by the U.S. Army Institute of Surgical Research are the Combat Application Tourniquet (C-A-T) and the SOF Tactical Tourniquet (SOFTT).
- Apply the tourniquet directly to the skin, 2 – 3 inches proximal to the hemorrhage site, but not over a joint space.
- Check for distal pulses—*they must not be present*—if the distal pulses are present, the tourniquet needs to be tightened. The distal arterial blood flow *must* be stopped, or compartment syndrome or an expanding hematoma may develop in the limb, both of which are avoidable complications.
- Note the time the tourniquet was put on the patient (this is crucial).
- There is significant pain associated with the application of a tourniquet as the tissues become ischemic and begin to die—this is not an indication of improper application.
- If the evacuation is going to take more than two hours and the patient is not in shock, the removal of the tourniquet should be considered if hemostatic agents are available.
- To remove a tourniquet, slowly loosen it after an alternative method of bleeding control has been put in place.
- If the patient is in shock, you must leave the tourniquet on until the patient arrives at definitive care—and yes, the limb may be lost.

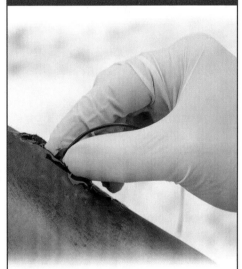

Direct pressure on an arterial bleed and using a commercial tourniquet

Extreme bleeding must be controlled quickly—direct digital pressure on a spurting artery and/or a tourniquet may be necessary. It is easy to improvise a tourniquet in the field. (More info in the soft tissue section.)

C/ chest pain

ALL chest pain

is considered cardiac in nature, a possible acute myocardial infarction (MI) [1], until proven otherwise. There are many harmless causes of chest pain, such as indigestion, heartburn, and pulled chest-wall muscles, but our concern with chest pain is the chance that it is cardiac-related.

No, it's not a button, it's an ordinary aspirin tablet—and it may be small, but it's mighty in the treatment of an MI.

ASPIRIN, whether round or capsule-shaped, is a medical wonder—working in so many ways that modern medicine wouldn't be the same without it. When a person is having a heart attack, fatty acid deposits in the blood vessels (atherosclerosis) can burst, and the body responds by sending platelets to the scene to form a clot—blocking the vessel and causing pain and tissue death. Aspirin reduces the clumping action of the platelets, helping to keep the vessel open and buying the patient precious time. It is a strong drug, not to be taken lightly.

Typical cardiac chest pain indicating acute coronary syndrome—signs & symptoms

- Left-sided, substernal chest pain, pressure, or tightness.
- The discomfort may radiate into the left arm, right arm, both arms, the lower jaw, etc.
- Discomfort is frequently associated with a sensation of shortness of breath.
- Discomfort is frequently associated with a cold sweat (diaphoresis).
- The chest pain or shortness of breath worsens with exertion.
- Vital signs indicate shock: rapid and shallow respirations, rapid and weak heartbeat, falling blood pressure, and the skin is pale, cool, and clammy.
- The patient may also have nausea, GI upset, and heartburn.
- In the case of angina pectoris, there may be some relief of symptoms with rest.

Principles of management

- The primary goal is to minimize the workload on the heart.
- Unless you are absolutely certain that the pain is not cardiac, evacuate ASAP.
- The patient should be kept at rest; exertion will make it worse.
- Transport them in position of comfort.
- Keep them calm and reassure them.
- If you have aspirin with you, give them one adult, 325mg or four 81mg aspirins.
- If they have a history of angina pectoris and they have sublingual nitroglycerin (NG) with them, you may assist them in taking their medicine as long as their systolic BP is >100 (radial pulse present).
- **GET HELP**—this patient needs to be evacuated ASAP (walking out may be appropriate).

1 Myocardial Infarction: "The Big One," as Redd Fox used to say on the 70s sitcom, *Sanford and Son*—the classic heart attack during which blood flow to the heart is blocked long enough for part of the heart muscle to be damaged or die.

ANAPHYLAXIS C/C

Anaphylaxis is the extreme of an allergic reaction. The body's systemic release of histamine causes massive vasodilation and bronchoconstriction, bringing on the symptoms of an acute anaphylactic reaction: shortness of breath, wheezing, difficulty breathing, and shock.

Signs & symptoms

- Initially, itching of the eyes and face which spreads to the rest of the body
- Swelling of the throat, lips, tongue, and face
- Difficulty breathing with a sensation of shortness of breath
- Difficulty swallowing
- Anxiety
- Wheezing
- Rash consisting of hives (urticaria) that are red, raised, and itchy
- Shock

Bee stings are a common cause of anaphylaxis.

Vital signs & physical exam

RR—tachypnea (rapid breathing) with wheezing
HR—tachycardia (rapid heart rate)
BP—hypotension (low blood pressure)
LOC—anxious, may go unconscious
Skin—flushed, diaphoretic (sweaty), hives
Pupils—PERRL (pupils equal, round, and reactive to light)

Treatment

Keep the patient alive:

- Treat the bronchoconstriction and the vasodilation by administering Epinephrine (adrenalin) 0.3cc of 1:1,000 intramuscular (thigh) by an autoinjector or EpiPen.

Solve the problem:

- Once the patient's breathing and ability to swallow have stabilized, solve the problem of too much histamines by administering an antihistamine: Benadryl (diphenhydramine 25 – 50mg) by mouth every 4 hours for 24 hours.

- Evacuate the patient for further evaluation and treatment regardless of how quickly they recover.

SHOCK

 No, this kind of shock has nothing to do with electricity

Shock is not a chief complaint

like the other problems described in this critical care section. No one has ever said, "My vasculature feels compromised." Instead, shock is a condition that you may discover as you monitor a patient's vital signs. Shock occurs when the cardiovascular system fails to provide sufficient circulation to every part of the body, causing tissues to eventually suffer from a lack of oxygen. If the cause goes untreated, and the shock is severe enough, it can kill.

The cardiovascular system consists of

Heart—pumps the blood
Blood vessels—carry and distribute the blood
Blood—carries O_2 and nutrients around the body

Shock is a compensatory mechanism designed to keep the brain well-oxygenated during times of cardio-vascular insufficiency by **vasoconstricting** the peripheral circulation, thus pulling blood into the body core. It also **increases the heart rate**, which sends more blood to the brain, and **increases the respiratory rate** to maximize the amount of oxygen in the blood. Initially shock is a life-saving condition that preserves blood flow to the brain, but shock kills if it continues for too long.

types of shock

Hypovolemic shock is caused by decreased blood volume due to blood loss, dehydration, sweating, diarrhea, vomiting, or a thermal burn.

Cardiogenic shock is caused by pump failure, a heart attack (an MI or cardiac arrest).

Neurogenic shock is caused by vasodilation, a loss of vascular tone. This vasodilation results in an increase in vascular space. The space in the vasculature for the blood volume becomes too large for the blood volume, creating the same effect as hypovolemic shock. This can be caused by a spinal cord injury, acute allergic reaction (anaphylaxis), or life-threatening infection (septic shock).

Shock is often an amorphous, misunderstood, and mis-attributed term. It is NOT feeling icky as a result of a flush of adrenalin in the moments and minutes after a traumatic event or accident. Shock is a specific medical condition, and it is ALWAYS the result of a major compromise to the circulatory system.

signs & symptoms of shock

➡ Individuals in shock may be awake, but, they seem distant, not in touch with reality.

➡ They may stare off into space or be unconscious.

➡ They may not know who you are or understand that you are there to help.

➡ They may not feel pain or respond to pain.

➡ They may have an obvious wound or injury that they ignore. (They may try to walk on a broken leg or use a broken arm.)

➡ They may not know how seriously injured they are.

➡ They may have a sense of impending doom.

vital signs for shock

LOC restless, anxious, may be disoriented, or unconscious.

RR rapid and shallow (the respiratory rate increases because the brain wants more oxygen).

RR rapid, weak, and thready (the heart rate increases to deliver more blood to the brain).

Skin pale, cool, and clammy (PCC) due to vasoconstriction of the capillaries in the skin, which helps to shunt blood away from the extremities.

BP begins to fall as the compensatory mechanism (shock) begins to fail.

The patient may **collapse** if they try to stand up.

They are typically **nauseated** and they may vomit.

treatment of shock

1. Check airway/breathing—no breath, no life.
2. Control bleeding to minimize blood loss.
3. Find and treat the underlying cause(s).
4. Treat all injuries to minimize pain.
5. Keep the patient lying flat in a position of comfort; you may elevate their legs.
6. Protect the patient from the environment and maintain body temperature.
7. Monitor vital signs, reassure the patient and get help.
8. Administer O_2 if available, 10 – 15lpm by non-rebreather mask.

PRIMARY SURVEY

1. Unconscious or conscious?
2. Not breathing or breathing?
3. No pulse or pulse?
4. Bleeding or not bleeding?
5. Life-threatening disability or no disability?
6. Environmental hazards or safe?

Unconscious

AIRWAY AND BREATHING

1. **Does the patient have an open airway and are they breathing?**
   - Open and clear their airway, if necessary.
   - If they are not breathing, give assisted ventilations, 1 breath every 3 – 5 seconds.

2. **Do they have adventitious breath sounds (wheezing, gurgling, crackling, or snoring)?**
   - If so, log roll them into the recovery position to open and drain the airway.

3. **Is their breathing adequate (respiratory rate less than 10 or more than 30 breaths per minute)?**
   - If outside those parameters, give assist ventilations, 1 breath every 3 – 5 seconds.

4. **Are they having an anaphylactic reaction?**
   - If so, administer Epinephrine: 1:1000 by auto-injector.
   - Follow with Benadryl (diphenhydramine) 50mg by mouth.

CIRCULATION

1. **Do they have a pulse?**
   - If not, perform CPR.

2. **Are they bleeding?**
   - Control major bleeding with direct pressure.

3. **Do they have the signs and symptoms of shock?**
   - Obtain a complete set of vital signs and monitor every 5 minutes.
   - If vital signs indicate shock, look for underlying causes, treat the underlying causes, and treat for shock.

DEFORMITY

1. **Unconscious patients should have their cervical spine and back protected from unnecessary movement.**

2. **Are they seizing?**
   - Protect them from injury.

3. **Do they have an underlying medical condition?**
   - Check for a medical alert bracelet or necklace.
   - If you suspect a diabetic emergency, give sugar.

Disaster strikes just after the first ascent of the Matterhorn, drawn by Gustave Doré, 1865.

WILDCARE™

RAPID CRITICAL CARE EVALUATION

Recovery position

Once the patient's airway is secure, their breathing is adequate, they have a pulse, their bleeding is under control, any disability treated, and they are protected from the environment, if they are still unconscious:

1. **Log roll them into the recovery position to protect and maintain their airway—be careful to protect their cervical spine and back.**

2. **Do they have any other potentially life-threatening injuries?**
   - Once in the recovery position, do a quick "chunk check"—perform a rapid hands-on assessment of their head, neck, chest (including checking for breath sounds), back, abdomen, pelvis, and femurs.
   - Treat any significant injuries found.

Conscious
AIRWAY AND BREATHING

1. **Can the patient speak?**
   - Is their speech clear and easily understood?
   - If not, are there any signs of stroke (CVA—FAST: if impairment of Face, Arms/legs, and/or Speech, Time is of the essence)?

2. **Are they choking?**
   - If so, clear their airway—perform abdominal thrusts, if necessary.

3. **Are they having an anaphylactic reaction?**
   - If so, administer Epinephrine: 1:1000 by auto-injector.
   - Follow with Benadryl (diphenhydramine) 50mg by mouth.

4. **Are they complaining of shortness of breath (SOB) or difficulty breathing?**
   - If so, perform a word dyspnea test: have them take a deep breath and count from 1 – 10. Record the results.
   - Ask them if they have a history of asthma—if so, and they have expiratory wheezing, they are most likely suffering from an attack.
   - Help them administer a bronchodilator (e.g., albuterol) with a hand-held metered dose inhaler (MDI). Repeat the dose every 5 minutes until breathing improves.
   - Document improvement by re-administering the word dyspnea test and recording the results.
   - You may also assist with air trapping associated with asthma by performing gentle lateral chest wall compressions on exhalation to force trapped air out.
   - Regardless of the source of the SOB, if word dyspnea does not improve to 5 or more, give assisted ventilations and evacuate.

5. **Listen to their lungs for breath sounds.**
   - Do they have adventitious breath sounds?
   - Are their breath sounds equal on the right and left?
   - Absence of breath sounds on one side indicates pneumothorax—if so, monitor for progression to tension pneumothorax and evacuate.

CIRCULATION

1. **Are they bleeding?**
   - Control major bleeding with direct pressure.

2. **Do they have the signs and symptoms of shock?**
   - Obtain a complete set of vital signs and monitor every 5 minutes.
   - If vital signs indicate shock, look for underlying causes; treat the underlying causes, and treat for shock.

3. **Are they complaining of chest pain or pressure?**
   - Is it associated with SOB?
   - Is the pain, pressure and/or SOB made worse with exertion?
   - If so, assume the symptoms are cardiac-related (Acute Coronary Syndrome) and treat as such: minimize stress, keep them at rest, and reassure them.
   - If there is associated pain, give one adult aspirin dose (one 325mg or four 81mg).
   - If they have a history of angina pectoris and they have sublingual nitroglycerin, you may assist them in taking their medication as long as their systolic BP is >100 (in the field, pedal pulses present).
   - Administer O_2 and evacuate.

DEFORMITY

1. **Is there an indication of changes in level of consciousness?**

2. **Did anyone witness a seizure, or do they appear postictal (altered state of consciousness after a seizure)?**

3. **Do they have an underlying medical condition?**
   - Check for a medical alert bracelet or necklace.
   - If you suspect a diabetic emergency, give sugar.

Unconscious or conscious
ENVIRONMENT

1. **Are they safe where they are?**
   - If not, move them safely out of danger.

2. **Are there general environmental dangers?**
   - Protect them from the environment, keep them dry, maintain normal body temperature.

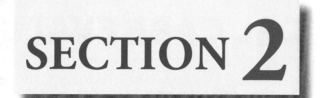

SECTION 2

ASSESSMENT AND MANAGEMENT OF TRAUMATIC INJURIES

Look close. Something's just not right here.

A TRAUMATIC INTRODUCTION

> **trau·ma** /'troumə/ *1: an injury (as a wound) to living tissue caused by an extrinsic (external) agent; 2: an often serious and body-altering physical injury, such as the removal of a limb.*

Trauma is often, well, traumatic—and can be dramatic, too: lacerations, amputations, impaled objects, burns, sprains, fractures, crush injuries, and others of their ilk, all sound (and are) universally bad. Who, after all, would want a part of their body to be "dislocated?"

While specific statistics are woefully hard to come by, anecdotal evidence suggests that wilderness misfortunes falling under the broad category of "trauma" are extremely common. As hikers, skiers, mountaineers, boaters, runners, campers, and mountain bikers, we are constantly slipping, tripping, and falling down, stabbing, poking, and burning ourselves, banging into things and having things bang into us, wrenching our joints, whacking our eyes and teeth, and delaminating our skin. For the immense pleasure of recreating in the outdoors, we happily risk beating ourselves up. Many (happily, most) of the resulting injuries are minor, can be treated quickly and easily, and won't spoil our trip; but some are serious, trip-ruining, life-threatening, rescue-initiating emergencies that take all our energy, skills and resources, and sometimes even require outside help. As a result, the trauma section of this book will be the biggest—and it will also be the section where the most hands-on instruction will be found: exciting stuff indeed!

We will break down trauma as follows:

Soft tissue injuries
- Injury or insult to the skin and immediately underlying tissues.

Joint injuries
- Strains, sprains, and aches and pains (e.g., tendonitis).

Dislocations
- When bones slip out of joint.

Fractures
- When bones break.

Orthopedic emergencies
- Injuries to the head, face, chest, pelvis, plus crush injuries and deformed fractures, and all related complications.

Each sub-section will include discussions of anatomy and physiology, signs and symptoms, prevention, recognition, and diagnosis, and immediate and long-term treatment options.

We will work our way from the outside in, beginning with the many ways that we can abuse our skin and the underlying tissues.

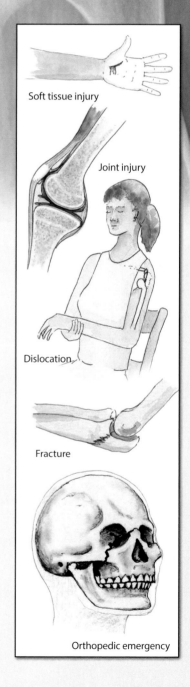

Soft tissue injury

Joint injury

Dislocation

Fracture

Orthopedic emergency

the Integumentary System

(our skin)

that thin, stretchy stuff that covers every square inch of us

Can we make skin?

No, we can't zip on new skin yet, but wonderful medical advances have been made in recent years, especially for replacing the skin on severely burned patients.

Some products use porcine (swine) small intestine tissue to create pliable sheets which serve as biocompatible scaffolds that the patient's body uses to facilitate healing of damaged tissue (particularly useful for burn patients).

A product called Integra® uses two layers—a base layer matrix of interwoven bovine collagen and a sticky carbohydrate molecule, and an upper layer of flexible silicon. Once applied to the burn area, the patient's own cells climb onto the matrix and grow a new dermis. The top layer of Integra® is then removed and a thin sheet of the patient's own epithelial cells is applied. Eventually, a new epidermis is reconstructed.

Another product, from Australia, Spray-on skin, incubates a small sample of the patient's healthy skin with an enzyme solution, loosening critical basal cells at the dermal-epidermal junction. The cells are suspended in a solution, which is then sprayed onto the wound, and the healing begins—amazingly, this spray can cover an area up to 80 times the size of the sample!

Our skin is so amazing—no other organ (yes, our skin is indeed an organ) can withstand the abuse, neglect, and daily beatings that our skin endures (of course, no other organ is on the *outside*).

- It holds us together—keeps the good things in and the bad things out.
- It is waterproof, breathable, stretchable, washable, wrinkle-resistant, and self-repairing.
- It is constantly rebuilding itself after being ravaged by abrasions, scratches, lacerations, burns, irritants (e.g., poison ivy), and insect bites.
- It is continuously protecting us from the invasion of disease-causing microbes, viruses, bacteria, and fungi.
- It prevents dehydration, helps with thermoregulation, and produces vitamin D.
- Without our skin, we would quickly die from dehydration, heat loss, and infectious disease—plus we would look really weird.

The skinny facts

- The skin is the largest organ in the human body.
- It covers our entire body.
- A typical adult has 1.5 – 2 square meters (16 – 22 square feet) of skin.
- It is replaced in its entirety every month or so.
- The thickness varies from 1.5mm (scalp) to 4mm (upper back).
- Skin makes up about 10% of total body weight.
- Skin cells die and are replaced at the rate of 30k – 40k per minute.
- Every cubic centimeter of skin contains:
  - 70cm of blood vessels
  - 55cm of nerves
  - 100 sweat glands
  - 15 oil glands
  - 230 sensory receptors (nerve endings)

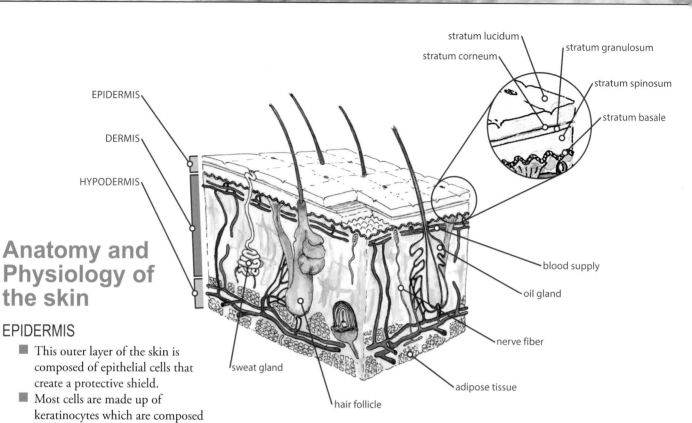

EPIDERMIS

DERMIS

HYPODERMIS

stratum lucidum
stratum corneum
stratum granulosum
stratum spinosum
stratum basale

blood supply

oil gland

nerve fiber

adipose tissue

hair follicle

sweat gland

Anatomy and Physiology of the skin

EPIDERMIS

- This outer layer of the skin is composed of epithelial cells that create a protective shield.
- Most cells are made up of keratinocytes which are composed of tough, fibrous proteins.
  - These cells arise from the basal layer at the base of the epidermis and migrate toward the surface of the skin.
  - As they reach the surface and are worn away, new ones replace them.
- Layers of the epidermis (from the outermost layer, inwards).
  - Stratum corneum
  - Stratum lucidum
  - Stratum granulosum
  - Stratum spinosum
  - Stratum basale
- Other cells that make up the epidermis include melanocytes that produce the skin pigment melanin responsible for skin color.
  - When exposed to sun, the melanocytes cause the skin to tan by producing more melanin.
- There are also Langerhan's cells, (macrophages) that help activate our immune system and protect us from infectious disease, and Merkel cells that provide sensory receptors for touch.

DERMIS

- The dermis is a tough, flexible layer primarily made up of connective tissue.
- This semi-fluid matrix of collagen, elastin, and reticular fibers binds everything together.
- The dermis is supplied with nerves, blood vessels, lymphatic vessels, hair follicles, and oil and sweat glands.
- It is attached to the underlying hypodermis.

HYPODERMIS

- The hypodermis is not actually part of the skin, but it supports the skin, shares many of the same functions, and suffers the same insults.
- It is made up of adipose tissue (fat) and has a rich blood and nerve supply.
- The hypodermis gives the skin its insulation and thermoregulation capabilities.

Functions of the skin

WATERPROOF

- Like waterproof-breathable fabrics, our skin keeps outside liquids from getting in, while controlling the rate that inside liquid gets out (via sweating).
  - When a full-thickness burn occurs, the waterproof layer is destroyed, and there will be significant fluid loss due to dehydration.

MICROBE RESISTANT

- Our skin prevents the vast majority of infections.
  - Only a few infectious diseases can penetrate intact skin.
  - When the skin is damaged (cut, burned), it allows temporary access to invading microbes.

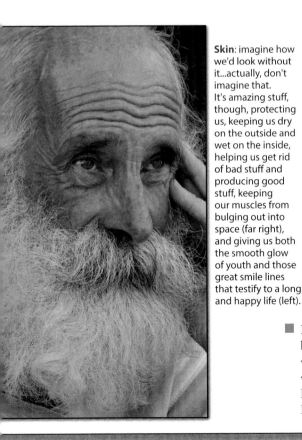

Skin: imagine how we'd look without it...actually, don't imagine that. It's amazing stuff, though, protecting us, keeping us dry on the outside and wet on the inside, helping us get rid of bad stuff and producing good stuff, keeping our muscles from bulging out into space (far right), and giving us both the smooth glow of youth and those great smile lines that testify to a long and happy life (left).

THERMOREGULATORY

- The skin controls our core temperature by adjusting blood flow and the rate of sweat production.
  - If we begin to overheat, the blood vessels in the skin dilate, increasing blood flow to the skin, which allows excess heat to dissipate (via radiation and convection).
- When the ambient air temperature rises above 80 degrees, the body (even at rest) can no longer dissipate heat via only blood vessel dilation, and sweating will begin.
- If we overheat more (e.g., during heavy exercise) the sweat glands will increase sweat production, which will evaporate and cool the skin (and the blood—which then returns and helps cool the core).
  - The evaporation of sweat off the skin accounts for up to 90% of our cooling efficiency in hot environments.
  - The rate of cooling from sweating is dependent on the temperature and humidity of the surrounding air—the higher the temperature and the lower the humidity, the more effective the cooling will be.
  - The risk of heat-related injuries is highest on days with high heat and high humidity.
  - When the humidity reaches 100%, evaporation (and the cooling) ceases—when treating heat-related injuries in this situation, external cooling will be needed.
- If we get too cool, the process will be reversed (the blood vessels will vasoconstrict and the sweat glands will turn off) thus preserving heat in the core and preventing hypothermia.

SENSORY

- Skin is laced with nerves and is capable of differentiating many different sensations.
  - Texture
  - Temperature
  - Vibration
  - Pressure
  - Pain

STORAGE AND SYNTHESIS

- Skin stores lipids and water.
- Skin produces vitamin D.
  - A form of cholesterol is converted to vitamin D by sunlight.
  - Vitamin D is important in the absorption of calcium in the small intestine.

EXCRETION AND ABSORPTION

- Sweat excretes urea (1/130th the concentration of urine).
- Medicine can be administered through the skin via ointments or by means of an adhesive patch (e.g., nicotine patch).

COSMESIS

- Skin helps give us our appearance.
- Our skin can help others to assess our mood, physical state, and attractiveness.

Muscle and skin make us (some of us, anyway) look like this.

Soft Tissue Injuries

A sprained ankle: the classic backcountry soft tissue injury. In a couple of days it will turn a delightful greenish-yellow. Initial treatment is **RICE**. Don't worry, we'll tell you what that means later.

Soft tissue injuries

are among the most common injuries that you will encounter, especially in a wilderness setting. Just stepping out the front door makes us vulnerable to all sorts of assaults on the non-structural parts of our bodies—we are constantly stumbling and bumping into things, bashing ourselves, slipping and skidding and falling down, scratching, scraping, burning, and slicing ourselves. It's all part of the fun, and it's why Band-aids were invented. Of course, not every injury is just a boo-boo that can be quickly solved by a mom with some iodine, an adhesive bandage, and a kiss. While many soft tissue injuries are indeed minor inconveniences that you can treat quickly with what you have in your first aid kit (and which won't end your trip, or even your day), others are life-threatening and will take all of your skills, effort, and resources (and perhaps the help of others).

SO, WHAT IS SOFT TISSUE?

Soft tissue is everything that isn't bone:
- Skin
- Muscle
- Fat
- Tendons
- Ligaments
- Nerves
- Organs
- Eyes
- Teeth

And the injuries associated with soft tissue include:
- Abrasions (scrapes)
- Contusion/hematomas (bruises)
- Incisions and lacerations (cuts)
- Avulsions (cuts that leave attached flaps)
- Amputations
- Punctures (stabbing injuries that close up)
- Impaled objects (things that stick in and stay there)
- Burns
- Blisters

Principles of treating soft tissue injuries

CONTROL OF EXTERNAL BLEEDING

Most soft tissue injuries are open wounds (e.g., laceration, avulsion), and stopping the bleeding is usually the most urgent need—you want to keep as much of the red stuff inside as possible. We will look at four ways to control bleeding; the first two are used together and often are all that is needed (direct pressure and pressure dressing); the third (digital pressure) may be needed if an artery is involved; the fourth (a tourniquet) is only used in extreme situations involving mangled or severed limbs.

1 DIRECT PRESSURE

- Apply pressure directly to the wound with your gloved hand.
- If possible, place some absorbent material, such as gauze pads, on top of the wound before applying pressure—it will act as a sponge and help hold the blood in place.
  - Because the vast majority of bleeding is venous, it is under low pressure, and can usually be controlled with gentle direct pressure.
    - It may take 10 – 20 minutes to completely stop the bleeding.
    - Once the bleeding has stopped, maintain direct pressure for ten additional minutes to allow blood clots to form.

2 PRESSURE DRESSING

- If a wound bleeds stubbornly, or you need to do other things for your patient, you can apply a pressure dressing, which will maintain light pressure for you.

3 DIGITAL PRESSURE

- If gentle direct pressure does not stop the bleeding in a reasonable amount of time, or if the bleeding continues and soaks through the dressings, inspect the wound to ensure that are you applying the pressure in precisely the right place.
- If the wound involves an artery (which is under far greater pressure than a vein) it will gush and spurt—this is a serious situation and should be apparent from the start.
- To control arterial bleeding, take a gloved finger and put it directly into the wound and pinch or compress the bleeding artery.
- Once the bleeding has stopped, continue digital pressure for an additional 10 minutes to allow time for a clot to form in the artery.

Arterial bleeding is under high pressure—blood will spurt out of the wound like a small, pulsing oil well. **Venous** bleeding is under low pressure—blood drains or flows out. **Capillaries** (the smallest vessels) only seep.

Note: blood is always red—the colors here (bright red for arterial blood and blue for venous blood) are only used to differentiate the systems.

Always maintain Body Substance Isolation (BSI)

Direct pressure (above) and **pressure dressings** (right) are used to control bleeding. Even when a cut is deep and bleeding profusely, using these two techniques—along with the body's remarkable ability to jump-start the healing process by sending the clotting troops to the wound site—venous bleeding can typically be controlled in 10 to 20 minutes. A pressure dressing should be used on wounds that bleed stubbornly. Use any elastic material and don't make the bandage so tight that it restricts circulation distal to the wound.

4 TOURNIQUETS

If all your efforts to stop the bleeding fail, you may have to use a tourniquet. Deciding to use a tourniquet is a desperate measure—you've determined that the patient will die without it. Although great technological advances have been made in recent years, resulting in the saving of many lives (especially advances in combat medicine made during the wars in Afghanistan and Iraq), a tourniquet is still considered a tool of last resort.

Tourniquets have been used for at least 2,000 years—the Romans used tourniquets (straps of bronze over leather) to control bleeding, especially during amputations. Throughout the 1700s, 1800s, and 1900s, many advances and refinements were made, and by the 1980s microprocessor-controlled tourniquets were in use. Modern automatic tourniquet systems are self-calibrating and self-contained and offer much greater safety than the older mechanical systems. There are two types of tourniquets: 1) surgical tourniquets, which provide a bloodless environment for increased precision, safety, and speed in the operating room, and 2) emergency tourniquets, which are limited to extreme emergency situations (e.g., combat) to control bleeding in the most severe injuries.

In wilderness emergency situations, it is unlikely that you will have a high-tech, microchip-driven tourniquet with you, and you will be forced to improvise. Please bear the following in mind.

- A tourniquet is very rarely needed—do not apply it to simple wounds involving only venous bleeding; virtually all bleeding can be controlled with direct pressure and, if needed, digital pressure. An example of a situation where a tourniquet may be needed would be a laceration of an artery (e.g., femoral or brachial) in a leg or arm.
- A tourniquet should only be used for extreme life-threatening arterial bleeding in an extremity that cannot be controlled any other way—for instance, if an arm or leg has been mangled or severed.
- If the decision is made to use a tourniquet, understand that you are making a life-over-limb decision—**the limb will likely be sacrificed to save the patient's life**.
- Tourniquets are used on extremities only.
- Because they compress the tissues overlying the artery with enough force to shut off that artery, tourniquets will produce ischemia (tissue death) to the distal tissues—which is very painful. Tissue death can begin in as little as 30 minutes.

Top: a modern military tourniquet—with so many soldiers receiving limb injuries because of improvised explosive devices (IEDs), tourniquet technology had to evolve quickly in order to save lives. **Bottom:** an improvised tourniquet: note that the patient's watch band has been used to temporarily secure the windlass (tensioning stick) after the wraps were taken—that's imaginative thinking.

Improvising a tourniquet in a wilderness emergency situation.

1. Find or create a wide band, at least 1 inch wide (a cravat works well).
2. Wrap the wide band around the extremity, approximately 1 – 2 inches proximal to the bleeding.
3. Tie a knot in the band.
4. Place a 6-inch stick or bar over the knot and tie a second knot.
5. Use the stick/bar as a windlass to tighten the band by twisting it.
6. Once the bleeding has stopped completely, secure the windless in place.
7. Write a capital "T" on the patient's forehead (this is the universal sign for "tourniquet in place").
8. Record the exact time the tourniquet was applied.
9. You can cold-pack the extremity to increase the duration of survivability, just like an amputation.
10. Evacuate immediately.

PREVENT INFECTION AND PROMOTE HEALING

Since almost all soft tissue injuries involve open wounds, it is vital to protect your patient from infection and do everything possible to encourage fast healing. For the most part, this is simple and straightforward—but do not take it lightly. Even a minor wound can become life-threatening (due to infection) if it is not treated properly.

 EXPOSE AND EXAMINE THE WOUND
- Is there evidence of **nerve damage** (demonstrated by loss of sensation)?
- Is there evidence of **muscle or tendon damage** (demonstrated by loss of function)?
- Is there evidence of a **severed artery** (demonstrated by the inability to control bleeding)?
    - If there is **evidence** of nerve, muscle, tendon, or artery damage, care for the wound properly, and plan to evacuate the patient as soon as possible—surgical repair will likely be needed.

2 **CLEAN AND DRESS THE WOUND**
- **Prepare** a dilute solution of iodine in water.
    - The amount you will need depends on the size of the wound—up to 4 liters may be needed.
    - The iodine will continue to kill bacteria that gets into the wound during the healing and evacuation process.
- **Examine** the wound closely and remove any gross debris (e.g., grass, sticks, dirt, rocks, glass, etc.). Forceps or tweezers will aid the process.
- **Clean** the wound with soap and clean water. Then rinse the wound several times with the dilute iodine solution 1) by pouring directly from a container, 2) by using a syringe, or 3) by improvising a device that will squirt the solution.
- **Dry** off the wound and cover with a sterile dressing or with a wet dressing containing the dilute iodine solution (the latter if the wound is still dirty).

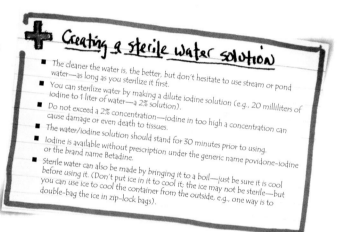

✚ **Creating a sterile water solution**
- The cleaner the water is, the better, but don't hesitate to use stream or pond water—as long as you sterilize it first.
- You can sterilize water by making a dilute iodine solution (e.g., 20 milliliters of iodine to 1 liter of water—a 2% solution).
- Do not exceed a 2% concentration—iodine in too high a concentration can cause damage or even death to tissues.
- The water/iodine solution should stand for 30 minutes prior to using.
- Iodine is available without prescription under the generic name povidone-iodine or the brand name Betadine.
- Sterile water can also be made by bringing it to a boil—just be sure it is cool before using it. (Don't put ice in it to cool it; the ice may not be sterile—but you can use ice to cool the container from the outside, e.g., one way is to double-bag the ice in zip-lock bags).

3 **LONG-TERM WOUND CARE**
- **Protect** the patient and the injured area from further injuries.
- **Monitor** for signs of infection: **tumor** (swelling), **rubor** (redness), **calor** (heat), **dolor** (aching), **purulence** (pus formation: a collection of white blood cells).
- Signs of a **worsening** infection: **lymphangina** (red streaks traveling up the lymphatic ducts), **lymphadenopathy** (swollen lymph nodes when the infection reaches them), **fever and chills** as the infection begins to spread systemically, **septic shock** (a dangerous medical emergency caused by decreased tissue perfusion and oxygen delivery as a result of severe infection; can lead to organ failure and death; the mortality rate is approximately 25% – 50%)
- Treatment if infection occurs:
    - **Apply** non-scalding hot water with Epsom Salts to the infection every 6 hours.
    - **Consider** starting an oral antibiotic, such as Keflex (500mg) every 6 hours.
    - If an abscess forms, **drain** it (see specific directions in the section on cellulitis).
- **Inspect** the wound and change the dressings every 12 hours (more often if dirty).
- If the wound is on an extremity, **check regularly** for circulation, sensation, and movement distal to the wound site.
- **Find out** when the patient last had a tetanus booster (if it's been more than 10 years, another booster will be needed quickly, within 48 hours, if possible).

Thorough cleaning is one of the most important aspects of wound treatment—a few minutes of concentrated effort can eliminate days of painful infection.

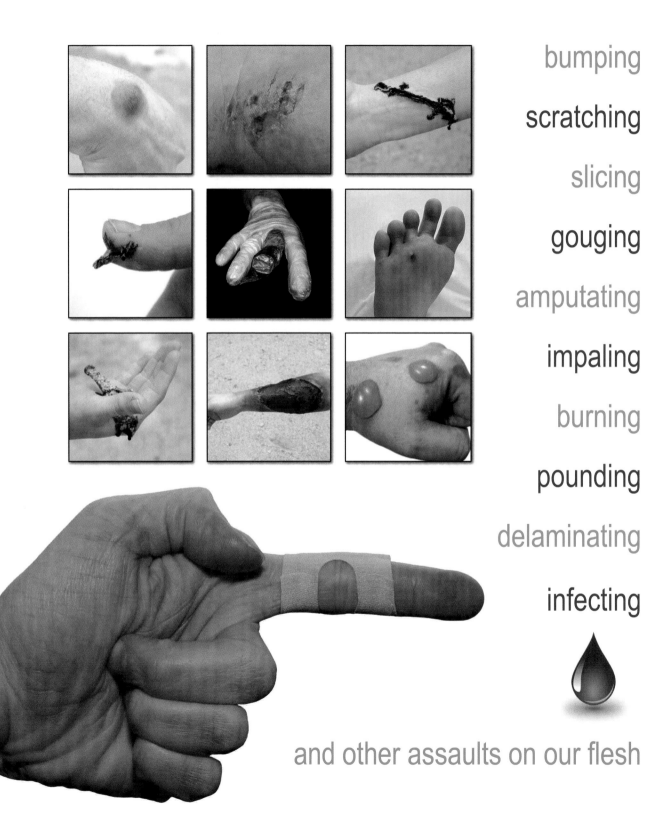

a rogues' gallery of

SOFT TISSUE INJURIES caused by

bumping

scratching

slicing

gouging

amputating

impaling

burning

pounding

delaminating

infecting

and other assaults on our flesh

WILDCARE™

Contusions and hematomas (bruises)

DESCRIPTION

- This is the common bruise that occurs from blunt trauma.
- Small blood vessels rupture in the skin and supporting connective tissues.
- A hematoma is a contusion where blood has accumulated in or under the skin—swelling is much more pronounced and can take weeks to resolve.

SIGNS AND SYMPTOMS

- Mild swelling
- Pain
- Discoloration (black and blue) due to blood seeping into the tissues

TREATMENT

The principles spelled out by the acronym, RICE.

1. Rest
2. Ice (cold compress)
3. Compress (elastic wrap)
4. Elevate

Rest, Ice, Compression, and Elevation (courtesy of friendly raccoons).

- As long as there is no risk of frostbite, a cold compress can be applied.
    - Cold causes vasoconstriction of the blood vessels, which also helps minimize bleeding.
- Because there are no open wounds to contend with, the primary treatment is to control the internal bleeding with gentle direct pressure.
    - This is most easily accomplished by the application of an elastic bandage (e.g., ACE wrap) over the injury site for 30 – 60 minutes (monitor the wound to ensure that the elastic wrap does not impair circulation).
    - Applying direct pressure to the injured vessels minimizes the amount of blood loss into the surrounding tissues.
- Elevate the injury to help reduce swelling.
- Monitor contusions and hematomas in cold weather—these injuries can freeze easier than undamaged tissue.
    - The "free blood" that has leaked into the tissue is no longer being re-circulated, making it and the surrounding tissues more susceptible to freezing.
    - In a cold environment, insulate the injured area to help prevent frostbite.

Abrasions

DESCRIPTION

- This is your classic bloody scrape—think "road rash."

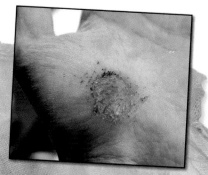

SIGNS AND SYMPTOMS

- This is often painful.
- The bleeding is capillary, and thus easily controlled with direct pressure and bandaging.

TREATMENT

- Abrasions can be dirty and contaminated so the focus is on preventing infection by properly cleaning the wound.
    - Scrub the wound with soap and water.
    - Tell the patient that this will hurt, but then just do it—scrub purposefully.
    - Allow the wound to dry before bandaging.
- Consider antibiotic ointment to reduce the risk of infection.

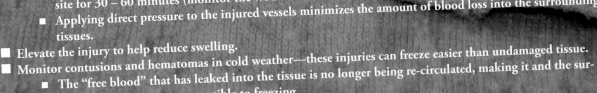

Incisions and lacerations

DESCRIPTION

An incision or laceration occurs when a cut is made by a sharp object.

SIGNS AND SYMPTOMS

- These wounds can be long and deep.
- The object's form and cutting action determine whether the wound is a straight, neat cut such as from a knife or glass shard (incision) or a jagged tear from a rock or chainsaw (laceration).
- Bleeding (which can be profuse, especially if an artery is cut) is the obvious, but not the only, concern.
- These wounds can cut through arteries, veins, nerves, muscles, ligaments, and tendons.
    - There is a risk of significant blood loss, infection, and loss of function.

Okay, this is fake—but imagine if it *was* real. Direct pressure is the key to squelching the bleeding.

TREATMENT

- Bleeding can be controlled with direct pressure and, if necessary, a pressure dressing to stabilize the wound for 20 – 30 minutes.
- Once bleeding has been controlled, remove the original dressing, and irrigate the wound thoroughly.
- Closely examine the area distal to the site of the wound for normal sensation and motion.
- If there is impaired sensation, movement, or loss of function, the extremity should be splinted in position of function to protect the damaged structures.
    - Any wound with loss of function will likely need surgery to repair the damaged muscle or tendon.
    - Evacuate the patient to definitive care immediately.
- Provide long-term wound care.

When to evacuate for stitches:

- Evacuate when a wound is gaping, especially if underlying muscle or fat is visible.
- Evacuate for any gaping wound greater than one inch long.
- When a wound requires a surgical repair of a ligament, tendon, muscle, or blood vessel—evacuate.
- When there are cosmetic concerns, especially on the face—evacuate.

A backcountry alternative:

- Super Glue (cyanoacrylate): Works well on straight, clean, short, non-gaping lacerations that are not under tension. To do this, approximate the wound edges and paint the Super Glue on top of the wound to hold it together. **Note:** if applied to the wound edges, the wound will not heal properly.

Avulsions (flaps)

DESCRIPTION

- A three-sided soft-tissue flap that is still attached.
- Because it is still attached, the flap is still getting circulation, although it may not be sufficient to sustain the life of the flap for long.
- Most avulsions are superficial and do not involve arteries, veins, nerves, muscles, ligaments, or tendons.

TREATMENT

- Control bleeding with direct pressure and/or a pressure dressing.
- Once bleeding has been controlled for 20 – 30 minutes, remove all dressings and clean the wound—rinse under the flap with sterile water.
- After the wound has been properly cleaned, if possible, place the flap back in its anatomical position to control bleeding, prevent infection, and promote healing.
- Properly bandage the wound.
- If the avulsion is large, it may also require splinting to protect the wound and support the dressings and bandages.
    - A large avulsion may also require stitches.
    - For large avulsions, or those involving arteries, veins, nerves, muscles, ligaments, or tendons, or that compromise function or need stitches, evacuate immediately.

DESCRIPTION

- A completely severed body part (e.g., a finger).
- The severed part is devitalized—it has no circulation and cannot survive for long without being reattached.
    - Amputated parts can survive up to 6 hours with proper care.

TREATMENT

- There are two wounds to manage: the base wound where the amputated part was removed from the body, and the amputated part itself.
- The base wound site is managed the same as any bleeding wound.
    - Control bleeding with direct pressure or a pressure dressing.
    - Clean the wound thoroughly.
    - Bandage.
- The amputated part must be cooled to slow down metabolism and extend survivability.
- Wrap the severed part in a moist sterile dressing and seal it in a plastic bag or other watertight container, and submerge the wrapped part in cold water—the closer to freezing the better.
    - Do not allow the part to freeze or come in direct contact with ice.
    - Do not submerge the part directly in water as the wound will absorb water and tissue will be destroyed.
        - Evacuate the patient and the severed part to the hospital as soon as possible.

PROPER PACKAGING will extend the viable life of a severed body part and increase the likelihood that reattachment will be possible. The ideal situation is to place the part inside two zip-sealed plastic bags (with the air squeezed out) and submerge the bags in a container filled with cold water and ice. If ice is not available, use the coldest water you can find (e.g., from a mountain stream) and change the water every 15 minutes (if possible). And hurry to the hospital—every minute counts!

A severed finger inside two-plastic bags and placed in ice water—this will preserve the tissue and increase the time that it remains viable.

Ridiculous...
sure, but we did get your attention. Perhaps the image below is more familiar. Take puncture wounds seriously (even minor ones)—they can be awesome little infection incubators. (Note secondary puncture vector in red circle above banana).

Puncture wounds

DESCRIPTION

- This is a small penetrating wound to the skin.
- The classic example is stepping on a nail.
- The object enters, then exits—if it stays in, it's an impaled object (see next page).
- Puncture wounds seal rapidly, so there is very little external bleeding.

TREATMENT

- Gently irritate the wound to promote some bleeding.
- Flush the wound with clean water.
- Bandage (a Band-Aid is often all that's needed).
- If possible, soak the affected area in non-scalding hot water with Epsom salts, 3 – 4 times per day, for 20 – 30 minutes each time, until healed.
- Monitor for signs of infection:
    - Redness
    - Swelling
    - Tenderness
    - Warmth

IMPALED

SOMETHING STUCK IN THE BODY THAT DOESN'T BELONG THERE

Minor nuisance mishaps (fishhooks), to rare, major, dramatic emergencies (ski poles, ice axes). And you thought puncture wounds were bad.

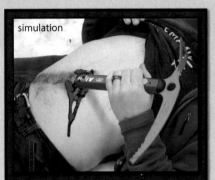
simulation

FAULTY USE OF CRAMPONS WHILE GLISSADING
New Hampshire, Gulf of Slides

In the Gulf of Slides a man was doing a seated glissade when he caught a crampon. He flipped and impaled himself on his ice axe through his midsection. He walked out to the AMC Pinkham Notch Camp with the axe still through his abdomen from the upper left to lower right quadrant. No organs were injured.

Analysis

"There is no good reason for glissading with sharp spikes on our feet." (Source: George Hurley, mountain guide)

From Accidents in North American Mountaineering, 1997, pg. 49.

GENERAL TREATMENT PRINCIPLES

◆ **It is usually best to remove an impaled object, if it comes out easily.**
- ◆ However, sometimes removing an impaled object (such as one that has damaged a major artery or is in a dense vascular area, like the abdomen) will put the patient at risk of severe bleeding—in cases like this the impaled object provides perfect direct/digital pressure (see sidebar).

◆ **Examine the object.**
- ◆ *How big is it?*
  - ◆ Is the object too big, too heavy, or too long?
  - ◆ Can the patient be moved and transported without the object shifting and causing more damage?
- ◆ *What is it made of?*
  - ◆ Can it conduct heat or cold? A metal object can increase the risk of hypothermia and frostbite—a good reason to consider removing it.
- ◆ *How is it shaped?*
  - ◆ Is it smooth, serrated, barbed, or some shape that would be difficult to remove?
- ◆ *Where is it embedded?*
  - ◆ If in an arm or leg, treatment is typically straightforward.
  - ◆ Has it damaged a major artery or vein? These injuries may bleed profusely when the object is removed.
  - ◆ In the chest or abdomen? Organ damage may have occurred, or major blood vessels may be damaged.
  - ◆ If the object appears to have penetrated the chest or abdominal cavity and is firmly stuck in place, since there is no way to determine what vital organs may have been injured, pad and immobilize the object.
  - ◆ If the object is loose and ready to fall out, gently remove it to eliminate its potential for causing more damage by moving around. If you remove the object, take it with the patient to definitive care to aid in evaluating the injury.
  - ◆ Head, face, or neck? If the object appears to have penetrated more than 1cm (1/2") and is firmly in place, leave it and package it to maintain its position.
    - ■ Evacuate.
    - ■ For impaled objects in the eye, see the eye injury section.

◆ **Infection is a major concern.**
- ◆ Microbes have likely been driven deep into the body.
- ◆ Clean the wound and surrounding tissue thoroughly.
- ◆ Gently irritate the wound to promote bleeding and to aid in flushing out the wound.
- ◆ If the wound is open, leave it open.
- ◆ Monitor for signs of infection.
- ◆ If more than 10 years have lapsed, the patient needs a tetanus booster.

OBJECTS

HOOKED ON YOURSELF

Errant back-casts, high-winds, yanking on hung-up pond-weeds, overzealous companions on opening day, little kids with no spatial awareness—there are more ways to impale yourself (or a bystander) with a fishhook than you can shake a pole at. Painful but rarely serious (eyes excepted), a fishhook in the flesh is an extremely common injury—common enough that it deserves its own treatment.

◆ **Method 1 (for a barbless hook)**
  ◆ If you're dealing with a barbless hook, just back it out the same way it went in—simple catch and release.

◆ **Method 2 (for a barbed hook)**
  ◆ Force the hook to continue through the skin until it re-emerges.
  ◆ Cut the barbed portion of the hook with pliers or wire cutters.
  ◆ Back the original part of the hook out the way it came in.
  ◆ This is a painful technique that requires a cutting device, but it is effective.

◆ **Method 3 (for a barbed hook)**
  ◆ Grab the shank and push the hook down and back, and it should pop out.
  ◆ This is a less barbaric—and less traumatic—method than the previous method and is the same method you use to remove a hook from a fish (although the fish isn't usually as big a baby about it).

◆ **Method 4 (for a barbed hook)**
  ◆ This "push-me-pull-you maneuver" is kinder, gentler, a little less painful, and causes less tissue damage than the previous methods for a barbed hook.
  ◆ Gently pull on the hook to feel how well it is seated.
  ◆ Attach a loop of fishing line to the bend in the hook close to the skin—this will aid you in pulling the hook out.
  ◆ Now, perform the maneuver (you will have to do two things at once—having a helper will make it a lot easier).
  ◆ Push the hook shank toward the surface of the skin.
    ◆ Pliers or a hemostat will make this easier.
    ◆ This will force the back of the bend of the hook to push the tissues deeper, helping to free the barb.
  ◆ At the same time, gently pull on the fishing line attached to the bend of the hook—parallel to the skin
  ◆ As the barb becomes free, the fishhook will come out.
  ◆ Do not yank during the maneuver—the hook may pop out and embed itself elsewhere.
  ◆ Note: even with your best efforts, tissue damage may occur.

The problem with most hooks is that they are barbed, which greatly increases their holding power (whether in a carp or the guy next to you)—especially when you are trying get them out. And, despite your best efforts, it's really hard to remove them without doing damage. Note: each of the techniques described also works with multiple hooks (e.g., treble hooks), although things will be more complicated.

Method 3 may require a fair bit of back and forth effort to remove the hook—which can be painful.

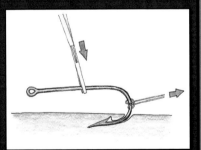

If you have a tool to grab the hook with, Method 4 will likely be the best choice.

Once the hook is out, treat the injury as a puncture wound.

BANDAGING MATERIALS

Dressings and bandages are soft items that are placed directly onto a wound to help protect the wounded tissues from further injury or insult. Common dressing and bandage materials include:

- **GAUZE PADS**—they come in a variety of shapes and sizes, from 12" x 9" trauma or abdominal dressings to smaller 4" x 4" or 2" x 2" square pads.
- **ROLLER GAUZE**—comes in a variety of widths and materials: 1" to 6" roller gauze is commonly used to hold gauze dressings and pressure bandages in place.
- **ELASTIC WRAPS**—available in widths from 2" to 6".
    - Very helpful to create pressure dressings
    - Perfect for stabilizing strains and sprains, and as the final wrap over splinting material to contain the entire splint
- **TRIANGULAR BANDAGES**
    - Tried and true, these large triangular pieces of cotton fabric are used to tie dressings and splints in place.
    - Cravat: a triangular bandage that has been folded into a 3" – 4" wide strips—"Cravat" is also the generic term used to describe any bandanna-sized triangular bandage—whether folded or not.

1. Gauze pad
2. Roller gauze
3. Elastic wrap (e.g., ACE)
4. Triangular bandage (in package)
5. Triangular bandage (as a cravat)
6. Masking tape (um...no)

SPECIFIC BANDAGES

- **SCALP**—used as an improvised hat to protect the head or to hold a dressing on the forehead or scalp in place.
- **TOOTHACHE**—used to hold a fractured jaw in place or to hold a dressing onto the side of the head or face over the temporal areas.
- **SHOULDER**—used to support and hold dressings onto the shoulder or upper arm.
- **ARM SLING AND SWATHE**—used to support and splint any injury to the upper extremity—by far one of the most useful and commonly used bandages.
- **HIP**—used to support and hold dressings onto the hip, buttocks, or upper leg.
- **KNEE**—used to support and hold dressings onto the knee.
- **SPRAINED ANKLE**—used to support and stabilize a sprained ankle. Can also be used as the ankle hitch for an improvised traction splint.

BANDAGING SEQUENCES

SCALP

TOOTHACHE

SHOULDER

BANDAGING USES

SCALP
- To hold dressings in place on the scalp
- To make an improvised hat (i.e., to protect from UV light)

TOOTHACHE
- To hold dressings in place on the side/temporal areas of the scalp
- To support a fractured mandible

SHOULDER
- To hold dressings in place on the shoulder and upper arm

SLING AND SWATHE
- To support the entire arm for comfort
- To hold bandages in place
- To support and immobilize fractures of the humerus, radius/ulna, and clavicle, or a dislocated shoulder
- To help immobilize and minimize the pain of a sprained shoulder, elbow, or wrist
- To help protect fractured ribs

KNEE
- To hold dressings in place on the knee
- To make improvised knee pads (spelunking anyone?)

HIP
- To hold dressings in place on the hip, buttocks, or upper leg

ANKLE
- See the Strains and Sprains section.

By its very nature, wilderness medicine often takes imagination and creativity—and improvisation is at the heart of it. You find a person who needs a sling/swathe but you don't have a backpack full of cravats? No problem! Just roll up their jacket and the rummage around for something to make a swathe with (e.g., a long-sleeved shirt), and you're good to go!

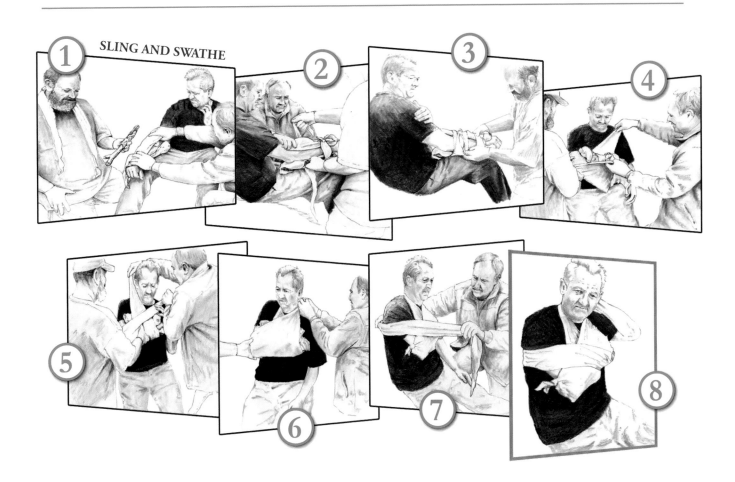

SLING AND SWATHE

1 2 3 4 5 6 7 8

HIP

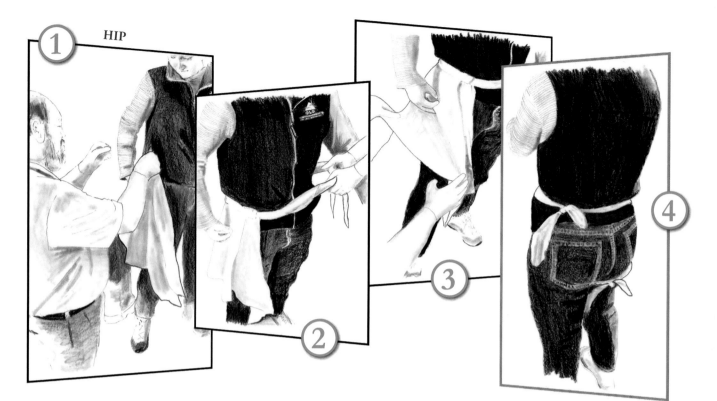

KNEE

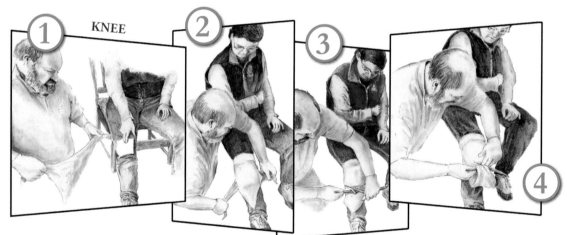

Burns

BURNS CAUSE SIGNIFICANT PAIN

and damage, plus long-lasting physical and emotional scars. Annually in the US there are about 1 million burn cases seen in emergency rooms, over 45,000 hospitalizations, and about 4,000 deaths. (The number of annual deaths has dropped significantly over the last 20 years due to increased use of smoke detectors and fire suppressant systems.) When a

THERMAL BURNS

Thermal burns are caused by an external heat source: fire, a hot stove, hot water, hot food.

- What you see is the extent of the burn.
- It is usually easy to estimate the depth and extent of the burn.

THERMAL

ELECTRICAL BURNS

Electrical burns are caused by resistance to electrical current flowing through tissue: lightning, contact with a man-made electrical source (e.g., household wiring). In addition to tissue damage at the contact point (the skin), electrical burns can cause additional problems.

- Respiratory arrest
- Seizures
- Fractures
- Extensive muscle damage—the current can extend well below the skin surface, so what may appear to be a relatively minor injury may actually be quite extensive beneath
- Can also have associated entry and exit wounds

ELECTRICAL

CHEMICAL BURNS

Chemical burns are caused by both the heat produced by some chemical reactions, as well as direct chemical interaction with the skin. Examples of strong corrosives (either strong acids or bases) that can cause chemical burns:

- Bleach
- Concrete mix
- Drain cleaner (lye)
- Metal cleaners
- Pool chlorinators
- Battery acid

CHEMICAL

RADIATION BURNS

Radiation burns are caused by exposure to alpha, beta, gamma, or X-ray radiation, typically in an industrial or medical setting. This ionizing radiation can cause damage to cells and their DNA—this is very rare, as the victim would have to be exposed to a radioactive source (e.g., the Fujita nuclear power plant accident, following the 2011 tsunami in Japan, caused ionizing radiation damage to some rescue workers).

A 2nd degree burn caused by scalding.

DETERMINING THE SEVERITY AND EXTENT OF THERMAL BURNS

Thermal burns are like many injuries—both the things that you do (and the pace that you do them) depend to a great extent on how bad the injury is. With burns, there are two things to determine:
1. The severity of the burn (how deep it goes into the tissue).
2. The extent of the burn (the surface area affected as a percentage of total body surface area).

In general, the deeper the burn and greater surface area it covers, the more severe the burn is. But it can be more complicated than that: a small full-thickness burn (that goes all the way through the hypodermis) may not be as severe (and thus, not require as fast and furious an evacuation) as a surface burn over a large area.

In addition to determining the depth and measuring the extent of a burn (below), there are other factors that you should consider when determining the overall seriousness of the injury—keep the following things in mind.

- Burn damage to the face, genitals, and airway make things more serious.
    - Genital burns can be very painful.
    - Even a minor burn to the airway can produce swelling significant enough to threaten the airway (this may take time to develop—pay attention).
    - Burns rarely cause immediate death, except when the airway is involved.
- Circumferential burns (burns that encircle a limb) can impair circulation distal to the burn site (over hours to days), requiring surgical escharotomy (cutting through the dead tissue of a full-thickness burn to relieve pressure and re-establish circulation distally).

SEVERITY
- SUPERFICIAL (1st degree)
    - Damage is limited to the top layer of the skin, the epidermis.
    - The area is red (erythema).
    - It is mildly painful.
    - It is tender to the touch.
    - There is an increase in warmth.
    - It can be itchy.
    - Sunburn is a good example of a superficial burn.
- PARTIAL THICKNESS (2nd degree)
    - Damage extends through the epidermis into the upper layers of the dermis.
    - The area is red because of vasodilation.
    - It can be very tender.
    - It is quite warm to the touch.
    - Painful blisters form (in minutes to hours).
    - Contact with boiling water is an example of a partial thickness burn.
- FULL THICKNESS (3rd degree)
    - The burn extends through the epidermis and dermis and into the hypodermis.
    - The area can be red, black, pale, or charred.
    - There is no pain because the nerves have been destroyed.
    - There is little or no bleeding because the vasculature has been destroyed.
    - Surrounding the burn area there will typically be additional areas of painful partial-thickness damage.

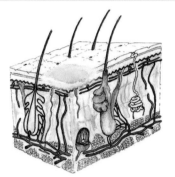

Superficial: damage just to the epidermis

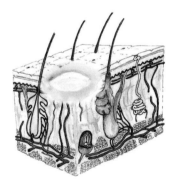

Partial Thickness: damage extends into the dermis; blisters may form

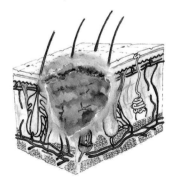

Full Thickness: damage extends into the hypodermis; subcutaneous tissue, nerves, and vasculature is destroyed

EXTENT

There are two common methods for estimating the percentage of total body surface area (TBSA) covered by a burn: the Rule of Nines and the Rule of Palm.

- The Rule of Nines
  - This method divides the body of a typical adult into 12 areas, and assigns either 4.5%, 9%, or 18% to each area, with the genitals taking up the final 1%, for a total of 100%.
  - Because it uses relatively large increments, this method is most useful for burns that cover an extensive area.
  - With modifications (see chart below) it can also be used for the obese, children, and infants (their proportions are different so the numbers are not divisors or multipliers of 9).
  - In the chart below, if you do the math, only the column for adults adds up to 100% (the others are close, but not perfect)—the Rule of Nines is not meant to be precise; it is an *estimating* tool.
  - Also, bear in mind that burns may cover more than one body part or may not fully cover a particular body part—for complicated or fragmented burn patterns, consider using the Rule of Palm.

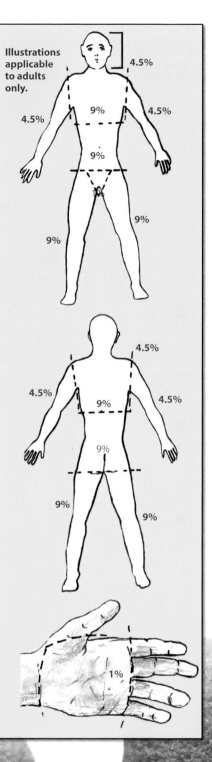

Illustrations applicable to adults only.

TOTAL BODY SURFACE AREA	Adults	Obese and Adults >80kg	Children	Infants
Anterior head	4.5%		8.5%	
Posterior head	4.5%		8.5%	
Head and neck		2%		20%
Anterior torso (9+9)	18%	25%	18%	16%
Posterior torso (9+9)	18%	25%	18%	16%
Each leg		20%		16%
Each anterior leg	9%		6.5%	
Each posterior leg	9%		6.5%	
Each arm		5%		8%
Each anterior arm	4.5%		4.5%	
Each posterior arm	4.5%		4.5%	
Genitalia	1%	0%	1%	1%

- The Rule of Palm
  - This is not the preferred technique because anatomical proportions are inconsistent with age groups and populations.
  - This method assumes that the area of an adult palm (not including the fingers) equals approximately 1% on a typical adult.
  - Because it measures in smaller increments, this method is *only* useful for burns covering a relatively small area.
  - *It should not be used* for children and infants because their proportionally smaller body sizes would give deflated values and underestimation of the total burn area—use the Rule of Nines for children and infants.

GENERAL TREATMENT PRINCIPLES

IMMEDIATE CARE FOCUSES ON FOUR AREAS

- Getting the heat out to minimize the extent of the burn
- Controlling all life-threatening problems
- Minimizing fluid loss from evaporation
- Pain control

LONG-TERM MANAGEMENT OF THE BURN PATIENT

- Fluid and electrolyte replacement
- Pain control
- Additional calories to aid in healing

SPECIFIC TREATMENT PRINCIPLES

The treatment sequence for burns (especially serious burns) is slightly different than for other emergencies (primarily regarding airway management). Rapid management of burn injuries makes a big difference in the patient's outcome. This is one emergency scene where several things must happen quickly and (nearly) simultaneously during your immediate response.

I: SCENE SAFETY

- Make sure the risk is over: remove the patient (and anyone else) from immediate danger.
- Determine the Mechanism of Injury (MOI).
- Make sure the source of the burn (e.g., burning material, corrosive chemicals, source of electricity) has been removed or its threat eliminated.

2: LEVEL OF CONSCIOUSNESS & ABCs

- Check the patient's LOC and ABCs—do this quickly—you must address the burn ASAP.

3: REMOVE THE HEAT SOURCE

- Safely remove the heat source.
- Soak all burns in cold water for 15 – 20 minutes.
- If a chemical burn, flush the area with copious amounts of water until all the chemical has been washed away. Protect yourself and others from the harmful chemical while you do this.
- If an electrical burn, make sure that the victim isn't still attached to the source of the electricity.

Get the heat out! Once the scene is safe the first order of business is to remove the heat source from the patient, or remove the patient from the heat source, to minimize tissue damage.

After you have completed steps 1 – 3, you can slow down a little as you move on, and, oddly, you will move on by going right back to the beginning and reevaluating the patient's ABCs: burn patients are different from other trauma patients.

4: PROTECT THE PATIENT'S ABCs

After the initial patient assessment, you must protect the patient's ABCs—because of the nature of burn injuries, the status of a patient's ABCs are more apt to change (deteriorate) while you are treating them, even if they initially seem stable.

- AIRWAY—is there risk of burn injury to the airway?
    - Look for ash and soot in the nose or mouth.
    - Look for charred nasal hairs.
    - Look at the lips and tongue for swelling.
    - Look at the face for evidence of burn injuries (e.g., singed eyebrows).
    - If there is evidence of a burn to the airway, constantly and closely monitor the airway.
    - Any airway problems will require immediate evacuation.
    - Cool, moist air can help to slow swelling.
    - Endotracheal intubation may be necessary (this is a definitive care procedure; you will probably not be prepared to do this in the wilderness).
    - Two airway-related problems:
        - Pulmonary edema if the heat reached the lungs—Monitor for signs of pulmonary edema: increasing shortness of breath (SOB), crackles.
        - Swelling of the airway—Monitor for signs of swelling: increasing difficulty breathing and/or snoring sounds.
- BREATHING—monitor for deterioration, and support with rescue breathing as necessary.
- CIRCULATION—monitor for problems: especially shock.
    - Be aware of fluid loss through burns.
    - If pulseless and breathless, perform CPR. (In the wilderness environment, you should stop CPR after 30 minutes if there is no response.)
- Assess for shock and treat accordingly.
- Check vital signs every 15 minutes (especially important in the case of a severe burn over a large part of the patient's body. Fluid loss through evaporation from the burn site can hasten shock.)

5: PERFORM A SECONDARY ASSESSMENT

- Start a SOAPnote
- Chief Complaint (CC)—careful, it may not be the burn.
- History of Present Illness (HPI)
- Vital Signs
- Patient Exam (burns are distracting—look for other injuries)
- AMPLE History
- Rescue Plan

BURNS—BY THE NUMBERS
- Deaths from fires and burns are the third leading cause of fatal home injury (Runyan 2004). The United State's mortality rate from fires ranks eighth among the 25 developed countries for which statistics are available (International Association for the Study of Insurance Economics 2009).
- On average in the United States in 2010, someone died in a fire every 169 minutes, and someone was injured every 30 minutes (Karter 2011).
- About 85% of all U.S. fire deaths in 2009 occurred in homes (Karter 2011).
- In 2010, fire departments responded to 384,000 home fires in the United States, which claimed the lives of 2,640 people (not including firefighters) and injured another 13,350, not including firefighters (Karter 2011).
- Most victims of fires die from smoke or toxic gases and not from burns (Hall 2001).
- Smoking is the leading cause of fire-related deaths (Ahrens 2011).
- Cooking is the primary cause of residential fires (Ahrens 2011).
- Males account for $4.8 billion (64%) of the total costs of fire/burn injuries.
- Females account for $2.7 billion (36%) of the total costs of fire/burn injuries.
- Fatal fire and burn injuries cost $3 billion, representing 2% of the total costs of all fatal injuries.
- Hospitalized fire and burn injuries total $1 billion, or 1% of the total cost of all hospitalized injuries.
- Non-hospitalized fire and burn injuries cost $3 billion, or 2% of the total cost of all non-hospitalized injuries.
- Groups at increased risk of fire-related injuries and deaths include children 4 and under (CDC 2010; Flynn 2010), older Adults ages 65 and older (CDC 2010; Flynn 2010), African Americans and Native Americans (CDC 2010; Flynn 2010), the poorest Americans (Istre 2001; Flynn 2010), persons living in rural areas (Ahrens 2003; Flynn 2010), persons living in manufactured homes or substandard housing (Runyan 1992; Parker 1993).
- Risk Factors: over one-third (37%) home fire deaths occur in homes without smoke alarms (Ahrens 2011); most residential fires occur during the winter months (CDC 1998; Flynn 2010); alcohol use contributes to an estimated 40% of residential fire deaths (Smith 1999).

source: CDC

6: TREAT THE BURN

- Remove or cut away clothing or debris in the burn site.
- Remove jewelry, watches, footwear, and anything else that could cut off circulation.
- Clean the wound: proper wound debridement is a crucial—and ongoing-process. Remove any foreign material and any devitalized (dead) tissue from the burn site as soon as possible—this helps minimize the risk of infection.
- Leave blisters intact.
- You may apply Aloe Vera (100%) or Silvadene cream (prescription).
- Dress the burn with a moist, sterile dressing.
    - If sterilized commercial dressings are not available, or you don't have enough, sterilize a cloth (e.g., towel) by boiling it or soaking it in a dilute Betadine solution (1 part of a 10% Betadine solution combined with 9 parts of sterile water yields a 1% solution) or 2% iodine solution (commercially available at that concentration).
    - Wrap the burn with additional sterile dressings to hold it in place.
    - If the burn area is greater than 9%, apply an occlusive dressing to prevent fluid loss by evaporation.
- Keep the patient hydrated.
- Keep the patient warm.
- Monitor the patient for infection.
- Watch out for signs of hypothermia—treat it immediately and aggressively.
- When should the patient be evacuated?
    - Consider evacuating for full-thickness burns larger than 1 inch (2cm).
    - Immediately evacuate any patient with the following burns:
        - Full-thicknesss (3rd degree) burns covering more than 5% of their Total Body Surface Area (TBSA)
        - Partial-thickness (2nd degree) burns covering more than 10% of their TBSA.
        - Full- or partial-thickness burns to the face, hands/feet, genitals, or burns covering any joint.
        - Burns that involve the airway.
        - Burn patients in shock who become hypothermic.
        - Circumferential burns.

A quarter is just about one inch in diameter—a good gauge.

CIRCUMFERENTIAL BURNS

- This is a rare complication in which a burn encircles a limb, isolating unburned tissue distal to the burn.
- If the skin is allowed to dry and contract in a burn that encircles a limb, the burn can act like a tourniquet and impair circulation distal to the burn site.
- The area distal to the burn site will become pulseless, painful, and edematous (swollen).
- Without treatment, the tissue distal to the burn site may die.
- This condition is treated by splitting the eschar (the tight, burned skin) parallel with the extremity, allowing it to expand (sometimes dramatically), which depressurizes the underlying tissue and reestablishes circulation.
- The process is not painful since the nerves at the eschar site are destroyed in a full-thickness burn.
- There are no protocols for doing this in a wilderness setting.

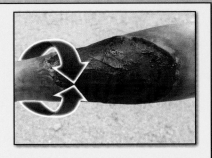

BURN TREATMENT OPTIONS
(top to bottom)

- A nasty third degree burn.
- A moist, sterile dressing (a towel, boiled and then cooled and soaked in a dilute Betadine solution).
- An occlusive dressing (minimized fluid loss through evaporation).
- Depending on the burn, an additional wet dressing can be applied over the occlusive dressing.
- Wrap the entire dressing packaged with an ACE wrap (not shown).

LONG-TERM BURN TREATMENT

- **Minimize fluid loss, maintain fluid and electrolyte levels.**
    - When you re-dress the wound, help minimize the amount of fluid loss via evaporation by covering full-thickness burns with an occlusive dressing (e.g., plastic food wrap—this is airtight and waterproof and helps maintain core temperature and prevent hypothermia). Start with an under-dressing, moistened with a 1% dilute Betadine (see treatment section for formula) or 2% iodine solution, and finish with an occlusive dressing, and a final wrap.
    - Use the Parkland Formula to estimate the fluid replacement over the first 24 hours: milliliters of fluid equals 4 x the % of body surface area (BSA) burned x the patient's weight in kilograms. Example—a 70kg adult with 10% of burned BSA would need 2.8 liters of fluid (4 x 70 = 2,800 cc/2.8 liters).
    - If IV crystalloid fluids are available, and IV access can be obtained, start an IV, through burned tissue, if necessary. Give ½ of the fluid in the first 8 hours, and the second half over the following 16 hours.
    - If IV fluids are not available, and the patient can tolerate oral fluids, use the same formula to estimate how much fluid is needed—and get them to drink the electrolyte solution!
    - You must replace electrolytes, too—use oral rehydration salts or rice water—cook rice with salt and continue to add water until the cooked rice dissolves into a milky-colored liquid (rice water is rich in electrolytes and carbohydrates).
    - If laboratory services are not available to monitor electrolytes and hemoconcentration, use vital signs and urine output to estimate fluid replacement—vital signs should stay in the normal range and adequate fluid volume should produce light amber urine. Minimal fluid output in an adult is at least 0.5cc/kg/hr, or at least 500cc per day (20⁺cc per hour). This minimal output cannot be sustained for long—urine output of 1000cc – 1500cc per 24 hours (50⁺/⁻cc per hour) is needed to maintain normal homeostasis.
- **Monitor vital signs.**
    - For severe burns, especially for extensive partial- or full-thickness burns, initially check vital signs every 10 – 15 minutes for the first two hours, then every 30 minutes after that.
    - If the vital signs deteriorate and indicate shock, treat the shock and evacuate the patient to definitive care immediately.

- **Control pain.**
    - Use a moist dressing as the outer layer—evaporation will provide cooling and comfort.
    - Administer Tylenol (acetaminophen or paracetamol) up to 3000mg total per 24 hours.
    - NSAID (aspirin, ibuprofen, naproxen): dosages vary depending on the med.
    - Note: Tylenol and an NSAID can be used together for very effective pain control.
    - Narcotics can be used and are extremely effective (codeine, hydrocodone, oxycodone).
- **Minimize the risk of infection.**
    - A burn is sterile for the first 24 hours—after that, the risk of infection increases.
    - It is easier to prevent an infection than treat one.
    - Re-dress the wound twice a day, if possible—or as often as necessary to prevent seepage through the dressing.
    - Use sterile dressings each time.
- **Keep the burn site clean**—reassess and debride the burn 2 - 3 times per a day.
- **Monitor blisters.**
    - Blisters form with partial thickness (2nd degree) burns.
    - If possible, leave them intact—they are sterile and leaving them intact helps minimize the risk of infection.
    - If a blister ruptures, gently debride the site by removing dead skin.
- **Provide proper nutrition.**
    - Cellular repair with any injury requires significant calories from carbohydrates and protein.
    - Burn patients have a very high calorie demand.
- **Use ointments**—most over-the-counter ointments and antibiotic creams do little or nothing to aid in the healing process of a burn, but two prescription creams are helpful in burn care.
    - Silvadene cream is an antimicrobial, water-soluble cream that contains silver sulfadiazine that is very soothing to the burn victim. It is a sulfa drug that should not be used on individuals who are allergic to these drugs. It should be washed off and reapplied during each reassessment of the burn site. Cover silvadene cream with a dressing and bandage and prevent exposure to sunlight
    - Bactroban cream is an antimicrobial, water-soluble cream that contains mupirocin. It is a very effective antistaphlococcal agent that should be washed off and reapplied during each reassessment of the burn site.

SUNBURN

Sunburn is a unique and very common form of radiation burn caused by the direct effects of intense sunlight on exposed skin—the ultraviolet wavelengths A and B (UVA and UVB) account for the damage.

- These wavelengths cause chemical changes in the skin cells.
    - These changes, in turn, cause the blood vessels to dilate and stimulate the melanocytes (melanin-producing cells in the bottom layer of the epidermis) to crank out melanin.
    - This increase in melanin is our body's way of protecting us from future exposure to the sun—and it manifests itself by tanning. When we are over-exposed, we burn.
- The damage from UV exposure stimulates pain receptors, and the vasodilation produces increased erythema (redness) of the skin, which, in severe cases, produces blisters.
- Duration of sun exposure, altitude, and exposure to reflective surfaces (snow, sand, ice, water) increases the risk of severe sunburn.
- The damage is permanent and cumulative.
- There is very significant long-term increased risk of skin cancer from severe sunburns.
- Repeated sunburns or chronic tanning increases aging effects with wrinkles, areas of pigmentation, thickening, and precancerous lesions.
- With time these can turn into cancers: basal cell[1] or squamous-cell[2] cancer or malignant melanoma[3].

PREVENTION

- Wear proper clothing, use hats, umbrellas and sun block, avoid the sun, and don't go to tanning salons.

TREATMENT

- Eliminate further exposure—find shade, put on clothing.
- Assess for signs of heat exhaustion or heat stroke.
- Hydrate with water and salt replacement.
- Use non-steroidal anti-inflammatory drugs (NSAIDs) such as aspirin, ibuprofen (Advil, Motrin) or Naprosyn (Aleve)
- Acetaminophen (Tylenol), although not an NSAID, helps relieve pain and can be taken along with an NSAID.
- Moisturize the skin with an aloe-based skin cream.
- If blisters occur, leave them intact.
- Certain medications do cause increased photosensitivity to UV light, thus increasing the likelihood and severity of sunburn—if you are taking one of these drugs, take all measures to prevent sun exposure (sidebar).

---

1   The most common skin cancer, typically on the head or neck, rarely metastasizes or kills but can cause tissue destruction and disfigurement.
2   Another common cancer usually arising from mutated cells lining body cavities: skin, lips, mouth, esophagus, bladder, prostate, lung, vagina, etc.
3   A less common but serious cancer of the melanocytes; aggressive, it readily metastasizes and accounts for 75% of skin cancer deaths.

(SOME) PHOTOSENSITIVE AGENTS

ANTIDEPRESSANTS: Amitriptyline (Elavil and others), Desipramine (Norpramin, Pertonfrane), Doxepin (Adapin, Sinequan), Imipramine (Tofranil and others), Isocarboxazid (Marpian), Maprotiline (Ludiomil), Nortriptyline (Aventyl, Pamelor), Protriptyline (Vivaetil), Trimipramine (Surmontil).

ANTIHISTAMINES: Cyproheptadine (Periactin), Diphenhydramine (Benadryl, and others).

ANTIBIOTICS: Doxycycline (Vibramycin and others), Griseofulvin (Fulvicin and others), Minocycline (Minocin), Quinolones (Cipro and others), Sulfa drugs (Bactrim, Septra, and others), Sulfasalazine (Azulfidine and others), Tetracyclines (Minocin and others).

ANTIPSYCHOTIC DRUGS: Promethazine (Phenergen and others), Thioridazine, Thiothixene (Mellaril), Trifluoperazine (Stelaz and others), Triflupormazine (Vesprin), Trimeprazine (Temaril).

DIURETICS: Acetazolamine (Diamox), Amiloraid (Midamor), Chlorothiazide (Diuril and others), Furosemide (Lasix), Hydrochlorothiazide (Hydrodiuril and others), Metolazone (Zaroxolyn), Thiazides (Diruil and others).

HYPOGLYCEMICS: Chlorpropamine (Diabinese, Insulase), Glipizide (Glucotrol), Glyburide (DiaBeta, Micronase), Tolazomide (Tolinase), Tolbutamide (Orinase and others).

NON-STEROIDAL ANTI-INFLAMMATORY DRUGS: Ketoprofen (Orudis), Naproxen (Naprosyn), Phenylbutazone (Butazolidin and others), Proxicam (Feldene), Sulindac (Clinoril).

OTHER DRUGS: Amiodarone (Cordarone), Captopril (Capoten), Carbamazepine (Tegretol).

Cellulitis

Cellulitis is a bacterial or viral infection of the dermal and subcutaneous layers of the skin characterized by diffuse and severe inflammation. It can be triggered by normal skin flora (an estimated 1 trillion bacteria live happily on and in our skin— most are harmless, some are beneficial), or by bacteria from external sources (the environment). Cellulitis often occurs where the skin has been broken by lacerations, abrasions, scrapes, burns, insect bites, surgical wounds, drug injection sites, or sites of catheter insertion. The elderly and those with compromised immune systems are particularly susceptible. The mainstay of therapy is antibiotics (both oral and IV); recovery can take two days to six months.

physiology

- Cellulitis most commonly occurs when Streptococcus or Staphylococcus bacteria (which commonly reside on our skin, where they typically cause no infection) enter the skin through a break.
- Once inside, they multiply, producing waste products called pyrogens.
    - Pyrogens are recognized by our immune system as coming from a foreign invading germ that is out to destroy us.
    - Although bad, these pyrogens trigger the chain of events of our defensive mechanism that causes localized vasodilation, increased circulation, and an increase in white blood cells (WBCs). If the process continues for too long, a fever develops as well (see sidebar).
- The vasodilation at the wound site increases the circulation to that area, which brings in more nutrients, antibodies, and white blood cells (WBCs)—all needed to help battle the invaders.
    - When peripheral blood vessels dilate, small gaps between the endothelial cells that make up the vessels open up, allowing WBCs to escape into the surrounding tissue and sera or fluid in the blood to also leak out.
    - This process will cause an increase in the classic signs of a skin infection: rubor (redness), tumor (swelling), dolor (pain), and calor (warmth)—all part of the immune system's first line of defense.
- In a process known as chemotaxis, WBCs increase and are attracted to the waste products (pyrogens) produced by the bacteria and the histamines produced by the mast cells.
    - The collection of WBCs at the infection site produces the pus or purulent material that can be seen draining from an infected wound.
- As the pyrogens get into the systemic circulation, they are detected by the thermoregulatory center in the brain, causing the brain to increase the systemic body temperature, bringing on a good old-fashioned fever— and this is helpful.
    - Bacteria multiply every 26 minutes at 98.6°F/37°C (see graphic at right), but as the core temperature rises, the rate of reproduction of the bacteria goes down, giving our WBCs a better opportunity to destroy the bacteria.
- If the infection from a wound goes unnoticed and untreated, the bacteria may overwhelm the immune system and get into the lymphatic drainage from the wound site.
    - The lymphatics then become infected, signaled by a tender, red streak, (lymphangitis), moving centrally up the extremity.
    - If the infection reaches the lymph nodes, the nodes proximal to the site of the cellulitis will become warm, swollen, and tender, (lymphadenopathy).
    - If the progress of the infection is not slowed or halted, it will eventually reach the central circulation and the heart.
    - Once in the circulation, it is distributed throughout the body within 60 seconds, causing septic shock (sepsis), high fever, shaking chills (rigors), tachycardia, hypotension, and death.

wound

multiplying bacteria

cellulitis

lymphangitis

sepsis, the heart, and the
spiral down to death

A DANGEROUS CASCADE OF INFECTION

The obvious red streaks at left are a result of a cascade of
badness from the original wound to bacterial rampage to cellulitis
to lymphangitis—the latter an inflammation of the lymphatic vessels
and channels which can be a serious medical problem. It is typically treated
with antibiotics and analgesics, although surgical aspiration and drainage may be
necessary. Left untreated, cellulitis deteriorating into lymphangitis can kill.

BACTERIA GONE NUTTY

Assuming that one little bacterium will replicate
itself every 30 minutes, over a 24-hour period
281 trillion offspring will be spawned (2^{48}). Speed
is everything—catch the little buggers after 6
hours, and you only have to kill 1,024 of them;
wait a day, and you have to kill all those trillions. To
make this more visual, if each bacterium
was the size of this book*, after 6 hours
they wouldn't quite cover a basketball
court.

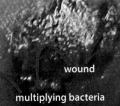

WFR
x 700+

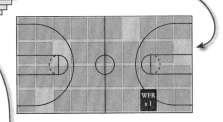

WFR
x 1

After 24 hours, they would cover New
Hampshire with *259 billion stacks* of
books, each stack over *700 books tall.*

Nothing here is to scale.

*  1 bacterium

cellulitis treatment

1. **Monitor** the wound site for the initial immune response to the multiplying bacteria:
   - ◆ **Rubor**—Redness of the skin caused by vasodilation.
   - ◆ **Tumor**—Swelling of the soft tissue by the fluids that are escaping from the dilated vasculature.
   - ◆ **Dolor**—Pain caused by the swelling of the tissues.
   - ◆ **Calor**—Warmth in the tissues from vasodilation.
2. As soon as cellulitis is suspected, **examine** the wound closely for any foreign material in the wound, and if found, remove it.
3. **Heat-soak** the area of cellulitis in non-scalding hot water with Epsom salts or table salt in the water. This is an old, tried and true technique for treating infections.
   - ◆ Heat-soak the area of cellulitis every 4 hours for at least 30 minutes, until the infection has resolved.
   - ◆ Heating up the area will slow the rate of reproduction of the bacteria and increase circulation to the area by further vasodilation.
   - ◆ The higher salt concentration in the water (compared to the tissue) helps draw the infectious material out due to osmosis—the fluid flows to the area of greatest salt concentration.
   - ◆ Epsom salt is used because it is harmless to the human tissues and lethal to bacteria.
4. **Evacuate**
   - ◆ As soon as possible, organize and evacuate the patient to advanced medical care for further evaluation and treatment, as they may need IV antibiotics or surgery at the site of the infection

if an abscess forms...

- ■ With cellulitis, the war that is being waged by the multiplying bacteria and the WBCs occurs in the layers of the skin.
- ■ WBCs gather at the site of the infection (chemotaxis), forming in a space within the wound—when this collection of WBCs and bacteria form an isolated, walled-off compartment, this is referred to as an abscess.
- ■ An abscess is more dramatic then cellulitis. While cellulitis is red, warm to the touch, slightly swollen, but not normally tender, an abscess has a definite area of swelling with induration (a distinct palpable margin around the abscess), redness, warmth, and tenderness to the touch.
- ■ If the bacteria do breech the wall of induration, just like with cellulitis, the infectious material will get into the lymphatics causing lymphangitis, lymphadenopathy[1], and eventually septic shock.
- ■ As long as the abscess remains sealed and pressurized, it is very dangerous and potentially life-threatening, and the immune system will have a very hard time winning the battle.
- ■ The abscess should be treated the same as cellulitis with non-scalding hot water salt-soaks (Epsom salt preferred).
- ■ In addition, the abscess needs to be incised and drained—this is as simple as creating a hole and allowing the infected, purulent[2] material in the abscess to drain out, thus decompressing the abscess.

THE LYMPHATIC SYSTEM works with the circulatory system by removing interstitial fluid from tissues, absorbing and transporting fatty acids and fats from the digestive system, transporting white blood cells to and from the lymph nodes into the bones, and transporting antigen-processing cells to the lymph nodes to stimulate the immune system. In addition to the ductwork shown, the thymus, bone marrow, spleen and other minor organs are involved.

top-down view

ABSCESS:
ANATOMY OF
A PUS POCKET
Induration
Skin
Pyogenic membrane
Pus
Granulation tissue
Fat

cross-section view

---

1   Swollen/enlarged lymph nodes.
2   Containing, discharging, or causing the production of pus (a whitish-yellow or yellow-brown collection of protein-rich fluid and dead cells).

...incising/draining an abscess

1. **Picture**—Assess and evaluate the abscess and surrounding anatomy.
   - Note the location, size, depth, and consider the surrounding anatomy.
   - If you are going to stick a hole in the skin to drain the abscess, you need to make sure that you avoid any obvious tendons, ligaments, nerves, or arteries.

2. **Preparation**—Clean and prep the area of the skin to be incised.
   - Thoroughly clean the area with soap and water and paint it with an iodine solution to minimize the bacteria count on the surface of the skin.

3. **Pain control**—If possible numb the skin with ice or inject with lidocaine.
   - If you are using a scalpel or other surgically sharp instrument, pain control is probably not necessary.
   - However, pain control can be achieved by either numbing the area with snow or ice (do not cause frostbite), or infiltrating the area with a 1% or 2% lidocaine injection.

4. **Puncture the abscess**—With a scalpel or sharp knife, pierce the abscess.
   - To avoid important underlying structures, keep incisions to about 1 centimeter and do the incision parallel to the long axis of the limb or body.
   - Since arteries, nerves, tendons and other important structures run lengthwise, this helps avoid cutting across one and severing it.
   - The puncture wound has to go deep enough to penetrate the abscess. This will be evident with the bloody, purulent material that will exude from the abscess
   - The purulent material can be, and most often is, very foul-smelling due to the anaerobic bacteria in it.

5. **Purge**—Drain the abscess.
   - Gently compress the sides of the abscess, along the margins of the induration to force the purulent material out.
   - Do not be overzealous—you do not want to breech the wall of the induration and push the infectious material deeper into the surrounding tissues.
   - With a pair of forceps or other small instrument, you can also gently explore the cavity of the abscess to break up any adhesions (loculations) and help evacuate the gunk.

6. **Purify**—Rinse the abscess out with iodine solution—this will help to remove all unwanted material and destroy the bacteria in the abscess.

7. **Protect**—Cover with a sterile dressing and monitor during evacuation.
   - Cover the surgical wound with a sterile dressing.
   - Change the dressing at least every 12 hours, and monitor for signs of cellulitis or further abscess formation.
   - Continue to treat with non-scalding hot water Epsom salt-soaks every 4 hours during the preparation for evacuation.

8. **Consider evacuating** the patient to advanced medical care, as they may need IV antibiotics and/or surgery.

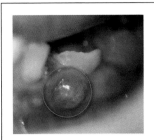

A DENTAL ABSCESS can be extremely dangerous if left untreated. It can perforate the bone causing osteomyelitis to extend into the surrounding soft tissue resulting in cellulitis. And it can spread to other parts of the body causing a dangerous cardiac infection, potential septicaemia (blood infection), and even meningitis. If a dental abscess forms on a backcountry trip—evacuate!

SOFT TISSUE INJURIES

Controlling bleeding

1. Direct Pressure: Apply pressure directly over the wound and compress to stop the bleeding.
2. Pressure Dressing: To maintain constant pressure, place something absorbent over the wound, about ½ inch thick, and then wrap it with an elastic bandage.
3. Digital Pressure: The rare spurting arterial bleeder may require digital pressure by placing a gloved finger directly into a wound to compress the lacerated artery and stem the flow of blood. Once bleeding has been controlled for 20 – 30 minutes, stop applying pressure so the wound can be inspected and cleaned.
4. Hemostatic agents: Very effective; see Critical Care.
5. Tourniquet: The last resort—but can save a life.

Long-term wound care

WOUND INSPECTION, CLEANING & BANDAGING

1. **Wound inspection and cleaning**—Once bleeding has been controlled for 20 – 30 minutes:
   - Remove dressings and closely inspect the wound.
   - Check circulation, sensation, and motion (CSM) distal to the injury.
   - Debride, removing any foreign material in the wound like sticks, grass, etc.
   - Clean around the wound with soap and water or with a dilute solution of iodine.
   - Clean the wound by irrigation with a forceful flow of sterile water or a dilute solution of iodine by using an irrigation syringe or water bottle.
2. **Dressing and bandaging**—Cover the wound with dry sterile dressings, and keep the area clean and dry.
   - Bandage the sterile dressings in place.
   - Change the dressings every 12 hours, and examine the wound for signs of infection.
   - If the wound is dirty, or you are unable to keep it clean and dry, cover the wound with a dressing soaked with a dilute solution of iodine (less than 2% strength), and change it every 6 hours.
   - Protect from further injury, freezing, and from contamination by proper bandaging.
   - If there are impaired CSMs distal to the injury, do all of the above, then splint (if applicable) and evacuate.

WOUND CARE *DON'TS*

- Don't tightly close a wound with butterfly bandages or suturing.
- Don't fill the wound with an antibiotic ointment.
- Don't leave a pressure dressing in place for more than 30 minutes.
- Don't allow the wound to freeze.
- Don't be afraid of causing a little pain to properly clean a wound.

SIGNS AND TREATMENT OF A SKIN INFECTION

1. **Early**—localized to the skin and wound area
   - Red (rubor)—due to dilated capillary beds, increased blood flow to the area.
   - Warm (calor)—due to the increased blood flow.
   - Swollen (tumor)—due to increased blood flow.
   - Tender (dolor)—due to swelling.
2. **Late**—severe and potentially life-threatening
   - Pus formation—a collection of white blood cells, may be draining from the wound.
   - Streaking up the extremity—due to infection traveling up lymphatics.
   - Swollen lymph nodes—infection has reached the lymph nodes.
   - Fever and chills—a sign that the infection is spreading systemically.
3. **Treatment of skin infections**
   - If possible soak in hot water with Epsom salt or dilute iodine solution.
   - Apply moist heat packs.
   - If the wound is closed, but swollen, gently open so it can drain.
   - The patient may need to be on an antibiotic, if lymphangitis or lymphadenopathy occur. If so, EVACUATE!

Specific injuries

CONTUSIONS
- Rest, Ice, Compression, and Elevation (RICE), to limit swelling.
- Protect and watch injury closely in cold weather as it will freeze quicker than undamaged tissue.

ABRASIONS
- Clean, debride, and wash thoroughly with soap and water.

LACERATIONS
- May bleed profusely or require pressure dressing.
- Control bleeding and maintain hemostasis for 20 – 30 minutes.
- Cleanse well with copious irrigation.
- To treat a large gaping wound, control bleeding, cleanse with irrigation as usual, approximate the edges, but do not close tightly.

AVULSIONS
- Control bleeding.
- Rinse under flap with sterile water irrigation; place flap in proper anatomical position and bandage.

AMPUTATIONS

- Wrap the amputated part in a moist sterile dressing and seal in a plastic bag.
- Immerse the bag in ice water and evacuate both the patient and the part to the hospital.

PUNCTURES

- Gently irritate to cause some bleeding to flush out wound.
- Monitor for infection. This is the most likely wound to become infected.

IMPALED OBJECTS

- Use common sense; if easily removed, remove it.
- Impaled objects **may be removed** if it is in an extremity, if it is metal in a cold environment, if it is too large or hard to cut off, or if it is in the cheek of the face (or the other one—buttocks) .
- An impaled object **should be bandaged in place** if it is in the skull, face, or neck, in the chest (possibly penetrating the lungs), in the abdomen (possibly penetrating the abdominal cavity and damaging organs).

BURNS

Get the heat out

- Remove clothing over and around the burn site; cool with cold water for at least 15 minutes.

Burns by degree

- **Superficial:** First and Second degree burns
  - The area of the burn will turn red and may form blisters, but the patient has full sensation.
  - Cold-soak the burn with water for 15 minutes.
  - Protect the burn with a dry, sterile dressing.
  - Evacuate if the burn area is more than the size of the patient's palm.
  - If the burn area is large and painful, cover with moist dressings for comfort during evacuation.
- **Deep:** Third degree burns
  - The area of the burn may be red, white, charred, and blistered, and the patient will have no sensation—the burn is deep enough to destroy the nerves.
  - All deep burns must be evacuated.
  - Cold-soak the burn with water for 15 minutes.
  - Cover with a moist dressing and waterproof bandage to prevent evaporation.
  - Hydrate—force fluids as burns can cause severe dehydration.

BLISTERS

- Use sterile techniques; deflate the blister; then protect with moleskin, antibiotic ointment, and tape.

Bandaging skills

MATERIALS

Dressing: Sterile material put directly onto a wound site.

Bandage: Piece of material that holds the dressings in place.

Cravat: A large triangular piece of material that is used in very clever ways to hold dressings.

Elastic bandage: Elastic material 2" – 6" wide that can be used to hold dressings and also to apply compression.

SPECIFIC BANDAGES

Scalp bandage: To hold a dressing on the scalp (or to look cool).

Temporal/Jaw: To hold a dressing on the side of the head, to support the jaw.

Shoulder: To hold a dressing on the shoulder or upper arm and maintain range of motion .

Arm sling: To support the shoulder, upper arm, elbow, forearm, or wrist.

Hip: To hold a dressing on the hip or buttocks and maintain full range of motion of the hip.

Knee: To hold a dressing on the knee and maintain full range of motion (or to pad the knees if you plan on spending a lot of time kneeling).

Sprained ankle: To support a sprained ankle, or for an ankle hitch for a traction splint.

We've gone to great pains to make the images in this book realistic—it was hard to find a volunteer for this one.

i injuries

Of all our senses, vision is probably the one we value the most. Because of this, eye injuries—even minor ones—are among the most common reasons for evacuation in the backcountry. If not treated properly, even simple eye injuries (e.g., a **subconjunctival hematoma**, above) can be a risk to vision and health. Major injuries (e.g., a **blowout fracture**, occurring at right) while not life-threatening, are nonetheless major traumatic events. Emergency eye care is also one area where long-term patient care is much different than short-term patient care.

E
F P
T O Z
L P E D
P E C F D
E D F C Z P
F E L O P Z D
D E F P O T E C
L E F O D P C T
F D P L T C E D
P E Z O L C F T D

[1] Fracture fragments and periorbital tissue herniating into the maxillary sinus

i anatomy

Why our vision is flipped, from right-side up, to upside down, and back to right-side up again, is a mystery—but in the end, our marvelous brain ensures that we see things just as they should be.

The human eye is a marvel of engineering. As the wavelengths of visible light pass through the cornea, it refracts them (bends them) so they can pass through the pupil. Then, like a camera aperture, the iris expands or contracts to control the amount of light that enters the eye and passes through the lens. The lens, in turn, shortens or lengthens its width to focus the light on the retina, which the light reaches after passing through the gel-like vitreous. The retina captures the image, (only inverted and with much greater discerning power than a modern digital camera), processes the image, and passes the data as electrical impulses though the optic nerve to the brain, reverting the image and passing it off to our internal recognition, interpretation, and motion-detection software. Visual memory storage takes place in our occipital lobe, where capacity is measured in exabytes (1 billion gigabytes)—which is so far beyond that of a typical PC that comparison is ridiculous.

Lens

The crystalline lens is a transparent, biconvex structure in the eye that, along with the cornea, helps to refract light to be focused on the retina. The lens, by changing shape, functions to change the focal distance of the eye so that it can focus on objects at various distances, thus allowing a sharp real image of the object of interest to be formed on the retina.

Vitreous & Aqueous Humors

The vitreous humor is the clear gel that fills the space between the lens and the retina of the eyeball (no line on drawing). The aqueous humor is a transparent, gelatinous fluid similar to plasma, and is located in the anterior and posterior chambers of the eye, in the space between the lens and the cornea.

Cornea

The cornea is the transparent part of the front of the eye that covers the iris, the pupil, and the eye's anterior chamber. Along with the lens and the anterior chamber, the cornea refracts light and it accounts for approximately two-thirds of the eye's total optical power (ability to focus light).

Retina

This is a light-sensitive tissue lining the inner surface of the eye. The optics of the eye create an image of the visual world on the retina, which serves much the same function as the film in a camera.

Optic nerve

This transmits the captured images to the brain.

Conjunctiva

An invisible, clear layer of tissue covering the front of the eye, except the cornea.

Iris

The iris is a thin, circular structure in the eye, responsible for controlling the diameter and size of the pupils and thus the amount of light reaching the retina. In response to the amount of light entering the eye, muscles attached to the iris expand or contract the aperture at the center of the iris, known as the pupil. The larger the pupil, the more light can enter. In humans, the color of the iris can be green, blue, or brown, hazel, gray, violet, or even pink.

Macula & fovea

The macula is an oval, yellow, highly pigmented area near the center of the retina (no line on drawing). It absorbs excess blue and ultraviolet light and acts as a natural sunblock for this area of the retina. Near its center is a small pit, the fovea, which contains the largest concentration of cone cells in the eye and is responsible for central, high-resolution vision.

Pupil

The black circular opening in the iris that lets light in.

Sclera

The opaque, white, fibrous, protective, outer layer of the eye.

Rods & Cones

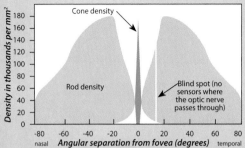

Density in thousands per mm²

Cone density

Rod density

Blind spot (no sensors where the optic nerve passes through)

-80 nasal -60 -40 -20 0 20 40 60 80 temporal

Angular separation from fovea (degrees)

The retina contains two types of photoreceptors: rods and cones. There are about 120 million rods in the human eye, and they are 1,000 times more sensitive than the cones—however, they cannot differentiate colors. The eye's 6 to 7 million cones provide color sensitivity, are concentrated in the macula, and are most densely packed in the 0.3mm, rod-free center—the fovea centralis (chart at left).

Because the rods are more sensitive, they help us with night vision, and because they are located off-center, they help with our peripheral vision—this explains why it is easier for us to see a star at night if we look slightly to one side. Rods are also better in detecting motion, but they cannot see red, which is why the light sources in dark environments (e.g., a photo darkroom, the display in a jet cockpit) are often red—the pupil can stay fully dilated.

Curious eye facts

▶ The human eye can process 12 to 15 separate image exposures each second, perceiving each of them individually.

▶ The visual cortex holds onto one image for about one-fifteenth of a second, so if another image is received during that period, an illusion of continuity is created, allowing a sequence of still images to give the impression of motion (movie frame rates vary from 24 to 60 frames per minute—the higher rates being used in HD TVs because they create less flicker and motion-blur.)

▶ The average person blinks their eyes once every six seconds, with each blink lasting about 0.25 seconds. Thus, on a 4.5 hour drive from Boston to New York City, your eyes will actually be closed for nearly 7 minutes (which may explain some of the erratic driving on I-95).

▶ If you were given glasses that flipped your vision upside down, over the course of a few days your brain would correct things so that you would perceive things as right-side up.

▶ Seeing is so important that about half of our brain gets involved.

▶ The muscles that control your eyes are the most active muscles in your body.

▶ A newborn's eye color is typically dark gray or blue—it takes up to a year for the melanocytes (melanin-producing cells) to react to light and fix their final color—brown is dominant, blue is recessive.

Optical illusions

Despite the eye's marvelous design, sometimes we "see" things not as they are—our eyes can be tricked. In the illusion below, if you look straight on, the image appears stationary, but if you look off to one side the image appears in your periphery to be slowly spinning.

View angle

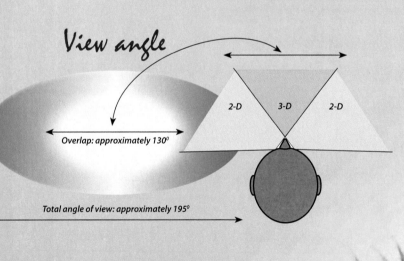

2-D   3-D   2-D

Overlap: approximately 130⁰

Total angle of view: approximately 195⁰

Color

A common color test: a color-blind person will not be able to see the number 57 in the center of this test image.

i examination

OBSERVE THE EYES FOR ANY OBVIOUS INJURY **1**

Is there periorbital swelling, a lacerated eyelid, subconjunctival hematoma (bleeding underneath the conjunctiva), a foreign body in the eye, or an impaled object?

INSPECT THE CONJUNCTIVA, PERIORBITAL TISSUES, AND EYELIDS **2**

Look at the pupils and the shape of the pupils, the white of the eye (the conjunctiva), the eyelids, and the tissue surrounding the eyes—are there any wounds, erythema (redness), ecchymosis (bruising), or swelling?

CHECK THE PATIENT'S VISUAL ACUITY **3**

Visual acuity is the ability of the eye to focus. It can easily be checked by having the patient read something with different sizes of print on it (e.g., a trail map, guidebook, dollar bill, energy bar wrapper). Check one eye at a time.

▶ Hold the printed material about 16 inches (the length or your forearm) in front of them in good light and have them read it from the biggest print size to the smallest.
▶ They should be able to read what you can read; in other words, their vision should be as good as yours.
▶ If they wear glasses or contacts, they should use them for the test.

CHECK THE PATIENT'S VISUAL FIELDS **4**

▶ With both you and the patient sitting, place your hands on their shoulders so that your arms are straight—this should place the patient about 2 feet in front of you.
▶ Have the patient stare at your nose—their vision must remain fixed on your nose during the exam.
▶ Remove your hands from their shoulders and move your hands through the four different quadrants of vision about halfway between you—up/down and left/right.
▶ Wiggle your fingers at the limits of peripheral vision— the patient should be able to see what you can see.
▶ This test will help identify any blind spots resulting from a temporary ischemic attack (TIA), cerebrovascular accident (CVA), trauma, or detached retina.

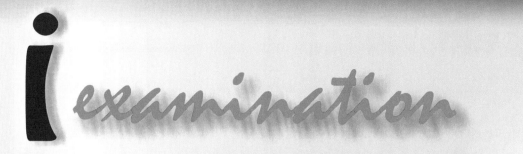

CHECK THE EXTRAOCULAR MOVEMENT (EOM)

▶ With both eyes open, have the patient look forward at your finger or a light that is held about 16 inches in front of their eyes.
▶ Instruct them to follow the finger or light as you draw a large capital "H" in front of their face.
▶ As you go through the motions of making the "H," make it large enough to force the eyes to the extremes of motion.
▶ You may have to hold their chin to keep them from turning their head to follow your finger.

5

CHECK THE PUPILS

Pupillary response is a basic vital sign skill that tests the pupils to see how well they respond to light and if they are equal.

6

- ▶ Pupils should be PERRL: Pupils Equal, Round, and Reactive to light.
- ▶ Be sure to look closely at the shape of the pupil and the condition of the iris, as eye trauma can distort the shape of the pupil and the iris.

LOOK FOR HYPHEMA

- ▶ While checking the pupils, take the time to look at the anterior chamber of the eye (the visible portion of the iris that is covered by the cornea).
- ▶ If the eye has suffered blunt trauma, blood can collect in the lower portion of the anterior chamber and can be seen in front of the iris—hyphema.
- ▶ Although this may look awful, and it does indicate an internal injury to the eye, hyphema rarely puts the vision at risk.

7

A hyphema looks dramatic indeed—fortunately it is typically not as serious as it appears.

i *injuries*

Corneal abrasion

A corneal abrasion occurs when something rubs up against the cornea of the eye removing several layers of cells. With one of the greatest concentrations of pain receptors in the human body, the cornea is very sensitive—an abrasion can be quite painful, and can feel worse than it is. While corneal abrasions are very common, fortunately they are also easily treated. With long-term care, the main problem is the risk of infection in the days following the injury while the abrasion heals. With proper care a corneal abrasion will usually heal in 24 – 48 hours (depending on the severity).

EVALUATION

1. Determine mechanism of Injury (MOI)—what caused the injury? Something happened to injure the eye: a branch hitting the face, a piece of sand or sawdust blowing into the eye, or a ball or a fist smacking the eye.
2. Immediately have the patient sit down and keep their eyes closed for several minutes to allow the wounded eye to calm down.
3. Instruct the patient not to rub their eye (the natural response) in case there is a foreign body under the eyelid.

Inverting an eyelid using a smooth, cylindrical object such as a Q-Tip is a useful skill for evaluating many eye problems—it allows you to search under the lid for injuries (scratches) and foreign matter (e.g., a dead bug, piece of bark).

4. Closely examine the face and the area around the eye for evidence of injury.
5. Eventually you will be able to gently open the eye. Once open, look closely for a foreign body, speck of dust, impaled object, or wound.
6. If possible, invert the upper lid and examine the area under it closely (left).
7. Check their vision in both eyes and look at the shape of the iris and pupil for evidence of a penetrating injury—A foreign body in the eye can cause a corneal abrasion as the patient blinks in an effort to get rid of the object from their eye.

Corneal abrasions can be almost impossible to see with the naked eye. In a clinical setting, fluorescein stain is used to highlight and fluoresce the abrasions under a cobalt blue light. In the backcountry this is not an option, so a presumptive diagnosis will have to be made on the basis of the discomfort and no other evidence of injury.

TREATMENT

1. Remove all foreign bodies. Flush the eye out with sterile saline while holding the eye open (tilt the head so that fluid drains away from the other eye). With a corneal abrasion, the patient may still describe the sensation of a foreign body, even after rinsing.
2. Treat to prevent infection (the greatest risk) by placing a broad spectrum ophthalmic antibiotic eye drop or ointment in the eye. In the wilderness setting, a good choice is Erythromycin Ophthalmic Ointment, a prescription drug that comes in a small tube that is easily added to a first aid kit. Place a ¼" ribbon of the ointment in the eye every 6 hours for 5 days. Continue administering the ointment, even after the patient becomes pain-free (often within 24 hours).
3. Put the eye at rest by fixing the patient's vision. Typically in the clinic setting, the eye would be at rest by placing an eye-patch over the affected eye for 24 hours. In the backcountry, where mobility is important, you can put the eye at rest and fix the patient's vision by giving them a small pinhole to see through.
4. Evacuate for medical attention if the abrasion is causing the patient severe pain and/or irritation—there may be more going on than you can determine.

Foreign bodies

This is a very common problem which most often resolves itself when the eye tears and the object (dirt speck, twig, etc.) rinses out. If not, you will need to try to remove the object. While this can be a little scary for both the caregiver and the patient, it is typically easy to accomplish and causes minimal discomfort.

TREATMENT

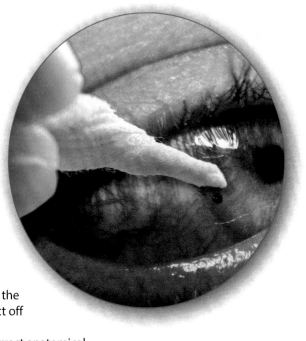

1. If the object does not naturally flush out, support the head and then hold the eye open by the lid and try to flush the object out with a gentle flow of sterile water.
2. If this doesn't work, use something soft (e.g., the twisted end of a bandanna) to gently try to prod the object and lift it out. Sometimes it may need some coaxing—try your best not to cause any further damage.
3. If the object is on the cornea, lifting it off may be painful—in the definitive care setting, anesthetizing eye drops can be used.
4. If the foreign body is stuck behind the upper lid (common), it can be more difficult to remove. Invert the eyelid by grasping the eyelashes. Use a stiff item (e.g., Q-Tip) and gently lift the object off and out (see previous page).
5. Once the object is removed, fold the lid back down into its correct anatomical position.
6. If the patient's eye remains painful after the removal of a foreign object, assume there is a corneal abrasion and treat accordingly.

Blunt trauma

This is the classic "baseball in the eye" injury. They eye has suffered direct trauma and the surrounding tissue swells dramatically to the point where the eye swells shut. When this happens to both eyes, the condition is known as "raccoon eyes."

TREATMENT

1. Identify the MOI and evaluate the patient to determine if there is any accompanying facial, sinus, jaw, or neck injury.
2. Inspect the periorbital tissues and manage any wounds as usual.
3. Apply gentle pressure to control any bleeding (not on the eyeball).
4. If the eyelids can be separated, examine the eyes closely.
5. Look at the shape of the iris (is it abnormal?) and for hyphema—both conditions can indicate a potentially sight-threatening injury.
6. Apply a cold compress to reduce swelling.
7. Evacuate.

Lacerated eyelid

A lacerated eyelid may involve the globe of the eye.

TREATMENT

1. Place a sterile dressing over the eyelid (do not apply direct pressure).
2. Cover both eyes to minimize sympathetic movement (the coordinated movement of both eyes).
3. Give pinpoint vision in the uninjured eye so the patient can still walk.

Impaled objects

Impaled objects in the eye are rarely life-threatening, but they can be sight-threatening. Occasionally, a foreign body will penetrate the globe of the eye and become impaled. Impaled objects in the eye rarely occur in the backcountry—these injuries are usually associated with urban environments where explosions throw shrapnel into the air, or where something breaks under tension at an industrial site and flings out a projectile. In the urban environment, the standard of care is to leave the object in place , stabilize it, and evacuate. When they do occur in the backcountry, the most common impaled objects are fishhooks or twigs embedded from a face-first fall.

TREATMENT

1. In the wilderness setting, grasp the object to see if it can be easily removed. Often, a twig or piece of glass will come right out. If an object (e.g., a fishhook) is really stuck, do not remove it—follow the protection instructions below.

Because all but the most easily-removed objects should be left in the eye while transporting the patient to definitive care, it is critical that the eye be protected so that the object cannot be bumped, which might cause devastating further damage.

2. If the object comes out, you will be left with a hole in the globe of the eye. The eye is filled with a thick, gelatinous fluid (vitreous humor), which supports the globe and holds the retina in place. Because of its high viscosity, it won't drain out—it has to be forced out.

3. Apply direct pressure to the wound to control bleeding, but do not apply so much pressure to the globe of the eye that it forces some of the vitreous humor out.

4. Protect and bandage the eye (have the patient and/or an assistant aid in keeping everything in place while you fix the bandages in place).

   ▶ Place a cloth doughnut over the injured eye and a gauze bandage over the uninjured eye.

   ▶ Place a cup or similar object over the injured eye.

   ▶ Capture the base of the cup and the gauze bandage with a cravat or cloth strip.

   ▶ Tie the cravat behind the head.

   ▶ Capture the body of the cup with a second cravat.

5. If the patient is ambulatory, leave a peep-hole in the dressing over the uninjured eye and in the cup over the injured eye—this fixes the patient's vision, but allows them to see while they walk (they will have to move their head, not just their eyes to see).

6. Evacuate.

Blowout fracture

This is an extreme form of blunt trauma where enough force has been applied to the eye and surrounding tissues to fracture the area of the skull that makes up the eye socket—in particular, the thin section of the maxilla that forms the orbital floor of the eye socket. Between the eyeball and the orbital floor are some of the extraocular muscles, which can also be damaged. In a blowout fracture, the injured eye will droop slightly, sit lower in the eye socket, and the eye muscle will become trapped, preventing upward eye movement. This will cause double vision, but the vision in each eye should remain intact.

TREATMENT

1. Cover both eyes to minimize eye movement—providing a pinhole if there is an uninjured eye.

2. Evacuate immediately and quickly—surgery will likely be needed.

Avulsion/open-eye injuries

A wound that penetrates the globe of the eye.

TREATMENT

1. Cover both eyes with a moist, sterile dressing.

2. Evacuate the patient lying on their back.

One of the common treatments for eye problems is to "fix" the patient's vision so that their eyes don't move unnecessarily. There are many ways to do this—here, good old duct tape over a pair of sunglasses does the trick. In order to see properly while they walk out, the patient must keep their good eye aimed right at the pinhole, minimizing movement in both eyes.

Subconjunctival hemorrhage

The white of the eye, the conjunctiva, is rich with blood vessels. Minimal trauma, including forceful coughing, can cause some of these vessels to rupture. When this occurs, blood will collect under the conjunctival epithelium and an area of bright red blood will appear that can be very dramatic looking. If the exam of the eye is otherwise normal, and vision is intact, this is a minor injury that does not threaten vision and heals without complication over the course of a week.

Detached retina

The retina is the layer of cells—the rods, cones, and supporting tissue—found in the back of the eye, which captures the images of the world (akin to the sensor in a digital camera). The retina is not physically adhered to the globe of the eye, but rather held in place by the vitreous humor. A detached retina is one that has partially or completely peeled off the back of the eye. This condition can occur as a result of blunt trauma or can occur spontaneously without any accompanying injury (as a result of numerous medical conditions).

SYMPTOMS
- ▶ Little or no pain.
- ▶ The person complains of a change in and loss of peripheral vision and will commonly describe this change as if a curtain were being drawn across their vision.
- ▶ Prior to loss of vision, they may have noticed flashes of light around the perimeter of their vision.

You will not be able to diagnose a detached retina by physical exam, but you can assume it based on the patient's description of their symptoms.

TREATMENT

1. This is a medical emergency with no field treatment—it is important to be able to recognize the condition as soon as possible.
2. Evacuate the patient immediately—this is a sight-threatening injury that will most likely require surgical intervention.

Chemical burns

TREATMENT

1. When someone gets any sort of unwanted chemical or contaminate in their eye (e.g., fuel, insect repellent, ashes from a camp fire) the treatment is to flush the eyes with copious amounts of clean water—"the solution to the pollution is dilution."
2. Do not delay by performing an eye exam—the longer the material is in the eye, the more potential damage it can do.
3. When rinsing the eyes, use a gentle flow of warm water across the bridge of the nose and away from the other eye—be careful not to rinse the pollutant from one eye to the other.
4. Gently rinse for 10 – 20 minutes and use several liters of fluid.
5. Once the eyes have been rinsed clean, do a thorough eye exam.
6. If there is any residual pain, a burning sensation, or foreign body sensation, apply a ¼" ribbon of Erythromycin Ophthalmic Ointment to the eye.
7. Cover the eye.
8. Consider fixing the patient's vision with pinhole glasses.
9. Consider evacuation.

Light burns

This is a painful condition where the eyes have been exposed to too much ultraviolet light—it is essentially a sunburn of the conjunctiva. The burn can occur very quickly, in just seconds, as with a welder's flash while arc welding, or slowly over a period of hours when exposed to highly reflective surfaces such as snow (snow blindness), sand, or water. Several hours after the exposure, the eyes become painful, and the whites of the eyes look sunburned (pink, irritated) and have a rough (cobblestone-like) surface. This is not a sight-threatening injury, but it is a painful injury that will take several days to heal.

PREVENTION

▶ This is a very preventable injury—wear sunglasses that block 100% of UV light.
▶ If sunglasses are destroyed, improvise pinhole glasses.

TREATMENT

1. Primarily, healing requires the tincture of time (hours to a day or two).
2. Control pain with cold, moist compresses.
3. Apply Erythromycin Ophthalmic Ointment every six hours to keep the eyes moist and promote healing.
4. Oral pain medications can be used in conjunction with ointment.
5. Avoid direct sun.

Eye infections

PERIORBITAL CELLULITIS occurs when an infectious agent, (e.g., staph bacteria), gets into the soft tissues surrounding the eye. These are potentially very serious infections that can spread quickly and, therefore, require aggressive treatment.

▶ The area around the eye becomes erythematous (red), swollen, and warm to the touch, and the area expands quickly over hours.
▶ Treat immediately with oral antibiotics. Doxycycline 100mg po bid for at least 7 days. If doxycycline is not available, other oral antibiotics can be used: any of the penicillins, cephalosporins such as Keflex, or quinolones such as Cipro should work in appropriate dosages.
▶ Warm, moist compresses may be applied during evacuation.
▶ Evacuate immediately.

CONJUNCTIVITIS is a common condition, typically caused by viruses, (may be bacterial).

▶ The affected eye will have mild conjunctival erythema (redness) with purulence (pus) on the eye lashes or in the corners of the eyes.
▶ Apply a broad spectrum antibiotic eye ointment or drop—Erythromycin Ophthalmic Ointment works very well (place a ¼" ribbon in the affected eye every 6 hours).
▶ Warm, moist compresses will aid in healing and comfort.
▶ Evacuation is not necessary unless the conjunctivitis does not improve within 24 hours, or if vision is affected.
▶ Note: conjunctivitis is highly contagious, so frequent hand washing is important. Also, avoid using the same towel, etc., as the patient.

EXTERNAL STYE (hordeolum) A sty occurs when one of the manubrium oil glands in the eyelids becomes infected, usually with staph bacteria.

▶ The area of the eyelid becomes swollen, tender, erythematous, and may have a whitish area or pustule in the center of the swelling—these can be quite tender.
▶ Do not attempt to incise and drain these; instead treat the sty with warm, moist compresses and apply a ¼" ribbon of Erythromycin Ophthalmic Ointment every 6 hours.
▶ Styes can take from several days to weeks to resolve.
▶ Add an oral antibiotic if periorbital cellulitis develops (see above).

Even just a few seconds of exposure to a the flash of a welding torch (top) can burn your conjunctiva. Other causes, such as reflected light from snow, sand, or water, can take several hours to create the same amount of damage. Prevention is the key: anticipate potentially damaging situations, and avoid them or protect yourself against them—out in the bright sunny world, nothing beats a pair of really dark sunglasses with side shades.

What to do when things go wrong in here . . .

INJURIES or infections to teeth run the gamut from annoying to debilitating to even life-threatening. While a headache or broken tooth, much like a blister from hiking in wet socks, can ruin your day, other issues can lead to a serious infection that requires not only immediate treatment but also evacuation to definitive care.

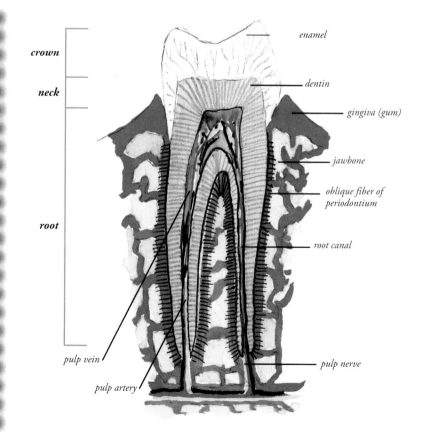

crown

neck

root

enamel

dentin

gingiva (gum)

jawbone

oblique fiber of periodontium

root canal

pulp nerve

pulp vein

pulp artery

ORAL INJURIES

Tooth anatomy

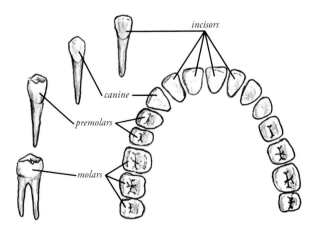

incisors

canine

premolars

molars

Emergencies which are not dangerous to a person's overall health, but which need to be managed for the health of the tooth.

- Fractured teeth
- Luxation
- Avulsion
- Oral infections

Emergencies which are very hazardous to the person's health and which can be very painful.

- Dental caries
- Abscessed tooth
- Osteomyelitis
- Subacute Bacterial Encocarditis (SBE)

Nuisance problems—can be painful and bothersome.

- Lost fillings, displaced crowns, cracked teeth
- Aphthous ulcers (canker sores)
- Cold sores

ORAL TRAUMA
GENERAL TREATMENT PRINCIPLES

1. Whenever a person has suffered enough trauma to their face to cause damage to their teeth, they should be closely examined.
2. Take a complete history.
3. Determine the MOI.
4. Examine the face, jaw, temporomandibular joint, and cervical spine.
5. Test the integrity of their facial structure: with a gloved hand, push on the hard palate between the upper teeth—movement indicates a significant facial fracture (Le Fort fracture—see facial trauma section).

Check the palate by visual inspection (left) and test its structural integrity by pulling and pushing the palate using the upper teeth (right); you should reach up behind the upper teeth and press on the palate directly, too.

ORAL TRAUMA
TOOTH FRACTURE

These are typically cosmetic injuries that can be easily repaired later. If the pulp (nerve tissue) has been exposed, there may be considerable pain. There are three classifications.

- **Root fracture**: The tooth broken off with ½ of the root still in the socket and ½ of the root broken free with the tooth.
- **Crown fracture**: The tooth is broken off at the base of the crown or gum line.
- **Chipped tooth**: Part of the crown, but not the whole crown, is chipped off.

TREATMENT

1. Control bleeding—it can be copious (but not dangerous—it looks worse than it is). Bleeding is easily controlled by direct pressure using a piece of gauze.
2. Save the fragments—any fragment is worth saving.
3. Keep the fragment moist by wrapping it in gauze with the patient's own saliva (not water, which can damage the soft tissue and nerves) and place it in a plastic bag.
4. Avoid handling the pulp (it is easily damaged).
5. Control pain: If the fracture is painful, reduce pain by reducing the exposure of the tooth to temperature changes, air movement, saliva, and the patient's tongue—seal off the exposed nerve ends by covering the exposed tooth with soft candle wax, using a commercial product like Cavit or Super Glue (Note: Super Glue, cyanoacrylate, has not been FDA-approved for this application). Clove oil (or eugenol, a derivative of clove) can be applied directly to the exposed pulp and will alleviate pain for several hours.
6. Evacuate.

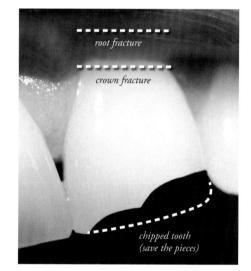

root fracture

crown fracture

chipped tooth
(save the pieces)

By adding just two small items to your first aid kid, you can greatly improve your ability to treat tooth injuries: clove oil (right—old bottle, may be expired), will provide pain relief for a broken tooth for up to two hours, and Cavit (below), can be used to make temporary repairs to injuries such as chipped teeth and lost fillings.

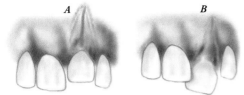

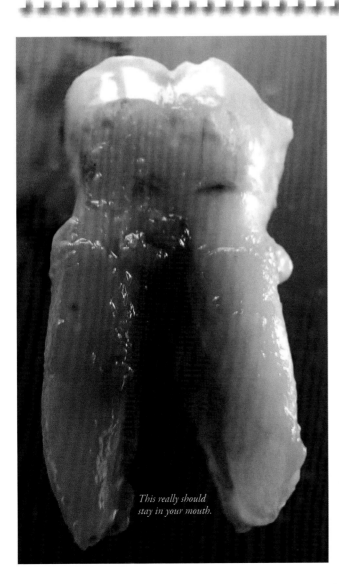

*Two examples of luxation: intrusion (**A**) and extrusion and displacement (**B**). An intruded tooth cannot be treated in the field; the person needs a dentist immediately. An extruded or laterally displaced tooth can be repositioned in the field prior to evacuation to a dentist.*

ORAL TRAUMA
LUXATION

A luxation occurs when a tooth is shifted out of anatomical position but is otherwise left intact.

- Treatment depends on the direction the tooth was displaced.
- After field treatment (if appropriate) all patients with luxation injuries should be evacuated immediately to the nearest dentist.

TREATMENT

1. **Intrusion**: the tooth appears shorter than the surrounding teeth. Do not field-manage this injury—leave the tooth as found and evacuate.
1. **Extrusion**: the tooth appears longer (taller) than the surrounding teeth. Grasp the tooth with a gloved hand and firmly push it back into the socket.
2. **Laterally displaced**: the tooth appears to be pushed ahead or behind the tooth row. Reposition the tooth to normal anatomical position.

ORAL TRAUMA
AVULSION

The entire tooth, including the root, has been removed from its socket.

- The best results occur when the tooth is replaced within 30 minutes.
- After two hours, the chance of the tooth surviving is minimal.

TREATMENT

1. **Rinse**: gently wash away any blood clots or debris with a gentle stream of fresh, clean water.
2. **Replace**: reposition the tooth in its socket in its anatomical position and press it down firmly—it should re-seat with a snap.
3. **Alternately**: place gauze between the teeth and have the patient bite down on it to help re-seat the tooth and hold it in place.
4. **If re-seating is unsuccessful**: treat the tooth as a fragment and package appropriately (see tooth fracture treatment).
5. **Evacuate**

This really should stay in your mouth.

A tooth avulsion can be a major oral injury, and re-seating the tooth isn't easy:

- *It is often hard to determine the correct anatomical position*
- *The process is painful—even after re-seating.*
- *The tooth may be loose in its socket and easily dislodged.*
- *Even when replaced successfully, get the patient to a dentist as soon as possible.*

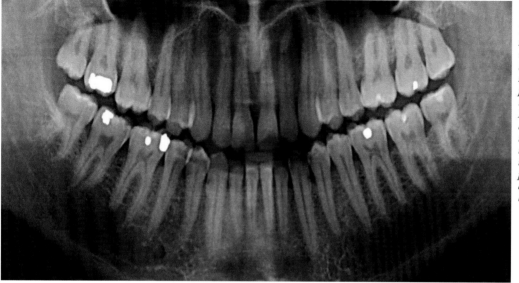

Yup, under all your skin and muscle, that's what your lower face looks like (note: there is some proportional and perspective distortion in this rather grotesque X-ray). Notice the clear delineation of the teeth—they're longer than you thought, aren't they? The bright white patches are where dental caries (cavities) have been filled.

ORAL INFECTION
DENTAL CARIES

The classic "cavity"—typically annoying, can lead to pulpitis, which in turn can lead to a far more serious infection

- Chemicals produced by bacteria break down the enamel and eventually reach the pulp.
- They typically occur as a result of poor oral hygiene and neglect of tooth care.
- Diet (too much sugar), saliva production (the more saliva, the fewer cavities), and genetics and morphology (some people are simply more susceptible) are also factors.
- Bad teeth, bad gums, and dental caries all affect an individual's overall health, to the point of being potentially life-threatening.

SIGNS AND SYMPTOMS

- Dental caries are not painful.
- Decayed enamel may appear as a different color or will be detected via X-ray.

- If the decay extends into the pulp of the tooth, pulpitis will occur, causing pain (the classic toothache), often associated with the pressure of chewing or temperature change (e.g., when eating ice cream).
- As an infection progresses, an abscess forms inside the tooth, creating pressure and a toothache with a constant, throbbing pain.
- If the infection spreads into the surrounding tissue or bone, the area around the tooth will swell and become warm and tender to the touch.
- The infection can also spread to adjacent lymph nodes, causing more swelling and pain.
- If the infection spreads to the valves of the heart, causing subacute bacterial endocarditis (SBE), the damage to the heart valves will result in a heart murmur as well as the systemic signs of sepsis: fever, chills, fatigue, weakness, tachycardia, and hypotension, and possibly even septic shock and death (this is a slow-moving disease that can take a year to be fatal).

TREATMENT

1. Treat the pain with an NSAID (ibuprofen, naproxen, aspirin) and acetaminophen (Tylenol).
2. If a simple dental caries evolves into a dental abscess, narcotic pain relievers such as Tylenol with codeine, hydrocodone (Lortab, Vicodin) may be needed.
3. If an abscess is suspected because of constant pain (right), the severity of the pain, or erythema (reddening) and swelling of the gums around the tooth, an antibiotic is appropriate—penicillin VK 500mg PO 3x per day (if the patient is allergic to penicillin, erythromycin 500mg PO 2x per day).
4. Apply a warm, moist heat pack.
5. Clove oil can also be applied to the cavity to ease pain.

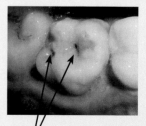

dental caries—cavities as a result of tooth decay

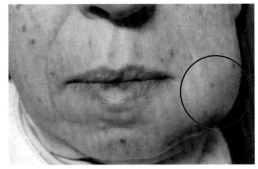

A tooth abscess—swollen, painful, requires treatment by a dentist.

Yes, even statues get toothaches...

ORAL INFECTION
TOOTH ABSCESS

A tooth abscess is pus enclosed in the tissues in and around the teeth

- Typically the result of a bacterial infection that has accumulated in the soft, often necrotic, pulp of the tooth.
- Can be caused by advanced tooth decay (i.e., dental caries), a broken tooth, periodontitis (gum disease), a failed root canal treatment, or a combination of these factors.
- Types of abscesses include gingival (involving only gum tissue, but not the tooth), periapical (which start at the apex of the root), and periodontal (which begin in the pocket of gingiva over 3mm).

SIGNS AND SYMPTOMS

- Continuous pain—extreme, gnawing, sharp, shooting, or throbbing.
- Localized swelling (can be dramatic).
- Tooth sensitive to percussion.
- Can include difficulty opening mouth, swallowing, or breathing.
- The tooth may be unresponsive to thermal changes due to necrosis of the pulp (nerves).
- Can have elevated temperature, rapid and weak pulse.
- There may be history of a toothache.

TREATMENT

1. Treat pain with NSAIDs.
2. Give antibiotics (see dental caries #3).
3. Evacuate for drainage: extraction, incision, or root canal—this is not something you can field manage.

ORAL
NUISANCE PROBLEMS

LOST FILLINGS, DISLODGED CROWNS, CRACKED TEETH

1. If the nerves have been exposed, treat with candle wax, Cavit, and/or clove oil.
2. Control pain with NSAIDs and Tylenol.
3. A mild narcotic may be necessary.
4. Evacuate for dental follow-up.

APHTHOUS ULCERS (CANKER SORES)

- These are very common.
- They are just a nuisance—rarely serious.
- Pain is usually mild and intermittent (typically associated with eating or drinking).
- There is no quick cure.

1. Warm saltwater gargles, several times a day, can help.
2. Commercial rinses are also available.

COLD SORES

- Cold sores are typically caused by the oral herpes virus.
- Estimates are that 80% of people harbor the virus.

1. Protect the lips from chapping and sunburn.
2. Use acyclovir (Zostrix) or other commercially available treatments.

PREVENTION OF NUISANCE PROBLEMS

1. See your dentist before an extended trip.
2. Consider using a mouth guard in any activity that can cause tooth damage (e.g., mountain biking).
3. Use lip balm and sunblock.
4. Bring meds if prone to canker or cold sores.
5. For extended trips, consider a dental first aid kit.

- Candle wax: to cover exposed pulp/nerves.
- Clove oil: applied to pulp, helps alleviate pain.
- Super glue: for small repairs (chips, fillings, crowns); also can be used to cover exposed pulp (not FDA-approved for this use).
- Cavit: commercially available temporary filling material.
- Plastic dental mirror: helpful to see problems.
- Toothbrush, dental floss, cotton balls, cotton-tipped swabs .
- NSAIDs and Tylenol.
- Antibiotics: penicillin VK 500mg 1 po qid x 10 days; Erythromycin 500mg po bid x 10 days.

the **Musculoskeletal System**

our muscles,
bones, tendons,
ligaments,
cartilage, plus
other stuff . . .

WILDCARE™

Far more complex than man's greatest technological achievements, the human body, with its pulleys, cables, and girders (not to mention its electrical, plumbing, sensory, and cognitive systems) is a marvel of engineering. Some mornings, just getting out of bed can seem amazing.

. . . the structural members that hold us together and allow us to move

Without our musculoskeletal system we would have all the structural integrity of a jellyfish—and it would give new meaning to the phrase, "Let's hang out." Unfortunately, we wouldn't be able to pass the chips, or operate the TV remote, or even speak to each other, so the party might end up pretty dull. But we're not jellyfish, we're human beings, designed with a harmonious combination of structural parts that give us form and function—and allow us to do important things, like flip burgers on the grill and text each other with our thumbs. The fundamental roles of our musculoskeletal system include:

- **MOVEMENT**
  - The contraction of muscles provides us with purposeful movement.
- **HEAT PRODUCTION**
  - The contraction of muscles produces heat.
- **PROTECTION**
  - The strength and flexibility of muscles protect many internal structures, including the bundles of nerves, arteries, and veins under the muscles.
  - Bones protect the underlying structures.
- **CALCIUM STORAGE**
  - The bones act as a large calcium store.
  - Calcium is an electrolyte that allows for the contraction of muscle and the conduction of nerve impulses.
- **HEMATOPOIESIS**
  - This is the process by which the various blood cells—red blood cells (RBC), white blood cells (WBC), and platelets—are produced in the bone marrow.
- **COSMESIS**
  - The muscular and skeletal structures contribute greatly to how we look.

MUSCULOSKELETAL ANATOMY & PHYSIOLOGY

Functionality

Bones
Provide structure, protection, motion, calcium storage, and red blood cell production.

Muscles
Provide the power for movement by contracting. Give our body form (cosmesis).

Tendons
Attach muscle to bone or muscle to muscle. They span the joints to help facilitate movement. They operate in conjunction with ligaments, bones, and nerves to do work.

Ligaments
Tough, fibrous bands that span the joints and attach bone to bone. They help hold the joints together and control range of motion.

Cartilage
Provides cushioning between bones at the joints. Acts as a lubricated, durable cap on the ends of bones so that the joint can flex and rotate smoothly with little friction. Provides durable support for muscle in areas where more flexibility than what bone offers is needed.

Joint detail

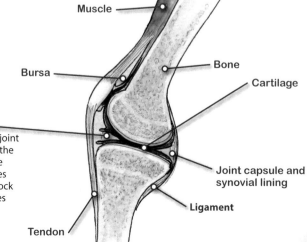

Muscle

Bursa

Bone

Cartilage

Synovial cavity (synovial fluid)
The lubricant in the joint space, produced by the synovial lining of the joint capsule: reduces friction, provides shock absorption, facilitates nutrient and waste transportation.

Joint capsule and synovial lining

Ligament

Tendon

WILDCARE™

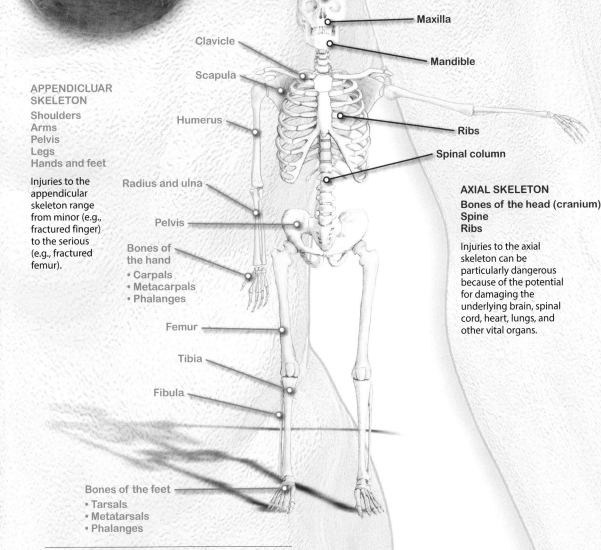

MUSCULOSKELETAL FACTS

At birth, we have over 300 bones; as we grow, some of these fuse together, so we end up with 206.

The human hand has 27 bones; the skull has 29; the whole leg has 31.

The largest bone is the femur (upper leg); the smallest is the stapes bone in the middle ear.

The femur is so strong that it can withstand axial loading (compression along the length of the bone) of over 3,000 pounds.

Most of the bones in the human body are about 75% water.

We replace our entire skeleton approximately every 7 years (virtually every cell in our body, in fact).

The human body has 230 movable and semi-movable joints.

There are approximately 630 skeletal muscles in the human body, almost all occurring in symmetrical, bilateral pairs (i.e., each side of your body has one of each muscle).

Each of us has approximately 43 muscles in our face—and the theory is that it takes fewer muscles (i.e., less effort) to smile than to frown.

Each of us has approximately 4,000 tendons and 900 ligaments (no wonder we creak and groan so much as we age).

Unlike muscle, which is constantly perfused with fresh blood, tendons and ligaments are not well vascularized—they take much longer to heal.

Bones are made up of living cells that form a composite that is stronger than aluminum. Calcium and phosphate, in a matrix with collagen, creates an elastic protein called calcium hydroxyapatite, The skeleton is constantly remodeling itself utilizing two types of cells: **osteoblasts** are constantly rebuilding new bone, and they are followed around by **osteoclasts** that are constantly reabsorbing bone. These cells allow the bones to heal and strengthen in response to stressors.

APPENDICLUAR SKELETON

Shoulders
Arms
Pelvis
Legs
Hands and feet

Injuries to the appendicular skeleton range from minor (e.g., fractured finger) to the serious (e.g., fractured femur).

AXIAL SKELETON

Bones of the head (cranium)
Spine
Ribs

Injuries to the axial skeleton can be particularly dangerous because of the potential for damaging the underlying brain, spinal cord, heart, lungs, and other vital organs.

Cranial bones
Maxilla
Mandible
Clavicle
Scapula
Humerus
Ribs
Spinal column
Radius and ulna
Pelvis
Bones of the hand
• Carpals
• Metacarpals
• Phalanges
Femur
Tibia
Fibula
Bones of the feet
• Tarsals
• Metatarsals
• Phalanges

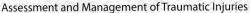

Assessment and Management of Traumatic Injuries

Types of musculoskeletal injuries

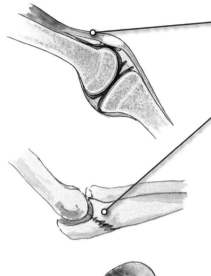

STRAINS AND SPRAINS

- Strains are overuse and/or over-stretching injuries, primarily involving muscles and tendons.
- Sprains involve the over-stretching of a joint (moving it beyond its range of motion) and typically cause damage to ligaments.

FRACTURES

- Sometimes abbreviated as Fx, a fracture is the break in the continuity of a bone.
- Fractures can result from high-force impact or stress, or from a seemingly trivial incident that occurs in people with bones weakened by disease (e.g., osteoporosis, bone cancer).
- There are two basic types:
    - Closed—fractures where the skin is not breached.
    - Open (compound)—where there is an accompanying wound that may expose the bone to contamination, risking infection.

DISLOCATIONS

- An injury where the bones in a joint become displaced or misaligned.
- Often caused by forceful impact or twisting action.
- There is always some accompanying soft tissue damage to the surrounding muscles, tendons, ligaments, and/or cartilage.
- Dislocations can be associated with a fracture.

ORTHOPEDIC EMERGENCIES

In addition to the common injuries listed above—most that involve the appendicular skeleton, there are a host of other ways we can beat ourselves up, many involving the axial skeleton and associated tissues and organs.

- Head trauma.
    - Increasing intracranial pressure (ICP), skull fracture, change in level of consciousness (LOC), concussion, superficial hematoma.
- Facial trauma.
    - Airway injuries, facial bone fractures, basilar skull fracture, injuries to the eyes, ears, and teeth.
- Chest trauma.
    - Chest wall soft tissue injuries, fractures of the clavicle, sternum, or ribs, pulmonary contusions and lacerations, hemothorax and pneumothorax, subcutaneous emphysema and tracheobronchial tear, pericardial tamponade, myocardial contusion, traumatic aorta rupture, impaled object, traumatic asphyxia.
- Pelvic trauma.
    - Fractures of the pelvic girdle and associated circulatory compromise.
- Crush injuries.
    - Damage to skeletal and soft tissues as a result of crushing trauma.
- Compartment syndrome.
    - A dangerous circulatory condition associated with crush injuries.
- Deformed fracture or dislocation
    - A threat to circulation distal to the site of the injury.

WILDCARE™

Evaluating a musculoskeletal injury

LOOK

- ▪ Is there normal movement and function?
- ▪ Is there any deformity or angulation?
- ▪ Is there any discoloration or swelling?
- ▪ Is there any guarding? They are trying to protect the injury—don't touch them.

LISTEN

- ▪ What happened—what was the mechanism of injury (MOI)?
- ▪ Where does it hurt—what is the patient's chief complaint (C/C)?
- ▪ Did the patient hear anything snap, crack, or pop?
- ▪ If the patient is unconscious, you will have to look for clues.

FEEL

- ▪ Is there point tenderness (pain felt when pressure is applied to a specific place—some injuries don't hurt unless palpated)?
- ▪ Is there crepitation (the crunching feeling or sound of broken bones grating against each other)?
- ▪ Is there any compromise in circulation, sensation, and movement (CSM), especially distal to the injury site?

TRAUMA S/S gamut

The relative size of the circles corresponds to the relative severity of the signs and symptoms—both within a type of injury, and when comparing types of injuries, the bigger the circle, the more prominent the sign or symptom.

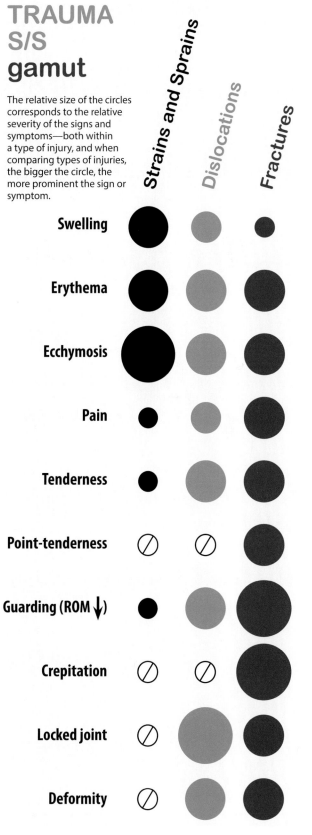

PURPLE

hematoma from a classic lateral ankle roll (inversion). In a few days it will turn a lovely shade of greeny-yellow akin to a bruised, overripe pear.

st**RAINS**
sp

STRAINS AND SPRAINS are the most common musculoskeletal injuries (particularly involving the ankle). They will be considered together because the mechanisms of injury are similar; they typically occur together; they are hard to differentiate in the field; and they share the same treatment.

STRAINS

- Pulls or tears of the **muscles** and/or **tendons**—the injury occurs when the muscle and/or tendon is stretched to the point of tearing, causing slight (micro) internal bleeding.
- Strains occur when muscles are forced beyond their capacity because they are over-worked, stressed, or tired (because of recent activity).
- Strains can also be caused when the muscle is stressed before being properly warmed up (starting a long trail run by sprinting 200 yards is a bad idea).
- Strains most often occur in the lower back and hamstring.
- Most strains can be treated effectively in the field.

SPRAINS

- Overstretching of joints beyond their normal range of motion that causes injury to the associated **ligaments**.
- Sprains most often occur in the wrist and ankle.
- Muscle strains usually accompany sprains.
- Sprains can be very painful, and ankle or knee sprains may require litter evacuation.

SIGNS AND SYMPTOMS OF BOTH STRAINS AND SPRAINS

- Pain at the site can be mild to severe, depending on the injury, but is generally not debilitating.
- There is typically diffuse tenderness in the injured tissues.
- Pain is exacerbated by movement of the injured joint.
- Swelling and discoloration vary from minor to significant, depending on the severity of the injury and the speed of treatment. Swelling tends to increase with time. The faster the treatment, the less soft-tissue damage will occur.
- There is often decreased range of motion (ROM) secondary to the pain. Although ROM may not be compromised, the patient may say that they cannot move the injured area because it's too painful.
- Localized internal bleeding from the injured tissue may cause ecchymosis (the spread of blood under the skin—a minor bruise) and hematoma (localized collection of blood outside the blood vessels—larger and more serious than ecchymosis).

ICE

applied quickly can greatly reduce swelling and tissue damage—if not available, look for the nearest cold stream.

Range of motion

TREATMENT

1. **EXPOSE** the injury. If an ankle sprain, carefully and gently remove the boots and socks and examine.

2. **RICE: Rest, Ice, Compression, Elevation**
   Rest—Do not use the joint, get the patient off their feet.
   Ice—Apply ice or a cold compress to the injured area. Do not apply ice directly to the skin—wrap it in cloth or plastic first. A cold mountain stream is a good option if ice is not available.
   Compression—wrap the injured area with an elastic bandage to reduce swelling—but do not compromise circulation.
   Elevation—elevate the injured area above the level of the heart (this helps reduce swelling).

3. **RICE** for one hour, then re-evaluate:
   For Range of Motion (ROM)
   - Have the patient gently work the joint through its range of motion (opposite page, bottom)—tell them to stop if they feel severe pain (with a sprain, there will be no point tenderness).
   - Do not move the joint yourself—because you cannot feel the patient's pain level, you may cause additional damage.

   For possible fracture
   - The same MOI can cause a fracture or a strain/sprain, and each injury can present with a rapid onset of significant swelling, bruising, and pain.
   - With a sprain, the pain is usually more generalized and on one side of the ankle (lateral most often)—a fracture will be more severe and localized, with point tenderness and guarding.
   - Palpate the injury site, checking for misalignment, deformity, or crepitus.
   - If you suspect a fracture, splint the joint and start evacuation—a litter-carry may be inevitable.

   For functional ability
   - If a patient with a sprained ankle is ambulatory after an hour of RICE treatment, allow them to walk (a litter evacuation is a long and tedious affair).

4. **EVACUATE**
   - Go slowly and take frequent rests. You may have to assist them over rough spots.
   - Consider improvising a crutch or cane to help them minimize additional stress on the joint.
   - Have others carry the patient's gear.

5. **SPLINT**
   - The strain/sprain may benefit from splinting, which helps protect it from further injury and helps alleviate and control pain.
   - When in doubt, treat as a fracture and splint.

A curious note: this is the same foot as the one in the stream photo.

ON A ROLL

Some 2000 times each mile a trail-runner's foot is planted, often just an inch or two from disaster—a little closer to that root and the right ankle may have rolled to the outside, collapsing into a classic lateral ankle sprain.

Medial sprain: rare

Lateral sprain: most common

OH

STICKS AND

F X

The symbol **F_x** is medical shorthand for "fracture."

Some activities just lend themselves to fractures. Here we might get a clavicle, a wrist, a forearm, or a tib/fib; shoot, we may even see a femur—it probably all depends on velocity (which sure looks pretty fast).

SNAP
STONES MAY BREAK YOUR BONES...

Three basic types of fractures

Fractures

A fracture occurs when enough force is applied to effect a break in the dense cortex[1] of a bone, causing pain and disruption of normal function. The pain results from the tear that occurs in the periosteum[2] surrounding the bone (the bone itself has no pain receptors).

Types of fractures

Although physicians differentiate between many kinds of fractures, because our treatment options in the backcountry are limited, the nuances are not that important. We're basically interested in answering two questions: **1)** Are the broken bones still in anatomical position? **2)** Is there an associated wound? And we keep the descriptions basic.

CLOSED (SIMPLE), IN-LINE FRACTURE
- There is a break in the bone's cortex, but the skin over the injury site is intact; the bones are in proper anatomical alignment; and there is no open wound.

CLOSED ANGULATED FRACTURE
- There is a break in the cortex, and the bone ends are angulated and not in anatomical alignment.
- Angulated fractures can be closed or open.

OPEN (COMPOUND) FRACTURE
- A fracture with an associated open wound—a break in the skin at the fracture site—with or without bone ends showing through the skin.

---

1 The dense outer shell of all bones: stiff and hard, it provides primary skeletal support for the body.
2 A membrane that lines the outer surface of all bones, except at the joints of long bones (bones that are longer than they are wide).

Diagnosing a fracture

Often, the mechanism of injury (i.e., typically some kind of impact) combined with the signs and symptoms will lead you to suspect a fracture.

1. **LISTEN TO THE PATIENT**—they will frequently say that they heard or felt a snap (a clear indication).

2. **LOOK**—expose the skin and examine the site.

   - Fractures may bleed internally, so there may be swelling and/or discoloration (ecchymosis).
   - There may be a wound associated with the fracture site: A) unrelated to the fracture, B) as a result of a compound fracture, C) from an impaled object.

3. **FEEL**—the injured limb

   - Check for CSMs distal to the injury site.
   - Check for proper anatomical alignment (when not associated with a joint, deformity indicates an angulated fracture).
   - Check for bilateral symmetry (i.e., compare the injured limb to the uninjured limb—asymmetry indicates a dislocation, a fracture, or both). See photo.
   - Palpate for point tenderness (can indicate a fracture).
   - Palpate for crepitation—the feeling of bones grating together (confirms a fracture).

Periosteum—a membrane that covers the surface of all bones, except at the joints of long bones (bones that are longer than they are wide, such as the femur).

When it comes to fractures, it's all about MOI. Hitting things or being hit by things cause virtually all fractures. In most instances (left) the MOI can be painfully obvious, but not always— e.g., elderly bones break easily.

The interior of our bones is *trabecular bone*: an amazing spongy matrix (calcium hydroxylate) of plates and rods that reduce weight and make room for blood vessels and marrow.

Basic goals for managing a fracture

All fractures will ultimately need to be seen by a physician—all will require treatment that cannot be done in the field, and some will require surgery. In the wilderness setting the goals are really simple.

1. **IF NECESSARY, USE TRACTION-IN-LINE (TIL)** to restore the fractured part to its anatomical position.

   ■ If this is not possible (e.g., because of shattered limbs or severely angulated fractures), immobilize in the position of greatest comfort and evacuate immediately.

   ■ With a closed, in-line fracture, TIL won't be necessary from an anatomical standpoint, but gentle TIL can help relax spasms and reduce pain until a splint is applied.

2. **CLEAN AND DRESS ANY ASSOCIATED WOUND,** minimize contamination, and dress the wound to protect it from infection.

3. **IMMOBILIZE THE FRACTURE** with a splint, making sure to preserve circulation.

4. **EVACUATE** to definitive care.

   ■ The rate of evacuation will depend, in part, on the severity of the fracture—for instance, a simple forearm fracture does not require as rapid an evacuation as a femur fracture would.

   ■ Check vital signs regularly, especially circulation distal to the injury.

Bone

Bone marrow and **vasculature**

FX

F X

Treating closed, in-line fractures

- These are common fractures that are relatively easy to treat in the field.
- There is no associated wound, relatively little soft tissue damage, and typically little or no circulatory impairment.
- The most common fractures involve the humerus, radius/ulna, tibia/fibula, fingers, or toes.
- A femur fracture, even if closed and in line, is a serious injury—field treatment and evacuation should be done as quickly as possible (see next section).
- Traction-in-line is not necessary (the bones are already in anatomical position), although gentle TIL can reduce spasms and relieve pain.

1. **SPLINT** in anatomical position.
2. **CONSIDER** administering pain medication.
3. **EVACUATE** (monitor CSMs distal to the injury).

Simple fractures (ulna, above) are treated simply. The bones are already lined up, so all you have to do is splint the fracture to stabilize the limb, provide pain mitigation, and get the patient to the nearest hospital.

Angulated radius/ulna fracture

Angulated fractures are serious. Deformity caused by misalignment damages tissues much more than an in-line fracture does and it can compromise circulation to such an extent that the limb's very survival is at risk: without blood flow, a limb will likely die after six hours.

A traction splint (background image) is reserved for a broken femur only—a dramatic and potentially very serious injury—see next section.

Treating closed, angulated fractures

- Angulated fractures are more complicated than closed, in-line fractures because the fractured bone ends are not in anatomical position and will need to be realigned before splinting.
- They can be accompanied by significant soft tissue damage, which can cause internal bleeding, impair circulation, and put the limb at risk.

1. **INSPECT CIRCULATION** by checking pulses, color, temperature, and sensation distal to the injury site. If any of the problems described below occur during treatment or evacuation: stop, reassess the situation, and solve the circulatory problem—otherwise, the limb is at risk.

   Pulses
   - For an arm fracture, check the radial pulse at the wrist.
   - For a leg fracture, check the posterior tibialis pulse, posterior to the medial malleolus, and/or the dorsalis pedis pulse on the top of the foot (the latter shown).
   - Compare the pulses between limbs (e.g., arm to arm, ankle to ankle)—they should be equal in strength.

   Color, temperature, and sensation
   - If circulation is impaired, you can anticipate that the extremity will become pale, cool to the touch, and that paresthesia (pins and needles sensation) will develop and eventually evolve into numbness. (Note skin color change in photo.)

   If circulation is impaired...
   - If your initial evaluation of pulses and color/temperature/sensation shows that circulation is impaired distal to the site of the injury (lack of pulses), inspect the injury to determine the cause. Early on, circulation is typically limited by deformity at the site of the injury—correcting this problem requires realigning the angulated fracture into proper anatomical position (see Step 2, next page).

2. **REALIGN THE ANGULATED FRACTURE**—every angulated fracture should be realigned so the bones move back into their anatomical position. If the circulation is compromised, this must be done immediately.

 A. Carefully examine the fracture site to determine the position of the bone fragments and determine what their normal anatomical position should be.

 B. Apply gentle traction-in-line (TIL), the operative word here is gentle—only about five to ten pounds of in-line traction force is required (about the same force as lifting two liters of water).

 C. Once gentle in-line traction has been applied for several minutes, and any muscle spasms have relaxed, begin moving the injured part into proper anatomical alignment to maintain (or reestablish) circulation.

3. **SPLINT THE FRACTURE**—once the fracture is in proper anatomical position, and there is good circulation distal to the injury site, splint the fracture (see splinting section).

4. **EVACUATE THE PATIENT**
 - Consider administering pain meds.
 - Monitor vital signs (especially circulation and warmth distal to the F_X).
 - If pulses fade or disappear, inspect the site of the injury, as swelling may have occurred which can cause the supporting splint to act like a tourniquet. If this happens, remove the splint, gently massage the area to re-establish circulation, and then reapply the splint, but not as tightly.
 - If good circulation cannot be restored (because of an accompanying crush injury, perhaps), evacuate the patient as quickly as possible—the limb is at risk and the patient will likely need immediate surgery.

Initially, traction is done without moving the fracture. Traction-in-line is a slow, steady pull that is initially in line with the direction the bones are pointing.

Hold the proximal portion in place and slowly move the distal portion in small increments. With each movement, ask, "Is that better or worse?" This question is very important because it is your guide to minimizing the risk of further injury. If the patient complains that the movement has made the pain worse, move back to the previous position and re-evaluate.

If the fractured, angulated bone-ends begin to stab or tear an underlying structure, such as a neurovascular bundle, there will be a dramatic increase in pain. If this occurs, STOP, back up to the previous position, and reevaluate. You may first have to rotate the distal portion gently in the direction of least resistance before trying to straighten it out again.

Maintain static traction for about five minutes; this allows the muscles to relax and the bone ends to separate slightly, then slowly move the bones into anatomical alignment.

A severe compound fracture can be very challenging to treat in the field—realignment will be complicated by the visual difficulties of the obvious trauma and the likelihood of extreme pain.

Treating open (compound) fractures

- An open fracture is complicated by an associated wound at the fracture site, typically caused by the bone ends breaking through the skin during the injury. The bone ends may or may not still be sticking out of the wound.
- Because of the associated wound, open fractures are easily contaminated and prone to infection— proper wound cleaning is critical.
- Open fractures have a greater likelihood than closed fractures of damaging the accompanying arteries and causing severe bleeding.
- The steps for treating an open fracture are the same as treating a closed angulated fracture, except that they begin by controlling bleeding and cleaning the wound. Bandaging the wound is integrated into the process prior to splinting.

1. **CONTROL BLEEDING**—stopping the bleeding is the first priority and should be done immediately. If an artery is damaged, the bleeding can be profuse and vigorous.
   A. Apply direct pressure and/or a pressure dressing at the fracture site. This should compress the soft tissues against the underlying arteries and veins and stop the external blood loss.
   B. While you are controlling the bleeding, evaluate circulation—if compromised, realignment (step 3) should resolve it.

2. **CLEAN THE WOUND**—once bleeding has been controlled, remove any foreign material from the wound and rinse it with a dilute Betadine solution (3 – 4 ounces of 10% Betadine solution in a liter of water). Make sure that any exposed bone ends are cleaned and rinsed, to decrease the risk of infection in the bone.

3. **REALIGN THE FRACTURE**—this will help close the wound and keep the injury warm, moist, and protected. If TIL does not reduce the bone ends back inside the extremity, protect the bone ends from freezing or drying out (bone is living tissue) with a sterile dressing moistened with a dilute Betadine solution and splint in place to prevent movement.

4. **BANDAGE THE WOUND**

5. **SPLINT THE FRACTURE**

6. **EVACUATE**

All fractures must be evacuated to the hospital—imaging, casting, and perhaps surgery will be required. Some patients will be able to walk; others will need a ride.

Upper extremity fractures

HUMERUS
- May be angulated with impaired circulation
- Straighten out with gentle TIL
- Splint with a sling supporting the forearm
- Keep the elbow at a 90-degree angle
- Allow the elbow to hang free

RADIUS/ULNA
- Fractures will commonly have a deformity
    1. Colles'—a distal fracture of the radius in the forearm with dorsal (posterior) displacement of the wrist and hand
    2. Smith's—sometimes known as a reverse Colles' fracture: the distal fracture fragment is displaced with respect to the forearm
- May need to straighten out with gentle TIL if circulation is impaired
- Splint with the wrist at 30 degrees of extension and the fingers at the MCP joints about 60 degrees of flexion, as if holding a can
- Wrap the extremity with a 6" ACE bandage to control bleeding from the fracture

ELBOW
- Can be a fracture/dislocation combination
- Can be very painful with a "gun stock" deformity
- Will have to be straightened if circulation is impaired distal to the injury
- Straighten with gentle TIL
    1. Hold the humerus stationary and apply gentle traction to the forearm
    2. Initially maintain the elbow at 90 degrees—once under traction the elbow should slide into anatomical position
    3. Slowly extend the forearm until circulation is restored (check pulse at wrist)
- Support with sling and swathe

For wrist and fingers, go to page 134

Note: A sling and swathe is the standard way to finish off most musculoskeletal injuries of the upper arm, lower arm, and wrist. We have shown the splinting sequence for the lower arm (radius/ulna) here; for a fracture of the upper arm (humerus), the splinting principles are the same: straighten with gentle TIL, splint, and apply the sling/swathe.

Lower extremity fractures

TIBIA/FIBULA
- This fracture may be angulated with impaired circulation distal to the fracture.
- It is easily reduced into proper anatomical position with TIL.
- Splint the leg in its proper anatomical position, and assure that the distal pulse is present.
- It's best to splint with a foam-pad-lower-leg-splint, keeping the patient's ankle at 90 degrees. Ensolite is flexible and soft, conforms easily, provides excellent insulation, and offers good support when molded to the extremity and tied in place.
  1. Remove the shoe and sock so you can inspect and monitor the foot for CSMs once the splint is in place.
  2. Fold the foam pad in half and adjust the length to fit the length of the leg, keeping the doubled-over portion at the foot end. The pad should extend at least 12 inches above the knee and 12 inches below the foot.
  3. Roll the foam around the leg and tie it in place above and below the knee.
  4. Fold the section that extends below the foot up against the sole of the foot. To aid in tying this section around the leg, pass a 6-foot piece of webbing (or rope/cord) through the folded section of the pad:
     - Take the webbing and cross it in front of the leg.
     - Wrap the webbing around the lower leg and cross it over the top of the leg.
     - Wrap the webbing forward around the folded section of the foam while holding the foot at the 90° position of comfort.
     - Finish by tying off the webbing on the front of the leg.

For patella, ankle, feet and toes, go to page 134.

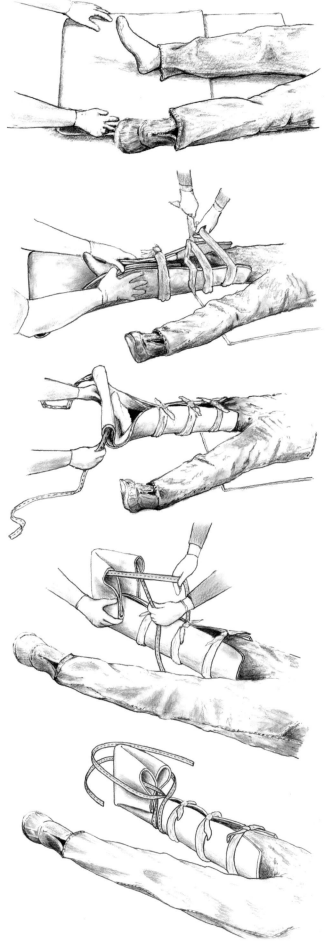

fractured

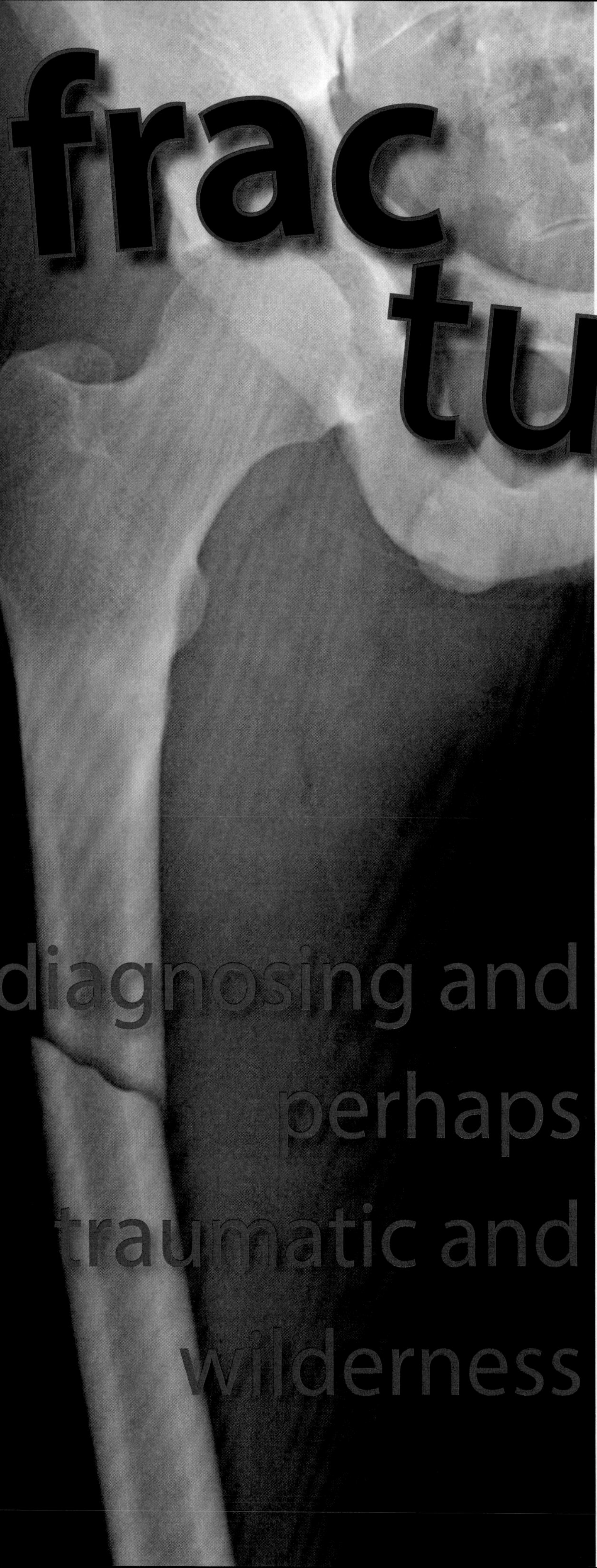

FEW THINGS SHOUT TRAUMA louder than the biggest break of them all: a busted femur. Break a smaller bone and you have an emergency—you'll need a splint, maybe a sling and swathe, and you might have to carry the patient out on a litter you improvise from branches and a climbing rope; but the tension will likely pass quickly, and things will settle down. The patient may even laugh at your jokes.

BUT BREAK A FEMUR and you may need a helicopter—and no one will be laughing.

diagnosing and treating

perhaps the most

traumatic and serious

wilderness fracture

THE LARGEST BONE in the human body, the femur, is packed with bone marrow, richly supplied with blood vessels, and is surrounded by (and supports) some of the strongest muscles in the body.

BURIED DEEP beneath the muscles, and lying in close proximity to the femur, is a neurovascular bundle containing major blood vessels (the femoral artery and femoral vein) and nerves.

IT TAKES TONS OF FORCE (literally) to break a femur, and it indicates that the body as a whole has sustained major forces.

THIS IS A VERY PAINFUL INJURY due to spasms of the large muscles of the upper leg.

IT CAN BE LIFE-THREATENING because of the potential blood loss into the area surrounding the fracture—typical blood loss is 1000 – 1500cc, and can reach 25% of total blood volume—as well as a risk of pulmonary emboli caused by fat emboli that can be released from the bone marrow. Proper splinting with a traction splint (for a mid-shaft fracture only) minimizes these risks and dramatically reduces the pain by controlling the spasms of the leg muscles.

THE THREE TYPES OF FEMUR FRACTURES, each with its own distinctive treatment:

At the proximal end—a broken hip

- Fractured hips are not life- or limb-threatening, and they do not cause a lot of pain, spasms, or internal bleeding.
- By placing padding between the legs and gently binding one leg to another to support the hips, they are easily splinted.
- This fracture does not require—nor should be treated with—a traction splint.

At mid-shaft

- This is the most dangerous and problematic—the big, bad, nasty one.
- A mid-shaft femur fracture is a potentially life-threatening injury.
- Severe bleeding can occur if the femoral artery is damaged.
- There is a risk of pulmonary emboli from blood clots that form in the bone marrow.
- Without traction there is up to a 50% mortality rate due to emboli (clots) blocking circulation in the lungs. Fat emboli from the bone marrow travel through the circulatory system and lodge in the lungs, where they can cause death from pulmonary emboli.
- All mid-shaft femur fractures must be treated with a traction splint.

At the distal end—the femoral condyles

- Fractures of the femoral condyles are usually avulsion fractures associated with knee injuries.
- Like hip fractures, they are not life- or limb-threatening and do not cause a lot of internal bleeding.
- They are easily splinted by immobilizing the knee in a position of comfort, which is usually with the affected knee flexed at about 20 – 30 degrees.
- Like a broken hip, this fracture does not require—nor should be treated with—a traction splint.

femur

signs and symptoms of a mid-shaft femur fracture

- Major MOI to the upper leg—it takes a lot of force!
- Pain and spontaneous muscle spasms. A mid-shaft fracture of the femur is a very painful injury, which commonly has associated muscle spasms of the quadriceps and adductor muscles of the upper leg. Pain and spasms can also be triggered by palpation and movement of the leg.
- Possible discoloration, swelling, tenderness, crepitation, deformity, angulation, or exposed bone ends at the fracture site.
- A significant loss of blood into the surrounding tissues can occur: 1000cc – 1500cc can be lost in 15 – 20 minutes.
- The patient is unable to bear weight on the injured leg.
- The patient does not want to sit up or move their legs, but they may be shifting side-to-side in an effort to get comfortable.
- Vital signs can indicate shock: tachycardia, tachypnea, hypotension, pale, cool, and clammy skin.

treatment principles

A MID-SHAFT FEMUR FRACTURE IS A MAJOR EMERGENCY that requires specialized skills and immediate action. While proximal (hip) and distal (knee) fractures are easily immobilized and splinted (see bullet points in previous spread), a mid-shaft femur fracture requires traction-in-line from the first possible moment—and that traction must be maintained without interruption until the patient arrives at definitive care (which could be many hours).

- Traction stabilizes the fracture and controls bleeding, thus minimizing the risk of fat emboli.
- A traction splint provides pain control by relaxing the muscles in spasm; and, when wrapped with an ACE bandage, it helps minimize internal blood loss. Improvised traction splints are for femur and lower leg fractures only—not for a fractured or dislocated hip, or for knee injuries.
- If you are involved with a backcountry evacuation of a patient with a traction splint on their femur, they will still fit well into commercial litters (if you have to improvise a litter, make sure it is big enough to contain both the patient and the entire traction splint—nothing should be hanging out).
- Check the patient's ABCs, then look closely for other injuries (it takes a lot to break a femur and there may be additional injuries).

treatment steps

- Cut away clothing so you can see the injury site.
- Pull manual traction-in-line (TIL) from the ankle—even if the fracture is open (compound): the ends of the bones should spontaneously reduce back under the skin. If they do not reduce, protect the exposed ends from freezing or drying out with a dilute iodine solution and an insulating bandage.
- Apply a traction splint (see opposite page).
- Complete the patient exam.
- Evacuate the patient (this may be complicated by time, distance, terrain, and personnel—evacuating patients with broken femurs can be a major undertaking that requires outside help).

An example of manual traction being converted to mechanical traction using an improvised splint made from a ski pole.

building a traction splint

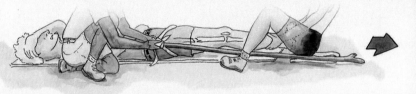

1 ■ attach ankle & waist hitches

- ■ Use cravats, webbing, belts, or cord.
- ■ Use an S-hitch around the foot—this is both secure and comfortable. Boot on, or boot off? Boot-on provides stability and warmth and keeps the S-hitch from compromising circulation, but makes it impossible to monitor CSMs at the toes. Boot-off allows you to monitor CSMs, but provides no insulation, little stability, and can be uncomfortable. Use your judgment.
- ■ The waist hitch is a simple loop around the injured leg at the groin. If you have a coffee mug or a similar container with a handle, place it on the outside of the patient's hip and tie the waist hitch through it.

2 ■ attach the traction support

- ■ Find a straight stick, ski pole, or similar object that is at least one foot longer than the patient's leg, and place it along the outside of the patient's injured leg.
- ■ Attach the hip end of the stick to the waist hitch by tying it directly, or placing it in the mug (mentioned above).
- ■ Tie a cord (or similar material) to the far end of the stick and attach it to the S-hitch with a trucker's hitch.

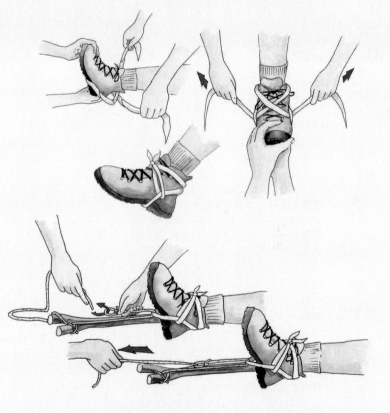

3 ■ apply mechanical traction & secure

- ■ Make a smooth transition between manual traction and mechanical traction—any interruption can cause spasms and pain. Secure the splint to the leg, making sure there is sufficient padding (for comfort).
- ■ Wrap the leg with two 6-inch elastic bandages, beginning at the ankle and ending at the hip—this helps stabilize the splint, reduces swelling, and keeps internal blood loss to a minimum (25% of blood volume can be lost into the fracture).
- ■ Add stabilization by tying the injured and the uninjured legs together.
  Monitor for signs of shock as well as circulation distal to the site of the injury.

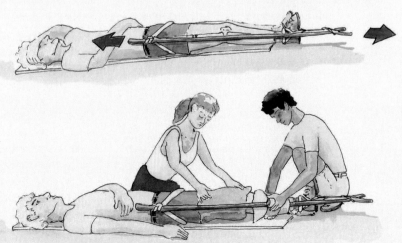

Sometimes it's the little things that matter the most. This wrist splint is *almost* perfect—but could be improved if the wrist was cupped downward a little more and if the SAM Splint came further forward to better support the fingers.

Continued from pages 128 and 129

WRIST

- The most common carpal fracture is of the scaphoid—the largest bone of the proximal row of wrist bones, situated between the hand and forearm on the thumb-side of the wrist
- Pain in the anatomical snuffbox (the little pocket formed by tendons at the base of the thumb) can indicate a fractured scaphoid
- Splint with the wrist at 30 degrees extension and fingers at 60 degrees flexion

HANDS AND FINGERS

- Reduce angulations with gentle TIL—this may require anterior or posterior pressure
- Buddy-tape the fractured finger with an uninjured neighbor, placing padding in between
- Splint fingers in a flexed position as if holding a soda can

With all splints, make sure the fractured bone(s) are in anatomical alignment, well padded, firmly immobilized, protected from possible further damage (e.g., kept warm to prevent possible frostbite), and that you regularly check CSMs distal to the fracture to ensure adequate circulation.

PATELLA

- A fractured patella and a ruptured patella tendon both make it difficult (but not impossible) to walk, as they can be splinted straight if the patient needs to walk a short distance
- The most comfortable splint is a posterior knee splint that maintains the knee at a 20 – 30 degree angle (see the knee splint on the opposite page).

ANKLE

- Use the Ottowa Rules—you may clear the ankle if:
  1. The patient is an adult (i.e., they can give an accurate and reliable patient history).
  2. There is no point tenderness.
  3. There is no laxity (a feeling of looseness) on inversion (turning the foot inward), eversion (turning the foot outwards), or while performing a drawer test.
  4. The patient can walk three steps.
- If more than 1 of the 3 malleoli are injured, it may be an unstable ankle—treat with a foam-pad-lower-leg-splint and immobilize the ankle at 90 degrees (see the tibia/fibula section).

FEET AND TOES

- March Fracture
  - This is a stress fracture of the 5th metatarsal from a long hike or march.
  - It presents with pain in the center of the lateral arch, 5th metatarsal.
  - Treat with a firm boot to support the arch and sole.
- Fractured toes
  - Use TIL to straighten.
  - Buddy-tape with padding between toes for support.
  - Support with stiff-soled shoes.

KNEE TRAUMA

We tend to *tweak* our elbows or *turn* our ankles, but we so often ***blow out*** our knees.

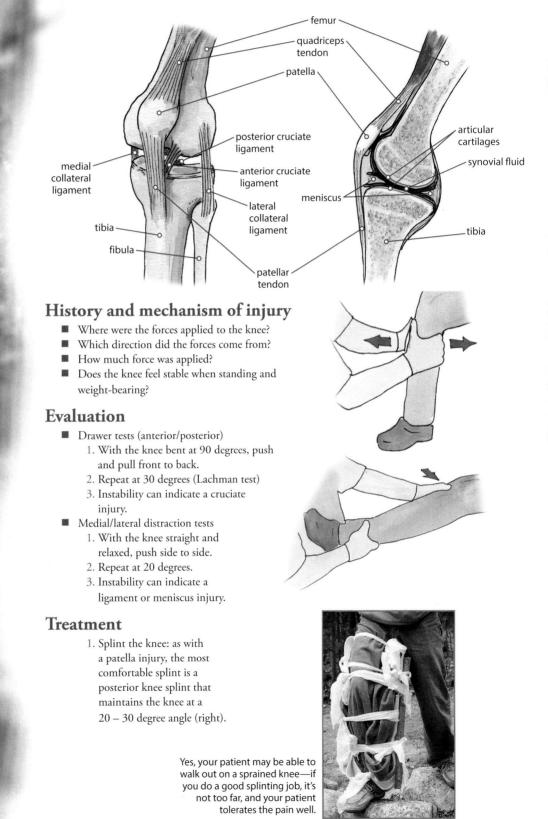

femur

quadriceps tendon

patella

posterior cruciate ligament

medial collateral ligament

anterior cruciate ligament

tibia

fibula

lateral collateral ligament

patellar tendon

articular cartilages

synovial fluid

meniscus

tibia

This is a very stressful place—forces of up to 550% of body weight can pass through a runner's knee! For a 150-pound runner this would equal a momentary impact force of 825 pounds with each foot-strike.

History and mechanism of injury

- Where were the forces applied to the knee?
- Which direction did the forces come from?
- How much force was applied?
- Does the knee feel stable when standing and weight-bearing?

Evaluation

- Drawer tests (anterior/posterior)
  1. With the knee bent at 90 degrees, push and pull front to back.
  2. Repeat at 30 degrees (Lachman test)
  3. Instability can indicate a cruciate injury.
- Medial/lateral distraction tests
  1. With the knee straight and relaxed, push side to side.
  2. Repeat at 20 degrees.
  3. Instability can indicate a ligament or meniscus injury.

Treatment

1. Splint the knee: as with a patella injury, the most comfortable splint is a posterior knee splint that maintains the knee at a 20 – 30 degree angle (right).

Yes, your patient may be able to walk out on a sprained knee—if you do a good splinting job, it's not too far, and your patient tolerates the pain well.

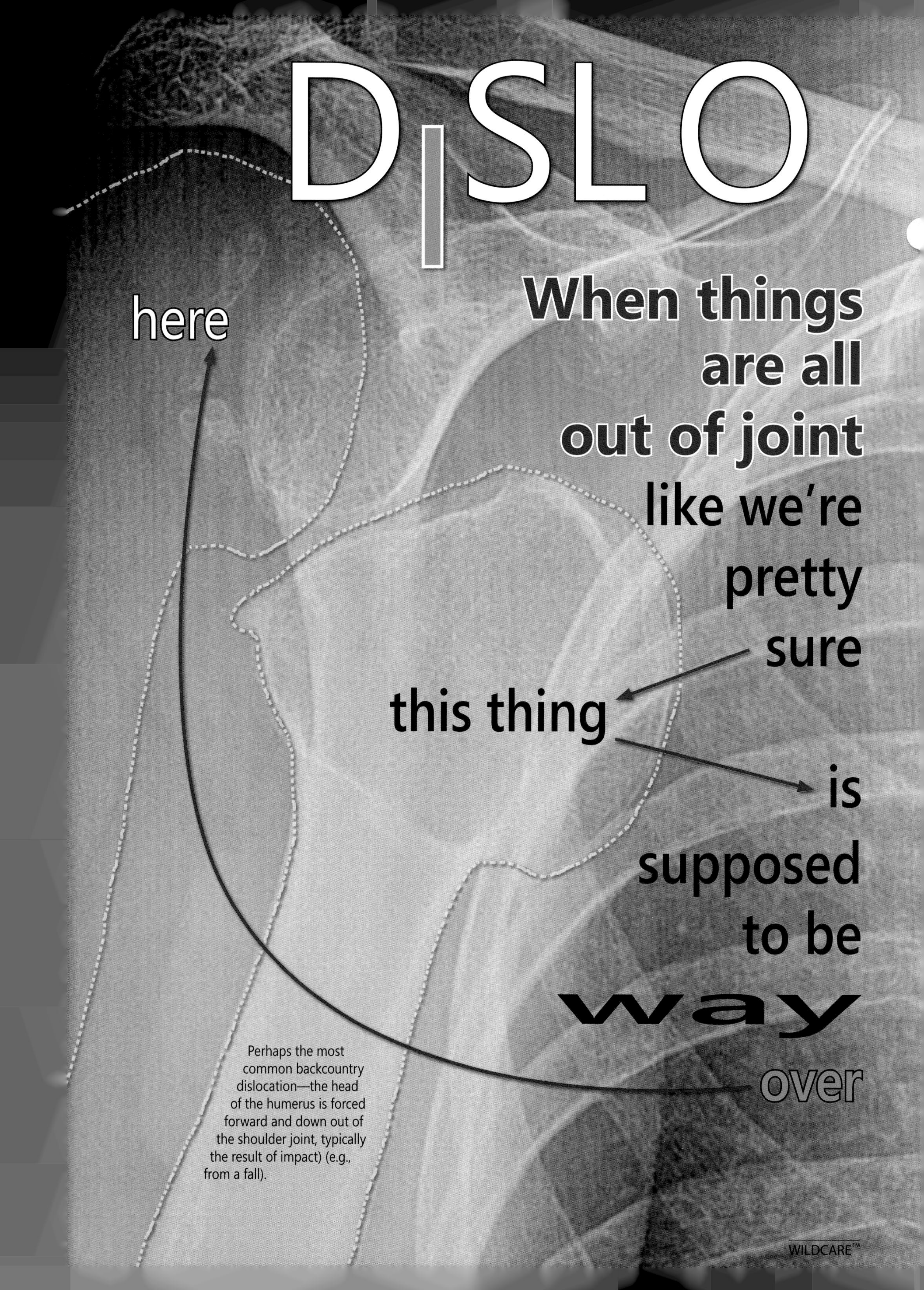

D|SLO

here

When things are all out of joint like we're pretty sure

this thing

is supposed to be

way

over

Perhaps the most common backcountry dislocation—the head of the humerus is forced forward and down out of the shoulder joint, typically the result of impact) (e.g., from a fall).

WILDCARE™

CATION

dislo cations

Dislocations occur when the bones in a joint become displaced, misaligned, or otherwise traumatized to the point where the joint pulls apart—the disruption is such that the correct anatomy is no longer maintained, and the joint's normal range of motion is reduced.

- All dislocations damage the surrounding soft tissues: muscles, tendons, ligaments, and/or cartilage.
- Dislocations can be associated with a fracture, and it can be very difficult to distinguish between a fracture and a dislocation—when in doubt, position the joint to maintain circulation distal to the injury, and splint.
- Dislocations are debilitating. They put the future function of the limb at risk because of compromised circulation.
- People who have had previous dislocations may experience less pain upon recurrence and may be more able to help you treat them.
- Dislocations sometimes reduce quickly and spontaneously. When they do not spontaneously reduce, they are often extremely painful.
- Reducing dislocations involves risk. If you attempt a reduction in the field, don't exceed the pain barrier—if what you are doing causes more pain, you are also causing more harm.

Signs of dislocation? Just give us a second...

signs symptoms

- **Pain:** generally very painful and diffused, rather than point-specific.
- **Reduced range of motion (ROM):** patient voluntarily says that they cannot move the joint.
- **Reduced CSMs:** due to compromised circulation—this can be a long-term-care concern.
- **Deformity:** the injury is typically, obviously, anatomically incorrect.

general treatment

■ **Urban:** immobilize in position found and transport.

■ **Wilderness**

1. Expose and examine the joint carefully.

2. Palpate for a possible fracture.

3. Check CSMs.
   A. Circulation distal to the injury site.
   B. Sensation at the injury site and distal to it.
   C. Movement: by working with the patient, determine motor function and range of motion (pain will be the limiting factor).

4. Pull traction-in-line (TIL) to reduce the dislocation.
   A. Use a steady, firm pull with slow and gentle movements (the muscles surrounding the joint will typically be in spasm, and any sudden movements will cause them to spasm anew).
   B. If necessary, have someone else or a fixed object immobilize the patient to provide counter-traction.
   C. The more time that goes by before a dislocation is reduced, the harder it will be to reduce—the quicker, the better.

5. Once the joint has been reduced into proper anatomical alignment, immobilize the joint with a splint.

6. RICE as appropriate.

7. Evacuate (all dislocations need to be seen by a physician).

8. Monitor CSMs distal to the injured joint every 15 minutes. If you find a compromise, carefully remove the splint, realign the joint until CSMs are restored, and re-splint.

We were going to make a list of all the different ways there are to dislocate ourselves, but the book just isn't big enough—suffice it to say that we humans can get pretty creative when it comes to trashing our various joints. Possibilities for this mountain biker include (clockwise from circle at far left): ankle, elbow, hip, shoulder, clavicle, fingers, wrist, knee—shoot, maybe all of them! Of course, he may also ruin his face.

 **common** dislocations

 Many excellent videos can be found online that demonstrate the treatment techniques outlined here.

SHOULDER DISLOCATION

- This is the most common dislocation. Anterior (forward) dislocation is far more common than posterior (rearward) dislocation.
- The shoulder will be locked and painful, and any movement of the humerus will increase pain.
- The appropriate technique depends on the position of the humerus and the position of the patient.
- If none of the techniques listed below are successful in reducing the dislocation, immobilize in the position of comfort and evacuate immediately.

SNOWBIRD REDUCTION TECHNIQUE

Typically, the patient with a shoulder dislocation will be found sitting up with their humerus beside their chest wall and their forearm flexed across their abdomen in the "guarding position."

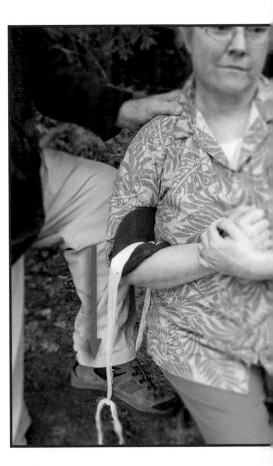

1. Place a wide, well-padded sling in the antecubital fossa (i.e., the anterior pocket of the elbow when the arm is flexed to 90%).
2. Put one foot in the sling to apply downward traction.
3. Slowly increase traction by pushing down on the sling with your foot, which leaves both your hands free.
   A. Place one hand on the opposite shoulder to keep the patient sitting up straight; have the other hand support the wrist on the injured side (or have someone stand behind them with their hands on the patient's shoulders to keep them sitting up straight).
4. While under traction, as the shoulder muscles relax, externally rotate the arm.
   A. If the shoulder does not reduce, continue traction and retry in several minutes.
5. Once reduced, support the arm and shoulder with a sling and swathe.
6. Evacuate.
   A. If ambulatory, the patient may walk out.
   B. Monitor circulation every 15 minutes during evacuation.

THE HANDS-ON-HEAD TECHNIQUE—MODIFIED MILCH TECHNIQUE

Use this technique if the patient is found with a dislocated shoulder, and their humerus is extended over their head—as can occur when kayaking or in a skiing fall. With an anterior dislocation the elbow of the bad arm will be projecting forward at about 45 degrees. The patient may be found sitting up or lying down—although they will need to lie down for this method to work (see below).

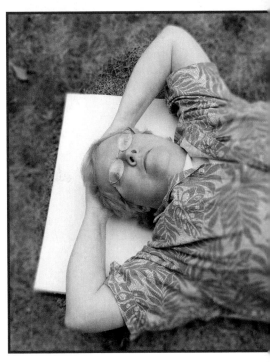

1. Have the patient place the hand of their good arm on top of their head.
2. Then (without your help) have them place the hand of their bad arm on top of their head and interlace the fingers of both hands.
3. With their hands on their head help them to lie down on their back.
   A. As they lie flat, the elbows, via gravity, will slowly flatten out, and the shoulder will likely spontaneously reduce.
4. Once the shoulder has reduced, place the arm in a sling and swathe to support the injured shoulder.
5. Evacuate.
   A. If ambulatory, the patient may walk out.
   B. Monitor circulation every 15 minutes during evacuation.

STIMSON'S HANGING ARM TECHNIQUE (DANGLE TECHNIQUE)

- ■ Requiring only a small weight (5 – 10 pounds) and a place for the patient to lie prone and dangle their arm (e.g., a picnic table), this is a very simple technique to reduce an anterior dislocation, and there are very few complications.
    1. Lay the patient prone on a padded surface with their injured arm hanging off the side.
    2. Attach the weight to their hand/wrist. Make this a passive attachment rather than asking the person to hold the weight—the idea is to get them to completely relax the arm.
    3. Tell them to relax their arm and shoulder and let gravity do the work. As the muscles relax, gravity will gently stretch the shoulder, and it will spontaneously reduce. This usually takes about 5 – 10 minutes. (During that time, make tea.)
    4. Once reduced, place the arm, with the forearm flexed across the body, in a sling and swathe to support the reduced shoulder, and evacuate.

CUNNINGHAM'S TECHNIQUE

- ■ This technique is performed with the patient sitting with support for their back (as in a chair).
    1. Have the patient sit up straight, with their buttocks and shoulders tight against the back support, their chest out, and with the affected arm hanging by their side and their elbow flexed.
    2. Apply gentle downward traction to the elbow, in line with the direction the humerus is pointing.
    3. Gently massage the trapezius muscle for 30 seconds, and then massage the deltoid, biceps, and triceps muscles. As the muscles relax and gentle traction-in-line is applied, the shoulder will spontaneously reduce.

ELBOW DISLOCATION

- ■ Can be a fracture/dislocation combination.
- ■ Can be very painful with a "gun stock" deformity.
- ■ May have to be straightened if circulation is impaired distal to the injury
    1. Straighten with gentle TIL.
    2. Hold the humerus stationary and apply gentle traction to the forearm.
    3. Initially maintain elbow at 90-degrees, once under traction. When the elbow has slid into anatomical position, slowly extend the forearm until circulation is restored.
    3. Check pulse at wrist.
    4. Support with sling and swathe.

From top: Stimson's and Cunningham's techniques for reducing a shoulder dislocation, and reducing an elbow dislocation (right).

Ouch!

HIP DISLOCATION

- This is considered an orthopedic emergency—immobilization and immediate evacuation is the only recommended field treatment.
    - This is a very difficult reduction, and to the best of our knowledge, has never been attempted in the field.
- While the hip is dislocated, the circulation is impaired to the femoral head.
    - This is not a life-threatening injury; the risk is to the femoral head which may require surgery to repair.
    - If the dislocation cannot be reduced, the hip will develop aseptic necrosis (death of bone tissue), requiring a surgical repair.
- Signs and symptoms
    - Hip flexion with internal rotation (the modesty position.)
    - The patient is unable to move their hip and usually has significant pain.
- Treatment
    1. We do not recommend attempting reduction for a dislocated hip.
    2. Splint the hip in the position of comfort with a pelvic binder and evacuate.

KNEE DISLOCATION

- Is often accompanied by severe ligament damage.
- Always requires surgical repair, but can be reduced in the field.
- Reduction is required to maintain circulation.
- A dislocated knee usually presents with the tibia being forced posteriorly.
    1. To reduce a knee dislocation, slowly and gently pull the tibia forward.
    2. Once reduced, splint the knee in the position of comfort, about 30 degrees
    3. Evacuate by litter carry.
    4. Monitor distal pulses during evacuation.

PATELLA DISLOCATION

- Usually dislocates laterally (to the outside).
- The patient's leg will typically be bent.
    1. To reduce, apply gentle and firm inward pressure while slowly straightening the leg.
    2. Once reduced, splint the leg in the position of comfort.
    3. Wrap the knee with an elastic wrap to support the joint and control swelling during evacuation.

ANKLE DISLOCATION

1. Pull traction-in-line (TIL), and slowly bring the foot up to 90 degrees.
2. Once the joint has been reduced, splint.

FINGER AND TOE DISLOCATIONS

- These can generally be easily and safely reduced.
    1. Pull TIL.
    2. If the joint does not easily reduce, you may need to apply some pressure directly over the joint to pop it back into anatomical alignment.
    3. Once the joint had been reduced, splint in the position of function.

To reduce a knee dislocation, gently and slowly pull the tibia forward and in-line.

For a patella, simultaneously apply inward pressure to the patella while gently and slowly straightening the leg. Let the patient help dictate how fast you go and how forceful you are—this is both a painful injury and a painful treatment process, so the patient needs to relax!

"Buddy taping" works great on little things like toes—and it works on fingers, too, although with fingers there is actually room for a splint.

THE SPINAL CORD
THE BODY'S COMMUNICATION SYSTEM

- It connects the brain to the rest of the body.
- The spinal cord is **protected** by the spinal column, which is made up of 33 individual vertebrae in five sections.
- The spinal column is very **flexible**.
- Injury to the vertebrae risks **damage** to the spinal cord.
- Damage to the spinal cord may be **debilitating** and **permanent**.

SPINAL

C1
C2

THORACIC SPINE
The 12 vertebrae of the chest

- Each vertebra is associated with a rib.
- Injury almost always comes from a direct blow.

CERVICAL SPINE
The 7 vertebrae of the neck

- C1 is called the atlas vertebra. It is ring-shaped and connected directly to the skull, allowing the head to nod, creating the "yes" motion.
- C2 is called the axis and it is peg-shaped. It creates a joint that allows the head to pivot laterally, creating the "no" motion.
- Injuries to the neck occur via axial loading with the neck in flexion.
- Any other possible spinal mechanism can injure the cervical spine.

SPINAL MECHANISM OF INJURY (MOI)

- **Falls:** especially falls when high speed is involved, when the victim lands on their head or shoulders (tumbling), or any fall 3x body height or more.
- **Automobile accidents:** combinations of high speed and impact/rapid deceleration.
- **Head injury:** Any blow to the head resulting in loss of consciousness is MOI for spinal injury.
- **Diving accidents:** A blow to the head from diving into shallow water can produce a dangerous combination of axial loading and impact to the spine.
- **Direct blows:** may be the result of a fall or impact with a moving object.

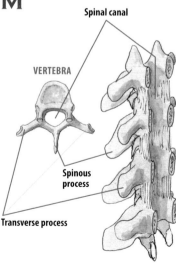

Spinal canal

VERTEBRA

Spinous process

Transverse process

MOI
(that's French for "Oh, my aching back)

TRAUMA

SPINE INJURY STATS in the US
12,000 new spinal injuries each year • Average age of injury is 40.2 years • 81% male • 66% Caucasian, 27% African American, 2% Asian • 42% motor vehicle accidents, 26.7% falls, 15.1% violence, 7.6% sports, 8.6% other—estimates from the *National Spinal Cord Injury Statistical Center*

T12

L1

L2

COCCYX
The 4 rudimentary vertebra at the termination of the spinal column

SACRAL SPINE
A wedge-shaped bone composed of 5 fused vertebrae

- There is no risk of spinal cord damage (the cord does not extend down this far).
- Peripheral nerve trunks can be damaged.
- Injury to the sacral spine is most often associated with a fractured pelvis.
- Injury to the sacrum/coccyx may indicate injury to the cervical or thoracic spine.

LUMBAR SPINE
The 5 vertebrae that span the rib cage to the pelvis

- The spinal cord extends down to L2. Below that is the cauda equina or "horse tail," made up of individual peripheral nerves.
- This is the most common spinal area to be injured.
- It is also the most common site of chronic injury.
- Injuries to the lumbar spine are the most common causes of worker's compensation claims.
- Injury occurs via a direct blow or by exceeding the range of motion.
- The highest risk of secondary injury is with rotation, especially at T12 – L1.

Axial loading

Flexion (bad)

PRINCIPLES
TO KEEP IN MIND

- The **greatest risk to the neck** is when the MOI causes flexion (as if the person were ducking forward—right) and axial loading with impact on the top of the head. This can cause a burst fracture of C4/C5 and put the spinal cord at risk. When moving a patient with a suspected neck injury, keep the head and neck in the neutral position and avoid forward flexion.
- The thoracic portion of the vertebral column is the **hardest to injure** because it is so well reinforced by the ribcage. It is most often injured by direct force.
- Injuries to the transition area (T12 /L1) pose the **greatest risk to the spine**—especially due to rotation, where the shoulders are rotated out of alignment with the hips. Keep the patient's hips and shoulders aligned when moving them.
- The lower back (lumbar to coccyx) is the **most common** area of the back to be injured. Approximately 85% of all back injuries occur in the lumbar spine, particularly L4/L5.
- It is always okay to move a patient into correct anatomical position (neutral position).
- **WARNINGS**
  - Unless the lack of MOI can be determined, treat **every patient** as if they have a spinal injury.
  - Remember, a person can **damage** their spinal column **without injuring** their spinal cord.

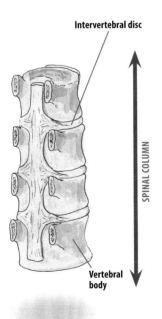

Intervertebral disc

SPINAL COLUMN

Vertebral body

TREATING SPINAL INJURIES

MECHANISM OF INJURY (MOI)

- In most situations, **mechanism of injury** alone is enough to demand full spinal inspection and immobilization.

- In most jurisdictions, urban medical protocols have stated that all patients transported from a motor vehicle accident (MVA) or a significant fall (3x body height) **require immobilization**, even in the absence of any other signs or symptoms. (This may be changing due to evidence-based medicine.)

SIGNS AND SYMPTOMS (S/S)

- **Pain** may be present in many ways and is often not spontaneous. Distracting pain may mask all pain response, making assessment unreliable until the distracting pain is reduced. Types of pain include:
  - Radiating—it shoots off in varying directions
  - Diffuse—pain is undifferentiated and ubiquitous
  - Pain with motion—it hurts when I move this
  - Point-tender upon palpation—it hurts where you poke

- **Loss of consciousness** indicates a possible head injury.
- **Guarding or muscle spasms**—my neck is stiff.
- **Paresthesia**—I feel pins and needles.
- **Numbnesss**—nope, I can't feel that.
- **Paralysis**—I'm unable to move that at all.
- **Spinal deformity**—things are out of place.
- **Swelling** along the spine.
- **Locked sensation**—it feels stuck.
- **Discoloration** along the spine.

THERE IS ONE BIG QUESTION...

The last thing he said:
"I'm stoked!"

The next thing that happened:
he got stoked (put in a Stokes litter).

don't IMMOBILIZE

IMMOBILIZE

The MOI & S/S **stop now red flag**

MOI and S/S?

Got **ANY** of these MOI factors?

Rapid deceleration

Fall 3x body height

Direct impact

Axial loading

Head trauma

And **ANY** of these signs/symptoms?

Then you should see the spinal trauma **red flag** (above) and

DO this...

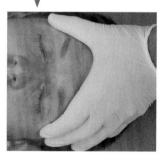

...and then **DO** this...

1. Immobilize the **C-spine**
2. Immobilize the rest of the **spine**
3. Place the patient in a **litter**

...and then **EVACUATE**

144

WILDCARE™

MOI but no S/S?

WAIT perhaps this spine is made for walkin...

If ALL YOU HAVE is MOI, you **MAY** be able to **CLEAR THE SPINE**

allowing

the person

to walk out...

ADVANCED SPINAL ASSESSMENT

- Due to the risks of weather, terrain, time delays, etc., and under certain assessment circumstances, it is possible to **clear the spine** of an ambulatory patient, enabling them to walk out without immobilization.

- Clearing the C-spine is a **controversial** skill. Unless you have been trained in this technique and have practiced the skills, you should not attempt to clear an injured person's spine when there is significant MOI.

- Clearing the spine is done in the presence of **MOI only**—the following tests must be applied and the criteria must be evaluated in the following order, and the patient must meet **all criteria**—if they fail **anything**, fully immobilize them and evacuate. If they pass everything, then wave the green flag and go.

1. **Reliability**
   - The patient is awake and oriented x 3.
   - They are not under the influence of drugs or alcohol.
   - They are not being adversely influenced by cold or heat.

2. **No distracting pain**
   - If the patient had a distracting injury or injuries (e.g., a fractured femur), treatment must have reduced the pain to a point where it is no longer a distraction.

3. **No signs or symptoms** (yes, the redundancy is intentional)
   - The patient does not complain of pain anywhere in their back.
   - They do not have radiating pain, paresthesia (tingling), or numbness in any of their extremities.
   - The have intact circulation, sensation, and motion in all four extremities.
   - They have no tenderness the length of their spine during the physical exam.
   - They do not exhibit any guarding and there is no paravertebral muscle spasm.

4. **Range of motion test**
   - This test is performed only if the patient has been found to be reliable, is without distracting pain, and has no signs or symptoms.
   - The rescuer supports, but does not move the patient through their range of motion.
   - If during the test, the patient experiences any pain, stiffness, or locking sensations, the test is over and the patient must be immediately and fully immobilized.
   - If the range of motion is pain-free, elicits no locking sensation, and is normal, you may consider the spine to be free of injury, and the patient does not need to be collared and backboarded.
   - Performing the test: the patient should lie flat on their back and perform the following movements, in order (the patient does the work—active range of motion).
     1. They slowly rotate their head to one side, and then to the other (it doesn't matter if you start to the left or right).
     2. They slowly extend their head to look up.
     3. They slowly flex their head down by bringing their chin to their chest (flexion).
     4. They arch their lower back off the ground   .
     5. They do half a sit-up (to 45⁰).

The range of motion test (including moving the head side-to-side, then up and down) is the last assessment criteria. It is essential that the patient directs the movement, and that they pass the test perfectly—when in doubt, immobilize and evacuate.

Head trauma: with change in Level of Consciousness (LOC) and increasing intracranial pressure (ICP**).**

Facial trauma: all kinds of nasty fractures, some that interfere with the patient's airway.

Chest trauma: many complex injury scenarios, some that can interfere with breathing or circulation.

Pelvic trauma: dangerous fractures that can cause severe internal bleeding and hypovolemic shock.

Abdominal trauma: lots of stuff that can go wrong, from nausea and vomiting to blunt and penetrating trauma

Plus: Crush injuries and Compartment syndrome: with their associated soft tissue damage and circulatory complications.

ORTHO PEDIC EMER GENCIES

UP UNTIL NOW, WE HAVE BEEN CONCERNED WITH THOSE BONES THAT STICK OUT TO THE SIDES: ARMS, LEGS, FINGERS AND TOES IT'S TIME TO GET TO THE CORE

These core structural injuries can be serious, life-threatening emergencies, and recognizing and managing them quickly in the wilderness is essential.

HEAD TRAUMA

OF ALL THE PLACES ON YOUR BODY TO DAMAGE, your head is just about the worst one to pick—there's just so much important stuff that goes on above your neck and between your ears. It's simple: if what's inside your skull doesn't work, nothing works.

Some head injuries are dramatic but minor (a big scalp laceration, a superficial hematoma), some are obviously major and scary (a fractured skull), and some are hard to see, insidious, and really dangerous (increasing intracranial pressure)—the minor stuff you can treat in the field, but the big stuff demands immediate and swift evacuation.

THE HARDWARE

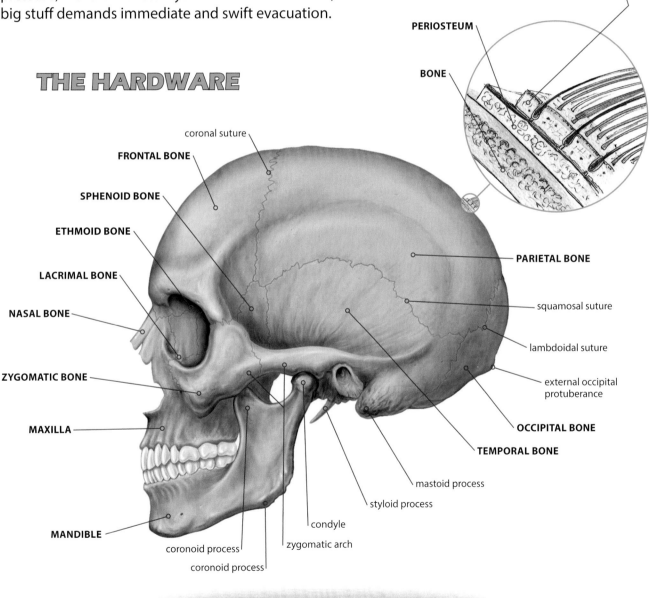

SKIN & SUBCUTANEOUS TISSUE
PERIOSTEUM
BONE

coronal suture
FRONTAL BONE
SPHENOID BONE
ETHMOID BONE
LACRIMAL BONE
NASAL BONE
ZYGOMATIC BONE
MAXILLA
MANDIBLE
coronoid process
coronoid process
zygomatic arch
condyle
styloid process
mastoid process
TEMPORAL BONE
OCCIPITAL BONE
external occipital protuberance
lambdoidal suture
squamosal suture
PARIETAL BONE

THE SOFTWARE

- The brain is contained inside the skull's cranial vault, which has a fixed volume; it cannot expand. Head trauma that causes swelling in the cranial vault can be life-threatening.
- The human brain weighs about 12 ounces (.75 pounds) at birth, grows to 90% of its adult weight by age five, and finally tops out at 3 – 4 pounds.
- The brain is 75% water, contains 100 billion neurons (with 1,000 to 10,000 synapses per neuron) and 100,000 miles of blood vessels, and feels no pain.
- The undamaged brain's intracranial pressure (ICP) is constant.
- The brain is surrounded by cerebrospinal fluid (CSF).

Blue lines denote the areas of the **motor homunculus** that control various parts of the body related to voluntary movement. The sizes of the body part drawings are relative to the size of the portions of the homunculus dedicated to that area—e.g., more of the homunculus is dedicated to the head and hands than to the arms and legs combined.

FRONTAL LOBE

Primary motor cortex: the motor homunculus, the "Little Man"
> Controls all the voluntary muscles in the body.

Premotor Cortex or motor memory:
> Is where we have the memory of motor skills and initiate and sequence movement.
> Performs the higher intellectual functions of planning, intention, emotion, mood, general behavior, and social skills.
> Gives appropriate emotional responses to sensory experiences.
> Is responsible for imaging and complex memories.
> Is responsible for olfactory function, sense of smell, memory of smells, and emotional response.

Damage to the frontal lobe
> Can interfere with the ability to execute a plan.
> Can interfere with social behavior, causing people to be rude or disruptive.
> Can affect movement in the primary motor cortex and premotor cortex.
> Can cause loss of motor memory (e.g., how to throw a ball).
> Can affect speech—in Broca's Area, speech will become labored and hesitant.

TEMPORAL LOBE

> Hearing, music, language.
> Auditory memory.

Damage to the temporal lobe
> Can affect hearing, speech, interpretation of sound and speech.
> Can affect hearing, memory, and global memory loss. The patient may not be able to recognize a familiar sound or voice.

BRAIN STEM

> Thermoregulatory center— controls core temperature.
> Cardiovascular center—controls the heart rate and blood pressure.
> Respiratory center—controls the respiratory rate and depth.
> Reticular activating center—controls level of wakefulness.
> Centers for coughing, sneezing, and vomiting.

Damage to the brain stem
> Can obviously be fatal as it would interfere with any one of several life-sustaining centers.

PARIETAL LOBE

> The knowledge and memory of sensations of touch, pain, and temperature.
> Spatial awareness—awareness of the location of the body in space.

Damage to the parietal lobe
> Can affect the perception of pain and temperature.
> Can affect knowing where the body is in space.
> Can cause a patient to ignore ("neglect") a body part.

OCCIPITAL LOBE

> The visual cortex—both recognition of sight and memory vision.

Damage to the occipital lobe
> Can affect visual acuity, cause visual memory loss, or cause blindness.

CEREBELLUM

> Coordination of movement, balance, eye movements.
> Planning and execution of movements.

Damage to the cerebellum
> Will cause incoordination, unsteady gait, coarse movements.

SUPERFICIAL HEMATOMA

This is the classic "egg" that quickly appears after you've been hit in the head by something (e.g., a falling coconut, a wayward fly ball in right field).

Though a relatively minor injury, it can cause dramatic swelling. Treat with a cold pack or ice to reduce swelling, and OTC pain meds.

SKULL FRACTURE

Every skull fracture should be considered a major medical emergency—there are just so many bad things potentially going on: the cracked bone itself, bleeding, edema (and associated increasing ICP; see next), brain injury, leakage of spinal fluid...you get the idea.

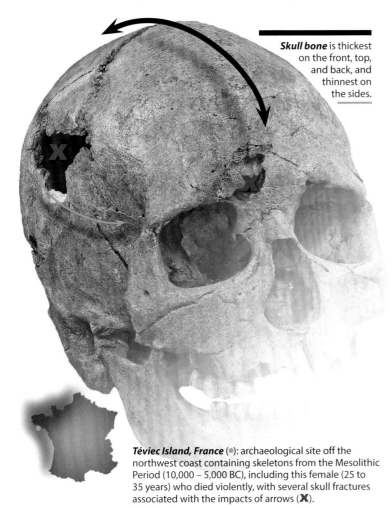

Skull bone is thickest on the front, top, and back, and thinnest on the sides.

Téviec Island, France (⬤): archaeological site off the northwest coast containing skeletons from the Mesolithic Period (10,000 – 5,000 BC), including this female (25 to 35 years) who died violently, with several skull fractures associated with the impacts of arrows (**X**).

SIGNS AND SYMPTOMS

> Depression of skull area (palpable).
> Visible crack beneath laceration.
> Penetrating wound (e.g., arrow, see image caption).
> Cerebrospinal Fluid (CSF: amber-colored, sticky) leaking from nose, ears, or from around the eyes. It may mix with blood, but it does not clot and dries slower. Do not attempt to stop the flow—it is being forced out by the increasing pressure.
> Battle's sign (bruising behind the ears)—a dangerous sign indicating a basilar skull fracture.
> Raccoon eyes (bruising around eyes)—not necessarily an ominous sign.

TREATMENT

1. Monitor ABCs and for signs of increasing ICP (see next) every 15 minutes.
2. Assume spinal injury and immobilize the spine if there is significant MOI.
3. Reevaluate with any change in LOC.
4. Ventilate if respirations are inadequate.
5. Administer Oxygen, 100%, 15 liters per minute, by non-rebreather, if available.
6. Evacuate immediately and as quickly as possible.

Skull bone

If **ICP** gets too high, there is only one place for the compressed tissues to go: down. It's just simple physics, and it can be deadly.

INCREASING INTRACRANIAL PRESSURE [ICP]

It's common for a part of the body to swell in response to injury (or illness)—in addition to possible bleeding, this localized edema floods the affected area with various types of beneficial fluids designed to flush out damaged cells and toxins, and promote healing. Most of the time there is plenty of space for this swelling to occur (superficial hematoma), but because the volume inside the skull is fixed by the hard shell of bone, in cases of head trauma where the swelling occurs in the tissues *inside* the skull, intracranial pressure increases. Quick recognition of increasing ICP is critical.

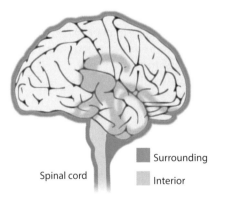

Spinal cord

Surrounding

Interior

IT'S NOT ALL JUST GRAY (OR PINK) MATTER

> The brain is surrounded by cerebrospinal fluid (CSF), a clear, sticky, sweet fluid (blue in diagram) that provides buoyancy (the brain is suspended in it), cushions the brain from impact, helps supply the brain with glucose, and helps maintain intracranial pressure.

PHYSIOLOGY

> Because the volume of the cranium is fixed, any bleeding or swelling inside the cranial vault will cause an increase in ICP.

> As ICP rises, the brain is compressed, in particular, the cerebral cortex and the brainstem: compression of the cerebral cortex causes behavioral changes, while compression of the brainstem causes changes to the victim's vital signs.

> If the ICP gets too high, the brainstem will herniate through the foramen magnum (the large hole in the occipital bone), resulting in death (via uncal herniation).

A motorcycle accident in South Sudan resulted in this nasty head laceration and closed, depressed skull fracture. Dramatic blunt trauma like this can cause damage to the brain (e.g., concussion, hemorrhage) that can result in increasing ICP. Fortunately, it did not occur in this case and this young man's outcome was good.

SIGNS AND SYMPTOMS

> Change in level of consciousness (deterioration).
> Headache—increases in severity with time.
> Nausea and vomiting that becomes cyclic.
> Amnesia—patient may have retrograde loss of memory.
> Seizures—risk of seizing increases with increasing ICP (late sign).
> Posturing indicates a brainstem injury (late sign).

VITAL SIGNS ASSOCIATED WITH INCREASED ICP

The vital signs do not change independent of each other—they predictably change together. When monitoring a patient with a head injury, pay particular attention to their LOC: as ICP rises, the patient's LOC will deteriorate from alert to painfully responsive. The earliest LOC changes include *uncooperativeness*, *irrational behavior* (potential refusal of care), *combatativeness* (like a "mean drunk"), and *disorientation*.

> *HR* slow, bounding
> *RR* increasing in both rate and depth, hyperventilation, or pattern breathing (see complete list, right), in order of occurrence, over time:
>> *Kussmaul's Breathing*—increasing hyperventilation, rapid and deep
>> *Cheyne-Stokes Breathing*—a cycle of breathing which gradually increases in rate and depth, followed by a gradual decrease in rate and depth, followed by a short period of apnea, then the cycle repeats
>> *Apneustic breathing*—pauses in the respiratory cycle at full respiration; this is the last stage (death follows)
> *BP* increasing, widening pulse pressure (systolic rises faster than diastolic)
> *Skin* variable based on environment and associated injuries—may be pink/warm/moist or pale/cool/clammy
> *Pupils* eventually become unequal (late sign)

TREATMENT

> Surgery is the only treatment—the only field treatment is O_2.
> Evacuate immediately by the quickest means possible.
> Maintain and protect the airway from vomitus and aspiration.
> Immobilize the C-spine and place the patient in the recovery position.

PATTERNS OF BREATHING ASSOCIATED WITH HEAD TRAUMA

NORMAL BREATHING

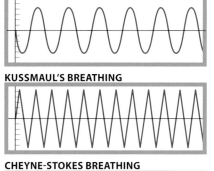

KUSSMAUL'S BREATHING

CHEYNE-STOKES BREATHING

APNEUSTIC BREATHING

BIOT'S BREATHING

ATAXIA BREATHING

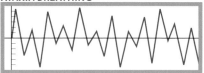

FACIAL TRAUMA

WHEN PUTTING YOUR BEST FACE FORWARD IS A ^Really **BAD IDEA**

WILDCARE™

GENERAL PRINCIPLES

FACIAL FRACTURES AND FACIAL TRAUMA ARE NOT PARTICULARLY COMMON BECAUSE ACCIDENTS THAT PRODUCE DIRECT FACIAL IMPACT OF SUFFICIENT FORCE ARE RARE. TYPICALLY, FACIAL FRACTURES ARE ASSOCIATED WITH HIGH-VELOCITY AND HIGH-IMPACT INJURIES SEEN IN AUTOMOBILE ACCIDENTS, MOTORCYCLE ACCIDENTS, FALLS FROM HEIGHTS, AND ASSAULTS WITH BLUNT WEAPONS. WITH THE EXCEPTION OF FALLS, THESE MECHANISMS OF INJURY ARE TYPICAL OF THE URBAN ENVIRONMENT.

- ☹ Facial trauma can damage the airway, facial bones, eyes, ears, nose, jaw, or teeth.

- ☹ Most facial injuries are primarily cosmetic; however, there are several injuries that can cause serious problems—especially those that compromise the airway.

- ☹ Suspect spinal and/or brain injury in patients with severe facial trauma.

GENERAL TREATMENT GUIDELINES

- ☹ Maintain airway. Do not try to insert an OPA or NPA in patients with severe facial trauma. Protect the airway from aspiration.

- ☹ Protect the cervical spine and place the patient in the recovery position.

- ☹ Remove impaled objects from the cheeks and apply direct pressure inside and outside the mouth.

- ☹ Apply cold compresses to closed injuries.

- ☹ Check for extraocular movement of the eyes by having the patient look right, left, up, and down (see Blowout Fracture).

- ☹ The rate of evacuation depends on both the overall stability of the patient and the stability of the patient's airway.

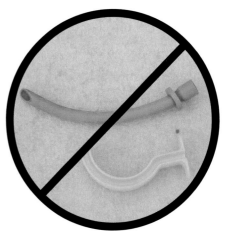

SEVERE FACIAL TRAUMA or basilar skull Fx? Leave NPAs and OPAs off your treatment option list—they are contraindicated because they may directly intrude upon brain tissue.

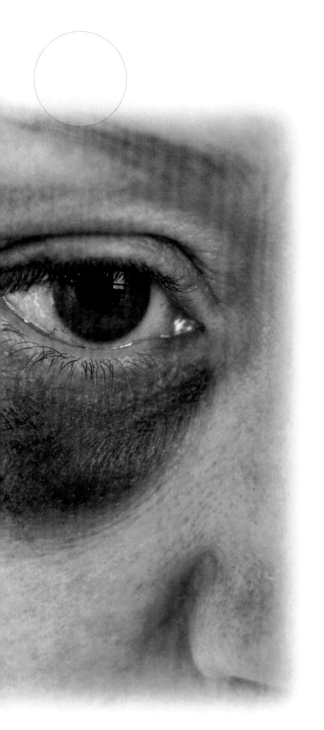

SYMPTOMS OF FACIAL TRAUMA

- ☹ Swelling of the soft tissues of the face can indicate an underlying fracture.

- ☹ Swelling of the soft tissues can make it difficult to breathe through the nose.

- ☹ Injuries to the cranial nerves can cause changes in facial sensation, as well as numbness or paralysis.

- ☹ Swelling of the soft tissues around the eyes can be dramatic, sometimes making it very difficult for the patient to open their eyes—it can also cause "raccoon eyes" (orbital bruising).

- ☹ A fracture of the floor of the orbit can interfere with eye motion and cause double vision (blowout fracture).

- ☹ Missing or broken teeth can indicate a fractured mandible.

- ☹ Malocclusion (improper alignment) of the teeth, when the jaw is closed, can indicate a fractured mandible.

- ☹ Cerebrospinal fluid leaking from the nose suggests fractures of the cribriform plate.

- ☹ Cerebrospinal fluid leaking from the ears, nose, or from around the eyes is evidence of skull fractures.

- ☹ A bloody nose may be the result of fractured nasal bones.

- ☹ Blood draining down the back of the throat can indicate compound fractures in the sinuses.

INJURIES TO THE BONES OF THE JAW, FACE AND SKULL

FRACTURED ZYGOMATIC ARCH

- ☐ The zygomatic bone forms an arch across the upper cheek just under the eye.
- ☐ Because it is an arch structure, a direct blow to the center of the arch can break the bone.

S/S

- ☐ The fracture site will be point-tender.
- ☐ Quite often, you will be able to feel a step-off of the displaced fracture in the center of the arch.

T

1. Support the jaw with a "mandible" bandage.
2. Evacuate.

FRACTURED MANDIBLE

- ☐ The mandible is the lower jaw, and fractures of the lower jaw are one of the more common facial injuries.
- ☐ The classic symptom associated with a fractured jaw is malocclusion—a misalignment of the teeth when the mouth is closed—the patient's "bite is off."

S/S

- ☐ Pain and point tenderness at the fracture site.
- ☐ Pain with jaw motion when the patient tries to open or close their jaw.
- ☐ The patient will have limited jaw motion; they can only partially open their mouth, and it is painful to do so.
- ☐ The patient usually has malocclusion.
- ☐ There may be broken or missing teeth.
- ☐ The patient will have swelling and discoloration at the fracture site.

T

1. Support the jaw with a "mandible" bandage.
2. Evacuate.

NOTE: the mandible can be a very difficult to stabilize, especially considering the power of the jaw muscles, so additional stabilization beyond that provided by a mandible bandage may be necessary. Fortunately, a person with a broken mandible (✖) or zygomatic arch (✖) is not likely to be very chatty—they will be very happy to keep their mouth shut.

NASAL BONE FRACTURES

- ☐ The nasal bones support the nose and are the easiest facial bones to fracture.
- ☐ The most common of the facial fractures, nasal bone fractures, are rarely dangerous or life-threatening by themselves.
- ☐ This injury is commonly associated with other facial injuries.

S/S

- ☐ The nose is often deformed and bent to one side.
- ☐ Epistaxis (a bloody nose), commonly occurs and is easily controlled with gentle pressure by pinching the nose—ten minutes should do it.

T

1. Sit the patient up, when possible, but do not tip their head back (it may cause blood to drain down their throat).
2. Apply a cold compress.
3. Tell the patient not to blow their nose for at least an hour.
4. Tell them not to swallow blood—it may cause vomiting.

BASILAR SKULL FRACTURE

These are rare fractures involving the base of the skull and can be life-threatening. Occurring in only about 4 percent of severe head injuries, the fracture involves the temporal bone, occipital bone, or clivus area around the foramen magnum.

(A) temporal bone

(B) occipital bone

(C) clivus area (centered in the back of the skull)

S/S

- ☐ Change in level of consciousness (LOC): the patient is usually unconscious and may be unresponsive.
- ☐ Although the fractures are usually linear, they can be depressed and can, therefore, be palpable.
- ☐ The leakage of cerebrospinal fluid (CSF) from the ears and nose is pathognomonic (distinctively characteristic) for a basilar skull fracture.
- ☐ A delayed sign is Battle's Sign.

T

1. Maintain a patent airway.
2. Administer oxygen.
3. Evacuate immediately.

FRACTURED ZYGOMATIC ARCH

- [ ] The zygomatic bone forms an arch across the upper cheek just under the eye.
- [ ] Because it is an arch structure, a direct blow to the center of the arch can break the bone.

S/S

- [ ] The fracture site will be point-tender.
- [ ] Quite often, you will be able to feel a step-off of the displaced fracture in the center of the arch.

T

1. Support the jaw with a "mandible" bandage.
2. Evacuate.

FRACTURED MANDIBLE

- [ ] The mandible is the lower jaw, and fractures of the lower jaw are one of the more common facial injuries.
- [ ] The classic symptom associated with a fractured jaw is malocclusion—a misalignment of the teeth when the mouth is closed—the patient's "bite is off."

S/S

- [ ] Pain and point tenderness at the fracture site.
- [ ] Pain with jaw motion when the patient tries to open or close their jaw.
- [ ] The patient will have limited jaw motion; they can only partially open their mouth, and it is painful to do so.
- [ ] The patient usually has malocclusion.
- [ ] There may be broken or missing teeth.
- [ ] The patient will have swelling and discoloration at the fracture site.

T

1. Support the jaw with a "mandible" bandage.
2. Evacuate.

NOTE: the mandible can be a very difficult to stabilize, especially considering the power of the jaw muscles, so additional stabilization beyond that provided by a mandible bandage may be necessary. Fortunately, a person with a broken mandible (✖) or zygomatic arch (✖✖) is not likely to be very chatty—they will be very happy to keep their mouth shut.

FACIAL BONE FRACTURES

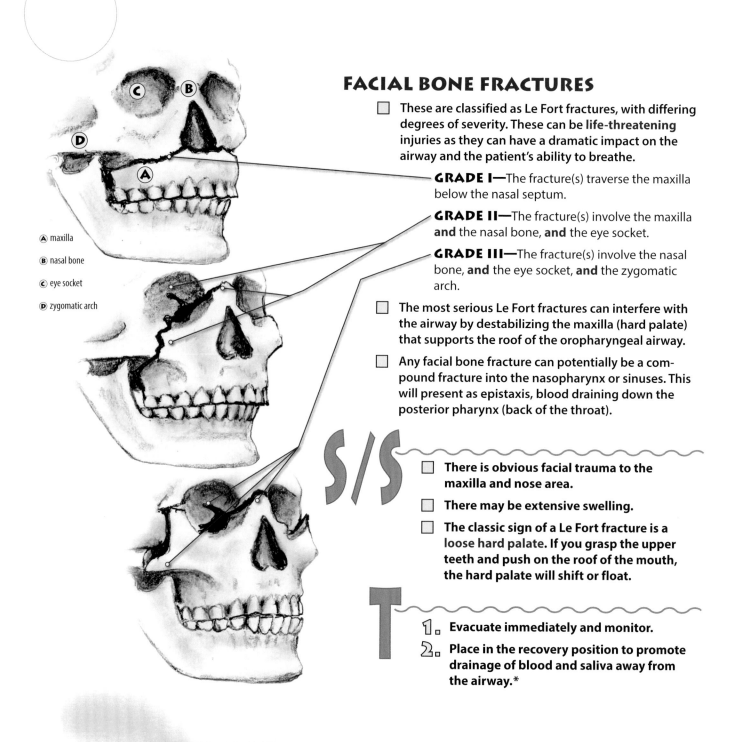

- ⓐ maxilla
- ⓑ nasal bone
- ⓒ eye socket
- ⓓ zygomatic arch

☐ These are classified as Le Fort fractures, with differing degrees of severity. These can be **life-threatening** injuries as they can have a dramatic impact on the airway and the patient's ability to breathe.

GRADE I—The fracture(s) traverse the maxilla below the nasal septum.

GRADE II—The fracture(s) involve the maxilla **and** the nasal bone, **and** the eye socket.

GRADE III—The fracture(s) involve the nasal bone, **and** the eye socket, **and** the zygomatic arch.

☐ The most serious Le Fort fractures can interfere with the airway by destabilizing the maxilla (hard palate) that supports the roof of the oropharyngeal airway.

☐ Any facial bone fracture can potentially be a compound fracture into the nasopharynx or sinuses. This will present as epistaxis, blood draining down the posterior pharynx (back of the throat).

S/S

☐ **There is obvious facial trauma to the maxilla and nose area.**

☐ **There may be extensive swelling.**

☐ **The classic sign of a Le Fort fracture is a loose hard palate. If you grasp the upper teeth and push on the roof of the mouth, the hard palate will shift or float.**

T

1. **Evacuate immediately and monitor.**
2. **Place in the recovery position to promote drainage of blood and saliva away from the airway.***

* YOU MAY WONDER why there is no mention here of stabilization. LeFort fractures often result in what is referred to as a "floating palate," which simply cannot be immobilized by any typical methods. Maintaining a patent airway, providing positive pressure ventilation (if possible), and evacuating immediately are the only treatments.

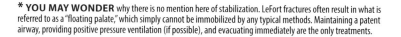

BLOWOUT FRACTURES OF THE EYES

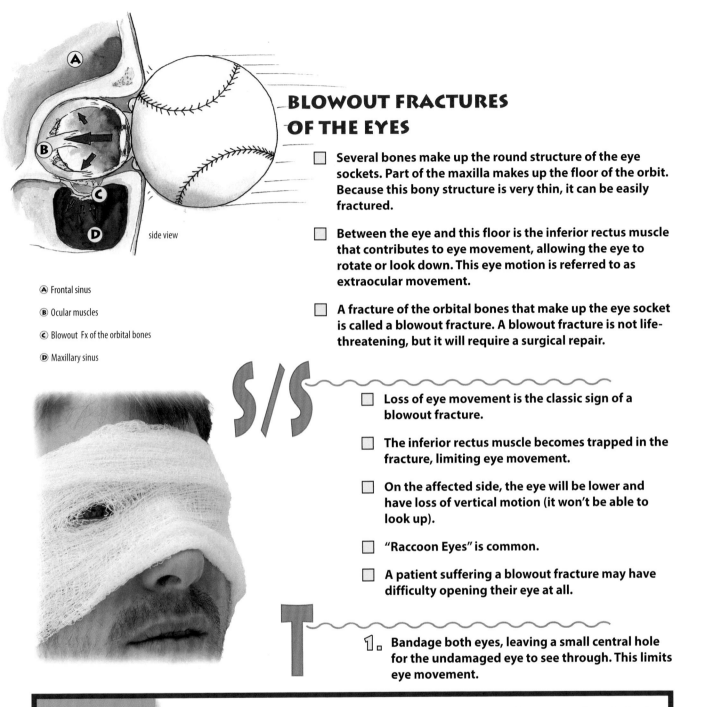

(A) Frontal sinus

(B) Ocular muscles

(C) Blowout Fx of the orbital bones

(D) Maxillary sinus

side view

- [ ] Several bones make up the round structure of the eye sockets. Part of the maxilla makes up the floor of the orbit. Because this bony structure is very thin, it can be easily fractured.

- [ ] Between the eye and this floor is the inferior rectus muscle that contributes to eye movement, allowing the eye to rotate or look down. This eye motion is referred to as extraocular movement.

- [ ] A fracture of the orbital bones that make up the eye socket is called a blowout fracture. A blowout fracture is not life-threatening, but it will require a surgical repair.

S/S

- [ ] Loss of eye movement is the classic sign of a blowout fracture.

- [ ] The inferior rectus muscle becomes trapped in the fracture, limiting eye movement.

- [ ] On the affected side, the eye will be lower and have loss of vertical motion (it won't be able to look up).

- [ ] "Raccoon Eyes" is common.

- [ ] A patient suffering a blowout fracture may have difficulty opening their eye at all.

T

1. Bandage both eyes, leaving a small central hole for the undamaged eye to see through. This limits eye movement.

CONCUSSION

Any head or facial trauma may include concussion—an injury that occurs when the brain impacts the skull during rapid deceleration, causing damage to the brain tissue itself.

> An injury to the brain results in the alteration of mental status (e.g., confusion and memory loss).

> Only 10% of concussions will have any loss of consciousness.

> Metabolic changes cause the brain to spend all the available glucose on repair which reduces the brain's overall ability to function.

> Concussions can occur with or without contact to the head.

> There can be microscopic damage to the brain, only detectable by S/S.

> Can be caused by repeated sub-concussive blows that accumulate over time.

S/S
- Headaches
- Blurred vision
- Ataxia
- Nausea & vomiting
- Dizziness
- Fatigue
- Insomnia
- Mood swings
- Anxiety
- Irritability
- Confusion
- Poor attention and focus abilities

NASAL BONE FRACTURES

- [ ] The nasal bones support the nose and are the easiest facial bones to fracture.
- [ ] The most common of the facial fractures, nasal bone fractures, are rarely dangerous or life-threatening by themselves.
- [ ] This injury is commonly associated with other facial injuries.

S/S

- [ ] The nose is often deformed and bent to one side.
- [ ] Epistaxis (a bloody nose), commonly occurs and is easily controlled with gentle pressure by pinching the nose—ten minutes should do it.

T

1. Sit the patient up, when possible, but do not tip their head back (it may cause blood to drain down their throat).
2. Apply a cold compress.
3. Tell the patient not to blow their nose for at least an hour.
4. Tell them not to swallow blood—it may cause vomiting.

BASILAR SKULL FRACTURE

These are rare fractures involving the base of the skull and can be life-threatening. Occurring in only about 4 percent of severe head injuries, the fracture involves the temporal bone, occipital bone, or clivus area around the foramen magnum.

Ⓐ temporal bone

Ⓑ occipital bone

Ⓒ clivus area (centered in the back of the skull)

S/S

- [ ] Change in level of consciousness (LOC): the patient is usually unconscious and may be unresponsive.
- [ ] Although the fractures are usually linear, they can be depressed and can, therefore, be palpable.
- [ ] The leakage of cerebrospinal fluid (CSF) from the ears and nose is pathognomonic (distinctively characteristic) for a basilar skull fracture.
- [ ] A delayed sign is Battle's Sign.

T

1. Maintain a patent airway.
2. Administer oxygen.
3. Evacuate immediately.

WILDCARE™

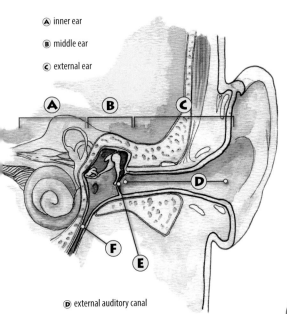

Ⓐ inner ear

Ⓑ middle ear

Ⓒ external ear

Ⓓ external auditory canal

Ⓔ tympanic membrane

Ⓕ Eustachian tube

RUPTURED EAR DRUM

☐ This is a tear in the tympanic membrane (E at left).

☐ Typical causes include infection, accidental perforation by a foreign object, or excessive pressure (as in barotrauma or an ear slap), head trauma, or acoustic trauma (explosion, extremely loud music).

☐ A ruptured eardrum can lead to middle ear infections and temporary hearing loss.

☐ A ruptured eardrum will typically resolve on its own, healing over a couple of months if the ear is protected, although surgical repair is sometimes needed.

S/S

☐ The patient will complain of decreased hearing and the sensation of air rushing in.

☐ Blood or CSF (clear fluid) draining from the ears indicates a head injury (a potential life threat).

T

1. Cover with a dry sterile dressing.
2. Allow fluids to drain—do not put anything in the ear.
3. Evacuate.

A BUG IN THE EAR CANAL

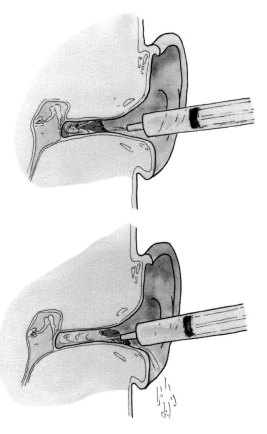

1. Stop the bug from moving by drowning it with vegetable oil or water.

2. Rinse the bug out of the ear. An irrigation syringe, such as the kind used for wound cleaning, will work great. Simply fill the syringe with warm water and squirt it in the ear. If you don't have a syringe, you can use many things to create a stream of water (e.g. a plastic bag with a corner snipped off).

3. With the bug-invaded person sitting up, gently spray a stream of water into the ear canal and rinse the offending intruder out. You can put a cup under the ear to catch the water and the bug, and prevent the patient from getting soaked.

4. Follow-up: Monitor the ear for signs of otitis externa (swimmer's ear, an inflammation of the outer ear and ear canal). This can be prevented by rinsing the ear out with isopropyl alcohol, which will dry out the ear canal.

EXTRAOCULAR MOVEMENT (EOM)

The following procedure will evaluate the eye muscles and blowout fractures of the facial orbits.

1. Have your patient follow your finger as you make a large letter "H" in the air.
2. The eyes should be able to follow the "H," and they should move together, symmetrically.
3. The successful execution of this maneuver noted in medical documentation as the "extraocular movements are intact" (EOMI).

ALIGNMENT OF TEETH

1. Examine the patient's teeth closely for missing teeth and for the alignment of their teeth and jaw as they open and close their mouth.

HARD PALATE

1. Examine the hard palate (roof of the mouth) by gently pulling on the upper teeth or by pushing on the roof of the mouth.
2. The area should be immobile—any movement or shifting is serious.

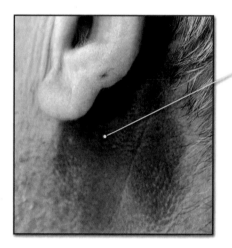

BATTLE'S SIGN

1. During the physical exam, look behind the ears to see if there is any discoloration (ecchymosis caused by blood collecting in the soft tissue).
2. Battle's Sign occurs over time; you need to check the area every 15 minutes to see if it develops.

RACCOON EYES

- This condition looks exactly as its name—bleeding from soft tissue trauma causes swelling and discoloration around the eyes.
- The result is that the patient appears to be wearing a mask similar to a raccoon.
- Raccoon eyes can look severe, and they can, (but rarely do), indicate an underlying major facial injury—but they are typically the result of soft tissue trauma.

CEREBROSPINAL FLUID (CFS)

Lying between the dura mater and pia mater (layers of meninges tissues), CFS surrounds the brain and spinal cord.

- Leakage of CFS occurs only with a skull fracture and a tear in the dura mater.
- Monitor the ears and nose for CSF leakage (clear, thick as maple syrup), as it indicates a skull fracture. Occasionally, it can leak out around the eyes as well.

DO YOUR ABCs

With suspected facial trauma, consider the following specific points (which go beyond your typical ABCDE assessment).

1. **Airway**—is the hard palate stable?
2. **Breathing**—do not try to blindly insert an OPA or NPA in the case of severe facial trauma. Rescue breathing and CPR may be difficult, depending on the stability of the patient's facial bones.
3. **Circulation**—is there any bleeding from the patient's nose; or is blood draining down the back of their throat from their sinuses?
4. **Deformity**—are there any obvious deformities of the face? If so, you should suspect spinal and/or brain injury.

TREATMENT EMPHASIZED FOR FACIAL INJURIES

1. Look in the patient's airway. If they are unconscious, and there is blood draining down the back of their throat, support their head and neck, and place them in the recovery position to encourage the blood to drain out of their mouth, not into their airway.
2. Constantly monitor the patient's breathing, and be prepared to suction their airway to keep it clear.
3. If they are conscious and there is blood draining down the back of their throat, tell them to spit it out (swallowing blood will make them nauseated and can cause vomiting).
4. Apply cold packs to closed injuries to encourage vasoconstriction and to minimize soft-tissue swelling.
5. If there is an impaled object through the cheeks, gently remove it and apply pressure to both the inside and the outside on the cheek.
6. Apply the appropriate bandage for the injury.
7. If the facial injury is severe, immobilize the spine with a C-collar and place the patient on a backboard or in litter.
8. Evacuate (the rate and destination may vary depending on the severity of the injury—a guy with a busted nose may be able to walk out and head to a local clinic; a Le Fort fracture victim must be rushed directly to the nearest hospital (and may need a ride in a helicopter).

BANDAGING FUNDAMENTALS FOR FACIAL INJURIES

- The goals with facial injury bandages are to provide stabilization and hold dressings in place to control bleeding
- Unlike limb injuries, which can be splinted, facial injuries cannot be splinted and must be treated with soft bandages.
- If a facial injury is severe, the patient should have a cervical collar and be placed on a backboard or litter.

Improvised cervical collar

- Typical "street collars" can become very uncomfortable during an extended carry-out.
- Improvised soft collars are very comfortable, effective, and provide warmth. The cervical spine can be easily immobilized with a blanket, fleece jacket, clothing, or a foam pad.
- Improvised collars can be quickly and simply made by rolling the material into a long tube, about 3 – 4 inches in diameter, placing it behind the neck, and wrapping it around the front of the neck, securing each side of the tube under their arms.

Backboards

- Backboards or litters are only necessary for carry-outs.
- They will become painful over time, so they require extra padding, especially behind the knees and in the lumbar portion of the back.
- Backboards are not required in litters.

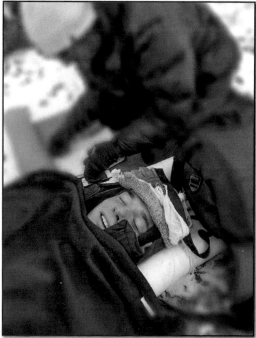

Patients with severe facial injuries will need to have their head and neck immobilized in a C-collar, which can be improvised in many ways. Evacuation will be necessary, and may include a litter (improvised or commercial) and perhaps even a helicopter.

CHEST TRAUMA
The 3rd leading cause of trauma-related deaths

Thoracic trauma is a common cause of disability and mortality—it is the leading cause of death from physical trauma after head and spinal cord injury. In about one-quarter of all trauma-related deaths, blunt thoracic injuries are the primary or secondary cause. Detailed descriptions of chest injuries are found as far back as the ancient Egyptian Edwin Smith Papyrus, which dates to around 1600 BC.

In the urban environment, many chest injuries are diagnosed with high-tech imaging (e.g., CT scans) and treated with interventions such as tracheal intubation, mechanical ventilation, and chest tube insertion (or surgery, in the case of penetrating injury). Because these tools are unavailable to us in the backcountry, our treatment is limited to the observations of the signs and symptoms (which, in the case of chest trauma, often change over time), stabilization of the patient, and quick evacuation.

Specific chest injuries

Chest-wall soft tissue injuries

Fractured clavicle

Fractured sternum

Fractured ribs

Flail chest

Pulmonary contusion

Pulmonary laceration

Hemothorax

Pneumothorax

Pericardial tamponade

Myocardial contusion

Traumatic aortic rupture

Impaled object

Traumatic asphyxia

CHEST TRAUMA AT A GLANCE

The **two classifications** of chest trauma: **blunt** chest trauma and **penetrating** chest trauma

Mortality from chest trauma alone: **10%**

Blunt chest trauma as a percentage of all trauma-related deaths: **25%**

Approximate percentage of patients presenting in an emergency department in respiratory distress (often the result of chest trauma) who will die: **50%**

Approximate percentage of patients in both respiratory distress and shock who will die: **75%**

Leading **causes of death** from trauma • 1—head trauma • 2—spinal trauma • 3—**chest trauma**

Chest Anatomy

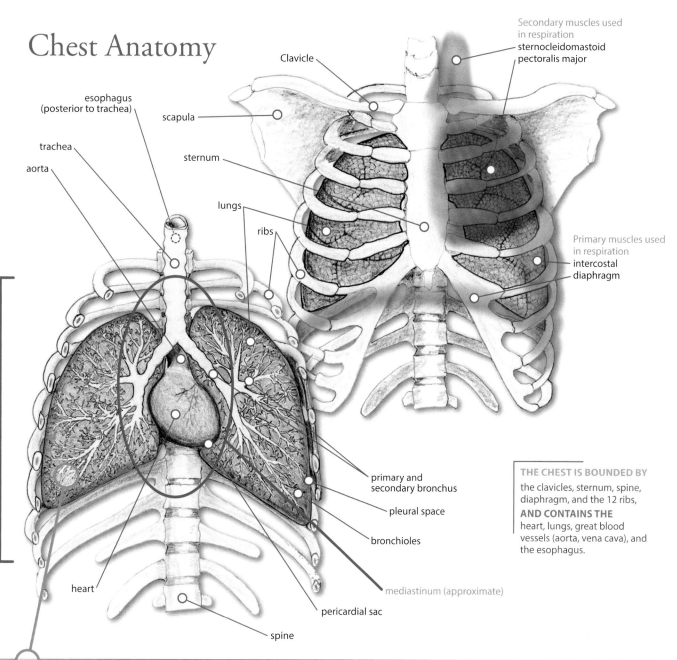

Secondary muscles used in respiration
sternocleidomastoid
pectoralis major

Clavicle

esophagus (posterior to trachea)

scapula

trachea

aorta

sternum

lungs

ribs

Primary muscles used in respiration
intercostal
diaphragm

thoracic cavity

primary and secondary bronchus

pleural space

bronchioles

heart

mediastinum (approximate)

pericardial sac

spine

THE CHEST IS BOUNDED BY the clavicles, sternum, spine, diaphragm, and the 12 ribs, **AND CONTAINS THE** heart, lungs, great blood vessels (aorta, vena cava), and the esophagus.

Inhalation/Exhalation

THE INS AND OUTS OF RESPIRATION

Each lung is sheathed by a delicate serous membrane, the pleura, in the form of a closed invaginated (sheathed) sac. The portion of the membrane that covers the surface of the lung and follows the wrinkles and fissures between its lobes is called the visceral pleura, and it is attached directly to the lungs.

The parietal pleura is a similar membrane that is attached to the opposing interior surface of the thoracic cavity.

The potential space between these two membranes is known as the pleural space, and it can hold 2 – 3 liters of air in an adult if the lung collapses.

The diaphragm contracts and drops, and the intercostal muscles are brought into play through contraction, creating negative pressure in the pleural space, which causes the lungs to expand and air to rush in—this is active inhalation.

Exhalation is purely passive: the diaphragm and other muscles relax, and as the elastic lungs recoil, positive pressure pushes air out.

JUST IN CASE YOU WERE WONDERING . . .

The average person (at rest) breathes about: 16 times a minute

- 16 times a minute
- 960 times an hour
- 23,040 times a day
- 8,415,360 times a year
- that's 673,228,800 to age 80...
- Whew!

The Circulatory System
(our heart and blood vessels)
the pump and all those pipes

that move the red stuff around
to reach each cell in our body
(bringing the good
and disposing of the bad)

The average adult has trillions of cells in their body, and without a continuous stream of oxygen, each of those cells would begin to die in as little as a few minutes or as long as several hours—depending on the type of cell. Fortunately, we have plumbing specifically designed to deliver a regular supply of oxygen (plus other necessary stuff, like white blood cells) to every nook and cranny from our eyelids to our toes. To gain an understanding of this complex system, we must examine the basic components.

- The heart—the pump.
- The blood vessels—the pipes.
- The blood—the red stuff.

Circulatory facts for the pathologically curious

Miles of blood vessels in an adult	60,000
Number of red blood cells	20 – 30 **trillion**
Number of blood cells produced each second	2.4 million
Heartbeats in a lifetime (75 years)	2.66 **billion**
Blood pumped in a day	2,000 gallons
Blood pumped in a lifetime (75 years)	54.8 million gallons
Time blood takes to circulate heart-to-toes and back	16 seconds
Man-made pump comparable to the heart	none

WILDCARE™

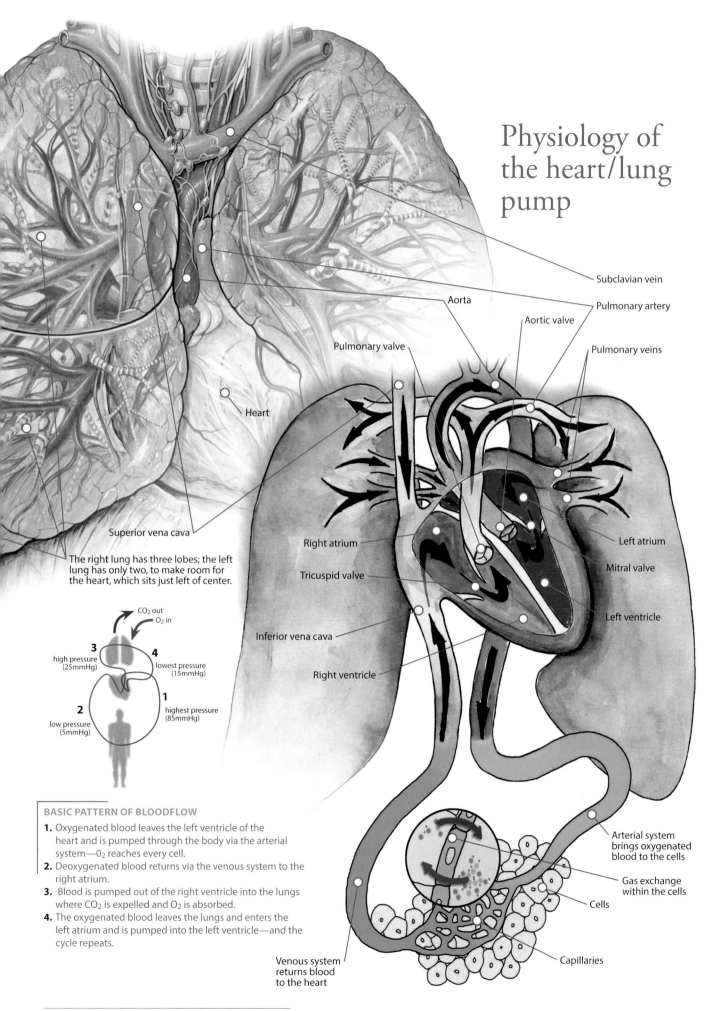

Physiology of the heart/lung pump

Subclavian vein

Aorta

Pulmonary artery

Aortic valve

Pulmonary veins

Pulmonary valve

Heart

Right atrium

Left atrium

Tricuspid valve

Mitral valve

Superior vena cava

Left ventricle

The right lung has three lobes; the left lung has only two, to make room for the heart, which sits just left of center.

Inferior vena cava

Right ventricle

CO$_2$ out
O$_2$ in

3
high pressure
(25mmHg)

4
lowest pressure
(15mmHg)

2
low pressure
(5mmHg)

1
highest pressure
(85mmHg)

BASIC PATTERN OF BLOODFLOW

1. Oxygenated blood leaves the left ventricle of the heart and is pumped through the body via the arterial system—O$_2$ reaches every cell.
2. Deoxygenated blood returns via the venous system to the right atrium.
3. Blood is pumped out of the right ventricle into the lungs where CO$_2$ is expelled and O$_2$ is absorbed.
4. The oxygenated blood leaves the lungs and enters the left atrium and is pumped into the left ventricle—and the cycle repeats.

Arterial system brings oxygenated blood to the cells

Gas exchange within the cells

Cells

Capillaries

Venous system returns blood to the heart

The heart

- A two-sided, four-chambered pump responsible for supplying all the body's tissues with oxygenated blood, nutrients, and heat, as well as removing and disposing of waste products and carbon dioxide produced by the cells.
- The heart is made of up of specialized coronary muscle cells that have the ability to contract in a coordinated fashion.
- When the heart contracts, it pushes the blood out through three circulatory circuits: systemic, pulmonary, and coronary.

SYSTEMIC CIRCULATION

- This is the largest of the three circuits, circulating blood from the heart to the rest of the body.
- As the heart contracts, blood is forced out of the left ventricle through the aortic valve on its way to the rest of the body via the aorta.
- The aorta soon divides into smaller arteries, those arteries to arterioles, and finally the arterioles to capillaries—gas and nutrient exchange occurs at the capillary level.
- The capillaries then merge together to form venules, and the venules merge to form veins.
- The veins then drain into the inferior and superior vena cava that return the blood to the right atrium of the heart, completing the round trip.

PULMONARY CIRCULATION

- Once the blood has returned to the right atrium of the heart, it is pumped through the tricuspid valve into the right ventricle and then out through the pulmonary valve to the lungs.
- As the blood leaves the heart via the pulmonary artery, that artery quickly divides down into capillaries that surround the alveoli of the lungs, where gas exchange happens.
    - Carbon dioxide (CO_2) is released into the lungs.
    - Oxygen (O_2) is absorbed by the red blood cells (RBCs) in the blood.
- The freshly oxygenated blood is then returned to the left atrium of the heart via the pulmonary vein.
- Once in the heart, the oxygenated blood is pushed through the mitral valve into the left ventricle where, as it is ejected out through the aortic valve into the aorta, it will restart the systemic circulation.

CORONARY CIRCULATION

- Just like any other muscle, the heart needs well-oxygenated blood and nutrients to survive and work continuously 24/7, beating (on average) once every second, 60 times per minute, 3,600 times per hour, 86,400 times every 24 hours, and 31,557,600 times per year.
- Blood is supplied from the heart to the heart by the coronary circulation.
    - As the blood leaves the heart, it is forced through the one-way aortic valve with the contraction of the heart, known as systole, (the measure of force of this contraction is called the systolic blood pressure).
    - When the heart relaxes between contractions, (the measure of force between contractions is call the diastolic blood pressure), the aortic valve closes and blood falls back against it.
    - Immediately adjacent to the aortic valve, built into the beginning or root of the aorta, are the openings of the coronary arteries, and it is through these that blood enters the coronary circulation.
    - Just like the rest of the body, the blood goes from arteries to arterioles to capillaries, where gas and nutrient exchange occurs.
    - It then exits the capillaries into venules, then into veins where the blood drains into the right atrium from the coronary veins.

WILDCARE™

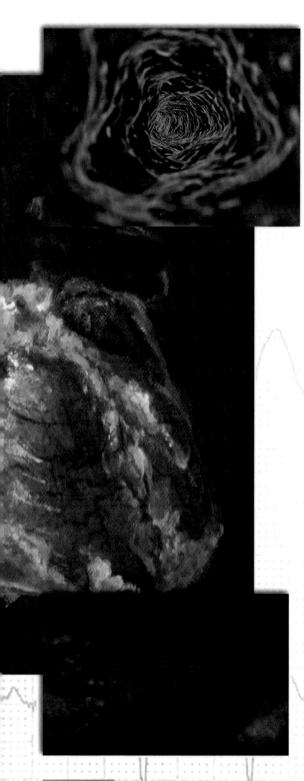

Arteries and veins

- The arteries and veins are the pipes that carry the blood around the various circulatory loops.
- Arteries carry blood **away** from the heart.
    - With the exception of the pulmonary artery, they carry oxygenated blood.
    - The arterial side of the circuit is the high pressure side, with an average systolic pressure of 120mmHg.
    - Arteries are strong, multi-layer tubes designed to withstand many decades of systolic pressure.
    - As arteries divide into smaller arterioles and eventually capillaries, the pressure decreases with each division.
- Veins carry blood **toward** the heart.
    - With the exception of the pulmonary vein, they do not carry oxygenated blood.
    - The venous side is under much less pressure, an average of 5mmHg pressure.
    - Veins are thinner, less muscular tubes designed for low-pressure blood flow.
    - Veins are equipped with one-way valves about every inch along their paths that keep bloodflow from reversing—this is especially important in our legs, where the low-pressure venous flow has to fight the pull of gravity.

Blood

- Blood is a complex liquid made up of many different parts that work together to bring oxygen and nutrients to the cells and carry away carbon dioxide and waste products.
- Red blood cells (RBCs)—carry oxygen.
- White blood cells (WBCs)—protect us against disease and help us fight disease if it occurs.
- Thrombocytes (platelets)—form clots that help control bleeding and promote the repair of damaged cells.
- The RBCs, WBCs, and thrombocytes are suspended in a watery liquid (blood plasma and serum) that also contains various proteins and antibodies that supplement the immune system and help us fight disease.
    - These proteins and antibodies help mediate allergic reactions, control bleeding, and promote healing.
    - If blood is allowed to sit and clot, the proteins in the blood responsible for clotting are tied up and precipitate to the bottom.
    - The remaining yellowish fluid is the serum.

CLOCKWISE FROM CENTER: the pump, the plumbing, and the fluid—in conjunction with the lungs; this is our body's system for connecting us to the gaseous external environment, exchanging life-giving oxygen for waste products every moment of every day for all our days. Automatic, self-regulating, and self-repairing, it is perhaps the most reliable and efficient machine ever devised.

General assessment and treatment principles

Because chest trauma can interfere with breathing, circulation, or both, it can be **life-threatening**. Initially, though their symptoms may look benign, patients with chest injuries can **deteriorate quickly** and must be **monitored** continuously. Unlike most other traumatic injuries, often the most serious sign/symptom of chest trauma is **shortness of breath** (SOB)—which can vary from minor distress to complete respiratory failure. Because of this, the ability to determine both the severity of the SOB and whether it is improving or deteriorating is paramount with the chest trauma patient.

Physical exam

- **LOC**—does it deteriorate?
- **Airway**—is it patent?
- **Breathing**
    - How well is the patient breathing?
    - What is the rate and effort?
    - Are there any adventitious breath sounds (wheezing, crackling)?
    - Consider assisting ventilations if the patient is in distress.
- **Circulation**
    - Do they have a pulse? What is the rate and quality? (Perform CPR if pulseless.)
    - Is there any obvious bleeding? (Control major life-threatening bleeding with direct pressure and pressure dressings.)
- **Blood pressure**—the key vital sign for chest trauma
    - The most accurate measurement requires a BP cuff.
    - A drop in blood pressure indicates bleeding in a major vessel or in the lung tissue.
    - A narrowing of pulse pressure (the difference between systolic and diastolic pressure) indicates direct damage to the heart.

Respiratory distress and failure

Respiratory distress is indicated:

- When the patient's respiratory rate is less than 10 or greater than 30 breaths per minute, and/or
- When they have word dyspnea severe enough that they can only count to 6 or less on one breath, and/or
- When they have adventitious breath sounds (wheezing, coarse crackles, stridor), and/or
- When they are unconscious (and have adventitious breath sounds).

Respiratory failure

This is the extreme of respiratory distress. It occurs when the patient runs out of the energy that it takes them to maintain the extra effort of breathing during the crisis and is indicated:

- When the patient's respiratory rate slows, and the depth of breathing becomes shallower and/or
- When the patient becomes cyanotic and/or
- When word dyspnea is 4 words or less with one breath (see right) and/or
- Adventitious breathing becomes softer as the depth of breathing becomes shallower (since each breath moves less air) and/or
- When the patient's O_2 saturation begins to drop (measured by pulse oximeter).

Word dyspnea

\'dis(p)•nē-ə\

Word dyspnea is measured on a 1 to10 scale, based on how high a person can count on one breath.

An average breath moves 500ml of air, and it takes the movement of at least 150ml of air to get fresh air to the alveoli (called the dead air space).

Assuming the patient will expel 50ml of air to say each number, ask the patient to take the deepest breath they can and begin counting from 1 to 10 as they exhale.

If they count to 3 (or less), they are not moving the minimum amount of air required to survive—this is a crisis situation.

If they can count from 4 to 6, a crisis is likely on the way.

If they can get past 7, there may still be a problem, but it is not critical (a healthy person should be able to count to 20 or more on one breath).

- **Hands-on exam specific to chest trauma (CHEST)**
  - **C**—crepitation (bone fragments grating)
  - **H**—hemorrhage (obvious bleeding), and bruising
  - **E**—equal respiratory motion (breathing symmetrical)
  - **S**—sucking chest wound (chest wall pierced, air leaks into the pleural space: pneumothorax)
  - **T**—tenderness (indicates thoracic damage), e.g., Fx ribs
- **Look**
  - Visually inspect the chest.
  - Look for wounds, bruising, deformity, and/or unequal chest-wall motion during breathing.
- **Listen**
  - Listen to the breath sounds, comparing them side-to-side.
  - If you do not have a stethoscope, put your ear on the patient's chest.
- **Feel**
  - Gently palpate the chest for tenderness, crepitation, and stability.
  - Auscultate (stethoscope) and percuss the lungs (thump the chest) for signs of pneumothorax (circles indicate correct positions—listen to both the front **and** the back of the thoracic cavity).

General patient care

1. Place the patient in a position of comfort that makes it easiest for them to breathe—typically sitting at 45 degrees (the Fowler's position, see below).
2. Stop and treat any life-threatening chest injuries before proceeding with the rest of the secondary assessment
3. Give O_2 via non-rebreather mask, or via a bag valve mask (BVM) if they require assisted ventilations (in the wilderness, assisted breathing may be mouth-to-mouth). ***There is never a good reason to withhold oxygen.***
4. Plug all holes: place airtight dressings over any holes in the chest and tape them in place, leaving one side open to prevent a tension pneumothorax (avoid petroleum gauze—it is not water soluble and surgeons have difficulty removing it).
5. Promote breathing: never bind or tape a patient's chest to support broken ribs, and don't sand-bag, tape, or otherwise restrict the paradoxical motion of a flail chest (this will limit the depth of breathing and worsen the patient's respiratory distress).
6. Evacuate ASAP—chest injuries accompanied by respiratory distress are life-threatening emergencies.
   A. Evacuate in the position of comfort—typically sitting up (the Fowler's position).
   B. Monitor all vital signs—pay particular attention to the patient's airway, breathing, and changes in pulse pressure.
   C. The rate of evacuation will be determined by the severity of the patient's injuries, their ability to breathe, and the rate of deterioration—the worse things get, the faster you go.
   D. If things get worse, ***go faster!***

UPRIGHT POSITION (90⁰)

FOWLER'S POSITION (45⁰)

SUPINE (180⁰)

Specific cardiothoracic trauma

Because so many of the signs/symptoms and treatments are shared by many of the injuries covered, we've consolidated things graphically at the end of the list—any S/S- and/or injury-specific information will be given for each condition within its description.

Chest-wall soft tissue injuries

These are simple soft tissue injuries to the superficial layers of the chest wall (skin, adipose tissue, intercostal muscles, or breasts), typically caused by a direct blow (e.g., from a fall). Although often appearing superficial, there may be more going on below the surface—examine the injuries closely and consider possible damage to the underlying anatomy (lungs and heart). You can estimate the depth of injury to be one half of the diameter of the surface injury.

Fractured clavicle

This is the most common fracture seen in emergency medicine. It is easily diagnosed because the clavicle is superficial—you can locate the point-tenderness and palpate the fracture (typically in the center to the distal 1/3). It is important to remember that just under the clavicle is a large neurovascular bundle containing a large vein, an artery, and nerves, as well as the apex of the lungs. As the clavicle breaks, a bone fragment can damage one of these underlying structures, causing bleeding, a pneumothorax, or subcutaneous emphysema. Subcutaneous emphysema occurs when air collects under the skin, indicating a tear in the trachea, airways, or the parietal and visceral pleura. A tear such as this allows air to leak out of the lungs into the pleural space and the adjoining tissues. Although this loose air is harmless, it can indicate a serious underlying injury. If this is a stand-alone injury, the patient will likely be ambulatory.

Fractured ribs

Fractured ribs are a common injury resulting from direct trauma to the chest wall. They are usually isolated injuries, which are easily managed. However, because the lungs lie directly beneath the ribs, bone fragments can pierce the chest and cause a pneumothorax, hemothorax, or both. Two treatment items are unique to this injury: first, don't wrap the ribs (this can interfere with breathing), and second, during recovery the patient should have at least four deliberate coughing sessions per day to prevent pneumonia (coughing forces air to move through all sections of the lung, removing CO_2 and reducing the likelihood of a bacterial infection).

Fractured sternum

Fractures of the sternum are relatively uncommon as they require a direct (and hard) blow to the sternum. For example, this injury can occur when an unrestrained driver hits their chest on the steering wheel during a head-on collision (where a bruise in the shape of the steering wheel may be seen). Also, avalanche victims occasionally experience sternal fractures. They are rarely serious, and do not require any specific treatment, but as always, it is important to monitor for signs of injury to the underlying structures—the heart and the lungs.

Flail chest

This is a life-threatening emergency—it is likely that there is damage to the underlying lung tissues, blood vessels, and the heart or lungs. The sternum and/or multiple adjacent ribs are broken in two or more places, creating a "free floating" segment of the chest wall (only the ribs example is highlighted at the right). There may also be extensive soft tissue damage. As the patient tries to inhale, the flail section gets drawn in by the vacuum, limiting the amount of air exchange. This asymmetrical movement of the flail section is called paradoxical motion. (Do not compress or immobilize the injured side during treatment—this will further limit air exchange.)

Pulmonary contusion

As the chest wall is injured, some energy from the blow is transmitted through the chest wall into the parenchyma (tissue) of the lungs resulting in bruising of that tissue. Over a period of hours, this will cause bleeding into the lung tissue and stiffening of that area of the lung, causing a progressive worsening of dyspnea. While not an emergency by itself, over time, it will contribute to the severity of the chest trauma and respiratory distress.

Pulmonary laceration

A laceration to the parenchyma of the lung can be caused by direct blunt trauma or a penetrating wound to the chest. Both the visceral pleura and parietal pleura may be involved, and there is an obvious risk of a hemo/pneumothorax or a sucking chest wound. Monitor closely for dyspnea that worsens over time.

Pneumothorax

A simple pneumothorax is a closed injury where air collects in the pleural cavity between the lung and the chest wall. The same mechanism that causes a hemothorax can also injure the airways, leaking air into the pleural space. As the air enters the pleural space, it rises to the top of the lungs, causing them to collapse from the top down—a collapsed lung. A simple pneumothorax can develop into a tension pneumothorax—a far more serious condition—so careful monitoring is critical.

Sucking chest wound

This is also called an open pneumothorax, and yes, it's as bad as it sounds—a penetrating (open) injury has occurred allowing air to enter the pleural space resulting in a pneumothorax. This is a potentially life-threatening injury, depending upon the extent of damage to the underlying structures and lungs.

Tension pneumothorax

This is a life-threatening emergency that begins as a simple pneumothorax, but as air continues to enter the pleural space, it compresses the lungs and heart and impairs respiration and/or blood circulation. As the lung is compressed against the mediastinum, the vena cava, and the uninjured lung, it interferes with the heart's ability to refill between contractions. It also squeezes the uninjured lung, limiting air exchange. If caused by an open pneumothorax, the wound will need to be dressed with an occlusive dressing, left open on one side so it can be "burped" to reduce pressure. A patient with a tension pneumothorax will require a thoracostomy or a chest tube—immediate and quick evacuation to definitive care is needed.

Hemothorax

When the parenchyma of the lungs and the visceral pleura are injured, the pulmonary vascular system will be injured, too. This causes blood to collect in the pleural space and, via gravity, settle to the base of the lungs.

Spontaneous pneumothorax

This is a spontaneous rupture of a congenital weak spot or bleb on the visceral pleura that causes air to escape into the pleural space and collapse the lung. This injury is not associated with any trauma, injury, or illness and is more common in smokers and tall, thin young men. This condition can also deteriorate into a tension pneumothorax—monitor the patient's condition closely.

Pericardial tamponade

This is a very rare, life-threatening injury that occurs when blunt force or penetrating trauma ruptures one of the ventricles and the heart bleeds into the pericardial sack. As the blood pools in the pericardial sac, it restricts the expansion and contraction of the heart. This decreases cardiac output and causes cardiogenic shock. The characteristic trio of symptoms for this condition (distant, muffled heart sounds, narrowing pulse pressure, and JVD) is called "Beck's Triad." This patient needs immediate surgical intervention—evacuate as quickly as possible.

Myocardial contusion

This is a bruising of the myocardium, the heart muscle, which occurs with direct trauma to the front of the chest. The bruising restricts coronary blood flow and decreases oxygen to the injured area. It is impossible to determine the extent of damage in the field—evacuate immediately.

Traumatic aortic rupture

This is an unusual and typically lethal injury with a specific mechanism of injury (MOI). As the aorta leaves the left ventricle, it arches back and travels down through the chest against the spine—a suspensory ligament holds the arch in place. During rapid deceleration accidents, such as a head-on collision motor vehicle accident, the aorta and the contents of the chest cavity swing violently forward tearing the aorta along the arch. Death occurs immediately after rupture of the thoracic aorta 75% – 90% of the time because of the severity of the bleeding, and 80% – 85% of patients die before arriving at a hospital. Typically there are no specific signs or symptoms—you suspect traumatic aortic rupture based on the mechanism of injury (MOI). Be especially suspicious in any accident involving rapid deceleration. This is an emergent life-threatening injury, and you only have a few minutes.

Impaled object

The symptoms of this (sometimes gruesome) injury will vary depending on which structures in the chest cavity were harmed. Do not remove the object—support and stabilize it with appropriate bandages. If the penetrating object has lacerated one of the pulmonary vessels of the heart, shock will set in quickly and progress rapidly (from internal bleeding)—a serious situation requiring immediate evacuation.

Traumatic asphyxia

This is an unusual life-threatening emergency associated with the sudden compression of the chest which can occur during an avalanche (right) or a head-on collision. The sudden crushing trauma to the chest rapidly forces blood from the heart, causing reverse blood flow into the veins of the neck and face. This damages the valves in the heart, which normally maintain one-way blood flow, and distends the veins in the face, neck, and eyes. It is a gruesome injury that is typically lethal, with death occurring in minutes.

We tend to think of chest trauma in terms of urban circumstances (car crashes, industrial accidents) but many chest injuries, including several of the unusual ones on this page, happen in the wilderness, too.

Automated External Defibrillator

Many heart attacks are the result of irregular heartbeats, ventricular fibrillation (VF). When cardiac arrest is caused by VF, a machine known as a defibrillator can deliver an electrical shock that disrupts or stops this irregular, lethal rhythm, allowing the heart to spontaneously develop an effective rhythm of its own. The sooner a patient in cardiac arrest caused by ventricular fibrillation receives a shock, the greater the chances for survival.

Public Access Defibrillators (PAD)

In an effort to increase survival rates, PAD programs are in place across the country and around the world. PADs can be found at airports, malls, sporting events, etc.

BLS | defibrillation | time is essential

1. Perform primary survey to confirm the patient is in cardiac arrest.
2. Begin CPR. If two or more rescuers are available, one performs CPR while the other obtains, prepares and attaches the defibrillator to the patient. The sooner the patient is **defibrillated** the greater the chance of success.
3. Follow the instructions to place pads and the defibrillator's prompts

   ■ "Stop CPR"—All rescue efforts cease while the machine analyzes.

   ■ "Stand back"—All persons must clear themselves of contact with the patient to allow the machine to deliver a shock of 200 joules of energy.

   ■ "Shock"—The machine may require you to push the "Shock" button.

4. Immediately restart CPR and recheck for pulse after 2 minutes of CPR.

   ■ If a pulse is present:
      1. Leave the machine attached to monitor the condition.
      2. Maintain an open airway and continue life-support procedures.
      3. Assist with ventilations if needed.

   ■ If no pulse:
      1. Leave the machine attached.
      2. Continue CPR.
      3. After 2 minutes the AED will prompt you to "Stop CPR" and will analyze the rhythm and advise if shock is needed.

5. Continue the process until further help arrives.

Cardiothoracic trauma

SYMPTOM
gamut

symptoms listed in order of <u>decreasing</u> frequency

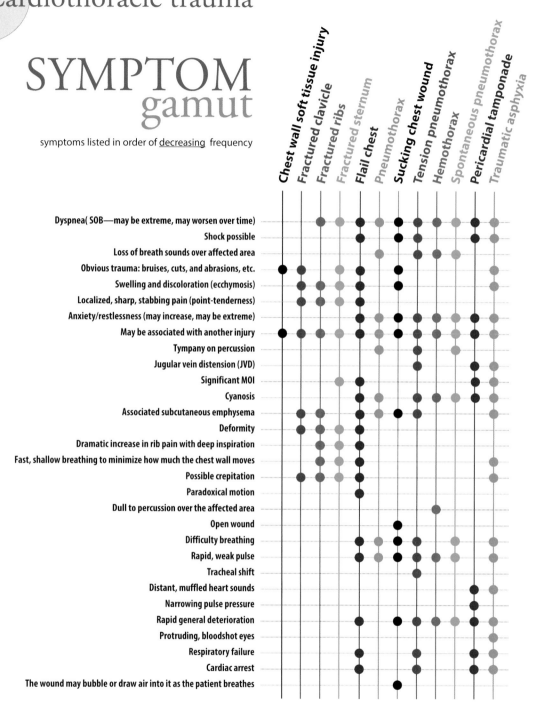

Column headers:
Chest wall soft tissue injury · Fractured clavicle · Fractured ribs · Fractured sternum · Flail chest · Pneumothorax · Sucking chest wound · Tension pneumothorax · Hemothorax · Spontaneous pneumothorax · Pericardial tamponade · Traumatic asphyxia

Symptoms (rows):
- Dyspnea (SOB—may be extreme, may worsen over time)
- Shock possible
- Loss of breath sounds over affected area
- Obvious trauma: bruises, cuts, and abrasions, etc.
- Swelling and discoloration (ecchymosis)
- Localized, sharp, stabbing pain (point-tenderness)
- Anxiety/restlessness (may increase, may be extreme)
- May be associated with another injury
- Tympany on percussion
- Jugular vein distension (JVD)
- Significant MOI
- Cyanosis
- Associated subcutaneous emphysema
- Deformity
- Dramatic increase in rib pain with deep inspiration
- Fast, shallow breathing to minimize how much the chest wall moves
- Possible crepitation
- Paradoxical motion
- Dull to percussion over the affected area
- Open wound
- Difficulty breathing
- Rapid, weak pulse
- Tracheal shift
- Distant, muffled heart sounds
- Narrowing pulse pressure
- Rapid general deterioration
- Protruding, bloodshot eyes
- Respiratory failure
- Cardiac arrest
- The wound may bubble or draw air into it as the patient breathes

NOTE: *pulmonary contusion, pulmonary laceration, myocardial contusion, traumatic aortic rupture, and impaled object have been left off the symptom and treatment charts. These first four are unusual (if not downright rare), nearly impossible to diagnose in the field, and cannot be readily treated. The symptoms and treatment for the last, impaled object, are obvious.*

WILDCARE™

Cardiothoracic trauma

TREATMENT gamut

treatments listed by order of care (i.e., ABCs to evacuation)

Conditions (columns):
- Chest wall soft tissue injury
- Fractured clavicle
- Fractured ribs
- Fractured sternum
- Flail chest
- Pneumothorax
- Sucking chest wound
- Tension pneumothorax
- Hemothorax
- Spontaneous pneumothorax
- Pericardial tamponade
- Traumatic asphyxia

Treatments (rows):
- Ensure and maintain adequate airway
- Administer 100% O₂ via non-rebreather mask for SOB
- May require assisted ventilations with BVM if distress or failure occurs
- Assist breathe with positive-pressure ventilations (mouth-to-mask if no BVM)
- Control bleeding (direct pressure)
- Look for an exit wound and treat as necessary
- Apply occlusive dressing (leave one side open as a valve—"burp" as necessary)
- Sling and swathe affected side
- Monitor for signs of potential lung/heart injuries
- Monitor shoulder/neck for swelling/discoloration (subq. emphysema)
- Monitor breathing and breath sounds for signs of pneumothorax
- Monitor for worsening dyspnea (SOB)
- Monitor vital signs and cardiac rhythm (EKG or rhythm strip)
- Treat for shock
- Prepare to do CPR
- Needle thoracotomy (if qualified and prepared)
- Beware of administering narcotics (may reduce respiratory effort)
- Place in position of comfort (maximizes respiratory effort)
- Evacuate for SOB or if there are indications of deeper lung injuries
- Evacuate (if not ambulatory, in position of comfort—typically sitting)
- Evacuate rapidly ASAP in position of comfort

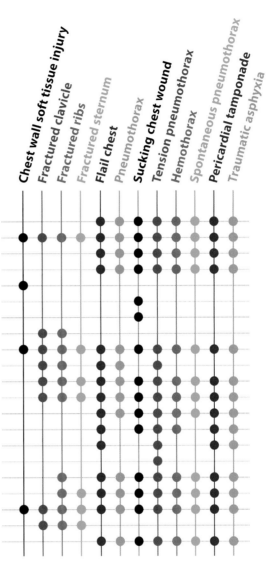

pelvis trauma

THE PELVIS is the lowest portion of the axial skeleton comprised of three bones (ilium, ischium, sacrum) that form a circular bowl that supports and protects the internal urinary, digestive, and reproductive organs. The sacrum forms the foundation for the spine while the ilium and ischium house the ball-and-socket joint for the upper terminus of the femur. The pelvis is richly lined with blood vessels which can be easily torn when a fracture occurs.

{ A fractured pelvis is considered a life-threatening injury because of the risk of internal bleeding and/or direct trauma to an internal organ. }

AN OPEN-BOOK pelvic fracture occurs when the pelvis is broken in two or more places, resulting in the pelvis falling open when the patient is supine (on their back).

REVIEW THE MOI
- The pelvis is usually injured by direct impact (e.g., a fall), or compression (e.g., being run over by a vehicle).
- Pain and guarding are likely.
- The patient will typically be in severe pain and unable to walk.
- The patient will generally prefer to lie still and will not be willing to move their legs, sit up, or roll side-to-side.

spine

sacrum

ilium

ischium

femur

- There are approximately 120,000 pelvic fractures reported in the US annually: of these, about 21,000 are open book fractures.
- An open book fracture has about a 25% mortality rate due to blood loss and the resulting hypovolemic shock.
- Typically, 2 – 3 units of blood are lost at the fracture site.

WILDCARE™

PHYSICAL EXAM

1. With the patient lying on their back, gently compress the lateral surfaces of the ilium downward, as if opening a book.
2. Then try to press the lateral surfaces of the ilium together, as if closing a book.
3. If the pelvis shifts during the open/close tests, or if the exam elicits pain, assume an open book fracture—**Do not let go**. Hold the pelvis closed until a pelvic binder can be applied or improvised. **A fractured pelvis should only be moved once** to minimize internal bleeding.
4. To test the hip: **Flex**, **Abduct**, and **Externally rotate** (FABER)—pain with the abduction and external rotation indicates injury to the hip joint.

TREATMENT

ANTISHOCK GARMENTS (MAST/PASG)

1. When you move the patient, do so very gently and as a unit while supporting the pelvis.
2. Use MAST/PASG or pneumatic antishock garments, if available. In addition to stabilizing the pelvis, they will help compress the abdominal contents, minimizing internal blood loss. The antishock garments don't have to be fully inflated, they only have to be inflated enough to support the pelvis and the patient. With this injury, internal bleeding can be severe enough to send the victim into hypovolemic shock.
3. Monitor distal pulses in the legs and use heat packs on the feet in winter to prevent frostbite. The inflated garment does stabilize the pelvis and tamponade bleeding very well, but it may also decrease circulation to the lower legs and feet.

SAM SLING

This is a commercial pelvic splint consisting of a broad band of padded material that fits around the pelvis and is adjusted to close an open book fracture and support the pelvis. It will automatically adjust the tension of the splint to the optimal pressure of 33 pounds,

IMPROVISED PELVIC BINDER

If commercial devices are not available, you can improvise a pelvic binder by folding a sheet or blanket 4" – 8" wide, or using a piece of foam pad, wrapping it around the pelvis, and then tying it in place circumferentially. The ties (webbing, cord, belts, strips of fabric, etc.) must be tight enough to close and support the pelvis, but not so tight that the fracture sites overlap, which can cause pain and bleeding.

1. Tie the legs together with padding between them.
2. Surround the pelvis with the wide material and the ties.
3. With your hands on the sides of the pelvis, gently close the pelvis until it feels tight. Adjust the tension on the ties to hold the pelvis in that position.
4. In the long-term care setting, you should also gently wrap the abdomen with two 6-inch-wide elastic bandages to shrink the potential space for blood to collect if internal bleeding occurs.
5. Treat for shock.
6. Administer oxygen, if available.
7. Provide a bolus of IV fluid for shock if indicated and available.
8. Monitor vital signs every 15 minutes.
9. Evacuate ASAP—transport the patient flat on their back with their knees slightly flexed for comfort.

abdominal

ABDOMINAL ANATOMY

- *Hollow organs*—these organs are most prone to penetrating trauma, and if they spill their contents into the gut, it can be very irritating and increase the risk of infection.
  - Small and large intestines
  - Bladder
  - Gallbladder
  - Stomach
- *Solid organs*—these are most prone to blunt trauma leading to blood loss.
  - Kidneys
  - Liver
  - Pancreas
  - Spleen

SIGNS AND SYMPTOMS OF ABDOMINAL TRAUMA

- Shock, from internal bleeding
- Abdominal wall rigidity (a reaction to the internal bleeding)
- Guarding, spasm of the abdominal wall muscles
- Distention from internal bleeding
- Obvious external trauma, wounds, and/or bruising
- Referred pain—pain may be referred to other areas, e.g., from the spleen to the left shoulder

GENERAL TREATMENT

1. Treat for shock.
2. Wrap abdomen with two 6-inch elastic bandages to apply counter-pressure.
3. Immobilize any penetrating objects.
4. Look for associated thoracic or genitourinary injuries.
5. Minimize food and water intake.

SPECIFIC TREATMENT FOR INTERNAL BLEEDING

Internal bleeding occurs when there is damage to the vascular system inside the body but with no open wounds. The most common internal bleeding occurs when blunt trauma to the abdomen (e.g., from direct impact from a fall or auto accident) results in damage to any of the internal organs.

1. Once bleeding is recognized, gentle pressure can be applied by the use of MAST/PASG devices or by wrapping the abdomen with two six-inch ACE wraps to gently compress the abdominal cavity (see pelvic trauma). This will decrease the potential space for the blood to accumulate and will apply counter-pressure to the torn vessels, slowing blood loss and allowing clots to form.

INJURIES TO EXTERNAL GENITALIA

- *Impact injuries*
  1. Examine for swelling or bleeding.
  2. Control bleeding with direct pressure.
  3. Apply cold to minimize swelling.
  4. Evacuate.
- *Lacerations*
  1. Control bleeding with direct pressure.
  2. Evacuate.
- *Burns*
  1. Cool immediately and keep cool.
  2. Apply a wet, sterile dressing.
  3. Evacuate.
- *Avulsions and amputations*
  1. Control bleeding with direct pressure.
  2. Save amputated part.
  3. Evacuate.
- *Impaled objects*
  1. Leave object in place.
  2. Stabilize with sterile dressing
  3. Evacuate.
- *Torsion of the testes:* This occurs when the spermatic cord to a testicle twists, cutting off the blood supply.
  Signs and symptoms
    - Sudden onset.
    - Swollen, red, painful scrotum—pain increases over time.
  Treatment
    1. Apply cool compress.
    2. Give pain meds.
    3. Support the testes.
    4. Evacuate (testes may die within 24 hours).

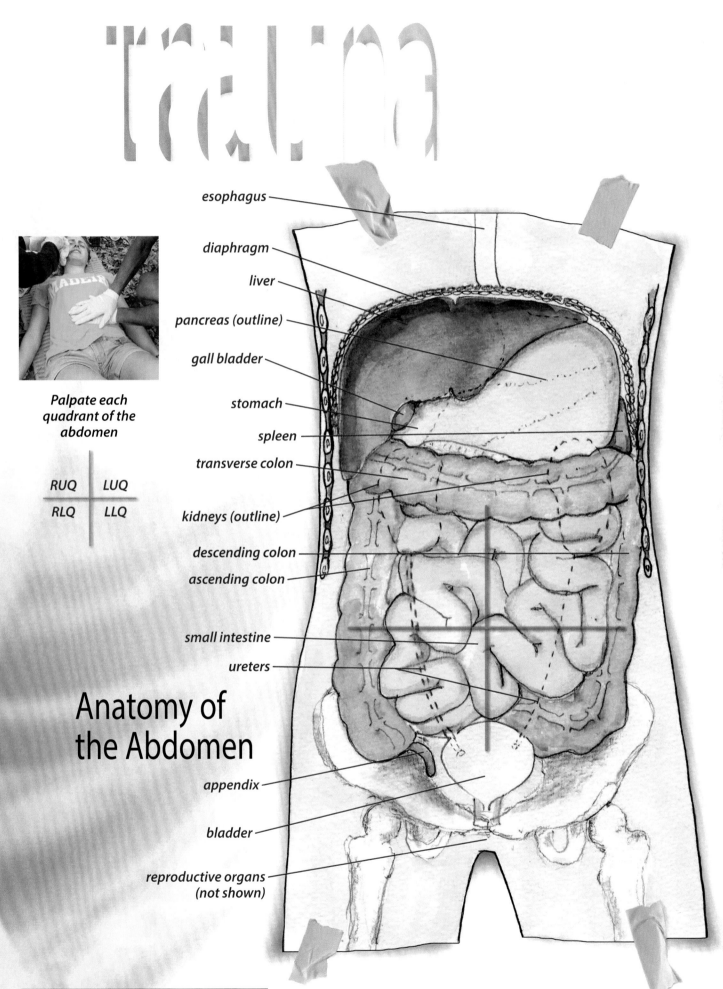

Trauma

esophagus

diaphragm

liver

pancreas (outline)

gall bladder

stomach

spleen

transverse colon

kidneys (outline)

descending colon

ascending colon

small intestine

ureters

appendix

bladder

reproductive organs
(not shown)

**Palpate each
quadrant of the
abdomen**

RUQ	LUQ
RLQ	LLQ

Anatomy of
the Abdomen

Crush Injuries

A crush injury occurs when part of the body is trapped between two solid objects and subjected to enough force to "crush" the tissues. The resulting injury can cause damage to the skin, supporting soft tissues, muscles, nerves, vasculature, and bones. The severity of the crush injury depends upon the forces involved, the quantity of tissue damaged, and the duration of entrapment—the more damage and the longer the entrapment, the more risk there is for long-term damage. This type of injury is an unusual wilderness injury, but a common disaster-related injury that occurs when buildings, bridges, and other structures collapse during earthquakes, floods, tornadoes, etc. The process of extricating the patient can take hours, and the longer the injured body part remains trapped and compressed, the more pronounced the long-term deleterious effects will be, not only to the crushed tissue, but more importantly, to the patient as a whole. Crush injuries can be life-threatening, even days after the initial injury (see bottom right).

SHORT-TERM TREATMENT

1. Manage the ABCs: Maintain a patent airway, monitor breathing, control bleeding.
2. Safely extricate the patient and the trapped body part (and control any additional bleeding).
3. Stabilize fractures.
4. Control pain.
5. Maintain core temperature.
6. Treat for shock.
7. Early systemic support of fluid volume and blood pressure will help to preserve life and protect the kidneys.

LONG-TERM TREATMENT

Long-term care/treatment can be complicated by kidney failure. The goal is to maximize renal function and minimize the risk of kidney failure secondary to the accumulation of the myoglobin proteins in the glomerulus of the kidneys. This requires adequate fluid volume to keep the urine dilute and to help ensure an appropriate blood pressure of 90mmHg systolic or higher to maintain circulation to the glomerulus.

*Man versus snowmobile**

A classic crush injury; the impact point is mid-calf (◉) and it took weeks to heal. Remarkably, the calf was the only injured part—gravity pulled blood that leaked from the crushed tissue down into the <u>uninjured</u> ankle (●).

Fluids can be given three different ways, orally, intravenously, or rectally.

- If the patient can tolerate taking fluids orally, great; if not, the next best option is by intravenous infusion.
- If IV fluids are not available or IV access cannot be established, fluids can be given per rectum, as they will be absorbed through the mucosal wall of the colon (the colon's job is to reabsorb fluids used in the digestive process).
- Adding small quantities of sugar and salt will aid in the absorption of fluids from the bowel.

Fluid requirement is based on urine output.

- A patient at rest with adequate hydration should produce a urine volume close to the amount of fluid intake. In the hospital, fluid intake and output is monitored.
- To remain healthy and get rid of the waste products produced by metabolism, minimal daily production of urine is 500cc (approximately 20cc/hour)—although normal daily urine production is 1,400cc (60cc/hour).
- To prevent kidney failure with crush injuries, maintain adequate urine production of at least 100cc per hour.
- If the kidneys are not working properly, the fluid going in will begin to accumulate in tissues, resulting in edema—the patient will quickly become edematous and can develop pulmonary edema.

The owner of this leg is the editor of this book—although happy to help, he declined to demonstrate a skull fracture (what a wimp).

LONG-TERM CONCERNS

The potential long-term consequence of crush injuries result in rhabdomyolysis—the release of large quantities of proteins from the damaged tissues into systemic circulation. The direct force of the crush injury and the extended hypoxia due to lack of circulation causes the affected muscle tissues to die. These dead tissues will begin to break down and release muscle proteins called myoglobins into the circulation, once circulation is re-established. This is a gradual process that continues over several days. The myoglobin proteins are large proteins and as the blood is filtered through the glomerulus of the kidneys, these proteins can plug up the filters, causing kidney failure. Long-term risks associated with crush injuries include:

1. *Significant blood loss and resulting hypovolemic shock.*
2. *Significant tissue loss requiring surgery or amputation.*
3. *Rhabdomyolysis from the tissue damage which can cause blockage of the glomerulus and kidney failure.*

In 1989, Buck Helm was rescued after 90 hours crushed beneath the earthquake wreckage of Interstate 880 in California...he died <u>22 days</u> later (organ failure).

COMPARTMENT SYNDROME

Physiology

- Each group of muscles is surrounded by a tough fibrous protective layer of fascia called the myofascial layer. This fibrous layer is flexible but not expandable.
- If there is bleeding within a muscle (such as can occur with a crush injury) the muscle compartment will become pressurized.
- The arterial pressure is higher (100 – 120mmHg) while the venous pressure is lower (5 – 10mmHg).
- As the pressure increases, due to compression, the venous circulation will shut off, but the arteries will continue to pump —blood is getting in, but not leaving.
- Eventually ischemia will result.
- This causes extreme swelling, tension, and pain.

Fasciotomy

In acute cases of compartment syndrome, surgery is required. A fasciotomy is a limb-saving procedure where the fascia is cut to relieve tension or pressure and help restore circulation. While it may appear extreme (above), it has a very high success rate. Once the swelling goes down the wound can be closed successfully (sometimes requiring a graft, above).

People likely to suffer injuries requiring a fasciotomy include :

- *Victims of motor vehicle accidents.*
- *Athletes who have sustained one or more serious impact injuries.*
- *People with severe crush injuries.*
- *People with severe burns.*
- *People who are severely overweight.*

Description

- Compartment syndrome is defined as the compression of nerves, blood vessels, and muscle inside a closed space (compartment) within the body.
- It leads to tissue death due to lack of oxygenation as the blood vessels are compressed by the raised pressure within the compartment.
- Compartment syndrome rarely occurs acutely because it is caused by pressure building up in the muscle compartments—which takes time.
- It is most commonly associated with crush injuries of the extremities—especially in the lower leg.

Treatment

- Prevention is key.
- When a crush injury occurs, make a wide ACE wrap over the injured extremity as part of the splinting process. This provides gentle compression, helping to minimize pressure build-up.
- Monitor circulation and sensation distal to the site of the injury.
- If, over the next several hours, compartment syndrome appears to be developing (swelling, tightness, pain):
  1. Elevate the extremity.
  2. Re-wrap the ACE with more compression.
  3. Cool the extremity with cold water or ice.
  4. Evacuate immediately—this is becoming a surgical emergency (see left).

SECTION 3

Changes in Level of Consciousness

Shortness of breath

Chest pain

Acute abdomen

MEDICAL EMERGENCIES

When something is certainly wrong, but you're not sure what . . .

MEDICAL EMERGENCIES

No, there's nothing wrong with your eyes—that headline is fuzzy.
In fact, this whole section is fuzzy.

There's no blood oozing, no bones sticking out, nothing burned or frozen.

You don't have to hold c-spine, apply pressure to a dripping wound,
snug up bandages, pull traction, or apply heat packs.

Instead of watching a snowboarder smack a tree (obvious trauma), you find an
otherwise normal guy slumped by the side of the trail, moaning softly.

"Hey buddy, excuse me, you okay?"

"What? Huh? Oh, I don't know. I just feel weird."

"Um . . ."

Okay, it's time to do some . . .

sleuthing

\\'slüth\\ (verb or transitive verb): the
act of carrying out a search or investigation, to gather
facts, to discover the meaning of or the cause of what is wrong.

Trauma is obvious: there is clear MOI (a big fall), a specific chief complaint (*"MY LEG!"*), and the problem can be quickly isolated with a hands-on exam.

Medical emergencies are more vague: there is no obvious MOI, no "snap-and-twist" chief complaint, and a physical exam may not reveal much—it's more like:

"Look, you're the doc—I just don't feel very ducky, okay."

The **patient interview** is key . . .

EXPLORE THE CHIEF COMPLAINT (C/C)

Common Chief Complaints (C/C) associated with a medical emergency:

- **A change in level of consciousness (LOC)**—neurologic
- **Shortness of breath (SOB)**—respiratory
- **Chest pain**—cardiovascular
- **Acute abdomen**—digestive/genitourinary

MAKE A DIFFERENTIAL DIAGNOSIS

The possibilities associated with the C/C:

- **A change in LOC**—hypoxia, poison, diabetes, seizure, stroke, behavioral, fever
- **Shortness of breath**—asthma, COPD/emphysema, pulmonary emboli, lung disorders (pulmonary edema, spontaneous pneumothorax, hyperventilation syndrome)
- **Chest pain**—coronary artery disease (angina, acute MI, hypertension), congestive heart failure, indigestion/acid reflux
- **Acute abdomen**—constipation, bowel obstruction, gallstones/kidney stones, peritonitis, genitourinary emergencies

HISTORY OF PRESENT ILLNESS AND AMPLE HISTORY

The question sequence to explore the C/C
The patient's current and past medical history } Please see the Secondary Assessment section in the front of the book.

For medical emergencies, this is your best friend

hey, my level of consciousness . . .

PERSON WITH A

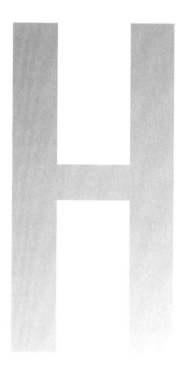

presents one of the most disconcerting and challenging problems in emergency medicine. In an urban setting, the standard is to maintain the airway, place the patient in a safe position, give oxygen, transport immediately, and do your best to try to find out what's going on. Fortunately, the patient will typically not deteriorate much more during the trip to the emergency department. This is one of the few areas where there may not be a lot that can be done in the prehospital setting, but early recognition and rapid transport can and will save brain cells.

By contrast, in the extended-care environment, with prolonged evacuation times, there is ample opportunity for the patient to get worse. To make things even harder, there may be little or no clue as to the underlying cause of their change in level of consciousness (obvious trauma or a cardiac event aside), and the patient may not be able to provide you with a chief complaint or medical history.

To be able to appreciate the various threats to our mental status, and to discern what happened and where the problem is, requires an understanding of the normal physiology and function of the human brain; familiarity with brain structure, circulation, metabolism, and the role of cerebral spinal fluid is crucial to recognizing, diagnosing, and managing some of the most difficult problems in medicine: the neurological emergencies. We will often refer you to other places in this book for additional and supporting information.

DETERIORATING LOC

AND THE PROBLEM TYPICALLY STARTS WITH THE LETTER

H

doesn't, um . . . feel so good . . . z z z

HYPOXIA
Too little oxygen getting to the brain—lack of O_2, poor O_2 exchange, heart failure, hypovolemia, cellular metabolic failure

HYPOGLYCEMIA & HYPERGLYCEMIA
Too little or too much blood glucose—diabetes

HYPOACTIVITY & HYPERACTIVITY
Too little or too much neuronal activity in the brain—seizures

HALLUCINATIONS
Illness (fever), abuse (alcohol, drugs), environmental emergencies, or trauma (esp. head) leading to behavior issues

HEAD TRAUMA
increasing intracranial pressure (ICP)—covered in the Trauma section

HYPOTHERMIA & HYPERTHERMIA
Too cold to think or too hot to function—covered in the Environmental Emergencies section

It's amazing what misery can come from trouble inside our little melon brains—please refer to the Critical Care section for a good overview of all the problems that begin with the letter H.

On to the details

Heart failure

Hypoxia in this situation is caused by the heart failing to beat with enough force to maintain blood flow to the brain and other vital tissues. Specifically, we are talking about an Acute Myocardial Infarction (AMI)—the classic heart attack. As the heart muscles fail, the strength of contractions and cardiac output decrease, resulting in decreased oxygen delivery to the brain and other vital tissues.

Along with the symptoms of hypoxia and the sensation of shortness of breath, the patient may also be complaining of chest pain, with radiating pain into the jaw, left shoulder and arm, abdominal pain, nausea, or a chest tightness. However, an acute MI may not have any chest pain; the only symptom may be the sensation of shortness of breath, anxiety, or a feeling of impending doom.

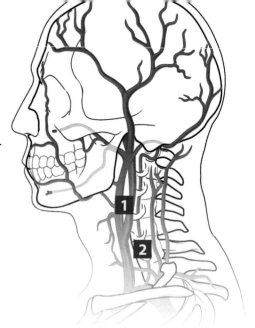

Cranial circulation is critical to life, and impairing it can lead quickly to unconsciousness, permanent damage, and death. The principle arteries are the carotids (1) and the vertebral (2).

Hypovolemia

Hypovolemia causes hypoxia because there is not enough blood volume to carry oxygen to the brain and other vital tissues. Hypovolemic shock results from a decrease in total blood volume, and the causes include blood loss, extended vomiting, diarrhea, dehydration, or thermal burns—the principle cause is often obvious. Hypovolemia victims show all the classic signs and symptoms of shock.

TREATMENT

The treatments for hypoxia are nearly universal, regardless of cause (for cyanide poisoning, see the specific additional treatment in that section, at left).

1 If you are dealing with an anoxic environment (i.e., you suspect poisonous gas), do not enter without proper equipment or until the area is well ventilated.

2 Remove the patient from the anoxic environment.

3 Maintain an open, patent airway—place the patient in the recovery position, if necessary.

4 If the patient's RR is <10 or >30 respirations per minute, administer high-flow O_2 and/or give artificial respirations. Even if a person is breathing well, if they are cyanotic you must provide oxygen.

5 If the patient is in cardiac arrest, perform CPR and Advanced Cardiac Life Support (ACLS).

6 Evacuate to definitive care.

Cellular Metabolic Failure

This is hypoxia caused by oxygen not being used up at a cellular level and an example is cyanide poisoning. Cyanide is an inhaled poison that blocks the use of oxygen at the cellular level. This is an unlikely wilderness etiology of hypoxia; however, this could occur in a disaster or terrorist setting. When inhaled, cyanide gas finds its way into each individual cell, where it disrupts oxidative phosphorylation and halts the production of high energy phosphate compounds (ATP). Since ATP is the chemical that we use to supply energy for other physiological processes, such as muscle contraction, the resulting cellular death can have devastating consequences. By preventing the existing oxygen in cells from being utilized, the oxygen will remain bound to the hemoglobin in the red blood cells, creating the odd situation of having maximum oxygen saturation, but no oxygen availability—people with cyanide poisoning will have very red skin.

TREATMENT

▶ The treatment protocols differ for cyanide poisoning than for other inhaled toxins. Cyanide smells like almonds, and this may be the only hint that you are in a toxic atmosphere.

▶ Do not expose yourself—you must have proper protective equipment to enter the cyanide gas area.

▶ This is one of the few emergencies that has to be managed prehospital. There is not enough time to transport the patient to the ER and make a difference.

▶ Cyanide poisoning is treated with a Cyanokit®—IV hydroxocobalamin (vitamin B-12), and oxygen.

POISON

Poisoning ranks second to motor vehicle accidents as a cause of unintentional injury death in the US—and among people 25 to 64 it is the leading cause of death (with over 90% of cases involving drugs).

General treatment

1. Verify that the scene is safe—especially important in cases of airborne poisons, e.g., CO_2, CO, cyanide, methane, chlorine, sarin, soman.

2. Identify the poison—what was the substance?

3. Identify the exposure method:
   ▶ Ingested
   ▶ Inhaled
   ▶ Airborne
   ▶ Injected

4. Identify the time of the poisoning:
   ▶ When were they exposed?
   ▶ How long have they been exposed?

5. Identify the dose:
   ▶ How much were they exposed to?
   ▶ How much did they take?

6. Determine the patient's last food and drink:
   ▶ What did they last eat or drink?
   ▶ How much did they last eat or drink?
   ▶ When did they last eat or drink?

7. Find out if alcohol or drugs was involved.

8. Get a physical description:
   ▶ Gender
   ▶ Age
   ▶ Size (obese?)

9. Determine the cause:
   ▶ Was the poisoning accidental or deliberate?
   ▶ Was it a suicide attempt?

10. Call the emergency department and give them all the information.

11. Call the poison control center and give them all the information.

12. Follow their instructions until help arrives.

INGESTED (most common)

INHALED (airborne)

ABSORBED (skin)

INJECTED (envenomation/needle)

Specific Treatment

INGESTED Drugs are most common.

1. Activated charcoal is the preferred treatment. It comes pre-mixed. Typical dose is 25 – 50ml.
2. Dilute the poison with water or milk.

INHALED e.g., CO_2, CO (most common), methane, chlorine, cyanide.

1. Ensure scene safety.
2. Remove the patient from the exposure.
3. Administer high-flow O_2 via non-rebreather or positive-pressure ventilations.

ABSORBED e.g., organophosphates, DEET

This can be a HAZMAT scene—be especially aware of pesticides. **SLUDGEM** (mnemonic for nerve agent poisoning: salivation, lacrimation, urination, defecation, gastrointestinal upset, emesis, miosis)

1. Ensure scene safety.
2. Remove the poison.
3. Remove any contaminated clothing.
4. Immediately decontaminate the patient with soap and water.

INJECTED e.g., reptile/insect envenomations (see Bites & Stings), drug overdose

1. Scrub and clean any obvious wounds.
2. Lightly wrap the wound site proximally with an elastic bandage.
3. Immobilize the extremity.
4. Monitor for signs of anaphylaxis and be prepared to treat it.

Number of people who die from unintentional poisoning each day in the US: **87**

Number of poisoning-related ED visits in 2010: **>830,000**

Number of calls to poison control centers in 2010: **2.4 million**

Men are **twice** as likely to die from unintentional poisoning than women. Among children, ED visits for medication poisonings (excluding misuse or abuse) are **twice** as common as poisonings from household products (e.g., cleaning solutions).

American Indians/Alaska Natives had the **highest death rate**, followed by whites and then blacks.

In 2005, poisonings cost **$33.4 billion** in medical and productivity costs.
* source: CDC

Diabetes is a group of diseases in which a person has a high blood glucose level, either because their pancreas does not produce enough insulin, or because the cells in their body don't respond properly to the insulin that is produced. Diabetes decreases the glucose supply to the cells and causes cellular starvation. While diabetes can typically be controlled by careful dietary monitoring and medication, emergency situations can still arise, and they can be serious, even life-threatening.

Key definitions

Insulin A hormone (beta islet cells of Langerhans) produced by the pancreas that transports glucose from the blood into the cells. Insulin lowers the blood sugar level.

Glucagon A hormone (alpha islet cells of Langerhans) produced by the pancreas which stimulates the release of stored glucose (glycogen) in the liver (glycogenolysis). Glucagon raises the blood sugar level.

Blood glucose level The amount of glucose in the blood. Blood glucose is measured by a glucometer. The level of blood glucose increases after a meal, then decreases as glucose is used by the cells.

Hyperglycemia Decreased insulin production results in high glucose levels in the blood and low levels in the cells.

Hypoglycemia Excess insulin production creates low glucose levels in the blood and low levels in the cells.

Normal physiology

1. As food is consumed carbohydrates are broken down into glucose molecules.
2. Glucose is absorbed into the bloodstream, elevating blood glucose levels (glycemia).
3. The rise in glycemia stimulates the pancreas to secrete insulin from its beta cells.
4. Insulin binds to specific cell receptors and facilitates entry of glucose into the cells: mitochondria uses O_2 to burn glucose and the resulting energy is used to produce adenosine triphosphate (ATP)—which transports chemical energy within the cells for metabolism.
5. As the pancreas secretes insulin and the cells burn glucose, the blood glucose levels in the blood decrease—which results in decreased insulin secretion.
6. This cycle repeats as a constantly self-adjusting metabolic balance: creating, storing, and releasing energy.

Sugars (dietary monosaccharides: glucose, fructose and galactose), are absorbed directly into the bloodstream during digestion and provide the fuel for life. Everything we eat is processed by the body and broken down into the simple sugars that drive metabolism—it's a delicate balance, and when things get out of whack, bad stuff can happen.

We often think sugar looks like the cubes at left ...but it really looks like this weird thing.

The diabetic's physiology

 AKA: Juvenile Onset or Insulin Dependent diabetes

- The immune system destroys the pancreas's insulin-producing cells—little or no insulin is produced.
- Insulin injections are a lifelong necessity to control blood sugar—without supplemental insulin Type I diabetes will eventually be fatal.
- It tends to occur at a young age (as a child or young adult).
- About 5% of all diebetics have Type I.
- Symptoms: increased urination (the body is attempting to get rid of excess blood sugar) and accompanying increased thirst, increased hunger (the cells are starving because of limited glucose), fatigue and weakness, blurred vision (elevated blood sugar causes the lenses of the eyes to swell).

 AKA: Adult Onset or Non Insulin Dependent diabetes

- The pancreas loses it's ability to effectively produce and release insulin.
- The body becomes resistant to insulin and blood sugar levels rise.
- Onset is later in life and can be linked to lifestyle/behavior choices (e.g., obesity, alcoholism).
- Typically managed with oral hypoglycemics, which lower blood sugar—Type II may not require insulin injections.
- About 95% of all diabetics have Type II.
- Symptoms (many are similar to Type I): increased urination, thirst, and hunger, fatigue, blurred vision, weight gain, frequent infections (e.g., UTI), slow healing of cuts or sores (there is little fuel for repairs).

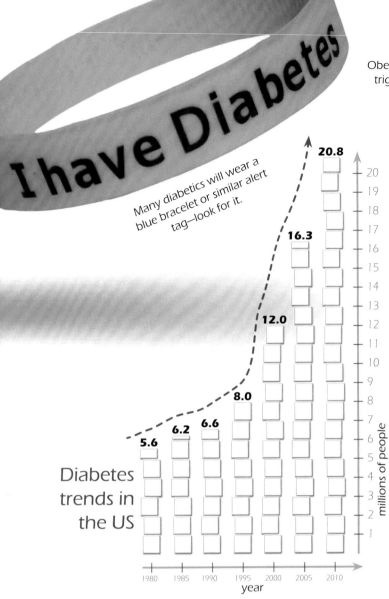

I have Diabetes

Many diabetics will wear a blue bracelet or similar alert tag—look for it.

Obesity is a primary trigger for Type II diabetes.

Diabetes trends in the US

millions of people

year

5.6 (1980)
6.2 (1985)
6.6 (1990)
8.0 (1995)
12.0 (2000)
16.3 (2005)
20.8 (2010)

Long-term effects

- Coronary heart disease
- An increased risk of acute MI
- Peripheral Vascular Disease with an increased risk of amputation
- Loss of vision due to retinal vascular problems
- Numbness and tingling (paresthesia) in the hands or feet due to nerve damage
- Sexual dysfunction

Diabetes diagnosis

- Diagnosis is based on blood glucose levels..
- Monitoring fasting blood sugar (FBS), and checking the response to a blood glucose challenge, also known as a glucose tolerance test (GTT).
- Fasting Blood Glucose
  Normal Glucose Tolerance: 70 – 99mg/dl
  Impaired Glucose Tolerance (pre-diabetes): 100 – 125mg/dl
  Diabetes: greater than 126mg/dl
- Oral Glucose Tolerance Test: Fasting blood sugar and a blood sugar check at two hours
  Normal Glucose Tolerance: less than 140mg/dl
  Impaired Glucose Tolerance (pre-diabetes): 140 - 200mg/dl
  Diabetes: greater than 200m/dl
- A second blood test, called a hemoglobin A1c (HgA1c), is also done. This will tell the average glucose level of the past several months.

Basic treatment

- Primary treatment goal: maintain tight control of blood sugar to minimize the long-term risk of diabetes and the risk of diabetic emergencies.
- Balancing blood sugar:

1. Food and diet—counting carbohydrates.
2. Exercise—increase physical activity to help achieve and maintain a healthy weight.
3. Oral medications and/or insulin.
4. Daily blood glucose testing.

Diabetic emergencies

- Diabetic emergencies occur primarily in diabetics that are insulin-dependent (Type I). Due to their dependency upon injectable insulin, they can find themselves with either too much or too little blood glucose.
- The organ that is most affected by too little blood sugar is the brain.
- The level of consciousness and the ability of the brain to function normally is dependent upon oxygen, glucose, temperature, pressure, and neuronal activity. Altering the proper levels of any one of these factors will result in a change in Level of Consciousness.
- Without a glucometer to determine the blood glucose level, the ability to differentiate between hyperglycemia and hypoglycemia can be difficult. Fortunately, emergency care for both conditions is the same until the blood glucose level is determined.

Hyperglycemic? Hypoglycemic? Or merely napping? Yeah, probably napping—but you can't tell just by looking. A change (deterioration) in LOC is a classic sign of a diabetic emergency.

Hyperglycemia

Hyperglycemia is elevated blood glucose due to lack of available insulin—also known as diabetic coma or diabetic ketoacidosis (DKA). There are two primary causes:

- The patient has not taken their insulin
- The patient has an infection such as a UTI or kidney infection that prevents the absorption and proper utilization of injectable insulin.

Signs/symptoms

The onset is gradual, over a period of 12 – 72 hours.
Food intake may have been excessive, but that does not have to be the case.
Hunger is usually minimal because the blood glucose is elevated.
Thirst (polydipsia) is intense, and as a result, the patient will be voiding frequently to try to pee off the excess blood glucose.
Signs of dehydration caused by the excessive urination: skin tenting, dry mucous membranes, tachycardia, hypotension, nausea, vomiting, and abdominal pain.

Change in Level of Consciousness—the patient may be irritable to combative, have slurred speech, an unsteady gait, and have the smell of alcohol (acetone) on their breath—they may appear drunk.

Vital signs

LOC: Altered LOC—may appear drunk or may be unconscious and unresponsive.
RR : As LOC deteriorates, the patient will develop deep, sighing respirations (Kussmaul's breathing). You may notice a sweet fruity or "alcohol" odor on their breath (acetone breath).

HR: Their pulse becomes weak and thready (hypovolemic shock)
BP: Low blood pressure (hypovolemic shock)
Skin: May be pale, cool, and clammy (hypovolemic shock)
Blood glucose level by glucometer will be elevated, >300 and usually >400mg/dl

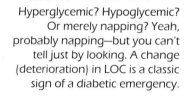

A glucometer is a daily tool for those who manage diabetes.

> **"Diabetes is one of the most costly and burdensome chronic diseases of our time and is a condition that is increasing in epidemic proportions in the U.S. and throughout the world."**
>
> —American Diabetes Association

Projected % rise in seven of the most common chronic diseases, 2003 – 2023

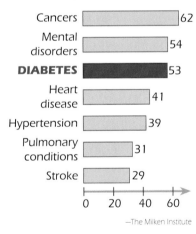

Cancers	62
Mental disorders	54
DIABETES	53
Heart disease	41
Hypertension	39
Pulmonary conditions	31
Stroke	29

0   20   40   60

—The Milken Institute

Diabetes $$$

2007: $174 billion

2012: $245 billion

Hypoglycemia

Hypoglycemia is a low blood glucose level also known as insulin shock. The condition is caused by either too little blood glucose or too much insulin—patients have either taken their insulin and not eaten enough to meet the energy demands, or they have taken too much insulin, and the blood glucose is quickly used up. This condition can also be brought on by over-exercising, excessive alcohol consumption, or aggressive dieting.

Signs/symptoms

Diagnosing a diabetic emergency is made easier by the fact that several of the signs and symptoms are opposite (see table below).

The onset is rapid—it can come on in minutes to hours.

Food intake is inadequate for their current energy needs as the blood glucose is quickly consumed.

Hunger pangs caused by the low blood glucose levels can be extreme, and the patient will crave sugar or carbohydrates.

Thirst is not intense, nor is there excessive voiding.

The patient may complain of a headache and/or dizziness. Change in Level of Consciousness can range from confusion to stupor to unconsciousness.

Vital signs

LOC: deterioration can be a rapid progression from dizziness to stupor to unconscious—the patient may appear drunk (rare).

RR: normal to rapid and shallow

HR: rapid and full

BP: normal

Skin: can be pale, cool, and clammy

Blood glucose level by glucometer will be low, < 60mg/dl

Signs & symptoms	Hyperglycemia (diabetic ketoacidosis—too much sugar, not enough insulin)	Hypoglycemia (Insulin shock—not enough sugar, too much insulin)
blood sugar	excessive	deficient
onset	gradual (12 – 48) hours	rapid (minutes to hours)
food intake	excessive	inadequate (common)
hunger	no hunger	extreme
thirst	intense	no thirst
insulin	inadequate (common)	excessive (common)
other causes	infection, stress, illness	exercise, alcohol, no food
other symptoms	nausea, vomiting, abdominal pain, polyuria, irritability, skin tenting	headache, dilated pupils, dizziness, confusion, stupor, unconsciousness
Vital signs		
skin	warm, dry, or pale	pale, cool, and clammy
pulse	rapid, thready	rapid, full
blood pressure	hypotension	normal
respirations	Kussmaul's breathing	normal to shallow
breath odor	acetone breath	normal
neurological	restless or "drunk"	weak to unconscious, may be combative

Note how often the symptoms of hyperglycemia and hypoglycemia are opposite.

Emergency treatment

for **hyper**glycemia and **hypo**glycemia

Initial treatment for a patient you suspect of having a diabetic emergency is the same: give them glucose immediately. If their blood glucose level is high, giving them additional glucose will not do any harm—and if they are hypoglycemic, it will help.

1. If the patient is conscious and can swallow, they should drink a sweet liquid such as orange juice with several teaspoons of sugar dissolved into it.

   - Liquids are preferred to solids because they are passed through the stomach and into the small intestine faster, allowing the glucose to be absorbed more quickly.
   - Any form of glucose and fructose can be used: sugar, honey, hard candy (dissolve in warm water)—anything sweet that can be put into a liquid form.
   - Obviously, NutraSweet and other sugar substitutes are of no value, as they do not contain any glucose or source of energy.

2. If the patient is unconscious, they obviously cannot swallow. In this case, the best method for sugar administration is to utilize the absorptive surface of the oral mucosa—gently rub any sugary paste onto the patient's gums—some of the glucose will be absorbed through the buccal mucosa of the lining of the mouth.

3. If the patient's LOC returns to alert (A&O x 3), **and** if it can be determined through taking patient history what caused the emergency, **and** the patient is able take over the management of their situation (e.g., has insulin and can inject), then you're done—however, if they do not rouse, or if their is **any** doubt about their recovery, transport the patient immediately for further medical evaluation and treatment.

4. Advanced Life Support (ALS) treatment: 50cc of D50W by IV and/or Glucagon 1mg IM

5. **Never** give insulin—although this is the cornerstone of treatment for hyperglycemia, administering insulin must be done in a hospital environment where the patient's blood chemistry can be monitored closely.

A natural sugar source, like orange juice (especially if cane sugar is dissolved in it), will raise blood glucose levels very quickly—a barely responsive hypoglycemic patient will come around in seconds. Because sugar substitutes (e.g., NutraSweet) contain no glucose, they are completely ineffective.

Myths busted

Diabetes cannot be passed from person to person—although there may be some genetic links, especially with Type II diabetes.

Diabetics do not have to avoid sugar—they must manage their blood sugar levels.

Eating sugar does not cause diabetes—but obesity is a risk factor and a high-sugar diet makes obesity more likely.

Diabetics do not need specialized diets—well-balanced nutrition is the goal.

Diabetics do not have to limit starch (e.g., breads, pasta)—those foods are part of a balanced diet.

Diabetics are not more likely to catch colds—however, flu shots are recommended for diabetics (any infection interferes with blood glucose management).

Insulin does not guarantee weight gain—glucose management far outweighs the risk of weight gain.

Seizures

SEIZURE (i.e., convulsion): a temporary disruption of the electrochemical impulses in the brain resulting in a change in level of consciousness or behavior.

POSSIBLE CAUSES OF SEIZURES

- Neglecting to take anti-seizure medications
- Congenital—patient born with a pre-existing condition
- Traumatic Brain Injury (TBI)
- Meningitis, stroke
- Tumor (space-occupying lesion)
- Alcohol or drug withdrawal, alcohol or drug overdose
- Fever—febrile seizures, usually in children
- Metabolic disturbances
- Sleep deprivation
- Hypoglycemia or hypoxia

SEIZURE TERMS

Aura

- A peculiar sensation (taste, smell, sight, feeling) that immediately precedes a seizure (moments to minutes)
- Can occur as long as an hour prior to the seizure, or just seconds before onset
- Seizure sufferers who experience auras typically experience the same type of aura each time they have a seizure
- Auras can help the patient protect themselves from injury by allowing them time to sit, lie down, pull over to the side of the road, etc.

Postictal

- Period of altered consciousness which occurs immediately following the termination of a seizure
- Typically lasts between 5 and 30 minutes—sometimes longer in severe cases
- Characterized by one or more of the following: exhaustion · altered ability to think clearly or concentrate (confusion) · short term memory problems · decreased verbal and interactive skills · other cognitive defects

Classic seizure presentation: supine, with body movement, typically most pronounced in the limbs.

TYPES OF SEIZURES

- **Generalized motor seizure (grand mal)**
  - Frequently preceded by an aura prior to onset of seizure activity
  - Tonic-clonic movement (uncoordinated muscle contraction and relaxation)
  - Postictal state may run the gamut of symptoms (left)
- **Absence seizure (petit mal)**
  - Most common in children
  - Very brief loss of consciousness—"staring off into space"
  - May be associated with eye blinking, lip-smacking, or jerky motions
  - Postictal state
- **Focal motor seizure**
  - Tonic-clonic twitching usually involving just one body part
  - May progress to a generalized motor seizure
  - Postictal state
- **Psychomotor seizure** (temporal lobe seizure)
  - Sudden alteration in personality
  - May be preceded by dizziness
  - May include hallucinations of sight, taste, sound, or smell
  - Postictal state
- **Status epilepticus**
  - More than 30 minutes of continuous seizure activity, or two or more seizures not separated by a period of consciousness
  - This is a medical emergency—transport to a hospital ASAP

TREATMENT OF SEIZURES

- Protect the patient from harm, but do not restrain them.
- Contain the patient in an area, if necessary.
- **Do not** place a bite-stick in the patient's mouth.
- Place the patient in the recovery position to maintain an open airway (below).
- Check for other injuries.
- Take a good history: talk with patient, relatives, bystanders.
- Be prepared to describe the seizure activity, including the direction of movement of the patient's eyes, to medical personnel.
- Administer oxygen, at a rate of 4 – 6 liters per minute by nasal cannula, if available.

stroke

CVA and TIA

A stroke in the right hemisphere of the brain causes left-sided paralysis, and vice-versa.

CEREBROVASCULAR ACCIDENT (CVA)

A CVA occurs when there is an interruption of blood supply to part of the brain due to a sudden vascular catastrophe caused by a blood clot (emboli) or hemorrhage (aneurysm).

signs / symptoms

CVA signs and symptoms vary depending upon which part of the brain is affected. The symptom complex may include one or more of the following:

- Loss of memory
- Inability to speak
- Facial paralysis
- Incontinence
- Frustration
- Headache
- One-sided weakness
- One-sided paralysis
- Unequal pupils

treatment

1. Maintain ABCs.
2. Place the patient in a position of comfort and be prepared to manage a seizure.
3. Reassure the patient.
4. If unconscious, place the patient in the recovery position.
5. Evacuate.
6. Administer oxygen at a rate of 10 – 15 liters per minute by non-rebreather mask, if available.

Both blockage (blue) and hemorrhage (red) can cause a stroke—blockage is the far more common cause, accounting for nearly 9 out of 10 strokes.

Top brain diagram: a stroke caused by an emboli— blood flow beyond the clot is restricted, causing ischemia and potential tissue death.

Bottom brain diagram: a stroke caused by hemorrhage via a burst aneurysm—bleeding into the cranium can cause direct damage to the brain.

TRANSIENT ISCHEMIC ATTACK (TIA)

This is a "temporary stroke" caused by insufficient blood flow to the brain that spontaneously resolves within 24 hours.

- The signs and symptoms are identical to those of a CVA, but they disappear in less than a day.
- The treatment is the same as for a CVA.

stroke / assessment

F **Face:** *is their face symmetrical when they smile?*

A **Arms:** *do they have bilateral symmetry, strength, and control?*

S **Speech:** *are there impairments: inability, slurring, decreased vocabulary?*

T **Time:** *if positive for any of the above (FAS), "time is tissue"—evacuate ASAP.*

stroke / facts

Stroke kills almost 130,000 Americans each year—that's 1 in every 19 deaths.

On average, one American dies from stroke every 4 minutes.

Every year, more than 795,000 people in the United States have a stroke. About 610,000 of these are first or new strokes. One in four are recurrent strokes.

About 87% of all strokes are ischemic.

Stroke risk factors include: diabetes, overweight and obesity, physical inactivity, excessive alcohol use.

Stroke is a leading cause of serious long-term disability.

(source: CDC)

behavioral

A behavioral emergency is a situation in which a person exhibits behavior that is unacceptable or intolerable to the patient, the family or the community. We must distinguish whether a behavioral emergency is triggered by an emotional disturbance, mental illness, or a medical problem.

MANY THINGS CAN AFFECT A PERSON'S BEHAVIOR

Situational stress

Medical illnesses
Infections of the brain or its coverings
Inadequate blood flow to the brain
Hypoxia
Hypoglycemia
Heat- and cold-related emergencies

Mental illnesses
Depression, panic attacks, paranoia, etc.

Trauma
Physical and mental—especially head trauma

Psychogenic substances
Alcohol
Depressants
Stimulants
Narcotics

S/S OF A BEHAVIORAL EMERGENCY

Intense fear—of a person, place or thing that would not normally be frightening

Anxiety—unconnected to current situation or to a specific person, place, or thing

Confusion

Behavioral changes—radical changes in lifestyle, values, or relationships

Anger—often misdirected, brief, and destructive

Mania—unrealistically optimistic outlook; a tendency to take unwarranted risks and/or to exhibit poor judgment

Depression

Withdrawal—loss of interest in anything that once was important to the patient

Loss of contact with reality—hallucinations
Sleeplessness

S/S OF A MEDICAL PROBLEM

Rapid onset of the problem

If hallucinating, the hallucinations are visual and not auditory

Memory loss or impairment

Pupils are dilated, constricted or unequal, or react sluggishly to light

Excessive salivation

Unusual breath odors

Unlike bleeding and fractures, this stuff is really hard to diagnose

WILDCARE™

emergencies

BEHAVIORAL EMERGENCIES: THE BIG FOUR

MAJOR DEPRESSIVE DISORDER (MDD)
A pervasive and persistent low mood that is accompanied by low self-esteem and a loss of interest or pleasure in normally enjoyable activities.

Clinical presentation
A person's current mood and thought content, in particular, the presence of themes of hopelessness or pessimism, self-harm or suicide, and an absence of positive thoughts or plans.

Treatment
1. Evaluate the patient's risk to themselves or others.
2. If there is a belief or an actual attempt at suicide, transport the patient immediately for evaluation.
3. If the patient is an adult that is A+Ox3, and they do not want to go to the hospital, remember that the police are a useful resource in the urban environment.

SCHIZOPHRENIA
Characterized by a breakdown in thinking and poor emotional responses.

Clinical presentation
Common symptoms include delusions, such as the feeling that someone is out to get you; seeing things that are not there; disorganized thinking; a lack of emotion and a lack of motivation.

Treatment
1. Reassure the patient.
2. Attempt to determine the cause of the emergency.
3. If it is a true behavioral emergency, transport immediately.

ACUTE STRESS REACTION
Occurs immediately after an emotionally traumatic incident.

Clinical presentation
Dyspnea, anxiety, irritability, nausea, guilt, isolation, and loss of concentration, appetite, interest in life, and carpal/pedal spasms

Treatment
1. Keep the patient calm.
2. Administer low or high-flow O_2 depending on SpO_2 (oxygen saturation in the blood— impossible to test in the field without a pulse oximeter)— when in doubt, give oxygen.
3. Place the patient in the Fowler's position.
4. Transport if necessary or if you are unable to control the patient.

DELIRIUM TREMENS
An acute episode of delirium (severe confusion and disorientation) that is usually caused by withdrawal from alcohol.

Clinical presentation
Nightmares, agitation, global confusion, disorientation, visual and auditory hallucinations, fever, hypertension, diaphoresis, and tachycardia

Treatment
1. Keep the patient calm.
2. Administer oxygen based on SpO_2 readings—when in doubt, give oxygen.
3. Transport for further care and evaluation.
4. Higher-level providers may administer benzodiazepines to help relax the patient.

Use caution with all behavioral problems— the patient may become Violent!

RISING SCALE OF TROUBLE

44°C (111.2°F) or more—almost certainly death will occur; however, a patient is known to have survived a temp of 46.5°C (115.7°F)

43°C (109.4°F)—continuous convulsions and shock, serious brain damage, cardio-respiratory collapse, death likely

42°C (107.6°F)—skin pale or flushed and red; severe tachycardia, BP may be high or low; severe delirium, vomiting, and convulsions can occur; patient may become comatose

41°C (105.8°F)—(medical emergency): fainting, vomiting, severe headache, dizziness, confusion, hallucinations, possible delirium, drowsiness, and heart palpitations

40°C (104°F)—profuse sweating, fainting, dehydration, weakness, vomiting, headache

39°C (102.2°F)—severe sweating, flushed red skin, tachycardia, increased respiration, fatigue; children and those with a seizure disorder are likely to convulse

38°C (100.4°F)—sweating, discomfort, slight hunger

37.5°C (99.5°F) normal daily variation (high)

37.0°C (98.6°F) normal daily (mean)

36.5°C (97.7°F) normal daily variation (low)

FEVER-CAUSING conditions

1. **Infections** (bacterial or viral)
2. **Tissue damage** (e.g., crush injuries)
3. **Alcohol** or **drug** withdrawal
4. **Environmental**: dehydration, heat exhaustion
5. **Other** (less common) causes: cancer, toxins, drugs such as amphetamines or MDMA (ecstasy)

FEVER

is one of the most common medical signs—a clear signal that the body is fighting something. And it can cause a deterioration in LOC. Although a natural body defense, if a fever becomes severe enough (at or above 40°C/104°F)—regardless of the underlying cause— it must be controlled. Extremely high temperatures can cause permanent brain damage and death.

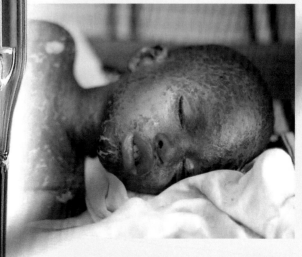

A child from the African nation of Guinea with measles (one of the word's most contagious diseases), which often presents with a fever up to 40°C/104°F. Though immunization is readily available, cheap, and efficacious, outbreaks are still common in developing countries. Measles killed 158,000 people in 2011.

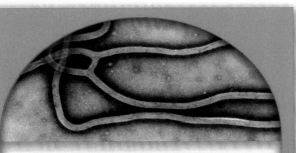

VIRAL INFECTIONS

- Viral infections are usually gradual in onset, starting out with minor symptoms that slowly worsen over the next day or two.

- Relatively short-lived, they last 4 – 7 days. Typically, the symptoms peak on day three and then begin to improve quickly, with 90 percent improvement by day six or seven.

- They have a tendency to cause a low-grade fever (up to 102-103°F [39°C]) that is easily controlled with acetaminophen or a non-steroidal anti-inflammatory drug (NSAID) such as Advil or Aleve.

- Viruses also tend to be tissue-specific, meaning they will infect only one type of tissue at a time.

- All of these common viral illnesses are marked by general malaise, fatigue, loss of appetite, and a low-grade fever.

EXAMPLES

The common cold (acute viral rhinopharyngitis)

- Attacks the respiratory epithelium that lines the sinuses, throat, and chest resulting in congestion, stuffiness, and a cough that may be productive of white or yellowish sputum.

- Viral pharyngitis will cause a sore throat, painful swallowing, and tender glands (lymph nodes) in the neck.

Viral gastroenteritis

- Is specific to the cells that line the intestinal tract and causes nausea, vomiting, and diarrhea.

We have all had a fever at one time or another that was associated with a sore throat or cough. These fevers are usually benign and self-limiting. But, in the wilderness setting, we need to try to determine if the infection is viral or bacterial in nature, as each is treated differently.

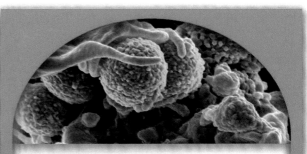

BACTERIAL INFECTIONS

- Bacterial infections are usually rapid in onset with symptoms coming on in 12 – 24 hours, and they tend to be more severe.

- Malaise is extreme, the fatigue is worse, the patient has a higher fever, the pain is greater—they are simply more uncomfortable.

- The patient looks sick and is referred to as appearing septic or toxic.

- Bacterial infections cause a higher fever (up to 104°F [40°C] and even higher), than viral infections, and are not as easily controlled with acetaminophen or an NSAID such as Advil or Aleve.

- Bacteria are not tissue-specific; they tend to disseminate to several areas at once.

EXAMPLES

Sinusitis

- Symptoms of sinusitis include facial or sinus pain, postnasal drip, sore throat, ear pain, fever, chills and fatigue.

- The physical exam will usually reveal a grayish, thick, postnasal drip running down the back of the throat.

Strep throat, tonsillitis, and bacterial pharyngitis

- These all cause a very sore throat, making swallowing painful and difficult, plus ear pain, and fever.

- The physical exam may reveal a whitish or grayish exudate on the tonsils and throat.

- Chest infections, bronchitis and pneumonia

- Chest infections, bronchitis and pneumonia, not only have a fever, general malaise, and fatigue, but may also cause shortness of breath, wheezing, and a cough that is productive of greenish, brownish, or blood-streaked sputum.

- The sputum tends to be more copious than with a viral infection.

Food poisoning (salmonella)

- A bacteria found in the intestinal tracts of humans and animals. Meat, poultry, dairy products, seafood, etc., that is not cooked to a safe temperature (145^0 – 165^0 depending on the food) may harbor live bacteria.

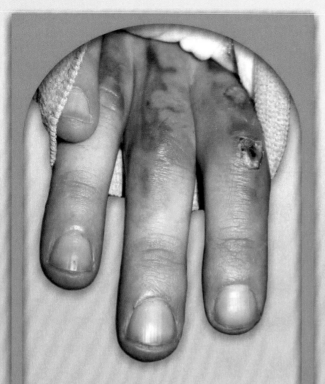

TISSUE DAMAGE

- Damaged tissues release proteins and other cellular components into the surrounding tissues which are removed by the lymphatics.

- These waste products of tissue damage (called pyrogens), stimulate the thermoregulatory center in the brain, elevating the core temperature and inducing a fever.

- Patient history is the key to finding the underlying cause—something has injured the muscles or tissues.

- Treat fever caused by tissue damage with an NSAID—it will control the fever and help control the inflammatory response to the injury.

- Acetaminophen can be added to aid in pain control if needed.

EXAMPLES

Direct trauma (severe bruising, crush injuries)

Frostbite

Muscle fatigue from overwork

Frostbite (top, Antarctica) and extreme muscle fatigue (left, Sydney Olympics) can both cause fever—a natural physiological response as the body works to flush toxins and heal damaged tissue.

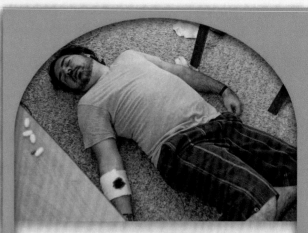

ALCOHOL OR DRUG WITHDRAWAL

- Alcohol and drug withdrawal are complicated and can be difficult to manage, especially in the wilderness setting.

- One of the classic signs of withdrawal is loss of autonomic control resulting in a rise in core temperature.

- This particular underlying cause will be discovered by taking a thorough patient history and asking the right questions. The patient must be honest—often they are honest in the hopes of getting alcohol or drugs to stop the withdrawal process.

- It is appropriate to manage this fever with tepid sponge baths or NSAIDs.

- Avoid using acetaminophen, as you do not know the condition of the patient's liver—chronic alcohol or drug use may have caused significant liver damage which acetaminophen would exacerbate.

ENVIRONMENTAL

- The final causes of fever are the obvious environmental concerns and risks of heat stroke, heat exhaustion, and dehydration.

- This will be discovered in the patient history as part of the events leading up to the fever.

- This type of fever is treated with hydration, oral electrolyte replacement solutions, shade, rest, and tepid sponge baths (these work extremely well).

- Don't give NSAIDs, especially aspirin, or acetaminophen to a heat stroke victim—heat stroke can damage the liver, and these drugs can make the damage worse.

FEVER treatment

PHYSICAL COOLING

Tepid sponge baths (with warm, not cool water), is an old-fashioned technique that works very well. Gently sponge the water onto exposed skin and let it air dry—evaporation cools the peripheral venous blood flow (simulating sweating) and helps lower core temperature.

MEDICATIONS

OTC non-steroidal anti-inflammatory drugs (NSAIDs) help to alleviate pain and control inflammation by direct action on prostaglandins, which are the chemical mediators of inflammation—NSAIDs are also very effective at lowering fever.

- Aspirin (acetylsalicylic acid)
- Advil and Motrin (ibuprofen)
- Aleve (Naprosyn)
- There are also many prescription NSAIDs.

Used in appropriate dosages, NSAIDs are very safe medications; however, as with any medication, it is important to know the potential adverse reactions and the warnings. Always ask about allergies before giving any medication—if the patient has had a bad reaction the past, do not administer the med.

POSSIBLE ADVERSE REACTIONS TO NSAIDs

- Anaphylaxis
- Gastrointestinal upset and gastritis. Gastrointestinal (GI) upset can be minimized by taking the NSAID with food. Reactions can vary from mild nausea or diarrhea to bleeding ulcers and a life-threatening GI bleed. Avoid giving NSAIDs to anyone who has a history of ulcers, irritable bowel syndrome (IBS), Crohn's Disease, ulcerative colitis, or any sort of inflammatory bowel disease.
- Asthmatics can be sensitive to NSAIDs (particularly aspirin). Their properties can exacerbate or precipitate an asthma attack.
- Renal or kidney problems can be made worse by NSAIDs. Avoid the use of NSAIDs in individuals with a history of renal insufficiency, kidney failure, or any form of kidney disease.

WARNINGS ABOUT NSAIDs

- All NSAIDs interfere with platelet activity—the ability of the blood to form clots and plug holes in the vasculature. The strongest anti-platelet drug is aspirin, which is why it is used to minimize the risk of an acute thrombotic event (venous clots that break loose and travel), such as during an acute MI.
- Platelet activity is important to control bleeding in acute injuries. For example, if someone has slipped or fallen and sprained an ankle or knee, they may have torn some of the supporting ligaments, and those tears are going to bleed. The area will swell and ecchymosis (black and blue) will form at the injury site. This is a time to avoid the use of aspirin or other NSAIDs, as they will prevent clot formation, which will increase bleeding into the damaged area.
- Aspirin is a very useful and powerful drug with several unique characteristics and warnings. It is a very strong anti-platelet, anti-arthritic, and an excellent anti-pyretic (fever) drug—but, it is not for everyone. Most importantly, aspirin and products containing aspirin should not be taken by children. Aspirin can precipitate Reye's syndrome—potentially fatal encephalitis—if the child has a flu-like, viral illness. The Centers for Disease Control recommends that aspirin and products containing aspirin be withheld from children younger than 19.
- NSAIDs should never be taken with other NSAIDs as this increases the risk of a GI bleed. For example, you should not take aspirin along with ibuprofen, Naprosyn, or other prescribed NSAIDs.

NON-NSAID ALTERNATIVES

- Tylenol (acetaminophen) is used similarly to NSAIDs, but it is not an NSAID because it has weak anti-inflammatory characteristics. It is not an anti-platelet, and it works by a different mechanism. However, acetaminophen is an excellent pain medication, and it works well to lower fevers. Because it has different pharmacological properties, it can be taken in conjunction with NSAIDs.
- Tylenol in appropriate doses is very safe in children and is commonly recommended to treat fevers and general aches and pains.

ADVERSE REACTIONS TO ACETAMINOPHEN

- Liver damage: acetaminophen can be hard on the liver, and, therefore, can exacerbate chronic liver diseases.
- Acetaminophen should be avoided in people with chronic liver diseases such as Hepatitis B or C, cirrhosis, or liver failure. In too high a dose acetaminophen is directly toxic to the hepatocytes (liver cells) and can cause liver failure.
- Because acetaminophen can be toxic to the liver, the maximum daily dose is 4000mg (4 grams). Doses greater than 4000mg per day will cause liver damage and possibly liver failure. Staying below this maximum daily dose can be tricky because acetaminophen is found in many other compounds, (other pain and allergy meds, cold remedies, etc.) and the cumulative effect may go unnoticed until liver damage has occurred.

STANDARD MEDICATION DOSAGES

- **Aspirin** 325mg; 1 every 4 hours as needed; should be taken with food.
- **Ibuprofen** (Motrin, Advil) 200mg; 1 – 2 every 6 hours as needed; should be taken with food.
- **Naprosyn** (another NSAID marketed as Aleve) 250mg; 1 every 12 hours as needed; should be taken with food.
- **Acetaminophen** (Tylenol) strengths vary from regular strength to extra strength; maximum dose of 500mg every 4 hours as needed until a maximum dose of 3000mg per day is reached.

Our understanding of how the respiratory system works (and how to make it work better) has certainly changed over the years; and treatment costs have risen as well—you won't get much to help your lung function for 39 cents these days.

short ness

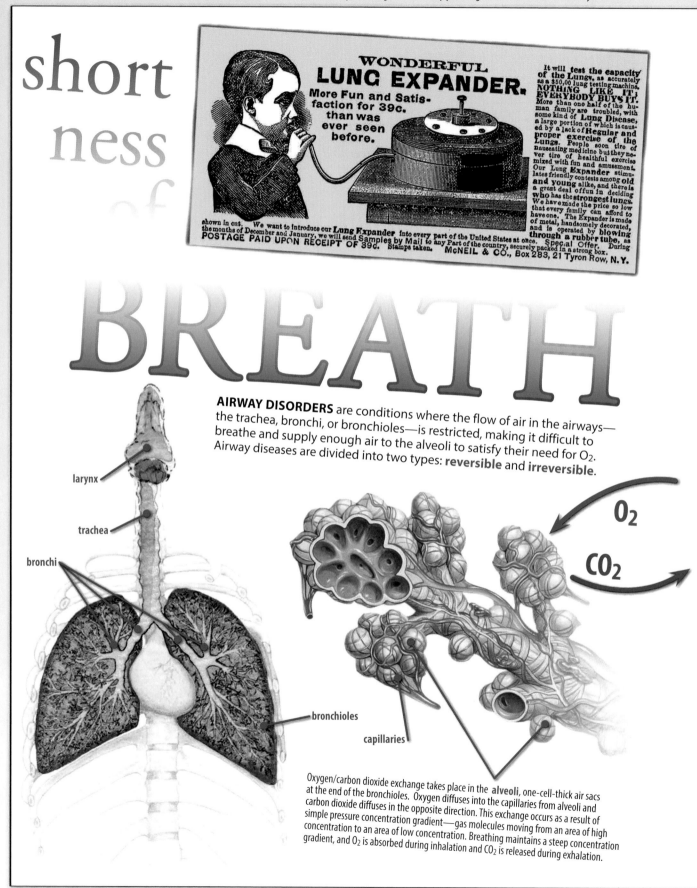

WONDERFUL LUNG EXPANDER.
More Fun and Satisfaction for 39c. than was ever seen before.

shown in cut. We want to introduce our **Lung Expander** into every part of the United States at once. During the months of December and January, we will send Samples by Mail to any Part of the country, securely packed in a strong box. **POSTAGE PAID UPON RECEIPT OF 39C.** Stamps taken.

It will **test the capacity** of the Lungs, as accurately as a $50,00 lung testing machine. NOTHING LIKE IT; EVERYBODY BUYS IT. More than one half of the human family are troubled with some kind of **Lung Disease**, a large portion of which is caused by a lack of **Regular and proper exercise of the Lungs**. People soon tire of nauseating medicine but they never tire of healthful exercise mixed with fun and amusement. Our Lung Expander stimulates friendly contests among old and young alike, and there is a great deal offun in deciding who has the **strongest lungs**. We have made the price so low that every family can afford to have one. The Expander is made of metal, handsomely decorated, and is operated by blowing **through a rubber tube**, as

McNEIL & CO., Box 283, 21 Tyron Row, N. Y.

BREATH

AIRWAY DISORDERS are conditions where the flow of air in the airways—the trachea, bronchi, or bronchioles—is restricted, making it difficult to breathe and supply enough air to the alveoli to satisfy their need for O_2. Airway diseases are divided into two types: **reversible** and **irreversible**.

O_2

CO_2

larynx

trachea

bronchi

bronchioles

capillaries

Oxygen/carbon dioxide exchange takes place in the **alveoli**, one-cell-thick air sacs at the end of the bronchioles. Oxygen diffuses into the capillaries from alveoli and carbon dioxide diffuses in the opposite direction. This exchange occurs as a result of simple pressure concentration gradient—gas molecules moving from an area of high concentration to an area of low concentration. Breathing maintains a steep concentration gradient, and O_2 is absorbed during inhalation and CO_2 is released during exhalation.

ANATOMY DETAIL: NARES TO TRACHEA

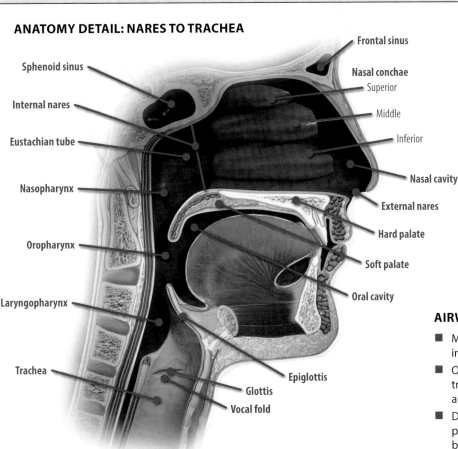

Sphenoid sinus
Internal nares
Eustachian tube
Nasopharynx
Oropharynx
Laryngopharynx
Trachea

Frontal sinus
Nasal conchae
Superior
Middle
Inferior
Nasal cavity
External nares
Hard palate
Soft palate
Oral cavity
Epiglottis
Glottis
Vocal fold

LUNG STATISTICS

- There are 300 – 400 million tiny alveoli.
- There are about 2400 kilometers (1580 miles) of capillary beds associated with the alveoli.
- The total surface area of the alveoli is about 80 square meters (95.6 square yards).
- At any given time there is about 1 liter (1 quart) of blood in the pulmonary circulation.
- Total lung capacity is about 6 liters.
- Vital capacity, the maximum amount of air in a deep breath, is about 4.6 liters.
- Tidal volume, the amount of air breathed in a normal breath is about 500mL (1/2 liter).

LUNGS

- The lung tissue is very sponge-like and elastic, able to expand and contract.
- This tissue consists of the alveoli, little air sacs where the gas exchange occurs, miles of capillary beds layered over the alveoli, and supporting tissue.
- The right side of the lungs contains 3 lobes and the left side has 2 lobes. The left is missing one lobe to make room for the heart and mediastinum.
- The interior of the rib cage is lined with the parietal pleura; the lungs are covered with the visceral pleura, and in between them is the pleural space. This is a potential space, lubricated with pleural fluid that allows the lungs to expand and contract freely.

RESPIRATORY MUSCLES

- The primary muscles of respiration are the intercostal muscles and the diaphragm.
- There are also accessory muscles, the pectoralis major and sternocleomastoid, to aid in expansion of the lungs if needed (use of these muscles indicates a respiratory emergency).
- Contraction of these muscles expands the lungs, creating low pressure in the lungs that draws the air in.
- Inhalation is an active process—contraction of the muscles pulls the lungs open.
- Exhalation is a passive process—the muscles relax and the lungs recoil due to their inherent elasticity. This creates higher pressure in the lungs, forcing the air out.

There is much more A&P information in the chest trauma section.

AIRWAYS

- Movement of air from the outside into the lungs.
- Oropharynx and nasopharynx > trachea > bronchi > bronchioles > alveoli.
- Dead air space: The space occupied by air that is in the trachea, bronchi, and bronchioles. You have to move at least 150ml of air to get to the alveoli.
- O_2 and CO_2 exchange occurs at the level of the alveoli.
- The trachea, bronchi, and bronchioles are made of smooth muscles and are held open by cartilaginous C-shaped rings.
- The airways are lined with cilia and goblet cells. By secreting mucus to keep the airway moist and sticky, dirt particles, pollen, and other debris in the air are trapped. This debris is then swept up and out of the airway by the cilia in a rhythmic sweeping motion referred to as the mucociliary escalator. Constantly sweeping upward, this motion moves the sputum and trapped particles up and out to keep the airway clean.
- During inhalation the air on the way to the alveoli is warmed to core temperature, becomes 100% humidified, and is scrubbed clean, trapping contaminants in the mucus lining the airways.

Asthma

Normal airway (right), restricted airway (left).

About 5,000 people die from asthma in the US each year.

ASTHMA AND OTHER RAD DISEASES occur when the airways become narrowed, causing a restriction of airflow.

- Asthma is recurrent and reversible with medication.
- Allergens in the airway cause swelling (bronchospasm) and increased mucous production, especially noted in the terminal bronchioles, which narrow before entering the alveoli, causing air to be trapped in the alveoli.
- When the air is trapped, the patient can inhale but cannot exhale, resulting in worsening shortness of breath (SOB).
- Asthma affects approximately 9% of the US population.
- Asthma accounts for about 25% of all emergency room visits per year in the US, or about 2 million visits per year (5000$^{+/-}$ deaths).

SIGNS AND SYMPTOMS

- Coughing
- Shortness of breath
- The patient has difficulty speaking: word dyspnea— the patient is unable to count to ten on one breath
- Expiratory wheezing—audible initially with auscultation
- Tripoding—the patient sits up and leans forward with their arms braced out in front to facilitate the use of their accessory muscles to aid in respiration
- Hyperinflation of the chest
- Cyanosis
- Shock
- Status asthmaticus—an asthma attack that won't stop; may be life-threatening

ASSESSMENT OF SEVERITY

Stage 1: Minor
- Sensation of shortness of breath
- No word dyspnea; the patient can count to 10 in one breath
- Little or no wheezing

Stage 2: Moderate
- Shortness of breath and wheezing
- Word dyspnea; the patient can count between 6 – 9 words in one breath
- Air trapping, and expiratory wheezing

Stage 3: Severe
- Rapid, shallow respirations
- Anxiety, and tripoding
- Word dyspnea—the patient can only count to 5
- Air trapping, rapid, shallow breathing
- Cyanosis
- Faint wheezing or no wheezing at all (not moving enough air to wheeze)
- Hyperinflation of the chest
- Shock
- Status asthmaticus

TREATMENT

1. Calm the patient, and remain calm yourself.
2. Place the patient in position of comfort (usually sitting or semi-sitting).
3. Take a good history—find out which medications, if any, the patient has taken.
4. Encourage pursed-lip breathing to create back-pressure and open the bronchioles.
5. If the patient has a rescue metered dose inhaler (MDI) albuterol or Xopenex, you can assist them in using it.
6. Give 100% oxygen, humidified if possible; you may need to assist with ventilations.
7. You can give the patient some relief and improve their breathing by gently helping them to exhale. This is an old-fashioned technique that was used before the days of the modern bronchodilator medications.
   - ▷ Have the asthmatic patient lie down and place your hands on the sides of their rib cage.
   - ▷ As they exhale, gently compress the chest wall. This helps to force out some of the air trapped distal to the bronchoconstrictions.
   - ▷ As they inhale, hold the chest wall compressed.
   - ▷ Maintain compression as they exhale and inhale through a total of three cycles.
   - ▷ After the third cycle, gently release the chest wall and allow them to take a deep breath.
   - ▷ This can be repeated as often as needed to aid in forcing out the trapped air and improving the depth of respirations.
8. Consider evacuation.
9. In the backcountry—use epinephrine for status asthmaticus, and always evacuate.

COPD

CHRONIC
OBSTRUCTIVE
PULMONARY
DISEASE

OBSTRUCTIVE AIRWAY DISEASES ARE IRREVERSIBLE because they destroy the alveoli, which decreases the available surface area for oxygen exchange. COPD refers to a group of lung diseases that restrict airflow and cause shortness of breath.

- The combination of emphysema and chronic bronchitis is the most common cause of COPD (asthma may also contribute).
- It is chronic, progressive, and irreversible—but symptoms can be controlled and minimized with medication, including supplemental O_2.
- It is commonly found in patients with a history of cigarette smoking.

EMPHYSEMA
DESCRIPTION

- This disease is characterized by deterioration of the alveolar walls, leading to decreased surface area for gas exchange.
- It is caused by smoking, smoke inhalation, or inhalation of lung irritants.
- The alveolar damage is irreversible.
- Smoking cessation or avoiding lung irritants can arrest the destructive process.
- If the destruction of the alveolar walls continues, eventually patients with emphysema will not have enough surface area for gas exchange and will have to live on supplemental oxygen—they will have to live with a nasal cannula in their nose to increase the concentration of O_2 above the 20% concentration in the air. Each additional liter (per minute) of O_2 adds 4% O_2.
- Anything that further compromises surface area, such as bronchitis, pneumonia, or pulmonary edema, will exacerbate a patient's symptoms and increase demand for supplemental O_2.

EMPHYSEMA SIGNS AND SYMPTOMS

- Weight loss
- Dyspnea on exertion
- Barrel chest

Intentionally pulling tobacco smoke into your lungs is a major cause/contributor to many major ailments (e.g., various cancers).

CHRONIC BRONCHITIS
DESCRIPTION

- This is a disease of the mucosa of the lower airway characterized by excessive mucus production.
- It is chronic when it occurs more than three months a year and has been going on for two years or more.

CHRONIC BRONCHITIS
SIGNS AND SYMPTOMS

- Dyspnea on exertion
- Pulmonary edema
- Wheezing
- Associated heart disease (in some cases)

COPD CRISIS
DESCRIPTION

- This is a flare-up or exacerbation of a pre-existing COPD condition.

COPD CRISIS SIGNS AND SYMPTOMS

- Increasing dyspnea, which may include paroxysmal nocturnal dyspnea—shortness of breath that comes on at night when a patient lies down to sleep and which forces them to get up to breathe
- Altered Level of Consciousness (LOC)—confusion, lethargy, combativeness, agitation
- Cyanosis
- Tripoding to allow use of accessory muscles in breathing
- Change in color of sputum from white to green or brown, which may indicate underlying bronchitis or pneumonia
- Cardiac dysrhythmias

COPD CRISIS
TREATMENT

1. Place the patient in the position of comfort—usually sitting up.
2. Administer 100% O_2 and titrate until the patient improves sufficiently. Start out with a nasal cannula at 4 – 6 liters per minute (LPM); if no improvement occurs, use a non-rebreather mask at 15 LPM.
3. You may have to assist ventilations if the patient's respiratory rate is less than 10 or greater than 30 breaths per minute. Assist-breathe with 100% O_2 via a bag valve mask (BVM).
4. Never withhold O_2 from a patient with COPD.

Pulmonary emboli

em·bo·lism

/'embə • lizəm/

NOUN 1. obstruction of an artery, typically by a clot of blood or an air bubble

A potentially life-threatening problem which occurs when free-floating emboli get into the venous circulation, travel through the right side of the heart, and lodge in the pulmonary arteries. When this happens, the lung tissue serviced by these arteries becomes blocked, preventing oxygenation of the blood. This is an emergent and dangerous situation that requires immediate hospitalization.

Clots are clearly visible in this autopsy photo.

Typcally originating in the legs or pelvis, a deep vein thrombosis (clot ●) breaks free and travels up through the chambers of the heart, lodging in the lungs where it blocks blood flow causing tissue death and stress on the entire cardiovascular system. Severe cases can lead to abnormally low blood pressure and sudden death.

Conditions that can potentially cause pulmonary emboli

STASIS

▶ Stasis is the slowing or stoppage of blood flow.
▶ Stasis occurs in patients who remain in bed for a long time without moving their legs.
▶ Blood pools in the legs and may clot.
▶ Some causes include **1)** being bedridden from injury, illness, or recent surgery **2)** sitting too long on an airplane, or in a car, bus, or train.

TRAUMA

▶ Trauma to the legs can result in a collection of blood in the tissues and veins.
▶ The risk of pulmonary emboli is especially high in patients with long bone fractures, blunt trauma, or who have recently had surgery.

HYPERCOAGULABILITY

▶ Hypercoagulability is an increased tendency to clot
▶ Causes of hypercoagulability include **1)** oral birth control pills or other hormone replacement therapy **2)** smoking and tobacco use **3)** pregnancy **4)** genetics—inherent clotting-factor problems

Signs and symptoms

These can vary greatly, depending upon the quality and size of the blood clots.

▶ Shortness of breath, with or without exertion (this is the only consistent symptom)
▶ Anxiety with a sensation of impending doom
▶ Diaphoresis (sweating)
▶ Sharp pleuritic pain (chest pain)
▶ Tachypnea (rapid breathing)
▶ Tachycardia (rapid heartbeat)
▶ Cough, initially a dry, non-productive cough
▶ Hemoptysis (coughing up blood) may develop
▶ Jugular venous distension (JVD), hypotension, and shock may develop

Treatment

1. Give 100% O_2 via non-rebreather mask.
2. You may have to assist ventilations with a BVM @ 15 LPM if the respiratory rate is less than 10 or greater than 30 breaths per minute.
3. Prepare for a possible cardiac arrest.
4. Place in the position of comfort.
5. Provide rapid transport to definitive care.

LUNG DISORDERS

PNEUMONIA, PULMONARY EDEMA, etc.

Pneumonia is the general term for a number of lung infections of various origins (viral, bacterial, or fungal) that result in pulmonary edema or fluid in the alveoli. This compromises oxygen absorption in the alveoli and causes decreased oxygen saturation.

GENERAL SIGNS AND SYMPTOMS

- Cough, often productive of a whitish or pink, blood-tinged sputum
- Shortness of breath—dyspnea and tachypnea
- Gurgling and crackles—fluid in the alveoli (they sound wet)
- Possible wheezing
- Fever and chills (associated with a respiratory tract infection)

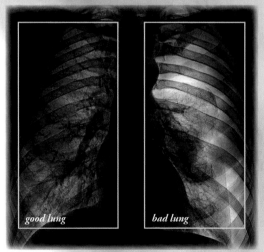

When the alveoli fill with fluid, their ability for gas exchange is diminished—the person is drowning from the inside.

PULMONARY EDEMA

Pulmonary edema is a collection of fluid in the bronchioles and alveoli of the lungs. The cause can be cardiogenic or noncardiogenic. Regardless of the cause, the result is the same: fluid collects in the alveoli resulting in a loss of surface area for gas exchange and a subsequent decrease in oxygen saturation.

CARDIOGENIC CAUSES

- Acute myocardial infarction
- Congestive heart failure (CHF)

NON-CARDIOGENIC CAUSES

- Aspiration or drowning
- Smoke inhalation or toxin inhalation
- Infection—Acute Respiratory Distress Syndrome (ARDS) or pneumonia
- Pulmonary contusions
- High Altitude Pulmonary Edema (HAPE)

TREATMENT

1. Place the patient in a position of comfort, usually sitting up, to help them breathe.
2. Provide 100% O_2 via non-rebreather.
3. You may have to assist ventilations with BVM @ 15 LPM if the respiratory rate is less than 10 or greater than 30 breaths per minute.
4. Evacuate.

SPONTANEOUS PNEUMOTHORAX

A spontaneous pneumothorax is the rupture of a congenital weak spot, or bleb (blister), on the exterior surface of the lung, allowing air to escape out of the lungs through the visceral pleura and into the potential pleural space. Because the lungs are elastic, exhalation is passive, and if there is a pneumothorax, the lungs will deflate as the air moves into the potential pleural space.

SIGNS AND SYPMTOMS

- Localized chest pain at the tear site.
- The onset of a sensation of shortness of breath (dyspnea) will be rapid.
- Dyspnea will worsen as the lung collapses (word dyspnea will worsen).
- There will be no breath sounds in the upper portion of the lung.
- If pneumothorax progresses to a tension pneumothorax, tracheal shift and jugular venous distention (JVD) will occur.
- Spontaneous pneumothorax is most common in tall, thin young men.

TREATMENT: as for pulmonary edema—plus treat for shock.

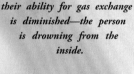

A healthy, inflated lung on the left, and a spontaneous pneumothorax (not a result of external injury) on the right—the bright white indicates where air has become insinuated into the potential pleural space between the lung and the interior chest wall.

good lung   bad lung

LUNG DISORDERS

CONTINUED

HYPERVENTILATION SYNDROME

Usually a psychogenic reaction from stress or anxiety causing increased rate and/or depth of breathing, resulting in excessive CO_2 loss and accompanying respiratory alkalosis. As the CO_2 level goes down, the pH of the blood goes up.

SIGNS AND SYMPTOMS

- Rapid and deep breathing
- Anxiety and/or a feeling of suffocation
- Dizziness
- Sweating
- Tingling around the mouth and lips
- Later, carpopedal spasms (claw-like formations of the hands, fingers, feet and toes)

TREATMENT

Hyperventilation syndrome is self-limiting and the symptoms will resolve if untreated. If you see the S/S in a child, suspect aspirin poisoning.

1. Calm and reassure the patient.
2. Treat the underlying emotional/anxiety concern, if known.
3. "Capture" the patient's breathing to slow it down (have them breathe into bag).
4. Get them to talk by taking a detailed history—this will help focus and calm them.
5. Do a thorough patient assessment to treat any physiological injuries.
6. If the patient passes out, they may stop breathing for up to 30 seconds.
7. If breathing doesn't resume, try painful stimulus.
8. If painful stimulus does not work, begin rescue breathing and call 911.
9. Consider additional medical attention—even after the crisis is resolved.

Breathing into a bag (we recommend a more conventional method than that shown at right) helps restore the balance of carbon dioxide in the body, which helps resolve hyperventilation. However, be careful: other conditions such as asthma or heart attack may have similar symptoms—and breathing into a bag could be dangerous.

SECTION SUMMARY

PHYSIOLOGICAL CAUSES OF SOB

Summary of the causes of decreased O_2 to the brain, causing a sensation of shortness of breath and resulting hypoxia. The primary chief complaint (C/C) will be shortness of breath.

AIRWAY DISORDERS

1. **Anoxia**—no oxygen!
   ▶ SOB and rapid change in LOC.
   ▶ There may not be enough O_2 in the air we breathe, thus, not enough O_2 in the alveoli for O_2 exchange to occur = anoxic atmosphere.
   ▶ This can be caused by gases heavier than air, such as methane.

2. **Obstructed airway**—O_2 can't get to the lungs
   ▶ The PT can't breathe.
   ▶ The airway can be physically blocked, preventing gas exchange = obstructed airway.
   ▶ The airway can be completely or partially obstructed by a foreign body, fluid, or asthma.

3. **Asthma**—can't get enough air in and can't get it all out!
   ▶ SOB and wheezing.
   ▶ Exposure to an allergen causes the airways to narrow and makes it harder to get the good air in and the bad air out.
   ▶ Can range from a minor sensation of shortness of breath and wheezing to a life-threatening attack with minimal air movement.

4. **Chronic Obstructive Pulmonary Disease (COPD)**
   ▶ Shortness of breath and dyspnea on exertion.
   ▶ Destruction of the alveoli has reduced the available surface for gas exchange.
   ▶ Commonly need supplemental oxygen to survive.

PULMONARY CIRCULATION DISORDERS

1. **Pulmonary emboli**— O_2 can't get to the blood!
   ▶ SOB gets worse with time.
   ▶ There is plenty of O_2 in the alveoli, but there is little or no blood flow through the pulmonary circulation = pulmonary emboli.
   ▶ Blood clots form in the upper legs, break loose, travel through the vasculature, the heart, and into the lungs, where they occlude blood flow, preventing the blood from being oxygenated.

2. **Carbon monoxide poisoning**—bad blood, no binding sites for O_2!
   ▶ SOB with change in LOC.
   ▶ There is plenty of O_2 and plenty of blood, but the blood is unable to absorb and transport the O_2 because the hemoglobin is bound up by CO = carbon monoxide poisoning.
   ▶ CO has a 200 times greater affinity for the iron in the hemoglobin molecule, and it binds permanently, eliminating that carrier molecule for O_2 transport.
   ▶ This accumulation can occur slowly over time.

3. **Hypovolemic shock**—not enough blood: low-volume shock!
   ▶ SOB, anxiety, with tachycardia and hypotension.
   ▶ There is enough O_2 but there may not be enough blood to transport the required amount of O_2 = hypovolemic shock.
   ▶ Something has occurred to reduce the blood volume: dehydration, vomiting, diarrhea, sweating, or blood loss.
   ▶ This reduction in blood volume reduces the O_2 carrying capacity of the blood.

4. **Cardiogenic shock**—the pump is failing: low-flow shock!
   ▶ SOB, anxious, with tachycardia, hypotension.
   ▶ There may be plenty of O_2 and ample blood, but the heart is not working well enough to meet the demands, thereby causing heart failure = cardiogenic shock.
   ▶ When heart failure occurs from an acute MI—the cardiac output of the heart decreases, which decreases the blood flow to the brain and the rest of the body.

5. **Neurogenic shock**—the pipe is too big: low-resistance shock!
   ▶ SOB, anxiety, tachycardia, hypotension.
   ▶ Plenty of O_2, ample blood, and the pump is fine, but the pipes have vasodilated. There is not enough blood volume to fill the pipes = neurogenic shock.
   ▶ Vasodilation can be caused by loss of communication with the brain due to a spinal cord injury (neurogenic shock), by excess quantities of histamine (anaphylactic shock), or by the toxins produced in an overwhelming infection (septic shock).

LUNG DISORDERS

1. **Pulmonary edema**—O_2 can't get into the alveoli!
   ▶ SOB and crackles.
   ▶ There is enough O_2 in the alveoli, but O_2 exchange is not occurring in the alveoli because the O_2 cannot cross the cell membrane into the blood, caused by an accumulation of fluid in the alveoli = pulmonary edema.
   ▶ Pulmonary edema can be caused by congestive heart failure, smoke inhalation, pneumonia, or high altitude pulmonary edema.

OTHER DISORDERS

1. **Cyanide poisoning**— O_2 can't be used by the cells!
   ▶ SOB and rapid change in LOC.
   ▶ There is plenty of O_2 in the blood, but the cells in the body are unable to use the O_2 on a cellular level = cyanide poisoning.
   ▶ Cyanide poisoning prevents the utilization of O_2 in the cells.
   ▶ This in turn prevents oxidative phosphorylation and the ability to burn glucose to produce energy. The body quickly becomes depleted of energy on the cellular level.

2. **Hyperventilation syndrome**
   ▶ SOB, paresthesia of the lips and hands, brought on by an overreaction to anxiety or fear, resulting in rapid breathing.
   ▶ Rapid breathing reduces the amount of CO_2, causing nausea, dizziness, and a tingling sensation of the lips, hands, and feet. It can also cause carpopedal spasms and unconsciousness.
   ▶ If they go unconscious, they will spontaneously recover.

chest pain

 the one chief complaint that gets everyone's attention in emergency medicine, for one simple reason—it may indicate that the person is having a **HEART ATTACK** and may truly be in significant trouble. Time is of the essence. Treat all chest pain as cardiac until you rule it out.

A&P of the cardiovascular system

For detailed anatomy info, see the chest trauma section

HEART: the pump

- Muscle (myocardial muscle)
- Conduction System to coordinate the contracture of the pump
- Valves to maintain direction of the blood flow through the heart

VASCULATURE: the pipes

- Arteries (carry blood away from the heart)
- Veins (carry blood toward the heart)
- Capillaries (the tiniest vessels that reach each cell)

BLOOD: the transport fluid and cells

- Serum (plasma without clotting factors)
- Plasma (the fluid of the blood without the cells)
- Red blood cells (RBC), white blood cells (WBC), and platelets

Cardiac chest pain causes/definitions

CAUSES
- Cardiac pain is caused primarily by ischemia of the myocardial cells. Ischemia is lack of blood supply to cells resulting in a decrease in oxygen and glucose supply.
- Hypoxia is decreased oxygen to the cells—which causes the chest pain.
- The heart does not have pain receptors—if it did you would constantly feel your heart beating. When individual myocardial cells do not have enough oxygen to function, they signal distress by referring pain to the surrounding tissues, which do have pain receptors.

DEFINITIONS of words and acronyms commonly used when discussing cardiac disease:
- **Atherosclerosis:** Narrowing of arteries caused by lipid deposits building up on the lining of the vessels
- **Arteriosclerosis:** Hardening of the arterial walls that occurs with aging
- **Hypertension:** High blood pressure that is high enough to likely cause cardiac damage over time—defined as either/or a systolic blood pressure over 140mmHg or a diastolic blood pressure over 90mmHg

ANGINA PECTORIS

A narrowing of the coronary circulation to a point where ischemia/hypoxia of the heart muscle occurs under exertion, causing chest pain.

SIGNS AND SYMPTOMS

- A previous history of angina
- Non-traumatic chest pain or discomfort (pressure, squeezing, fullness in the center of the chest)
- Occurs/increases with exertion (indicates stable angina)
- Occurs at rest (indicates unstable angina)
- Shortness of breath (SOB)— during exertion: stable; during rest: unstable
- Possible nausea
- Sweating (diaphoresis): Does it occur with the chest pain and shortness of breath
- Dizziness (indicated low blood pressure (hypotension)
- Changes in symptoms or an increase in severity may indicate a more serious heart condition—unstable angina; seek definitive care immediately

ACUTE MYOCARDIAL INFARCTION (MI)

A partial or complete blockage of an area of a coronary artery resulting in ischemia or death to that part of the heart muscle supplied by that coronary artery—the classic heart attack. An MI can be caused by plaque rupture or a blood clot.

SIGNS AND SYMPTOMS

- Non-traumatic, substernal, left-sided chest pain, pressure, or tightness—the discomfort may radiate to the jaw, arm(s), or back.
- Dyspnea (SOB) present at rest, worsened by exertion
- Pale, cool, and clammy skin
- Diaphoresis
- Vital signs: rapid and shallow respirations, rapid and weak heartbeat, falling BP
- Sense of "impending doom"
- Hypotension
- Nausea
- GI upset
- Heartburn
- Cardiogenic shock (inadequate circulation)

CONGESTIVE HEART FAILURE (CHF)

CHF typically occurs with an acute MI in the left ventricle (75% of all MIs). Normally, the blood flow out of the right ventricle and into the lungs equals the blood flow out of the left ventricle and into the systemic circulation. An AMI in the left ventricle causes ischemia of the myocardium, decreasing cardiac contraction, resulting in less blood flow out of the left ventricle. With more blood leaving the right ventricle than there is leaving the left ventricle, back-pressure in the pulmonary circulation results, causing fluid in the pulmonary vessels to leak out into the alveoli resulting in pulmonary edema—CHF

SIGNS AND SYMPTOMS

- Respiratory distress, with increasing SOB
- Cardiogenic shock with particularly pale to cyanotic skin
- Crackles—pulmonary edema on auscultation of lungs
- Cough—as the CHF worsens, the cough will become productive of sputum that may be frothy and tinged with blood
- The patient is not willing to lie flat, as it makes breathing harder

Patients often feel crushing pressure

Nausea and vomiting

Two of the most common symptoms associated with illness and stress are nausea and vomiting. Nausea is that vague uneasy sensation that you are going to vomit. Vomiting is the action by which the stomach contents are expelled out of the mouth.

The causes of nausea and vomiting are many and include infections, viruses, food poisoning, appendicitis, and peritonitis, as well as motion sickness, intestinal blockage, concussion, migraines, and anxiety. The symptoms can also indicate very serious life-threatening illnesses such as a heart attack, meningitis, encephalitis, kidney disease, liver disease, brain tumors, or cancer.

The sensation of nausea and the action of vomiting are controlled by the vomiting center in the brain, the area postrema. The area postrema receives signals from four locales around the body—three are in the gastrointestinal tract: the mouth, stomach, and intestines. These react to taste as well as toxins in food, which can cause food poisoning. The fourth locale is the brain, which constantly monitors the bloodstream for the chemicals of infections as well as certain medications that can cause nausea and vomiting.

The vestibular (balance) apparatus in the ears, when out of kilter, can also cause dizziness, nausea, and vomiting. And the brain can even induce nausea and vomiting from unpleasant sights, smells, and even thoughts.

Nausea and vomiting are symptoms of an underlying problem. Fortunately, the problem is usually benign and self-limiting.

The primary concerns are the risks of dehydration from not drinking enough, and electrolyte depletion from vomiting. If associated with diarrhea, the loss of electrolytes becomes an even greater risk.

PRINCIPLES OF MANAGING NAUSEA AND VOMITING

1. Try to prevent dehydration by taking small sips of a clear fluid often (ginger ale, fruit juices, or electrolyte drinks like Gatorade). This is preferred to drinking a larger volume less frequently because an upset stomach will only tolerate small amounts of fluid. Cold fluids are tolerated better than hot fluids.
2. Herbal remedies: Solutions of a ginger, peppermint, or chamomile tea will help to control nausea.
3. Over-the-counter (OTC) medications:
   - Pepto-Bismol® (bismuth subsalicylate) will help to calm the stomach and control diarrhea. Pepto-Bismol® cannot be used in someone who is allergic to aspirin. It should not be used in children and teenagers younger than 18-years-old if there is a chance that the illness is associated with viral influenza or chickenpox due to the risk of Reye's Syndrome, a left-threatening encephalopathy.

Yes, this subject is decidedly nasty—fortunately, it's typically not serious.

   - OTC antihistamines such as dimenhydrinate, diphenhydramine, and meclizine may help with nausea and vomiting caused by motion sickness.
4. Prescription drugs for nausea and vomiting:
   - A variety of medications for nausea and vomiting are used depending on the underlying diagnosis and cause. Two of the most common drugs for treating nausea and vomiting are phenergan and compazine. Both are available as suppositories so they will not contribute to the problem of nausea.
     → Phenergan (promethazine) suppository 25mg, one per rectum every 12 hours as needed for nausea and vomiting.
     → Compazine (prochlorperazine) suppository 5mg, one per rectum every 12 hours as needed for nausea and vomiting.
5. Once the patient is feeling better and their appetite has returned, advance the diet slowly with small quantities of bland food, such as the BRAT diet—Bananas, Rice, Applesauce, and Toast. Avoid greasy, hard-to-digest foods for 24 hours.
6. When to seek help:
   - Although nausea and vomiting are typically benign and self-correcting, you should seek help if they are associated with:
     → A fever greater than 102.5°F/39°C
     → A change (deterioration) in level of consciousness
     → Seizure activity
     → Bright red blood or digested blood (the latter looks like coffee grounds) in the vomitus
     → Vomiting that is frequent and copious and causes the patient to become progressively dehydrated
     → Symptoms lasting more than 24 hours that are not easily controlled

ABDO PAIN — DECISION TIME

When to evacuate to definitive care

It's time to combine all the information that you have gathered: the HPI, physical exam, and vital signs, and decide on your action plan

Okay, now what?

IMMEDIATE EVACUATION

Seek out medical assistance immediately if they have abdominal pain   any one of the following ...

- S/S of shock:
  - Rapid, weak, pulse
  - Rapid, shallow, respirations
  - Pale, cool, clammy skin
  - Delayed capillary refill
- Rebound tenderness on physical exam
- The abdominal wall is rigid and tender to deep palpation
- They have obvious distention and tenderness of the abdomen
- They have blood in their vomitus
- They have blood in their stool (bright red blood or black tarry stools)
- High volume watery diarrhea
- A fever greater than 103°F (40°C) with shaking rigors
- They are pregnant, with abdominal pain

CONSIDER EVACUATION

Consider evacuation if they have abdominal pain   ...

- The pain has lasted, without improvement, for more than 24 hours
- The pain suddenly increases in intensity over several hours
- The pain has gone from generalized to localized
- Vomiting has lasted for more than 24 hours
- Diarrhea has lasted, without improvement, for more than 24 hours

An understanding of abdominal anatomy may be helpful here: please see the abdominal trauma section.

Care while seeking medical assistance

- Handle the patient gently and transport the patient in the position of comfort
- Do not give them anything to eat or drink unless they are dehydrated
- If dehydrated, IV fluids are preferred, but if not available, give them frequent small sips of clear fluids as tolerated
- Treat them for shock if necessary with O₂ and fluids
- May control vomiting with compazine or phenergan rectal suppositories, if available
- May control a high fever, temperature above 104°F (40°C), by using acetaminophen orally or rectally, or by using tepid water sponge baths

If evacuation and outside medical assistance is not needed

- Allow them to rest in a position of comfort
- Complete stomach rest— nothing by mouth for 2 hours
- After 2 hours, give small amounts of clear liquids every 10 – 15 minutes
- If tolerating fluids well, may slowly increase for the next 24 hours
- Do not feed them until they develop an appetite—once they have an appetite advance their diet slowly, with bland, easy-to-digest food: the BRAT diet (bananas, rice, apple-sauce, toast, etc.) for the next 24 hours
- Evacuate if symptoms worsen

SECTION 4

You are here, and you are very cold.

ASSESSMENT AND MANAGEMENT OF ENVIRONMENTAL EMERGENCIES AND INJURIES

WE ARE A NAKED, hairless, warm-blooded, tropical animal that must make and take a microenvironmemt with us everywhere we go so we don't die. We are not designed for the cold, yet we live in all the climates of the world—including some brutally cold places like Siberia, Patagonia, and Minneapolis. Huh...

THE HUMANIMAL

Brains, sweat glands, and fleece made from soda bottles, versus instinct, panting, and a warm burrow

THE HUMAN ANIMAL— Unlike a bull moose, who loves cold climes and has antlers to keep him warm (okay, it's the hair, not the antlers), as soon as we head toward the poles from San Diego, St. John, or Nairobi, we must make do by bringing with us clothing, shelter, and a heat source— otherwise, we just turn into Popsicles.

If you're standing naked on a Minneapolis sidewalk in January or out in the African bush in the top of summer, your only hope of staying alive (and tolerably comfortable) comes down to three things.*

Thermoregulation

Hydration

Nutrition

* Of course, you may also need some friendly advice about some basic life issues.

"This thing is heavy, I think it's time to shed."
—Luke Sekera-Flanders, SOLO intern

Thermoregulation **maintaining thermal equilibrium**

As the name implies, this is a balancing act between heat production, heat conservation, heat transfer, and heat loss designed to maintain the optimum core temperature of 98.6°F (37°C).

THERMOGENESIS

There are three ways to produce heat: metabolism, exercise, and behavior.

Metabolism—the set of chemical reactions that happen in living organisms to maintain life. These processes allow organisms to grow and reproduce, maintain their structures, and respond to their environments.

- Metabolism uses oxygen to burn calories which sustain life and produce heat.
- The vast majority of calories that we burn are carbohydrates or starches—sugars, glucose, and fructose.
- In order to keep the metabolic fires burning, we must keep stoking the fire with glucose and fructose by snacking often on simple sugars rather than proteins and fats—this helps maintain a higher blood sugar level.
- In a well-fed state, we maintain a 24-hour emergency supply of glucose, stored in our liver as glycogen. This 24-hour supply is at rest—on a cold winter day that store can be depleted in 5 to 6 hours.
- Metabolic activity is regulated by the thyroid, which uses the hormone thyroxine (T3 and T4) to establish the rate at which we burn calories.
- Basal metabolism is the minimum amount of energy required to maintain vital functions in an organism at complete rest.
- When the body senses a need to increase the metabolic rate (due to a cooling core temperature, or exercise) the thyroid can increase calorie consumption up to five times the normal rate.

Exercise—Muscle activity produces heat.

- Voluntary muscle activity is willful exercise: hiking, skiing, running, climbing, etc. Exercise can produce excess heat that must be vented or dissipated.
- Involuntary exercise (shivering) is a natural, involuntary response to early hypothermia in warm-blooded animals which occurs when the core temperature drops.
  - Shivering is designed to maintain homeostasis—its sole function is to produce heat. It can increase heat production up to 10 times the normal rate.
  - Shivering requires oxygen and glucose to work—you must fuel the fire. If fuel runs out, shivering will slow and eventually halt, and dangerous hypothermia will likely set in.

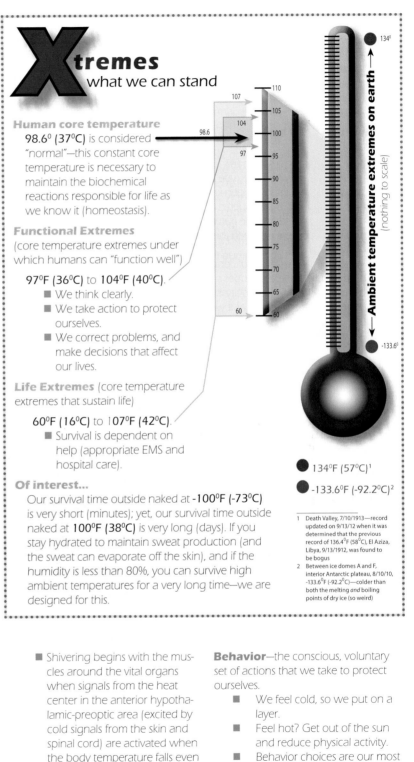

Xtremes
what we can stand

Human core temperature

98.6° (37°C) is considered "normal"—this constant core temperature is necessary to maintain the biochemical reactions responsible for life as we know it (homeostasis).

Functional Extremes (core temperature extremes under which humans can "function well")

97°F (36°C) to 104°F (40°C).
- We think clearly.
- We take action to protect ourselves.
- We correct problems, and make decisions that affect our lives.

Life Extremes (core temperature extremes that sustain life)

60°F (16°C) to 107°F (42°C).
- Survival is dependent on help (appropriate EMS and hospital care).

Of interest...

Our survival time outside naked at -100°F (-73°C) is very short (minutes); yet, our survival time outside naked at 100°F (38°C) is very long (days). If you stay hydrated to maintain sweat production (and the sweat can evaporate off the skin), and if the humidity is less than 80%, you can survive high ambient temperatures for a very long time—we are designed for this.

Ambient temperature extremes on earth (nothing to scale)

134°
-133.6°

● 134°F (57°C)[1]
● -133.6°F (-92.2°C)[2]

1 Death Valley, 7/10/1913—record updated on 9/13/12 when it was determined that the previous record of 136.4°F (58°C), El Aziza, Libya, 9/13/1912, was found to be bogus
2 Between ice domes A and F, interior Antarctic plateau, 8/10/10, -133.6°F (-92.2°C)—colder than both the melting and boiling points of dry ice (so weird)

- Shivering begins with the muscles around the vital organs when signals from the heat center in the anterior hypothalamic-preoptic area (excited by cold signals from the skin and spinal cord) are activated when the body temperature falls even a fraction of a degree below a critical temperature level.
- Unfortunately, shivering produces no useful work, and can actually interfere with the performance of important tasks (e.g., starting a fire, walking).

Behavior—the conscious, voluntary set of actions that we take to protect ourselves.

- We feel cold, so we put on a layer.
- Feel hot? Get out of the sun and reduce physical activity.
- Behavior choices are our most important defense against becoming too cold or too hot.

Assessment and Management of Environmental Emergencies and Injuries

Evaporation

Evaporation

- Evaporation is the transfer of heat via the vaporization of a liquid. For this discussion: the evaporation of water from the surface of the skin.
  - All warm-blooded animals use the evaporation of water to cool.
  - Fur-covered mammals and birds pant, evaporating water out of their lungs, thus cooling the pulmonary circulation. Short, shallow breaths move air in and out of the upper airways without causing gas exchange in the alveoli. This avoids the risks and consequences of hyperventilation—blowing off too much CO_2. As the CO_2 level goes down, the pH of the blood goes up (see hyperventilation syndrome).
- Humans sweat, and the evaporation of water from the skin (our largest organ, accounting for approximately 10% of our body weight) cools the blood flowing in the venous circulation below it, and thus, the systemic circulation, removing excess heat from the core.

- One gram-calorie equals the amount of energy necessary to raise 1 gram of water 1 degree Celsius. One kilocalorie equals the energy necessary to raise 1 kilogram (1,000 grams) of water 1 degree Celsius.
- Heat transfer ranges from 0% – 90% depending on how warm the object is, how warm the water is, the moisture content (humidity) differential, and the surrounding vapor pressure.
  - The greater the moisture differential and the lower the vapor pressure, the greater the rate of heat loss.
  - The higher percentage of humidity, the slower the rate of evaporation.
  - The lower the vapor pressure, the drier the air, the faster water will evaporate, and the greater the rate of heat loss.

- If we begin to overheat, our thermal regulatory center in the brain sends out a signal to the sweat glands in the skin, and they secrete sweat onto the surface of the skin.
- As the sweat evaporates, it will remove the heat from the blood flowing through the capillaries in the skin, cooling the blood that returns to the core.
- We must stay hydrated to keep this heat pump going.

Hydration *The ocean within*

THE WET FACTS

- We live in our own sea made up of salt water and electrolytes.
- Water helps maintain homeostasis (including thermoregulation).
- Life is totally dependent upon water—you can survive three days without water (months without food).
- Water is used in the digestion and in the absorption and utilization of nutrients.

ELECTROLYTES

- Sodium (Na), chloride (Cl), potassium (K), calcium (Ca)
- Together, electrolytes help maintain cellular fluid volume and effect electrical conduction.
- Sodium, chloride, and potassium allow nutrients and water to cross cell membranes.
- Sodium is primarily found in the extracellular fluid surrounding the cells.
- Sodium chloride is table salt—so we get it in our diet by eating salty foods.
- Potassium is primarily an intracellular fluid, and is found in many fruits and vegetables, especially bananas.

- Calcium allows muscle contraction (including the heartbeat) and nerve conduction via the myocardial cells in the heart. Calcium is found in all dairy products, meats, and many vegetables. Our skeletal system is made out of a matrix of calcium—if our serum calcium level begins to drop, we absorb some out of our bones.
- Electrolytes are maintained in our body in exact quantities and proportions—too little or too much causes problems.

Oh, we like to think of ourselves as solid. *"He's a **SOLID** citizen,"* we say, or, *"She's a **SOLID** performer."* But the drippy reality is we're mostly just juice.

About 57% of us is water. (about 40 quarts water for a 155lb person). Daily requirements: ½ your body weight in ounces—a 155lb person needs about 70 ounces (4.5 pints per day). Fluid requirements increase dramatically when exercising (see chart next page).

✳ The principle behind all electrolyte drinks is to provide the athlete with a fluid that contains water, sugar, sodium, chloride, and potassium.

DETERMINE YOUR OWN HYDRATION REQUIREMENTS

1. Weigh yourself (naked).
2. Do your intended exercise for up to several hours without drinking.
3. After 2 – 4 hours (no more than 4), weigh yourself again (naked—this is important because your clothing can absorb and retain lots of water lost from sweating).
4. The lost weight will be water.
5. Calculate the fluid loss (a gallon of water weighs 8lbs).
6. Use the result to estimate your fluid replacement needs while exercising.
7. Increase or decrease your water intake based on intensity level.

Water losses per day			
H₂O loss Mechanism	Normal Temperature	Hot Temperature	Heavy Exercise
Skin	350ml	350ml	350ml
Respiration	350ml	250ml	650ml
Sweating	100ml	1400ml	5000ml
Urination	1400ml	1200ml	500ml
Defecation	100ml	100ml	100ml
TOTALS	2300ml	3300ml	6600ml

Variables

- Water requirements will vary with activity, sweat output, and altitude.
- Exertional heat loss ranges from 1 – 3 liters/hour for up to 4 hours without replacement. A person can lose up to 10% of their body weight from sweating in 4 hours—this can be deadly.
- Altitude has a very low vapor pressure, which increases the evaporation rate. You can lose up to 1 cup/hour via respirations (6 quarts—1.5 gallons) in 24 hours.
- Hydrate often and drink more than you think you will need.
- Do not rely on thirst to tell you when to drink.

Electrolyte replacement: sodium (70%), potassium (20%), and calcium (5%).

If you wait until you're thirsty, you're already dehydrated

Nutrition

- About **70%** of daily caloric intake is expended in the operation and maintenance of the body (metabolic processes and thermoregulation).

- The remaining **30%** is expended in movement.

- The **only fuel burned** in our cellular furnace is **glucose** or **fructose**.

- In a **well-fed state**, we maintain a **24-hour emergency supply of glucose** in our liver as glycogen.

- That 24-hour supply is **at rest**; on a cold winter day in just **5 to 6 hours** you can **deplete** that store.

CARB/FAT/PROTEIN		
Carbohydrates	Fat	Protein
60% of daily nutritional requirements	10% of daily nutritional requirements	30% of daily nutritional requirements
4 calories/gram	9 calories/gram	4 calories/gram
200 – 400 grams/day (800 – 1600 calories/day)	20 – 60 grams/day (180 – 540 calories/day)	30 – 55 grams/day (120 – 220 calories/day)

Typical Daily Calorie Needs
Normal daily activity: 2000 – 2500 calories/day
Winter outdoor sports: 3000 – 4000 calories/day
When exposed to the cold, we can increase our basal metabolism—our fuel consumption—five times
High-altitude mountaineering: 4000 – 6000 calories/day

" Swedish snowmobilers who thought they had discovered a car wreck found inside a man very much alive, two months after the car was snowed under by a sudden storm.

The man, Peter Skyllberg, 45, was barely breathing and could utter little more than a few short words. Police are not sure why he was in the forest in the first place. They found no food or water in the car and concluded that the man had probably eaten snow at some point. "
dailymail.co.uk
21 February, 2012

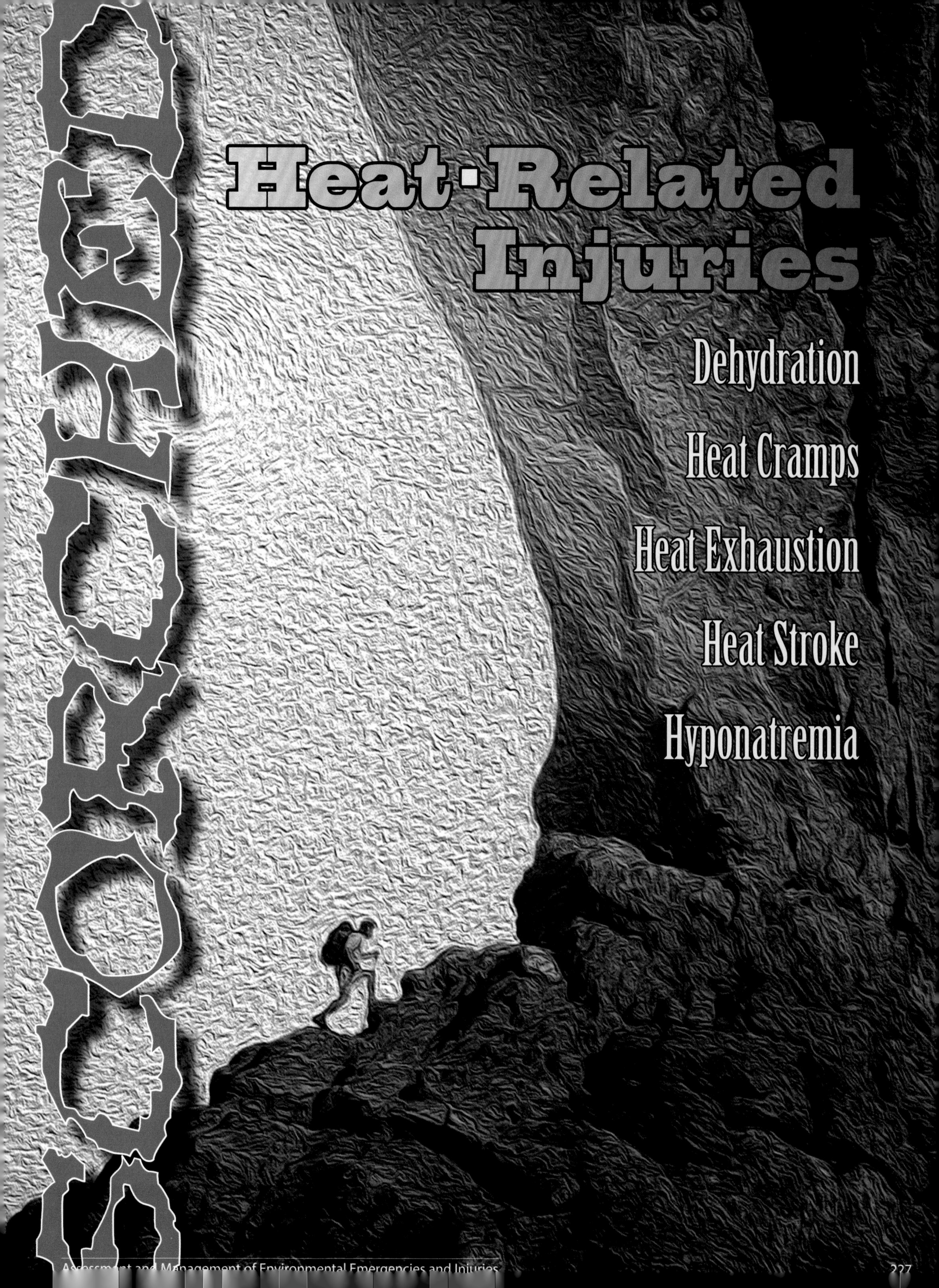

Heat-Related Injuries

Dehydration

Heat Cramps

Heat Exhaustion

Heat Stroke

Hyponatremia

Heat-related injuries

are some of the most common emergencies seen in the outdoor setting, and in virtually every circumstance they can be prevented because they are so often related to behavior. An understanding of the risks and preventive measures can go a long way in reducing the frequency and severity of these emergencies.

Causes

- Excessive dehydration from sweating and salt-loss (without replacement) in a warm environment to the extent that the sweating mechanism can no longer function.
- A high-humidity environment where sweat cannot evaporate off the skin—causing the cooling effect to be lost.
- Failure to take precautions or recognizing early warning signs while exercising in a hot environment.
- Contributing factors include:
  - ☑ Age (the very young or very old are more susceptible)
  - ☑ Poor health
  - ☑ Fatigue
  - ☑ Prior history of heat illness
  - ☑ Use of certain medications
  - ☑ Alcohol consumption
  - ☑ Heart disease
  - ☑ Overexertion in a hot environment
- Heat illness is a continuum—if unrecognized and untreated, mild illness can progress to a life-threatening emergency.

Heat-related deaths

The CDC reports that 3,442 people died in the US between 1999 and 2003 from heat-related injuries. This is less than anaphylaxis (approximately 7,000 during the period), but far more than lightning (756 from 1990 to 2003)—two outdoor-related emergencies that typically get more press.

Average heat-related deaths/year: **688**

Causes:
- ☑ Exposure to excessive heat   65%
- ☑ Hyperthermia as a contributing factor   35%
- ☑ Age
  - less than 15   **7%**
  - 15 to 64   **53%**
  - more than 64   **40%**

States with highest incidence:

MO

NV

AZ

Dehydration 10/2*

S/S *signs & symptoms*
- Headache and mild nausea
- Irritability
- Dark urine
- Thirst

T *treatment*
1. Rehydrate with water and electrolytes (e.g., Gatorade).
2. Improvise: 1 liter of water, 1 teaspoon salt, 8 teaspoons sugar.
3. Pre-made oral rehydration solution (ORS).
4. ½ a banana or ½ cup of orange juice can also be added to help supply potassium.
5. Maintain hydration for the long term.

Heat Cramps 6/1

S/S *signs & symptoms*
- Muscle pain and cramping, usually in the legs, caused by dehydration and electrolytes depletion.
- Usually occurs after exercise.

T *treatment*
Treatment is the same as for dehydration.

---

* **First number:** how common it is from 1 (rare) to 10 (very common)

Second number: how dangerous it is from 1 (typically minor) to 10 (can be life threatening)

Heat Exhaustion 4/3

physiology

- Is caused by working in a hot environment.
- Is a combination of salt and water loss secondary to sweating in hot conditions.
- Heat exhaustion typically occurs in people who are not acclimatized to heat.
- Those not used to working in a hot environment will lose salt (sodium chloride: NaCl) more rapidly than someone whose physiology has adjusted to working in hot conditions. Sodium plays an important role in maintaining cell wall integrity and membrane permeability, and is essential in maintaining normal homeostasis on a cellular level. If the amount of sodium in the extracellular fluid decreases, system-wide cellular dysfunction will occur, causing flu-like or exhaustion symptoms.
- The combined loss of water and a decrease in sodium is known as hyponatremia (see Hyponatremia).
- Heat exhaustion is not a life-threatening emergency: it is relieved by rest, hydration, and electrolyte replacement.

signs & symptoms

- Fatigue (which can be profound)
- Thirst
- Possible dizziness
- Increased heart rate
- Increased respiratory rate
- Pale, clammy skin
- Muscle cramps
- Nausea with possible vomiting
- Level of consciousness: minor mood changes that can vary from a simple headache and slight anxiety to agitation, confusion, and syncope.
- Pulse: with dehydration and volume contraction, heat-exhaustion patients will have a compensatory increase in pulse—the greater degree of dehydration, the faster the pulse.
- Blood pressure: at rest, their BP will be stable, but they may have mild orthostatic hypotension (low blood pressure) that is quickly remedied when they are supine. Orthostatic dizziness— dizziness caused by low blood pressure (the familiar "head rush" you get when you stand up quickly after being at rest).
- Respirations: breathing rate may be mildly increased, primarily from a symptomatic hyperventilation caused by anxiety.
- Skin: the capillary beds in the skin may vasoconstrict in reaction to the hypovolemia resulting in pale, cool, and clammy skin. Alternately, the skin may be warm and flushed in reaction to the heat.

treatment

1. Even without treatment, the patient will most likely spontaneously recover on their own over several hours. With appropriate treatment, recovery will be much faster.
2. Rest in a cool place.
3. Find shade if possible.
4. Remove any excess clothing that may trap heat.
5. Apply cool cloths to body (e.g., damp bandanna on forehead).
6. Replace lost fluid and salt (see dehydration treatment). At least 1 – 2 liters of oral rehydration solution (ORS—see the dehydration section).
7. Monitor body temperature.
8. The patient should recover within 6 – 8 hours.
9. Once recovered, the patient can cautiously resume activity.
10. If the symptoms of heat exhaustion are ignored and the person continues to work and sweat hard, it can progress to heat stroke

The young and old are most susceptible to heat stroke.

Okay, this is a big nasty one—thankfully, it's fairly rare. In the wilderness environment, most people quit exerting themselves long before heat stroke sets in. In the urban environment, heat stroke deaths make the news when competitive athletes (marathon runners, football players) push themselves (or are pushed by others) way beyond the danger point. With understanding, preparation, and vigilance, heat stroke is *always* preventable. But once it really gets going, it's almost impossible to stop outside of an emergency department.

■ Heat stroke is a *life-threatening* emergency.

■ If not treated immediately, it will quickly progress to *coma and death*.

■ The time from the onset of symptoms to *death* can be as little as *15 minutes* after the sweating mechanism fails and the core temperature begins to rise.

■ For those who survive, heat stroke can cause *permanent disability*—a number of tissues can suffer end-damage from the increased core temperature.

types

Classic
- Dehydration in a hot environment caused by the person "over-sweating" without replacing lost fluids, which leads to the failure of the sweating mechanism, causing the core temperature to rise rapidly.
- The patient is losing water faster than they are replacing it.
- Once the sweating mechanism fails, cooling stops and the core temperature rises rapidly.

Exertional
- Exercising in a hot and high-humidity environment where the sweat mechanism cannot function because the sweat cannot evaporate; again, the core temperature rises rapidly. The sweat, even though copious, cannot evaporate fast enough, and the patient overheats.

When the sweating stops...LOOK OUT!

pathology

- Brain: encephalopathy (swelling of the brain) is the norm.
- Liver: hepatic (liver-related) injury is common, and the liver is most susceptible to early damage.
- Interesting note: the liver is a biochemical factory that is so busy with chemical reactions that it is normally 1 degree C warmer (2 degrees F) than the rest of the body.
- Because it runs warmer anyway, the liver has less of a temperature buffer and permanent damage is possible (and can occur faster).
- Kidneys: Renal failure is common due to myoglobinuria (the presence of myoglobin, an iron- and oxygen-binding protein in the muscle tissue of most mammals, in the urine) from rhabdomyolysis (the rapid breakdown of skeletal muscle due to injury to muscle tissue).
- Muscles: Damage results from rhabdomyolysis (see previous bullet).
- Blood: Coagulopathy (clotting disorders) due to disseminated intravascular coagulation (DIC) is common.
- Death occurs when the core temperature exceeds 107 degrees/41.6 degrees—the point at which the tissues of the brain are destroyed.

signs & symptoms S/S

- The patient will be "red, hot, and mad" due to vasodilation as the body tries to deal with the increase in core temperature.
- The skin is red, hot, and may be dry (classic) or sweaty (exertional).
- The patient cannot continue to sweat because they are dehydrated, or because evaporation is impossible (i.e., high humidity).
- The patient will have a change in level of consciousness (LOC): they will be disoriented, confused, combative, and may hallucinate wildly. These changes are caused by core temperatures above 104F/40C.
- The patient may have seizures.
- The patient may not be able to urinate.
- The patient will have an increased heart rate.
- The patient will have an increased respiratory rate.

treatment

Heat stroke needs to be recognized early and treated aggressively. The duration and degree of temperature elevation determines the level of organ damage and the ability for the patient to recover.

1. Remove the patient from the heat and sun and place them in a cool, shady place.
2. Remove clothing down to underwear.
3. Cool them immediately by soaking with cool water and fanning to accelerate evaporation.
4. Vigorously massage limbs to encourage hot blood to flow to the extremities where it can cool.
5. Beware of shivering, as shivering produces heat. If they begin shivering, stop cooling them until they stop shivering, then resume cooling at a less aggressive rate.
6. May consider paralytics to control shivering. Consult Medical Control.
7. Lorazepam 0.5 – 1mg IV/IM or diazepam 2mg IV or 5mg IM.
8. Avoid vasopressors and anticholinergic drugs.
9. Hydrate once conscious.
10. Do not allow the patient to exercise.
11. Evacuate immediately to definitive care (don't let the patient walk out on their own—you may have to improvise a litter).
12. Continue cooling during transport.
13. Administer high-flow oxygen by non-rebreather mask, if available.
14. Adult: IV therapy: 1 – 2 liters of normal saline, wide open (maintain systolic BP > 90mmHg).
15. Pediatric: IV therapy, bolus with 20 ml/kg normal saline to maintain hemodynamic status.
16. Monitor the EKG.

Prevention · differential diagnosis · risks

prevention

1. Stay well-hydrated.
2. Replace electrolytes.
3. Wear proper clothing (including a hat).
4. Rest often when exerting yourself in a hot environment.

differential diagnosis

- Classic or exertional due to a hot environment, or a hot and humid environment.
- Infection—meningococcemia (an acute and potentially life-threatening infection of the bloodstream), Plasmodium falciparum (malaria).
- Pontine or hypothalamic hemorrhage (intracranial bleeds: CVA).
- Drug intoxication—cocaine, amphetamines, phencyclidine, theophylline, tricyclic antidepressants.
- Alcohol or sedative withdrawal.
- Severe hypertonic dehydration (primarily a loss of water).
- Thyroid storm—a life-threatening condition that occurs rarely in 1 – 2% of patients with hyperhyroidism that raises the HR, BP and body temperature to uncontrollable levels. A patient suffering a thyroid storm must be immediately transported to a hospital.

risk factors

- Poor acclimatization to heat or poor physical conditioning.
- Dehydration, febrile illness , chronic illness (DM, HTN), obesity.
- Medications: antihistamines, antipsychotics, antidepressants.
- Alcohol or other recreational drugs.
- Environment: high humidity, poor air circulation.
- Hyponatremia.

"A runner who died after crossing the finish line at the Rock 'n' Roll San Antonio Marathon and ½ Marathon likely suffered heat stroke, according to autopsy results released by the Bexar County medical examiner's office. Jorge Fernandez, 32, died on Nov. 13, 2011 after completing the 13.1-mile race. His death was ruled an accident; the cause was 'probable heat stroke,' the medical examiner's office said."

San Antonio Express-News, November 14, 2011

* **First number**: how common it is from 1 (rare) to 10 (very common)

Second number: how dangerous it is from 1 (typically minor) to 10 (can be life-threatening)

Hyponatremia ^{1/7}*

P physiology

- Our bodies are composed of about 57% water, but it isn't plain water—it is an electrolyte solution containing sodium, chloride, potassium, calcium, and others. These electrolytes aid in passing nutrients through our cell walls and in maintaining cellular fluid volume and effective electrical conduction.
- Sodium is found primarily in the extracellular fluid surrounding the cell, while potassium is primarily an intracellular fluid. These electrolytes change places, acting as a pump to bring other nutrients into the cell.
- Calcium helps in muscle contraction, nerve conduction, and is used by the myocardial cells of the heart to contract and produce the heartbeat.
- In certain circumstances electrolytes can become depleted, and if depleted too far, this can be life-threatening.
- Hyponatremia, also called "water intoxication," occurs when free water (plain water, without electrolytes) is over-consumed.
- The excess water dilutes the existing sodium in the extracellular fluid, causing "dilutional hyponatremia."
- The kidneys react to the excess fluid by increasing urine production.
- This causes us to lose sodium, adding to the dilutional hyponatremia problem, lowering the extracellular concentration of sodium and causing a downward cascade of symptoms, which increases the severity of hyponatremia. The loss of sodium interferes with and slows cellular metabolism.
- This is a potentially life-threatening problem.

P prevention

- Hyponatremia is easy to prevent.
- Don't over-consume free water—drink fluids with electrolytes in them.
- There are many sports drinks that do an excellent job, Gatorade being perhaps the most well-known. Oral rehydration solution can also be improvised (see the dehydration section).
- Eat nuts (salted best) and fruits (bananas are great).

A 22 year-old male fitness instructor finished the 2007 London Marathon, collapsed, and despite immediate emergency medical care, died. His serum sodium was markedly low, and the cause of death was found to be hyponatremia.

Clinical Journal of Sport Medicine Blog, April 9, 2012

S/S signs & symptoms

- Similar to heat exhaustion, but can be much more serious.
- Nausea and vomiting.
- Lethargy.
- Orthostatic hypotension.
- Stupor.
- Coma.
- Seizures.
- If the symptoms are ignored, death can result. There have been several high-profile deaths in recent years involving both athletes and water-drinking contests.

T treatment

Sme as for heat exhaustion.

Prevention for • heat-related illness

P prevention

- Prevention of heat-related injuries, in particular, heat stroke, is very important because of the risk of permanent injury or even death.
- Maintain adequate fluid and electrolyte (salt) intake.
- Monitor the group for fluid and electrolyte intake.
- Be aware of changing environmental conditions. Allow time to acclimate to new environments.
- Wear proper clothing, including a hat.
- Avoid overexertion in hot and humid conditions: above 90F.; at or above 70% humidity.
- Rest often, especially in extreme environments.
- Do not allow outside pressure to push you beyond safe limits.

*
First number: how common it is from 1 (rare) to 10 (very common)

Second number: how dangerous it is from 1 (typically minor) to 10 (can be life threatening)

Arid and hot climates are beautiful.
But they can be deadly.
Explore smart.

Go to Google Earth to see where the
background photo was taken (○)

N36.126755555555 | W115.5031138888

Traversing the south face of Bridge
Mountain, on the way to the NE Arête
(   ), Spring Mountains, Nevada

Temperature: 100 degrees
Wind: not a whisper
Water: none for 20 hours (other than what was carried)

Cold-related Injuries

Hypothermia

Frostbite

Non-Freezing Cold Injuries

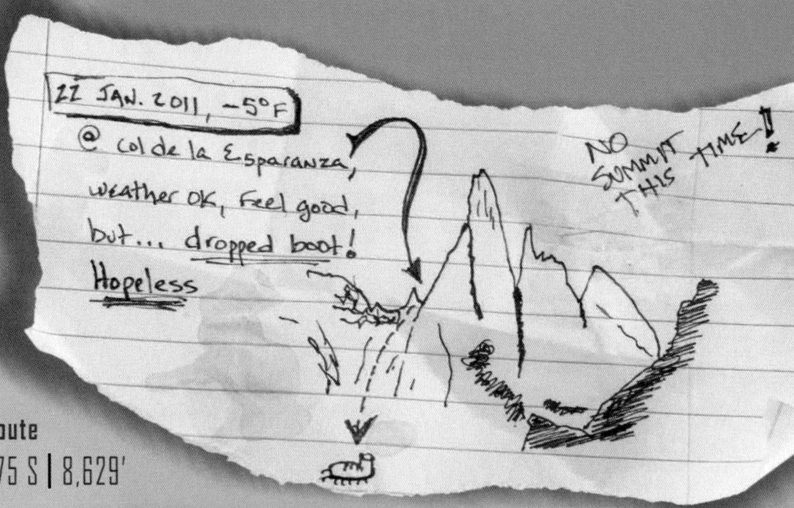

22 JAN. 2011, -5°F
@ col de la Esperanza,
weather OK, feel good,
but... dropped boot!
Hopeless

NO SUMMIT THIS TIME!

Cerro Torre ▪ Patagonia ▪ The Compressor Route
col de la Esperanza: 49.295281 W | 73.1008675 S | 8,629'

(dotted line shows path of wayward boot)

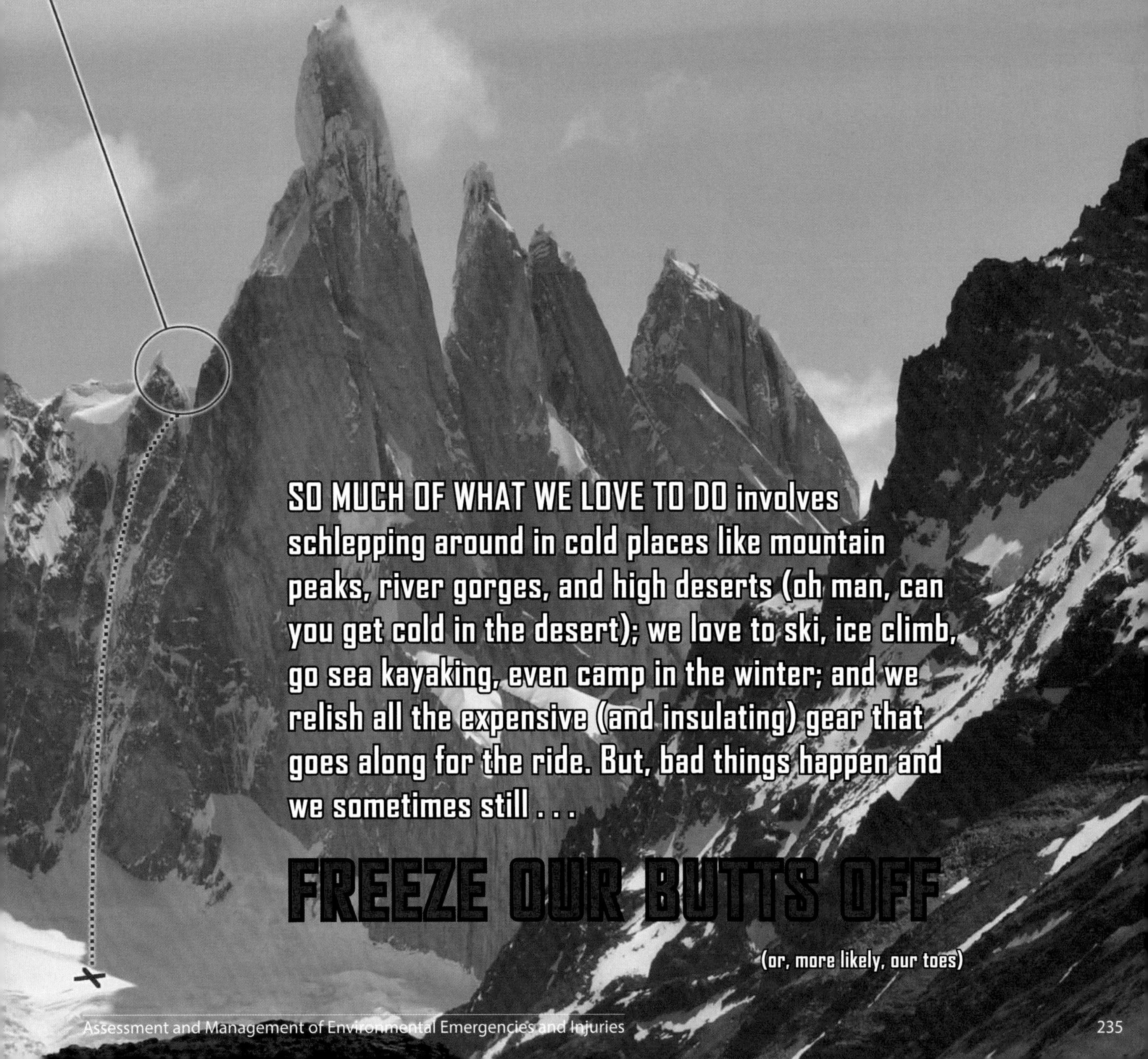

SO MUCH OF WHAT WE LOVE TO DO involves schlepping around in cold places like mountain peaks, river gorges, and high deserts (oh man, can you get cold in the desert); we love to ski, ice climb, go sea kayaking, even camp in the winter; and we relish all the expensive (and insulating) gear that goes along for the ride. But, bad things happen and we sometimes still . . .

FREEZE OUR BUTTS OFF

(or, more likely, our toes)

Hypoth

Stages of HYPOTHERMIA

The long slide from, "I'm fine," to coma

98.6°F (37°C)

PHYSIOLOGY: Walking and talking. Normal, all systems go.

COGNITION: We are mentally sharp, paying attention to details, monitoring our environment, and responding appropriately.

BEHAVIOR: We are physically coordinated, feeling strong and capable, making appropriate gear and clothing decisions, setting a pace appropriate for the conditions, eating and hydrating properly.

97°F (36°C)

PHYSIOLOGY: Brain functions slow.

The thermoregulatory center in the brain, sensing the heat loss, will initiate several defensive actions. It will vasoconstrict and reduce blood flow to the skin, creating an additional thermal layer to prevent further heat loss.

Piloerection occurs—our hairs stand on end in an attempt to create an insulating layer of dead air space.

The rate of metabolism will increase, burning more glucose to produce more heat.

COGNITION: Judgment begins to fail.

We become more focused on the trail in front of us and less aware of the weather and our surroundings. Enthusiasm wanes and apathy sets in.

BEHAVIOR: Protective instincts fade. We don't make the best gear and clothing decisions. We don't make the best food and hydration decisions.

Our mood and reactions change; we become more withdrawn.

96°F (35.5°C)

PHYSIOLOGY: All systems are on full alert, and the body is doing everything possible to rewarm itself from the inside.

Shivering begins as a constant, uncontrollable, fine motor tremor, and is caused by opposing muscle groups acting against each other. Shivering produces heat, but it is wasteful exercise that doesn't produce useful work—and interferes with other activities that require precision: swinging an ice axe, lighting a stove, pulling up a zipper.

Decreased fine motor skills—we begin to lose dexterity and our speech starts to slur.

Metabolism increases to meet the new fuel demands.

COGNITION: Mental abilities are falling rapidly. Decision-making, judgment, and "common sense" begin to fail. Self-preservation instincts are replaced with a "summit or bust" mentality.

BEHAVIOR: In the face of changing weather (e.g., drop in temperature, increase in wind), we may not take any constructive action (e.g., putting on another layer). We may leave clothing or equipment behind.

HYPOTHERMIA IS THE LOWERING OF THE BODY'S CORE TEMPERATURE to a level where normal brain and muscle functions are impaired. It typically happens when several things occur simultaneously: low temperatures (<40F/4.5C), wet conditions (damp clothes), lack of fuel and hydration (food and water), and physical fatigue. This cascade of problems causes our thermoregulatory system to fail—it just can't keep up with the heat loss (see the thermoregulation information in the Human Animal section).

94°F (34.5°C)

PHYSIOLOGY: Shivering is at its maximum, but other systems are slowing.

Metabolism is peaking, but fuel is being burned at such a furious rate (up to five times) that the stores will not last long (4 – 5 hours, rather than the typical 24). When the stores are used up, shivering (and thus, heat production) will slow, and eventually cease.

COGNITION: We are not aware of being cold. We believe that we are thinking clearly, but we're not. Simple problem-solving is impossible (we can't do basic addition/subtraction). When confronted with obvious problems—we're off the trail and thrashing about in a spruce trap—we may agree, but we really don't care.

BEHAVIOR: Coordination fails—tripping and falling begins. We have trouble staying on the trail and easily become lost.

We don't take care of ourselves—if we lose a crampon or a mitten or get a load of snow down our back, we don't do anything about it.

Still, we remain goal-oriented—onward to the top.

92°F (33.3°C)

PHYSIOLOGY: Shivering becomes intense.

COGNITION: Mentally, we are beginning to shut down. We enter a dream-like state where nothing seems real.

BEHAVIOR: We're unable to walk—though we may still be crawling toward the goal. Speech becomes very difficult.

90°F (32.2°C)

PHYSIOLOGY: Shivering becomes convulsive and begins to fail. Shivering is violent for a minute, then absent for a minute. We are running out of fuel and energy and shivering will soon cease.

COGNITION: We can still be aroused, and will try to answer questions, but our speech will be slurred, perhaps beyond recognition.

BEHAVIOR: Curling and mumbling. We adopt the fetal position—the body's last-ditch effort to protect the core and minimize heat loss.

As things deteriorate, we become less and less arousable, and as the final glucose stores are burned, our shivering mechanism begins to fail.

86°F (30°C)

PHYSIOLOGY: We become unconscious, ashen, and gray.

We enter a "Metabolic Icebox" (essentially suspended animation). All systems have slowed to minimize the consumption of oxygen and sugar.

The blood is now 190% thicker than normal, preventing a palpable pulse.

Heart sounds will be absent.

Respirations will slow to 3 – 6 per minute—so slow and shallow that they may be impossible to detect.

We may appear dead: pulseless and breathless, with cold, stiff skin, and fixed pupils.

You may have heard the expression that a person "is not dead until they are warm and dead"—this is the state that this expression refers to.

If you place a cardiac monitor on our chest, we will be in sinus bradycardia—this is not pulseless electrical activity (PEA)—we should not be shocked or given any drugs.

COGNITION: We are comatose and unresponsive to verbal or painful stimuli.

BEHAVIOR: We initiate no action.

SHIVERING: the universal sign for "I'm cold." When it stops, you're in real trouble.

Types of HYPOTHERMIA

98.6

97

96

94

92

90

86

SUBACUTE/MOUNTAIN/ACCIDENTAL HYPOTHERMIA

This is the most common type of hypothermia, and the condition typically develops over just a few hours.

It is often the result of a mishap (e.g., getting benighted on a winter hike), accident (e.g., broken ankle while ice climbing), or any series of poor decisions that leave a person cold, tired, dehydrated, and hungry.

It follows the classic downward spiral described in the opening spread.

NICE DAY, getting dark, though... Oh Snap! There goes your ankle. Can you spell h-y-p-o-t-h-e-r-m-i-a?

CHRONIC HYPOTHERMIA

Comes on slowly over days or weeks.

It is brought on by the combination of a cold environment and poor nutrition and occurs primarily in the geriatric population.

Older, sedentary people need a much warmer environment (the thermostat should be set close to their age). To save fuel, elderly people often turn the thermostat down way too low.

As the elderly cool, their metabolism will not increase enough to meet the demand. As we age, our appetites change and we may not be consuming enough calories to keep warm.

They may not shiver in response to the cold.

Mentally, they may exhibit symptoms similar to dementia.

Once rewarmed, they will return to a normal physical and mental state.

OKAY to spend a night or two in here, but, um...not a month.

ACUTE OR "SHELL" HYPOTHERMIA

This is caused by a sudden plunge into cold water (think ice fisherman on thin ice).

The "shell" cools suddenly, impairing muscle function and coordination.

The core temperature remains normal.

Death can occur after an hour or so, not because of deep hypothermia, but rather because the rapid cooling of the muscles prevents the victim from the kind of purposeful movement that allows them to stay afloat—death occurs from drowning.

It is a myth that a person plunged into ice cold water will die within three minutes because of hypothermia—you may drown, but you will not die quickly from hypothermia.

FUN, GLACIAL RUNOFF, but get pinned against a boulder for an hour and your shell will go numb (no, no, not the boat).

WILDCARE™

Treatment of HYPOTHERMIA

FOR MILD TO MODERATE HYPOTHERMIA (the patient is still conscious and responsive—their core temperature has not dropped below 92F (33.3C).

1 Remove the patient from immediate danger and further exposure.

2 Create shelter: tent, bivouac, snow cave.

3 Get them dry and keep them dry.

4 Remove their wet clothing, dry them off, and re-insulate them with dry clothing.

5 Place the patient in a hypothermia wrap and protect them from the ground.

6 If conscious and can safely swallow, feed the patient sickly sweet fluids, such as Jell-O in warm water or warm Gatorade. Have them sip constantly. You cannot give them too much water or sugar. Hypothermia victims cannot digest solids. If unconscious, do not try to feed them orally.

FOR SEVERE HYPOTHERMIA (patient unconscious and likely in the fetal position). Do the above, plus:

1 Avoid excessive movement or jarring.

2 Give rescue breaths.

! DO NOT DO CPR! The myocardium of the heart is very susceptible to fibrillation because of elevated potassium levels surrounding the cells. **Bumping or jostling** can cause the heart to go into **ventricular fibrillation**. It is almost **impossible** to defibrillate a hypothermia patient.

1 Protect from the ground with a waterproof layer (tarp) and foam.

2 Protect with multiple layers of dry insulation. Use extra insulation at the head and feet. Poor circulation in the feet can lead to frostbite.

3 Surround with a windproof/waterproof outer layer.

HYPO-WRAP

4 May add external heat sources near the feet, armpits, or hands (wrap in socks).

Prevention of HYPOTHERMIA

- Know your enemy: be prepared for wet, wind, and cold.
- Wear fabrics that stay warm when wet. Do not wear cotton—the phrase "cotton kills" really has validity: cotton loses almost all its insulating ability when wet.
- Get dry and stay dry—it can be difficult to re-warm a damp or wet person, and it can be extremely difficult to keep a damp person warm.
- Stay well-hydrated.
- Snack often on quick-burning carbohydrates (energy bars, candy, etc.).
- Carry bivouac gear and know how to use it.
- Be attentive to yourself, to your companions, and to the environment—pay particular attention to mental-status changes.
- Turn around before you get in trouble. This is a difficult point to determine, but there are almost always early warning signs.
  - → Someone in the party is moving slowly or complaining of being cold and/or tired.
  - → Weather/route conditions are not what you expected or are changing for the worse.
  - → You fall behind the schedule of your plan for the day.
  - → Someone (anyone) says something like, "I don't feel good about this."

Assessment and Management of Environmental Emergencies and Injuries

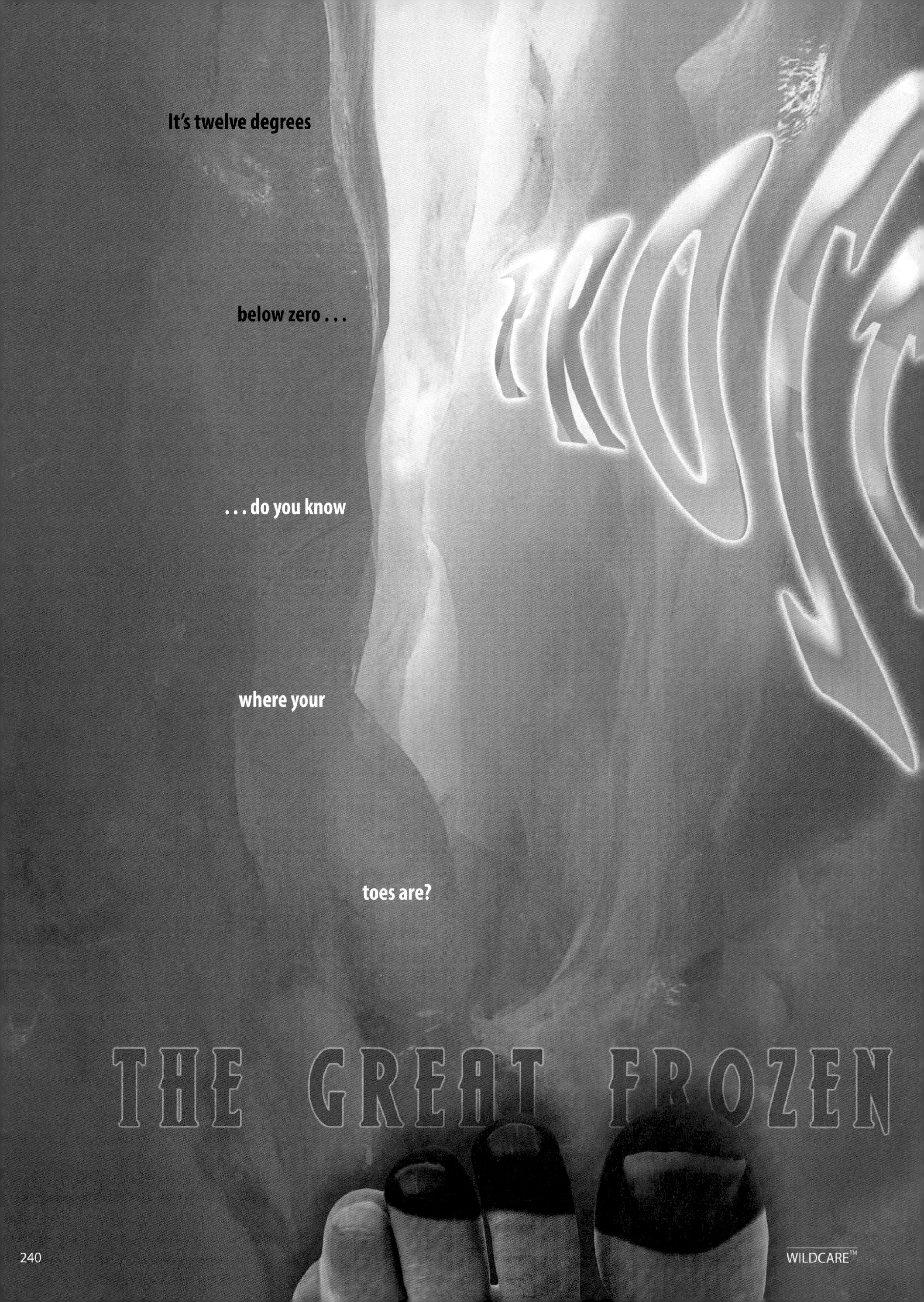

It's twelve degrees

below zero . . .

. . . do you know

where your

toes are?

THE GREAT FROZEN

WILDCARE™

BITE

On a bitter January weekend in 1982, Hugh Herr and Jeff Batzer completed a long ice climb on New Hampshire's Mount Washington, became disoriented above timberline, and were lost in a blizzard. Three days later, and after one of the most massive searches in the state's history, with gale force winds and temperatures plunging as low as -25°, and after the tragic death of one rescuer in an avalanche, Herr and Batzer were discovered by a showshoer who wasn't even part of the search team. Barely alive, but saved, the two young men suffered terrible frostbite: Herr losing both legs below the knee, Batzer losing most of his fingers.

MENACE LURKS

FROSTBITE

is the localized freezing of tissue caused by the combination of **below freezing ambient air temperature** and **constriction of blood vessels** which shunt blood away from cold areas of the body. Since water expands when it freezes, tissue destruction occurs when the cells freeze and burst. There are varying degrees of frostbite based on ice formation in the tissues and the extent or depth of the freeze. For wilderness medicine, the field treatment can be divided into three diagnostic and treatment categories based on ice formation in the tissues: superficial, partial, or deep. These are similar to the severity or degree of a burn.

SUPERFICIAL FROSTBITE

is localized vasoconstriction, but no ice forms in the tissues.

Signs and symptoms
- The area is cold, numb, and pale, but still soft and pliable.
- Although not frozen, the tissue is still damaged.
- The tissues, while not frozen, have a decreased blood flow, and thus are not getting enough oxygen.
- If not re-warmed quickly (<6 hours) permanent tissue damage can occur (see immersion foot/trench foot).

Treatment
1. Inspect the area closely and inspect the insulation—determine the cause.
2. Make sure that the frostbitten area is dry.
3. Re-warm in the field using skin-to-skin contact.
   A. Hands/feet in armpits/groin.
   B. Never massage, rub with snow, or use an external heat source.
3. Warm the patient.
   A. From the inside with high-carb snacks, warm Jell-O, etc.
   B. From the outside with additional dry insulation (e.g., new mittens). If they are capable, have them do isometric exercises.
4. Hydrate the patient.
5. Correct any problems before resuming activity (e.g., change to warmer boots, dry mittens, etc.).

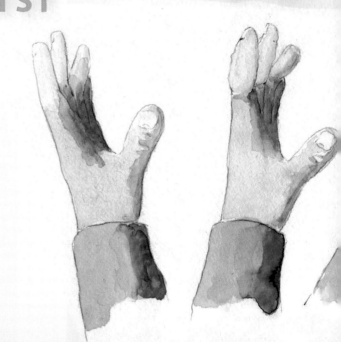

1ST DEGREE

2ND DEGREE

---

what's the difference?

Human digits freeze and tissue dies, but cold-climate animals (e.g., timber wolves) seem to pad along just fine . . . and they're naked!

There's much more fatty tissue in the canine foot—which doesn't freeze as easily as other tissue.

Their blood vessels are arranged so they act like living heat exchangers: arteries are very close to the networks of venules, facilitating the transfer of heat from venous to arterial blood—helping to maintain reasonable peripheral and core temperatures.

Canine feet can withstand temperatures as cold as -31ºF (-35ºC).

Similarly designed systems are seen in other animals, such as foxes and penguins; and some insects such as snow fleas (they're actually springtails) have antifreeze proteins in their blood!

WILDCARE™

PARTIAL-THICKNESS FROSTBITE is localized vasoconstriction and cooling with some ice crystal formation.

Signs and symptoms
- The area is the same as 1st degree: numb, pale, but still pliable.
- There is pain with thawing.
- Fluid- or blood-filled blisters appear (blebs).

Treatment is the same as superficial, except:
1. If a bleb forms, protect it with a bandage and evacuate the patient.
2. Do not puncture the bleb.
3. Protect the frozen part from re-freezing, which can occur quickly and cause further damage.

FULL-THICKNESS FROSTBITE is deep freezing involving muscles, tendons, nerves, and other tissues.

Signs and symptoms
- The area is numb, cold, white or waxy, and hard to the touch.
- Tissues are frozen solid (rock hard) and ice forms in the cells—the tissues are destroyed.

Treatment
1. Do not rewarm in the field—the goal is to prevent further damage.
   A. The thawing of frozen tissue can release large quantities of proteins that can cause high fevers and renal failure.
   B. Once thawed, the area is useless.
   C. A deeply frostbitten foot can still be walked on—if it is thawed in the field, a litter carry will be necessary.
   D. Thawed tissue will be extremely painful.
   E. If thawed tissue is refrozen, additional damage will be done.
2. Inspect the area closely.
3. Remove any wet of frozen clothing or boots.
4. Dry and re-insulate the area to prevent further damage and freezing.
5. Feed high-carbohydrate foods and give warm, sweet liquids.
6. The deeply frozen person is also likely to be hypothermic—treat accordingly.
7. Evacuate to definitive care, preferably a trauma center that specializes in cold injuries (severe cases may require surgery (amputation).

3DEGREE **RD**

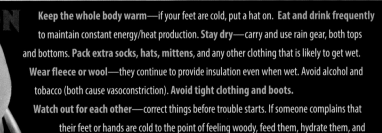

PREVENTION

Keep the whole body warm—if your feet are cold, put a hat on. **Eat and drink frequently** to maintain constant energy/heat production. **Stay dry**—carry and use rain gear, both tops and bottoms. **Pack extra socks, hats, mittens**, and any other clothing that is likely to get wet. **Wear fleece or wool**—they continue to provide insulation even when wet. Avoid alcohol and tobacco (both cause vasoconstriction). **Avoid tight clothing and boots.**

Watch out for each other—correct things before trouble starts. If someone complains that their feet or hands are cold to the point of feeling woody, feed them, hydrate them, and get them moving! A few minutes of strenuous exercise (doing short laps up and down a steep terrain) can bring a person quickly back from the brink of frostbite.

Umm . . . wear boots.

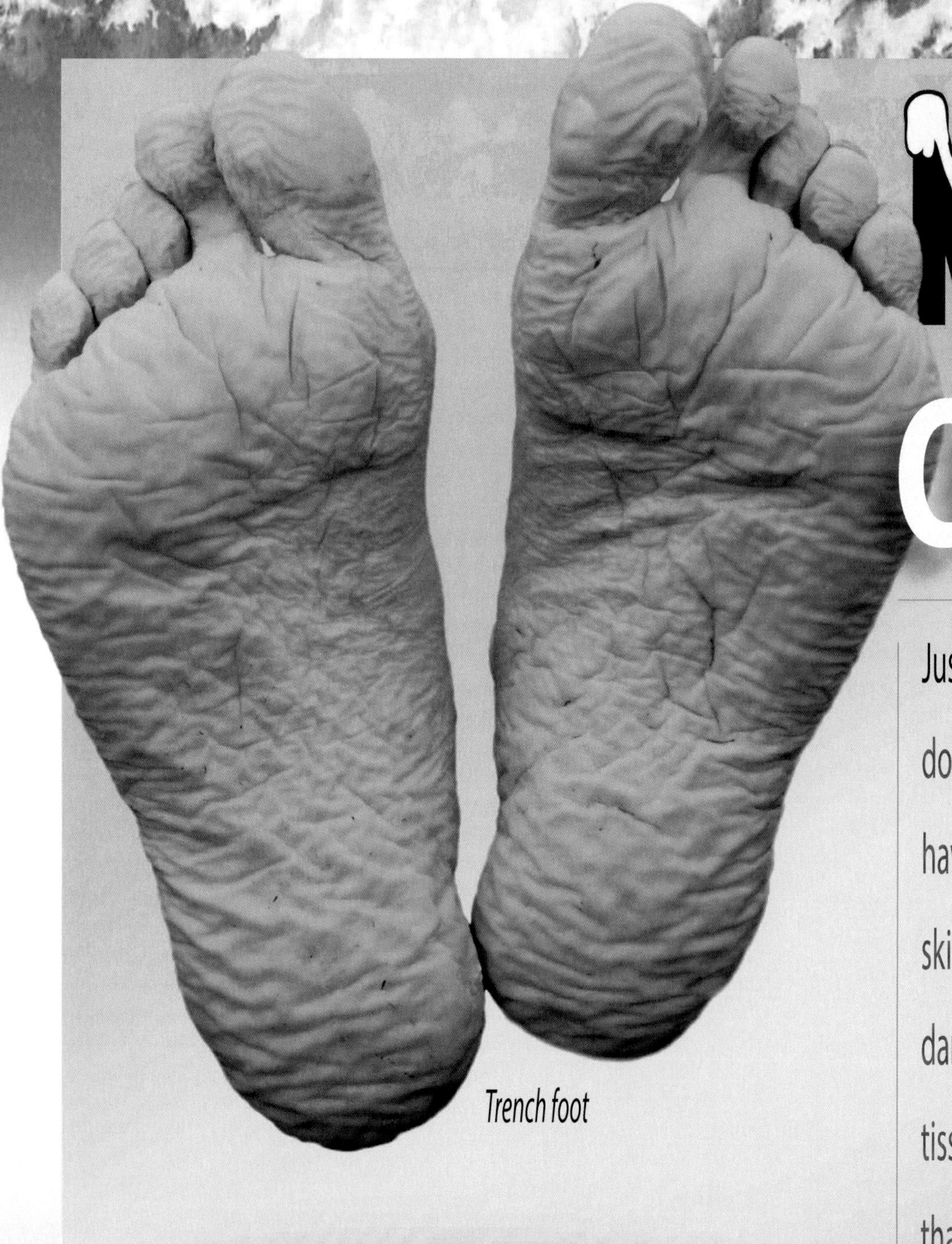

Trench foot

Raynaud's Syndrome

NON-

COLD

Just because it's above 32^0 doesn't mean that we won't have problems. When our skin is exposed to cold, damp temperatures, tissue damage can result that is painful, chronic, and difficult to treat. These injuries are not life-threatening, but they can be limb-threatening.

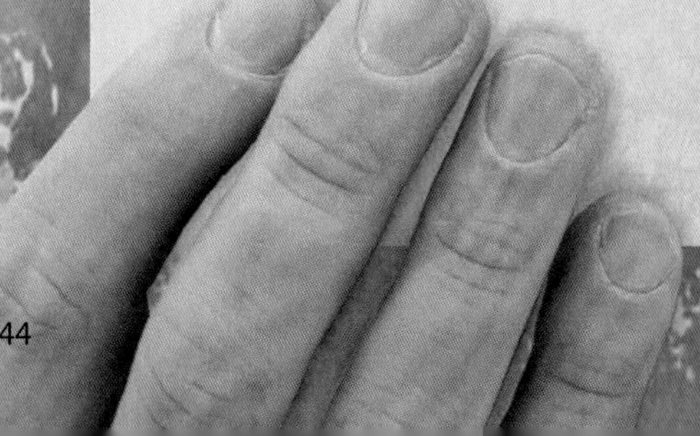

FREEZING INJURIES

Raynaud's Syndrome

Raynaud's Syndrome is a peripheral vascular disorder marked by abnormal vasoconstriction of the extremities on exposure to cold or emotional stress—a hypersensitivity reaction to cold exposure.

We are tropical animals and adapt to the cold environment by creating a micro-environment around us—it may be below zero outside, but it needs to be in the 70s next to our skin. We create this micro-environment by using: shelter, clothing, and external heat sources.

- Raynaud's was first described by French physician Maurice Raynaud.

- It is fairly common, occurring in about 5% of the population.

- It is 4x times more common in women than in men.

- Raynaud's tends to worsen with age.

- Once it occurs, it will recur whenever the affected parts are exposed to cool temperature—for example, swimming in 60 degree water.

- Raynaud's may be the result of genetics and/or of a prior injury such as frostbite.

- When Raynaud's occurs, the risk of frostbite increases.

PHYSIOLOGY

Because we are tropical, we have a relatively poor protective response to cold exposure.

All the vasculature in the affected part of the extremity (e.g., the tips of fingers, toes, ears, or nose) partially closes down, not just the capillaries and small-diameter vessels.

It appears that the problem is with the sympathetic innervation of the arteriovenous anastomoses (the growth of connective collateral vessels that serve the same volume of tissue as the capillaries), which shunt blood away from the cold area. We are designed to let our fingers freeze and fall off in order to preserve our core and brain temperature—where our vital organs lie.

An aside—certain mammals, such as dogs and cats, do the opposite: they vasodilate the blood vessels going to the cold areas to keep them warm. They do this because they have fur to insulate them.

SIGNS AND SYMPTOMS

- Pale, waxy, or blueness in extremities, usually fingers or toes, which typically occurs within 10 – 30 minutes of cold exposure (see image at right).
- Numbness and/or paresthesia (pins and needles).
- Sweating ceases as the body tries to keep the core warm.
- In severe cases, blisters can form due to the production of free radicals as a result of the tissue damage.

- Each time the cycle of cold/vasoconstriction to warmth/vasodilation takes place in the Raynaud's susceptible person, the vasoconstriction seems to occur with less stimulation and re-warming symptoms seem to be worse and more painful.

Classic Raynaud's: bloodflow shuts down and leaves tissue (often on the fingers and toes) pale-to-cyanotic, wax-like, and numb. It's more annoying than dangerous, and the rewarming process can be painful.

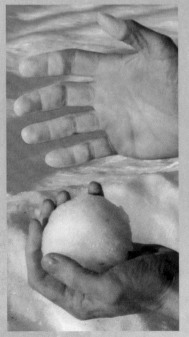

ASSESSMENT

Before you can treat and manage Raynaud's Syndrome you must make a proper diagnosis—is this primary Raynaud's caused by cold exposure, or is it secondary Raynaud's where the Raynaud's is a symptom of another disease or a drug side effect?

Some possibilities:

- Scleroderma—mixed connective tissue diseases, polymyositis, dermatomyositis
- Lupus (SLE)—a systemic autoimmune disease causing the immune system to attack and damage tissue
- Rheumatoid arthritis
- Buerger's disease —recurring progressive inflammation and thrombosis (clotting) of small and medium arteries and veins of the hands and feet
- Polycythemia—a disease state in which the proportion of blood volume that is occupied by red blood cells increases
- Cryoglobulinemia—a medical condition in which the blood contains large amounts of cryoglobulins (proteins) that become insoluble below normal body temperature (<37^0C/98.6^{0}F)
- Carpal tunnel syndrome
- Drug-induced: beta blockers, ergotamine, methysergide, vinblastine, beleomycin, oral contraceptives
- Estrogen replacement therapy without progesterone

PREVENTION

- Avoid or limit cold exposure and protect the effected area with effective (dry) insulation.
- Avoid situations where Raynaud's could be triggered.
- If possible, avoid medications that can make Raynaud's worse: beta-blockers, ergotamine, methysergide, vinblastine, bleomycin, and oral contraceptives.
- Avoid nicotine, caffeine, alcohol, and over-the-counter decongestants.

TREATMENT AND MANAGEMENT

- Treat the whole patient—keep them warm, fed, and hydrated.
- Re-warm the tissue. When the circulation is re-established there will be a hyperemic (reddening) response in the skin with throbbing pain that typically lasts 5 – 10 minutes; itchiness sometimes occurs.
- Calcium channel blockers are considered to be the most effective pharmacological treatment. Nifedipine XL 30 – 90mg po qd, is the drug of choice. If not effective or if side effects occur, try other calcium channel blockers: diltiazem 30 – 120mg po qid, or felodipine 2.5 – 10mg po qd. Verapamil has not been shown to be effective.
- Try retraining your body to reduce the tendency to shunt blood away from your exremities using a method developed by renowned cold weather expert, Dr. Murray Hamlett (below).

Hamlett's method for managing Raynaud's

This is a non-invasive, non-pharmacological method to attempt to retrain the neurovascular response to cold exposure. Remember Pavlov's dog—the dog that would have a hunger response and drool when the researchers rang a bell? Well, guess what—there is a good chance that your vasculature can be trained to vasodilate rather than vasoconstrict when exposed to the cold.

EQUIPMENT

- 2 – 4 foam coolers (depending upon whether you are doing just your hands or your feet, or all four extremities at once).
- A source of warm water.
- A cool environment: 32F – 40F (0C – 4.5C).

SETUP AND DRESS

- Dress to be comfortable for the inside environment (70 degrees).
- Do not add layers when you go outside—you want your body to cool off. You must allow your head and trunk to cool off while keeping your hands/feet warm.

STEPS

1. Fill the foam coolers with warm water, 105° – 110°F (40° – 43°C); place one set inside the house where it is warm and one set outside where it is cold.
2. Start inside: make yourself comfortable and sit down with your feet and/or hands in the warm water for 2 – 5 minutes.
3. Wrap you hands and/or feet in a towel to keep them warm and go outside
4. Sit down, allowing your head and body to sense the cold, while placing your hands and/or feet in the warm water for about 10 minutes.
5. After 10 minutes, go back inside and repeat the inside treatment.

- The process works best if you do 3 – 6 cycles per day (in for 2 – 5minutes, out for 10 minutes, then in for 2 – 5 minutes) every other day for a total of 50 cycles (i.e., 8 – 16 days).
- This method is inexpensive and very safe. If it works or helps, great; if not, you've lost nothing but a little time, and you now have some coolers for picnics.

Chilblains is characterized by inflammation: rubor (redness), calor (heat), tumor (swelling), dolor (pain), and pruritus (itching)—considering what these toes look like, we probably didn't need to explain this.

Chilblains

Chilblains (also known as pernio) occurs when a predisposed individual is exposed to cold, humid and/or damp conditions. The capillary beds are damaged, causing redness, itching, inflammation, and blisters (acral ulcers—ulcers affecting the extremities).

PREDISPOSITIONS

- Individuals with close family members who have/had chilblains
- People with circulation problems
- People with lupus
- People whose homes are drafty and cold (not well-insulated)
- Tobacco smokers
- Very thin individuals

PATHOPHYSIOLOGY

- The process usually starts with an initial injury, such as frostbite, and the onset of symptoms is typically 2 – 24 hours after exposure.
- Tissue damage occurs to the capillary beds and to the neurovascular apparatus that controls vasomotor response.
- As an extremity re-warms and the vasculature dilates, fenestrations (small gaps) open between the endothelial cells, allowing intravascular fluids (plasma) to leak out into the surrounding tissue.
- The immune system reacts to this fluid leakage, causing blister formation, erythema, swelling, tenderness, itchiness, a burning sensation, and tender blue lumps.
- This lays the foundation for future vasoconstriction and vascular shunting of blood away from the affected cold area—chilblains will often come on faster and be worse with subsequent exposures.
- Long-term, localized, violaceous (purple) plaque forms that is thick, tender, slightly cyanotic, and with a shiny appearance.
- Chilblains typically heals within several days—but it can become chronic if environmental conditions persist.

TREATMENT

- The same as for Raynaud's.

DIFFERENTIAL DIAGNOSES

Other disorders with symptoms similar to chilblains.

- Chronic myelomonocytic leukemia
- Anorexia nervosa
- Dysproteinemia
- Macroglobulinemia
- Cryoglobulinemia, cryofibrinogenemia, cold agglutinins
- Antiphospholipid antibody syndrome
- Raynaud's disease

Tasiilaq is the most populous community in southeast Greenland. In coastal areas of the world like this, where damp and cold conditions are persistent for much of the year, chilblains occurs in about 10% of the population, and more frequently in women.

Trench foot

Trench foot and immersion foot are synonymous. This is a nonfreezing cold injury to the extremities (typically the feet and lower legs) caused by vasoconstriction of the peripheral circulation, resulting from prolonged exposure to cold, damp, and unsanitary conditions—being cold and wet for more than six hours (e.g., standing in ice water). The term trench foot was coined during WWI when so many injuries occurred as troops in Western Europe were forced to stand for hours in trenches half-full of cold water. During WWI, WWII, and the Korean War, there were over 1 million casualties from trench foot and frostbite. Today, hunters, hikers, kayakers, construction workers, snowmakers, or anyone who works or plays in cold, wet environments are at risk.

PHYSIOLOGY

- Ischemia (caused by vasoconstriction) for more than six hours leads to tissue death. This leads to gangrene, nerve damage, and loss of tissue.
- After six hours of compromised circulation, the capillaries and supporting tissues of the skin begin to die from hypoxia (lack of oxygen).
- Immersion in cold water is not necessary: wet socks, wet insoles, or wet boots can put feet at risk in temperatures between freezing and 62^{0}F (17^{0}C).
- Immersion foot injuries are permanent and very painful.
- The colder the water, the shorter duration is needed to cause injury.
- The injury can result in extensive tissue loss (amputation may be necessary).
- Several things can increase risk and exacerbate the injury: blunt trauma, tight footwear, nicotine and alcohol consumption.

The poster (top) was created by the Office for Emergency Management, Office of War Information, Domestic Operations Branch, Bureau of Special Services, and distributed to troops during WWII from 1943 to 1945. Soldiers often spent days at a time in trenches (bottom) which were often knee-full of cold muck. One of the simplest keys to maintaining heath and battle-readiness was basic foot hygiene. Napoleon famously said, "An army marches on its stomach", but no army marches far if the soldiers' feet are continuously cold and wet, no matter how many canned wieners they eat.

Trench Foot presents as pale to cyanotic, cold-to-the-touch, wet, and macerated (saturated, spongy, wrinkled) tissue (simulated here); there may or may not be a clear demarcation between damaged and undamaged tissue. While it is common to associate frostbite with amputation, trench foot can be an equally serious injury, with an equally devastating outcome.

SIGNS

- Initially: cold, wet, numb, macerated extremities (softened by immersion—what your skin looks like under a Band-Aid).
- There may be an obvious line of demarcation between the affected tissue and healthy tissue.
- Feet become numb and turn red (erythema) or blue (cyanosis) as a result of compromised vascular supply.
- As the condition worsens, the affected tissue may begin to swell.
- Advanced trench foot presents with blisters and open sores which can lead to fungal infections.
- If advanced trench foot is left untreated, necrosis (tissue death), gangrene (advanced and widespread necrosis), and putrefaction and liquefaction (necrotic tissue digested by enzymes, eventually becoming liquefied) will set in. Tissue will begin to slough off.
- Nerve, muscle, and epithelial cells are the most susceptible to the effects of hypoxia resulting from immersion foot.
- A permanent injury, immersion foot can cause as much tissue damage as frostbite.
- The risk of a secondary bacterial infection is very high.

TREATMENT

- If the damage is minor and appropriate treatment is done immediately, complete recovery is normal—although it will be painful.
- As the extremity begins to rewarm, color will return and the feet will become red, hot to the touch, hyperhidrotic (excessive sweating), swollen, and painful. The pain can be excruciating and difficult to relieve—even narcotics may not bring relief.

1. Remove the patient from the cold and wet environment. Place them in the supine position. Get them dry and keep them dry—remove wet garments and dry the affected area.

2. Re-warm them (can be very hard, skin-to-skin contact is best. Once rewarmed, keep the area warm).

3. Do not do massage and do not immerse the affected tissue in warm water—it will be too painful.

4. Elevate the feet to minimize swelling and tent any sheets or blankets over the patient's feet—even the weight of sheets on the feet will be painful. If possible, direct a fan toward the feet as they will be hot and very sweaty.

5. For pain control, try narcotics, although they will most likely not be very helpful. **Amiltriptyline** has been shown to be effective: 50 – 150mg at bedtime. Much of the rewarming symptoms have been shown to be caused by the release of histamines in the damaged tissue—early administration of **antihistamines** may give some relief. Free radicals are being formed in the tissues, so radical scavengers such as **aspirin**, **ibuprofen**, or **allopurinol**, if given early, may be of some benefit. **Heparin** and **steroids** have not been shown to be efficacious.

6. If vesicles (similar to blisters) form, leave intact.

7. Evacuate the patient immediately, and keep them fed and hydrated.

PREVENTION

- Keep hands and feet dry.
- Change socks regularly and sleep in dry socks at night.
- As with other cold-related injuries, a person who has contracted trench foot will be more susceptible to it in the future—take extra care.

Winter wisdom—preventing hypothermia, frostbite, and non-freezing cold injuries

- If possible, avoid medications that limit or impair circulation.
- Avoid nicotine, caffeine, alcohol, and over-the-counter decongestants.
- Keep your hands and feet warm and dry.
- Do not tolerate any degree of numbness or loss of sensation in your extremities.
- Stay well-hydrated.
- Maintain blood sugar—fuel for the fire. Carry and eat lots of carbohydrates; you burn glucose to stay warm.
- Drink more than you think you need; do not rely on thirst to tell you to drink.
- Keep your body and head warm.
- Understand how to properly layer clothes and footwear.
- Know your personal limits and equipment.

- Have proper-fitting clothing and boots—avoid tight, constricting clothing socks, and boots.
- Wear multiple layers, including socks.
- Carry spare mittens and socks.
- Control the rate of sweating.
- Keep the whole body warm, dry, well-fed, and well-hydrated. Pay particular attention to keeping your hands and feet warm and dry—at the first sign of numbness, rewarm.
- Have a plan: bring emergency gear, monitor the weather, have a turnaround time (and stick to it—don't let "summit fever" get in the way of making wise decisions. Your destination will be there next year, we promise.)
- At the first sign of trouble, take action
- Keep an eye on the "other guy"—he's always the one who will get into trouble without admitting it.

CRACK THE SKY

A cloud-to-ground lightning strike traveling at upwards of 3,700 miles per second momentarily equalizes the electrical-charge differential between the T-storm and the earth below it. The flash of light that we see travels 186,000 miles per second, while the sound of thunder follows at a rather pedestrian average of 1/5 of a mile per second.

why lightning and people

average 15 miles in diameter • average forward speed 20 mph\

can be over 60,000'

-40°C/-40°F

-15°C/5°F

typically 5,000'
above ground

5°C/41°F

Positive charges build up
in the top of the T-storm
and on the ground...

a negative charge builds
up in the cloud base...

cool, dry downdrafts and
warm, moist updrafts
meet, ice particles rub
against each other
and create electrical
polarization and
instability—equalization
is inevitable...

a stepped leader (from
the cloud) and an upward
streamer (from the ground)
complete the circuit:

[FLASH > BOOM]

...things momentarily
stabilize, and then the
cycle repeats until the
storm plays out.

tornado alley

10 20 30 40 50 60 70 80 90
approximate thunderstorm days per year
(AK and HI <10)

T-STORMS: the anatomy of
BOOM

THERE'S NOTHING STATIC about nature's electricity factory—the thunderstorm. Without getting too meteorological about it, lightning is the result of atmospheric instability—specifically the increasing charge differential between the top (+) and bottom of a thunderstorm (-) and the earth below it (+), and the environment's tendency to balance itself. Cloud-to-cloud lightning briefly equalizes the differential within the cloud itself (or between adjacent clouds); but as electrical tension builds (as a result of the convective clash between warm/cold and wet/dry and the static build-up of grating ice, super-cooled water and soft hail (called graupel), eventually, the insulating effect of the layer of air between the base of the clouds and the earth is overcome and a cloud-to-ground strike occurs.

And what we see as a single flash is actually a sequence of many electrical events. Ionized channels form, called leaders, and the negative leader moves downward toward the earth; when it gets close enough, another leader (upward streamer) moves upward. When the two meet, "attachment" occurs and a circuit is formed, creating a channel (a path of least resistance). At this point a much greater current will propagate from the earth back up the leader into the cloud—this return stroke is the luminous lightning discharge that we see. Although usually perceived as a single flash, most lightning strikes are made up of multiple strokes, typically three or four—all taking place in about a quarter of a second.

LIGHTNING—QUICK FLASHES

- There are four types of thunderstorms: **single-cell** storms (single storm with one updraft), **multicell clusters** (a mature central storm with dissipating storms on the downwind side), **multicell lines** (elongated lines of T-storms along a cold front), and **supercells** (enormous, severe storms with a mesocyclone—a deep, persistently rotating updraft; these are the classic, anvil-topped, tornado-spawning monsters of the central US).

- Lightning strikes the earth about 1.4 billion times a year (45 times /sec)—about 20 million strikes are detected in the US each year (1 every 1.5 seconds, 10 – 15% reaching the ground).

- The boom of thunder that follows the strike is the shock wave created by the rapid increase in pressure as the lightning super-heats the air to over 50,000°F (five times hotter than the sun).

- Lightning flashes produce ozone (O_3), which protects the earth from ultraviolet radiation.

- Lightning travels over the surface of an object unless there is an internal conductor—nerves and blood vessels are good conductors, unfortunately.

- The average lightning bolt is 2 3 miles long, the longest recorded was 118 miles long.

Assessment and Management of Environmental Emergencies and Injuries

251

Lightning-related injuries

From 1988 – 2011, annual deaths from lightning in the US averaged 49.

From 2001 – 2010, annual injuries from lightning in the US averaged 360.

Odds of being struck by lightning in the US in a given year: 1/1.8 million; in a lifetime: 1/10,000.

Ways to get hit: **direct strike** (just like it sounds...a direct connection between you and the cloud; **splash** (an indirect connection that occurs subsequent to the initial strike, e.g., the bolt hits the tree and splashes onto you; **step voltage or ground current** (a connection between you and the ground as the electricity dissipates.

Lightning never strikes the same place twice—tall objects like buildings, towers, mountain tops are struck frequently.

Lightning only strikes the tallest objects—while taller objects are more likely to be struck, lightning can strike virtually anywhere, even on the ground just a few feet away from a tall object.

Wearing or holding metal objects make you much more likely to be struck by lightning—small metal objects (e.g., golf clubs) do not significantly change the strike point of a lightning bolt.

Lightning will not strike a body of water—the ocean, lakes, and ponds are frequently struck.

If you are caught in a thunderstorm while on or in the water, just getting to shore will ensure your safety—shorelines are dangerous places; move at least 100 yards inland.

Rubber shoes or automobile tires are insulators that protect you from being struck by lightning—as it has already proven by its ability to travel through miles of insulating air, lightning is extremely powerful; in order for rubber to be truly protective, it would have to be hundreds of feet thick.

People struck by lightning carry an electric charge and should not be touched—they carry no charge; give care immediately.

Lightning only strikes when it's raining—rain is not necessary and lightning can strike at any time, even if a storm looks merely threatening.

You can't be struck by lightning if the storm is far off— so called "blue sky" lightning can strike as far as 15 miles out from a storm.

INJURY CAUSES

- Direct effects of electricity on the nervous system
- Heat that is caused by the resistance of the current across or through the body
- Concussive effect of the shock wave of thunder
- Explosive force on other objects, hurling debris and causing blunt trauma

MINOR

- Confusion—amnesia (hours to days)
- Temporary deafness, temporary blindness, temporary loss of consciousness
- Cutaneous burns, contusions, minor blunt trauma, and related injuries
- Muscular pain
- Tympanic membrane rupture
- Mild transient hypertension (high blood pressure)
- Cognitive damage to learning, thinking, or memory

MODERATE: temporary to permanent

- Cataracts
- Disorientation, combativeness, coma
- Loss of motor function
- Mottled skin
- Diminished or absent pulses due to hypotension
- Fractures, spinal cord injuries, spinal fractures
- Respiratory arrest which can lead to cardiac arrest
- Seizures
- 1st and 2nd degree thermal burns
- Basilar skull fracture

SEVERE: temporary to permanent

- Cardiac arrest—asystole, ventricular fibrillation
- Direct brain damage
- Hematologic disorders—disseminated intravascular coagulation (DIC: bunches of small clots form throughout the body, hijacking the blood's clotting proteins—if a new injury occurs, the clotting platelets will not be available)
- Basilar skull fracture (at the base of the skull), in lightning victims typically in the temporal lobe resulting in bruising behind the ears (Battle's Sign)
- Sleep disorders, irritability
- Atrophic spinal paralysis (flaccid paralysis of involved muscle groups and later atrophy of those muscles)
- Generalized weakness
- Post-traumatic stress disorder (PTSD)
- Memory disturbance—short term
- Concentration disturbance—loss of focus, easily distracted
- Memory disturbance long-term
- Cognitive powers—decreased mental manipulation, decreased problem-solving
- Decreased multi-tasking
- Behavior issues: sleep disturbance, phobic behavior (paranoia), personality change (depression, bipolar)

SNAP
A GUINNESS WORLD RECORD

Between 1942 and 1977, Roy Sullivan, a park ranger in Shenandoah National Park, survived lightning strikes on seven different occasions, gaining him the nickname "Human Lightning Rod."

BOOM ⚡

A CASE STUDY

Gunnison County, CO, September 2005
Jason Crawford was struck by lightning while riding his dirt bike. The bolt melted his helmet, fractured his skull, and burned his chest and left arm. He made a full recovery. Remarkably, 90% of people receiving a direct lightning strike survive—albeit sometimes with permanent damage.

Assessment and treatment

SCENE SAFETY
- Scene safety
- Safety of victim
- Safety of rescuer(s)
- Safety of remaining group

PRIMARY ASSESSMENT—ABCs
- Is the victim conscious?
- Are they breathing? If not, give artificial respirations.
- Do they have a pulse? If not, begin CPR. (Because lightning can trigger cardiac arrest in people with no underlying or chronic heart disease, CPR is more successful in cases of lightning strike.)

SECONDARY ASSESSMENT
- **Vital signs**: Pay particular attention to LOC (deteriorating LOC is a bad sign). Monitor every five minutes until conscious and coherent.
- **Physical exam** (must be thorough and detailed): Pay particular attention to the following:
  - Skin: check for burns
  - Check ears for blood in the canal
  - Check for Battle's sign
  - Evaluate for spinal injuries
  - Evaluate for musculoskeletal injuries
  - Monitor peripheral pulses

TREATMENT
- Protect airway
- Splint fractures
- Dress wounds
- Evacuate
- Protect spine
- If conscious, force fluids
- Administer O_2 via nasal canulla at 6lpm, if available
- Administer IV—normal saline at 500 – 1000cc/hr, if available

Lightning: gorgeous, dramatic, powerful, deadly

LAWS OF LIGHTNING
- Lightning is unpredictable and uncontrollable.
- Lightning follows the path of least resistance.
- Lightning is most likely to strike the highest object around.

RULES TO LIVE BY
- When a thunderstorm approaches, go inside.
- If outside, stay away from the highest objects: mountain peaks, ridges, boulders, hilltops, tall trees, towers and large metal objects, utility poles, ski lift towers, bridge superstructure, fences, etc.
- Don't sit under overhangs or go into shallow caves; stay out of large open areas (fields).
- Lightning flows like water, so stay out of gullies, washes, and stream beds.
- Put on your rain gear and prepare for foul weather.
- Move at least 100 yards away from any shoreline.
- Find a low spot and sit on something insulated (foam pad) with your legs crossed.
- Spread your group out: do not hold hands or sit back-to-back; by spreading out, you minimize the risk of multiple victims if a direct strike does occur .
- **The 30 – 30 Rule:** when you see lightning, count the seconds from the flash until you hear thunder, and divide the number by five to estimate the distance in miles. Speed of light: 186,000 miles per second (visible strike instantaneous). Speed of sound: 770mph (about 1,000 feet per second, or five seconds per mile). If the time difference between the lightning flash and the thunder is 30 seconds or less (indicating the storm is about six miles away), take all precautions immediately.
- Wait until 30 minutes after the last strike to resume your activities.
- If on water, if possible, get off the water and move at least 100 yards away from the shore. Lightning is absorbed by fresh water, however in salt water the lightning will travel along the surface longer due to the increased conductivity thus making a person on salt water at greater risk of strike.
- If you have to stay on the water, put on a personal flotation device (PFD).
- Prepare for the winds of the squall line and the potential to be capsized.
- Sit in the center of the boat and stay away from the mast and metal shrouds and stays.
- **Indications that you may be about to be struck by lightning:** hair stands on end, skin tingles, light metal objects vibrate, you may smell ozone, you may hear crackling or a "kee-kee" sound.

Drowning

DEFINITIONS

THE OLD DEFINITION OF DROWNING: "Death by drowning is considered to be death secondary to asphyxia while immersed in a liquid, usually water, or within 24 hours of submersion." Along with this definition, there have been a variety of terms which tried to define and describe the consequences of being immersed or submerged in water, such as wet drowning, dry drowning, active or passive drowning, secondary drowning, near drowning, and silent drowning.

AT THE 2000 WORLD CONGRESS ON DROWNING, a new definition was agreed upon that essentially eliminated all these terms. The new definition: "Drowning is a process resulting in primary respiratory impairment from submersion in a liquid medium."

SUBMERSION
From an emergency care standpoint, submersion means to be completely under water—the airway is below the surface of the water.

IMMERSION
A person has been dunked under the water temporarily, but their head and airway are now above the surface of the water.

NEAR DROWNING
Survival for at least 24 hours after a submersion episode—there still may be serious complications.

The difference between submersion and immersion is subtle, but those few inches can make the difference between life and death.

PATHOPHYSIOLOGY
SEQUENCE OF EVENTS

1. The drive to breathe can cause gasping for air, swallowing, aspiration of water, and voluntary apnea (breath-holding).
2. This eventually leads to involuntary breathing and the inhalation of water, causing laryngospasm.
3. If the laryngospasm eventually relaxes, water rushes in, and this is referred to as a "wet drowning."
4. 15% don't relax, resulting in a "dry drowning."
5. The laryngospasm leads to a loss of consciousness.
6. Asphyxia follows leading to respiratory arrest, then cardiac arrest, then death.

FRESH WATER ～～～～ SALT WATER
IT'S ALL A MATTER OF OSMOSIS

- Water is drawn in the direction of higher salt concentration.
- If there is fresh water in the alveoli of the lungs, the water will rapidly move out of the alveoli and into the capillary vasculature surrounding the alveoli because there is more salt in the blood than in the fresh water.
- If there is salt water in the lungs, the higher salt concentration in the alveoli will draw water out of the pulmonary capillaries and into the alveoli.
- Both scenarios will also cause the surfactant* lining of the alveoli to be rinsed or washed out of the lungs.
- The result of drowning in fresh water versus salt water is the same, and it does not affect the emergency care skills needed to manage and resuscitate these patients.

*Surfactant is a detergent-like compound that is essential to breathing because it has a unique property that helps to push and hold open the alveoli. Without surfactant, when we exhale and the alveoli shrink in size, they will stick together like two sheets of glass with a thin film of water between them, making it much harder to inhale and fill the alveoli with fresh air.

An alpine lake in the British Isles.

Along a salty ocean coastline.

In 2000, an estimated **409,272** people drowned worldwide, which makes drowning the second leading cause of unintentional injury death globally after road traffic injuries. The nearly half million annual deaths do not include floods and transportation-related deaths. **97%** of unintentional drownings occur in low- and middle-income countries. **Males** are more likely to drown than females—risky behavior and alcohol are likely contributors. **Children** under five have the highest drowning mortality rates. Commercial fisherman and subsistence fisherman in low-income countries have the highest risk of drowning on the job. Catastrophic floods kill tens of thousands annually

RESCUE PRINCIPLES

1. REACH—extend your reach by using something long and rigid that the victim can grasp.

2. THROW—throw a rope, or something they can grasp to help stay afloat, and pull them to shore.

3. ROW—get in a boat and row out to them. Don't try to get them into the boat; instead have them hang onto the boat and row them back to shore.

4. GO—the last option is for you to swim out to them, try to give them something to grasp, and tow them back to safety.

   A. Remember, if you decide to grab them and swim them back to shore, a victim who is panicking may overwhelm you and drown you as well!

   B. Do not attempt to rescue a struggling victim if you do not have training in water rescue. This training is readily available through the Red Cross.

TREATMENT

1. Do they have an OPEN AIRWAY? If not, open it.
2. Are they BREATHING?
   A. If not, begin artificial respirations (this can be done while still in the water).
   B. If breaths won't go in, massage throat to relax laryngospasm.
   C. Be prepared for water to come up from the lungs after breaths.
3. CIRCULATION—do they have a pulse?
   A. If not, begin CPR.
   B. This requires a firm surface.
   C. Expect the patient to vomit during CPR—don't let them aspirate vomitus.
4. CERVICAL SPINE (inspect, protect if significant MOI is suspected).
5. HISTORY (ask bystanders, if available).
   A. How long was the person in the water?
   B. What is the water temperature?
   C. Is the water contaminated? Take a sample.
6. Is there RELATED TRAUMA (e.g., neck injury from diving)?
7. Treat for HYPOTHERMIA.
8. EVACUATE. Transport all drowning victims, even if fully conscious and coherent, to the local emergency room for further evaluation and monitoring.

THINGS THAT AFFECT SURVIVAL

AGE the younger the better.

DURATION SUBMERGED the shorter the better.

WATER TEMPERATURE the colder the better.

WATER PURITY the cleaner the better.

TIMING OF CPR the sooner the better.

DRY VS. WET DROWNING dry drowning victims have a higher survival rate.

If the victim's LARYNX can be relaxed quickly enough and they are resuscitated, they are more likely to survive without complications. In a wet drowning, the larynx spasms and shuts after water has entered the lungs.

WET DROWNING VICTIMS, even if resuscitated, face complications such as damage to the surface lining of the lungs, and pneumonia. Once out of the water, these patients are not yet out-of-the-woods.

If they have ASPIRATED WATER, they are at risk of having some of the surfactant rinsed out of their lungs, which will cause respiratory distress and secondary drowning in minutes to hours.

SECONDARY DROWNING is death caused several to many hours subsequent to the initial incident by the damage done to the lungs and circulatory system.

Additionally, wet drowning victims are at high risk of ASPIRATION PNEUMONIA.

Overcrowded and unsafe vessels account for many drowning deaths (specific data unavailable). Approximately 3,000 to 4,000 drowning deaths occur in the United States each year, of which 1,500 are children. Most children drown in their own homes in less than one foot of water. About half of the boating accidents in the US that result in drowning involve alcohol. Drowning victims are usually found close to shore in shallow water, lying still and floating face down. Most drownings are unwitnessed; therefore, how long the victim has been submerged or unconscious in the water is very hard to determine.

Dive Injuries

managing pressure under pressure

dissolved gas issues, decompression sickness & barotrauma

When we humans dive beneath the surface of the water, weird things happen to our bodies—it's the reverse of the old fish-out-of-water bromide. Aside from the obvious (there's no air down there), most problems that arise from living and recreating underwater are directly related to pressure differentials between the human body and the surrounding watery, variable-pressure environment (the deeper you dive, the greater the ambient pressure).

Dissolved gas issues are those which result from breathing gas under pressure. The gas (e.g., nitrogen) is absorbed into tissues with various detrimental effects. Nitrogen narcosis, by far the most common, happens to virtually all divers and is temporary, reversible, and causes no lasting damage. The more dangerous dissolved gas injuries will be covered under decompression sickness.

Barotrauma refers to tissue damage caused by the difference in pressure between an air space inside the body and the pressure in the fluid (liquid or gas) surrounding the body. Barotrauma typically occurs to air spaces within a body when that body moves to or from a higher pressure environment, such as when a SCUBA diver, a free-diving diver, or an airplane passenger ascends or descends, or during uncontrolled decompression of a pressure vessel. Damage occurs in the tissues around the body's air spaces because gases are compressible, but human tissues are not (because they are essentially fluid, which is incompressible). During *increases* in ambient pressure, the internal air space provides the surrounding tissues with little support to resist the higher external pressure. During *decreases* in ambient pressure, the higher pressure of the gas inside the air spaces causes damage to the surrounding tissues if that gas becomes trapped.

Decompression sickness (DCS, "the bends"): as a diver descends and while at bottom depth, nitrogen is absorbed into tissues until a pressure balance is reached. During ascent the nitrogen diffuses from the tissues, and if the diver ascends too rapidly, nitrogen bubbles will expand in the tissues as the pressure decreases—causing an extremely painful and potentially fatal condition.

OF THE APPROXIMATELY 27 MEN KILLED during the construction of the Brooklyn Bridge from 1870 to 1883, at least three died from what was described then as caisson disease, now known as decompression sickness. The first man, John Myers, described as a "heavy set German laborer", died on April 22, 1872 after working in a caisson at a depth of 75 feet below the surface of the East River.

THERE ARE AN ESTIMATED 150 FATAL DIVING ACCIDENTS in the US, each year—approximately 1 out of every 200,000 dives. Like those in other high-risk adventures sports (e.g., skydivers, mountain climbers), SCUBA divers must manage the risks of their sport via a combination of education and training, the proper use of sophisticated equipment, and good judgment. Nonetheless, significant risks remain for divers—they recreate underwater, after all.

history

The discovery and understanding of pressure-related injuries began over 100 years ago. It was first widely described when construction workers on bridge projects (e.g., the Brooklyn Bridge) began to work inside caissons (sunken, pressurized structures that allowed people to work under water)—in fact, what was to become known as "the bends" (decompression sickness) was originally called "caisson disease." The symptoms of the disease occurred when the workers left the compressed atmosphere of the caisson and rapidly reentered normal (decompressed) atmospheric conditions. The first documented cases occurred in 1841 among miners working in shafts pressurized to keep water out. Julius H. Kroehl, a submariner pioneer, died of decompression sickness after an experimental dive in the Sub Marine Explorer in 1867. In 1869 a death was reported from decompression sickness after the diver went beneath the water with a pressurized helmet.

scuba

- Originally an acronym for Self-Contained Underwater breathing Apparatus, Scuba has become a recognized word.
- Scuba diving began with the development of the Aqua-lung by Emile Gagnan and Jaques-Yves Cousteau in 1943.
- Scuba divers inhale a compressed gas (air or mixed gases for deeper dives) through a regulator from a tank on their back and exhale into the water.
- The sport is unregulated (no pun intended) so accurate numbers are hard to come by—PADI (the Professional Association of Dive Instructors) and Undercurrent Magazine, estimate that between one and three million people in the US take five or more dives each year. Scuba diving is one of the fastest growing sports worldwide.
- Early on, divers needed to record their depths and times by hand and calculate decompression rates themselves using dive tables. Modern scuba equipment uses computers to do the math, making the sport much safer by minimizing user error—although accidents still occur.
- It is estimated that 1 in every 10 dives has some sort of minor emergency or problem, yet the risk of dying is still very small (see left).
- Understanding how to prevent, recognize, and treat dive-related emergencies is essential for anyone who ventures into the undersea world. This is an alien environment (like high altitude) that humans are not designed to live in.
- Diving takes special equipment, knowledge, and skills. Emergencies typically occur far from shore, hospitals, rescue personnel, and decompression chambers.

Ye Olde Gas Laws

Boyles Law: P1V1 = P2V2 *

- At constant temperature, the volume of a gas varies inversely with absolute pressure, while the density of a gas varies directly with absolute pressure. Increasing the pressure (e.g., during a diver's descent), will decrease air volume, potentially causing squeeze injuries. Gas volume decreases by 50% for every 33fsw (feet of seawater).

- Decreasing the pressure (e.g., during a diver's ascent), will increase the air volume, potentially causing expansion injuries. Gas volume increases by 100% for every 33fsw.

- Boyle's Law is important to divers because it relates changes in the volume of a gas to changes in pressure (depth) and defines the relationship between pressure and volume in breathing gas supplies.

Henry's Law: p = k_H c

- Where **p** is the partial pressure of the solute in the gas above the solution, **c** is the concentration of the solute and **kH** is a constant with the dimensions of pressure divided by concentration. The constant, known as the Henry's Law constant, depends on the solute, the solvent, and the temperature.

- Henry's Law states: At a constant temperature, the amount of a given gas that dissolves in a given type and volume of liquid is directly proportional to the partial pressure of that gas in equilibrium with that liquid.

  An equivalent way of stating the law is that the solubility of a gas in a liquid is directly proportional to the partial pressure of the gas above the liquid.

- The classic example of Henry's Law is found in carbonated soft drinks. With the container capped, the gas above the liquid is almost pure carbon dioxide (CO_2) as a pressure slightly above atmospheric pressure. The liquid itself also contains dissolved CO_2. When the container is opened, some of the gas escapes with a hiss, relieving the pressure above the liquid,. Because the partial pressure of CO_2 above the liquid is now lower, some of the dissolved CO_2 in the liquid comes out as bubbles; and if left open, the concentration of CO_2 in the air and in the liquid will equalize (and you'll have flat soda).

- When the above scenario occurs in a diver's body, the consequences can be fatal as the diver's blood turns into a nitrogen fizz.

These are the gas laws most important to divers.

* P = pressure
V = volume
T = temperature.

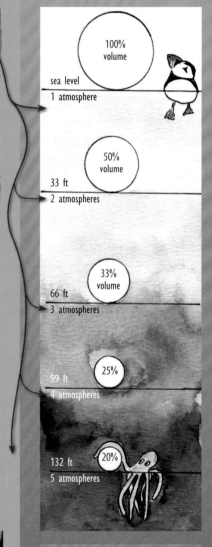

1 square inch   gravity

1 atmosphere of pressure (atm) at sea level at the earth's surface (14.7psi)

DEPTH	PRESSURE
0 ft (sea level, 1 atm)	14.7 psi
33 ft (2 atm)	29.4 psi
66 ft (3 atm)	44.1 psi
99 ft (4 atm)	58.8 psi
132 ft (5 atm)	73.5 psi

the weighty issue of measuring apparently nothing

Look up at the heavens on a crystal clear night, and it's easy to assume that the space between you and the stars is empty. You're gazing right up through the apparent nothingness of the atmosphere, but believe it or not, all that air above you weighs a ton, so to speak, and underwater things are under even more pressure.

The force per unit area exerted against a surface by the weight of air above that surface in the earth's atmosphere is 14.7 pounds per square inch (psi) at sea level—which is designated as 1 atmosphere (atm).

In diving, an additional atmosphere is added for every 33 feet of descent: thus at 99 feet, you are at a pressure of 4 atmospheres (1 atmosphere at the surface, plus 1 additional atmosphere for each 33 feet). Once you drop beneath the surface, the pressure increases because of the weight of the water in the column above you, not the air.

Regardless of the makeup of the fluid which is exerting the pressure, be it the atmosphere or the ocean (and yes, the earth's atmosphere is a fluid), the pressure is measured in psi.

ATMOSPHERIC ABSOLUTE (ata)
atmospheric pressure at sea level (ata) equals:

14.7psi (pounds per square inch)

29.9inmg (inches of mercury)

760mmHg (millimeters of mercury—Torr)

1033g/cm2 (grams per centimeter squared)

1013.3mbar (millibars)

10.08msw (meters of sea water)

33fsw (feet of sea water)

34ffw (feet of fresh water)

dissolved gas issues
BREATHING GAS UNDER PRESSURE

- As Henry's Law tells us, as pressure increases, the amount of gas that can be dissolved into a fluid also increases.
- The deeper you dive, and the longer you stay at depth (bottom time), the more nitrogen is dissolved into your body's tissues.
- As you ascend back to the surface, the pressure decreases and the nitrogen is released out of the tissues. If the rate of ascent is too fast, nitrogen bubbles will form in the tissues leading to various symptoms associated with decompression sickness—see below.
- The other dissolved gas injury we will cover, carbon monoxide (CO) poisoning, is extremely rare.

NITROGEN NARCOSIS

- Nitrogen narcosis is a reversible alteration in consciousness that occurs while scuba diving at depth.
- Narcosis produces a state similar to alcohol intoxication or nitrous oxide inhalation, and can occur during shallow dives, but usually does not become noticeable until depths beyond 30 meters (100 feet) are reached.
- It is sometimes called the "rapture of the deep" because it feels pleasant and victims may not initially be aware that they are in trouble.
- The symptoms of nitrogen narcosis have been called the "Martini Effect" or "Martini's Law" because for every 50 feet of depth, the effect is similar to drinking a martini on an empty stomach: slightly giddy, woozy, a little off-balance.

SYMPTOMS OF NITROGEN NARCOSIS

- Because of the perception-altering effects of nitrogen narcosis, the onset may be hard to recognize (especially in yourself).
- In its early stages, narcosis results in relief of anxiety, a feeling of tranquility and mastery of the environment.

DEPTH (feet)	Nitrogen Narcosis symptoms
33 - 100	Mild impairment of performance of unpracticed tasks ● mildly impaired reasoning ● mild euphoria possible
100 - 165	Delayed response to visual and auditory stimuli ● reasoning and immediate memory affected more than motor coordination ● calculation errors and wrong choices ● idea fixation ● overconfidence and sense of well-being ● laughter and loquacity (in a chamber), which may be overcome by self-control ● anxiety (common in cold, murky water)
165 - 230	Sleepiness ● impaired judgment ● confusion ● hallucinations ● severe delay in response to signals, instructions, and other stimuli ● occasional dizziness ● uncontrolled laughter ● hysteria (in chamber) ● terror in some
230 - 300	Poor concentration ● mental confusion ● stupefaction (groggy, insensible) with some decrease in dexterity and judgment ● loss of memory ● increased excitability
300 and deeper	Hallucinations ● increased intensity of vision and hearing ● sense of impending blackout and euphoria ● dizziness ● manic or depressive states ● a sense of levitation ● disorganization of the sense of time ● changes in facial appearance ● unconsciousness ● death

TREATMENT OF **NITROGEN NARCOSIS**

1. If you suspect you are getting "narced" (*nar•kt*) or see suspicious behavior in someone else, ascend immediately at the proper rate and taking appropriate rest stops. The effects of narcosis should disappear almost immediately upon ascent—going up as little as 10 feet may be enough to clear your head.
2. If the symptoms do not resolve after ascent, then narcosis is not the cause and prompt professional medical attention is advised.
3. Do not dive again for at least 24 hours.
4. There is no known long-term or permanent damage, and no increased susceptibility.

PREVENTION OF **NITROGEN NARCOSIS**

- Follow safe diving practices.
- Use properly maintained equipment.
- Use proper buoyancy (this reduces physical effort).
- Descend slowly (there is some evidence that rapid compression increases narcosis risk).
- Do not overwork mentally or physically while diving—avoid task overloading and keep your dive agenda simple.
- Over-learn tasks—proactive everything, including emergency procedures, until they are second nature.
- Use a slate—don't rely on your memory. Write your dive plan down and any other useful information (e.g., what camera settings you'll use).
- Schedule regular gauge checks (especially important below 100 feet, where air goes fast)—if your partner misses a check or seems uninterested, suspect narcosis and test them (see sidebar).
- Schedule buddy checks—eye contact and OK signs every three or four breaths, for instance.
- Use proper communication, watch for visual clues in others—if you see suspicious behavior, ascend immediately with the person at the proper rate.
- Be warm, rested, and confident (cold, fatigue, and anxiety increase narcosis risk).
- Be sober and drug-free: do not consume alcohol within 24 hours of diving, and watch out for drug interactions (e.g., motion sickness medications can increase narcosis risk and intensity).
- Keep focused.

CARBON MONOXIDE POISONING

- This is a rare problem which can occur if the intake for a compressor used to fill scuba tanks is not protected from contamination by carbon monoxide.
- If an internal combustion engine (a nearby automobile, the engine that powers the compressor) is running near the air intake, the air can become contaminated.
- Breathing a small quantity of carbon monoxide under pressure can cause life-threatening problems. The binding attraction of carbon monoxide to the hemoglobin in red blood cells is 200 times stronger than that of oxygen. A diver breathing from a contaminated tank can quickly become overloaded with carbon monoxide—robbing the body of oxygen.

"YO, DUDE, YOU OKAY?"

First of all, assume you'll be narced. The degree of narcosis is a function of depth, but it's unpredictable and there is no such things as a "safe" depth. Susceptibilities vary between divers and between dives. Typically, only slight impairment occurs until 60 feet, and it may not be noticeable until 100 feet. Virtually all divers experience significant narcosis at 130 feet, although it is still typically manageable—and is easily detected by an unaffected observer or an objective test.

TESTS FOR NARCOSIS

FINGER TEST Agree on this prior to the dive: every few minutes, hold up a number of fingers to your partner (e.g., three). They must respond with the same number of fingers, plus one. Give all five fingers, and your partner will have to use both hands to respond correctly—very clever.

SLATE TEST Every few minutes each of you writes you and your partner's depth and psi on your slate. Then each of you point to your own and your partner's numbers on each slate—the slates have to agree. This test evaluates both divers at once, and also encourages regular gauge checks.

BEHAVIOR TEST Diving is really fun, but it's not supposed to be goofy. If you or your partner is acting silly, or seems euphoric or dizzy, stop them and evaluate them—use one of the tests above, or some other cognitive test, like having them do a math addition problem on their slate. If things don't add up (sorry), go up.

A FINAL ADMONITION

PREVENTION IS THE KEY Be a cautious diver. Don't push your limits. Approach new maximum depths in increments of 10 feet. The first diver to 130 feet doesn't win. Stick to your dive plan. Test yourself and your partner for symptoms of narcosis. If anything doesn't feel or look right, it probably isn't—go up carefully and go home and dive again another day.

WHAT IS A DIVE CHAMBER?

Several of the conditions described in this chapter reference a dive chamber as part of the treatment. A dive chamber, or hyperbaric chamber, is a sealed vessel large enough for people to enter and exit that uses a compressed gas supply to raise the internal air pressure. Of the two types, decompression and recompression, the latter is used to treat decompression sickness and other diving-related medical conditions. They are primarily used when a diver has ascended from a deep dive to the surface too quickly and experiences decompression sickness (which may take hours to present). The patient is placed inside a hyperbaric chamber, and the pressure is raised to simulate depth, allowing the patient to stabilize. The pressure is then decreased over time (sometimes over many hours) while the patient is monitored, until they are medically stable at one atmosphere. Recompression chambers are found at many hospitals and other treatment centers throughout the US and a directory of them can be found at www.hyperbariclink.com.

If the symptoms of decompression sickness present in the hours following a dive, evacuate the person to the nearest medical facility equipped with a recompression chamber as soon as possible—when you dial 911, be sure to make it clear that you suspect decompression sickness to minimize delay to the appropriate facility. In circumstances where a recompression chamber is far away, the person should be evacuated to the nearest hospital first, for initial stabilization, then transferred. Some rescue teams (near popular diving destinations) have portable chambers that can help stabilize the patient during transport to definitive care.

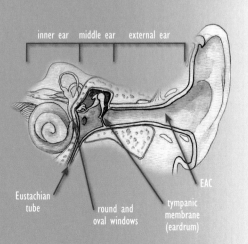

inner ear   middle ear   external ear

Eustachian tube

round and oval windows

tympanic membrane (eardrum)

EAC

SYMPTOMS OF **CARBON MONOXIDE POISONING**

- Cherry-red lips, cheeks and fingernails
- Dizziness
- Headaches
- Staggering
- Confusion
- Paralysis
- A diver with carbon monoxide poisoning will likely feel ill
- Carbon monoxide poisoning can cause rapid loss of consciousness and death

TREATMENT OF **CARBON MONOXIDE POISONING**

1. Immediate and controlled ascent
2. Fresh air
3. High-flow oxygen with positive-pressure ventilation, if available
4. Evacuation to the nearest dive chamber (see left)

PREVENTION OF **CARBON MONOXIDE POISONING**

- Only get your tanks filled from a licensed dealer.

barotrauma

COMPRESSION INJURIES

- Another law, Pascal's Law states that pressure applied anywhere to a confined incompressible fluid is transmitted equally in all directions throughout the fluid. Because fluids are (essentially) incompressible, fluid parts of the body (e.g., brain, muscles, vasculature) will experience the pressure without changing size or shape—this is harmless. But air is compressible, so an increase in pressure during descent will decrease the volume of air in the air-filled cavities of the body, which can cause compression (squeeze) injuries.
- Areas of the body susceptible to squeeze injuries include the ears (external ear canal, middle ear, inner ear), the sinuses, the lungs, and to a lesser extent, the stomach, intestines, bowels, and even beneath dental fillings.

EXTERNAL EAR SQUEEZE *(barotitis externa)*

- When the external ear canal (EAC) is occluded by cerumen (ear wax), ear plugs, or a wet suit hood, barotitis externa can occur.
- Since the EAC cannot vent, the air-filled space will shrink as the external pressure increases and the EAC will become edematous and hemorrhagic.

SYMPTOMS OF **EXTERNAL EAR SQUEEZE**

- The initial symptom is pain in the outer ear.
- Swelling and bleeding can also occur.

TREATMENT OF **EXTERNAL EAR SQUEEZE**

1. Stop descending and ascend until you are pain free.
2. Remove any obstruction, or remove the hood to allow the pressure to stabilize.
3. Inspect the EAC for bleeding.
4. Test the person's hearing to make sure you are not dealing with a more serious injury—if hearing is impaired, seek medical help.
5. Cortisporin Otic Solution or other steroid ear drops may be applied to ease pain and speed healing.
6. Do not dive for at least one week.
7. The ear should be examined by a physician.

MIDDLE EAR SQUEEZE *(barotitis media)*

- During descent, the increasing pressure can cause pain in the middle ear.

- The Eustachian tube running from the sinuses into the middle ear ventilates the middle ear, equalizing daily pressure changes (for example, the change felt when driving up or down a mountain road).

- If the Eustachian tube does not vent properly, the increase in external pressure will cause the volume of air in the middle ear to shrink, and the tympanic membrane will bow inward causing pain.

- If a diver ignores this pain, the increased pressure in the middle ear can cause mucosal bleeding, edema, and a possible tympanic membrane rupture.

- In the event of a rupture, water will rush into the middle ear resulting in severe vertigo caused by caloric (cold water) vestibular stimulation.

SYMPTOMS OF MIDDLE EAR SQUEEZE

- Deep pain in the ear
- Possible swelling and bleeding
- Hearing loss, from partial to complete, if the eardrum ruptures
- Dizziness

PREVENTION OF MIDDLE EAR SQUEEZE

- Descend slowly and relieve any pressure early by using the Valsalva or Frenzel maneuvers to help open the Eustachian tubes (right).
- Do not descend with pain.
- Long-acting decongestants or antihistamines can be used for three days prior to the dive to help keep the Eustachian tubes open.

TREATMENT OF MIDDLE EAR SQUEEZE

1. If pain develops, ascend to a depth where the pain improves and re-try the Valsalva or Frenzel maneuvers to equalize pressure in the ears.
2. If the ears cannot be equalized, ascend to the surface and terminate the dive—you're done for the day.

INNER EAR SQUEEZE *(barotitis interna)*

- Barotitis interna occurs when the pressure differential between the middle and inner ears causes an implosion or explosion of the round or oval windows that separate the middle and inner ears.

SYMPTOMS OF INNER EAR SQUEEZE

- Sudden onset of:

  - Severe vertigo
  - Roaring tinnitus (ringing in the ears)
  - Nystagmus (involuntary eye movement)
  - A sense of fullness in the affected ear
  - Hearing loss from partial to complete

- The above symptoms do not improve with ascent

TREATMENT OF INNER EAR SQUEEZE

1. Safely ascend to the surface immediately.
2. Give antivertigo drugs: meclizine (Antivert) or diazepam (Valium).
3. Follow up with an ear, nose, and throat specialist before diving again.

TO VALSALVA OR FRENZEL... UM, PARDON ME?

The increasing pressure in your ears can easily be equalized by performing one of these two maneuvers.

VALSALVA: forcibly exhale against a closed airway—pinch your nose and attempt to exhale. With this method, there is a slight risk of auditory damage due to overpressurization, so be careful.

FRENZEL: pinch your nose, place your tongue against the roof of your mouth as far forward as possible, move the back of your tongue gently upward (as if starting to swallow). There is no risk of overpressurization with this method.

REPEAT these maneuvers until the pressure equalizes—you may have to perform one or the other of them after every few feet of descent.

WHY NOT JUST SWALLOW?

Sure, it works in the car when you're driving up and down big hills, but it's virtually impossible to swallow with a regulator in your mouth.

Boyle's Law in a bottle: you take a full breath of pressurized air at 33 feet (top bottle, 1 atmosphere), and hold that breath while ascending to the surface. The volume of air doubles, and so does the volume of your lungs (bottom bottle)—and as can be seen, the potential for disaster is obvious.

EXPANSION INJURIES

- The decrease in surrounding water pressure during ascent allows the volume of air in air-filled cavities of the body to expand (e.g., lungs). If not managed, this can cause expansion injuries.
- Ascent injuries can also happen as the nitrogen that is dissolved in the tissues begins to be released. If the dissolved nitrogen comes out too quickly, nitrogen bubbles will form, resulting in one of the various types of decompression sicknesses.
- All expansion injuries are dangerous; some can be life-threatening.

PULMONARY OVER-INFLATION SYNDROME (POIS)

- Also known as pulmonary overpressurization syndrome (POPS), or a burst lung, this is damage caused by overinflation of the lungs.
- This typically occurs when a person ascends rapidly while holding their breath: the gas in the lungs expands during ascent and if the tissues are expanded beyond their limits, the alveoli rupture. This isn't hard to do—our lungs are quite delicate and can be easily damaged by pressure.
- Remember Boyle's Law: gas volume doubles for every 33 feet of ascent in salt water (34 feet in fresh water, because it is less dense).
- One of the principles constantly reinforced in dive training programs is to never hold your breath while ascending—gently blowing out as you ascend will keep the pressure down and ensure that the lungs don't expand beyond their limits.
- POIS can manifest with a variety of signs and symptoms.

PNEUMOMEDIASTINUM/INTERSTITIAL EMPHYSEMA

- The alveoli rupture, allowing air to forcefully leak into the mediastinum, the pericardium, and up into the neck.

SYMPTOMS OF PNEUMOMEDIASTINUM/INTERSTITIAL EMPHYSEMA

- Subcutaneous air in the tissues resulting in crepitus on compression of the skin and neck
- Change in the voice due to the swelling of the tissues around the vocal cords
- Dyspnea (shortness of breath) because the lungs are no longer being properly ventilated
- Pericardial air which can be seen on a chest x-ray

TREATMENT OF PNEUMOMEDIASTINUM/INTERSTITIAL EMPHYSEMA

This is typically not dangerous and will typically self-correct , however:

1. 100% O_2 will hasten recovery.
2. If symptoms deteriorate, evacuate the patient to a dive medical facility.
3. Monitor the patient for other sequelae (e.g., pericardial tamponade).

PNEUMOTHORAX

- The alveoli rupture, allowing air to forcefully leak into the pleural space.
- It can progress to a dangerous tension pneumothorax (increased impairment of respiration and/or blood circulation).

SYMPTOMS OF PNEUMOTHORAX

- Dsypnea from mild to severe, with cyanosis.
- Diminished-to-absent breath sounds on one side, with tympany on percussion on the same side.
- If severe, tracheal shift and jugular vein distention can be present.

TREATMENT OF PNEUMOTHORAX

1. Monitor for worsening dyspnea and subcutaneous emphysema.
2. Monitor for developing tension pneumothorax—perform a chest tube thoracotomy or needle thoracostomy for severe tension pneumothorax.
3. Administer 100% O_2 by non-rebreather—this may require artificial ventilation.
4. Evacuate immediately to a dive-medicine facility.

ARTERIAL GAS EMBOLISM (AGE)

- The most serious of all dive injuries, AGE is frequently fatal, and is second only to drowning in fatalities among sport divers.
- AGE occurs when the alveoli rupture, and the resulting air bubbles enter the pulmonary circulation.
- The bubbles travel to the left side of the heart; and from the left ventricle they can migrate into the coronary or cerebral circulation. This can cause an Acute Myocardial Infarction (AMI) or a Cerebrovascular Accident (CVA).
- One of the hallmarks of AGE is that it virtually always presents within 10 minutes of surfacing. In a study of 24 AGE cases involving US Navy divers in which the time was known, 9 incidents occurred during ascent, 11 occurred within one minute at the surface, and four occurred after 3 – 10 minutes at the surface—AGE presents quickly and often dramatically.
- AGE is not depth dependent and can occur after diving to a depth of as little as 2m (6ft)—if a diver has inhaled pressurized air and does not exhale while surfacing. (See sidebar.)

SYMPTOMS OF ARTERIAL GAS EMBOLISM

- Neurological symptoms associated with CVA (air in the cerebral circulation).
  - Change in mood or affect; confusion
  - Visual disturbances
  - Hemiparesis (weakness on one side of the body) or hemiplegia (paralysis of the arm, trunk, and leg on the same side)
  - Vertigo
  - Seizure
  - Unconsciousness—sudden loss of consciousness before surfacing is to be considered AGE until proven otherwise
  - Cardiopulmonary arrest

TAKE A DEEP BREATH

Taking a breath at the surface, diving to any depth, and then returning to the surface without exhaling will not cause AGE. The air in your lungs will compress during the dive and then expand to its original volume (but not beyond) when you return to the surface. So snorkel like a dolphin and don't worry about expansion injuries.

FREEDIVERS GO REALLY DEEP

The current world record depth for a No Limits Apnea (NLA) dive is 214m (702ft), accomplished by Herbert Nitsch on June 14, 2007, in Spetses, Greece. In this sub-discipline of freediving (diving as deep as possible on a single breath), the diver takes a breath at the surface, descends using a weighted sled, and then ascends with the help of an inflatable bag.) This is extremely dangerous, for many reasons, but there is no risk for AGE or other expansion injuries.

Wreck diving is particularly dangerous—there are lots of things to get tangled up in, bewildering and tight places to swim through, disorienting silt that won't dissipate, and so much cool stuff to see that it's easy to get distracted and forget basic diving procedures.

THE LAST DIVE . . .

On October 12, 1992, Chris and Chrissy Rouse, a father and son dive team with extensive experience, dove onto the wreck of a German submarine in 230 feet of water off the coast of New York. They became trapped in the wreck. When they finally escaped, they did not have enough compressed air left to take the necessary decompression stops as they ascended—both shot straight to the surface and the waiting dive boat. It was clear when they surfaced that both were in severe distress from decompression sickness.

A 911 call was made and a rescue helicopter arrived an hour and a half later. Chris, 39, the father, was pronounced dead at the scene. Chrissy, 22, was still alive, coherent, and talking. He was not in pain, but was paralyzed from the chest down and foam was found in a blood sample.

Recompression began approximately three hours after the ascent. Chrissy was put on pure O_2 and compressed to 60 feet in a chamber. He experienced extreme pain as circulation returned. He was recompressed to the equivalent of 165 feet and then gradually ascended to 30 feet in the chamber over five and a half hours. When he lost consciousness, he was recompressed back to 60 feet. He died shortly thereafter of heart failure. The autopsy revealed that his heart contained only foam.

The doctors concluded that nothing short of recompression to a depth of 300 — 400 feet, saturation treatment lasting several days, a complete blood transfusion, and deep helium recompression would have given Chrissy a real chance to survive.

- Symptoms associated with AMI (caused by air in the coronary circulation)
  - Apnea (momentary suspension of external breathing); dyspnea (shortness of breath)
  - Chest pain; chest pressure
  - Dysrhythmia (irregular heartbeat); asystole (no cardiac electrical activity—flatline)

TREATMENT OF ARTERIAL GAS EMBOLISM

1. Recompression ASAP
2. 100% O_2 while evacuating to a dive medical facility
3. Transport supine and monitor the patient's airway

ASTHMA

- A history of asthma is a contraindication for scuba diving (asthma types, symptoms, severity, and patient history vary, so this is not an absolute prohibition—asthmatics should consult with a physician who is familiar with diving to determine if it is an appropriate activity, and if so, what precautions and limitations apply).
- There is significant increased risk of POIS/POPS or arterial gas embolism.
- While diving in the ocean, it is very easy for salt water to get into the mouthpiece. When the regulator pushes air into the lungs, it will produce a fine mist of salt water that is then inhaled. This saline mist can act as a trigger, causing the bronchial constriction associated with asthma. The area of bronchial constriction will then cause air trapping, and during ascent the air will not be able to escape, creating an area of over-pressurization and potentially a burst lung. This is usually rapidly fatal.

decompression sickness
SEVERE DISSOLVED GAS INJURIES

- If bottom time (time at depth) is long enough and the ascent is too quick, nitrogen bubbles will form—where the bubbles form and where they lodge dictates the form of decompression sickness (see table).
- By obstructing small blood vessels, nitrogen bubbles can cause an acute MI (heart attack) or CVA (stroke).
- The bubbles can also effect changes in blood chemistry and can stretch and damage tissues.
- Unlike dissolved gas and compression injuries, the onset of the symptoms of decompression sickness occur in the hours after the dive has been completed—the dive itself may be essentially normal. An exception is when a diver makes a rapid emergency ascent; when this happens, the symptoms can be immediate, severe, dramatic, and tragic (see Last Dive sidebar).
- Symptoms of decompression sickness present within 12 hours of surfacing—80% of the time the symptoms will present within 1 hour, while 95% will present within 4 hours.
- The history of DCS classification began with simple descriptive terms like "bends" (musculoskeletal involvement,) "chokes" (pulmonary involvement), and "staggers" (neurological involvement,) and evolved into a class designation: Type I (simple: skin, musculoskeletal, lymphatic) and Type II (serious: with neurologic involvement and worse outcomes), and then evolved further into the body-system-based classification of today—which is diagnostically more useful because neurologic involvement may develop after initial presentation; and both Type I and Type II DCS have the same initial management.

SYMPTOMS OF **SPINAL CORD DCS**

- The most common form of DCS in divers, this presents as paresthesia (pins and needles) in the extremities with ascending numbness and eventually paraplegia (impairment in sensory or motor function in the lower extremities).

- Symptoms can include urinary retention, fecal incontinence, and priapism (continuous erection).

SYMPTOMS OF **CEREBRAL DCS**

- Cerebral DCS presents with classic CVA symptoms that can include memory loss, facial paralysis, hemiplegia, hemiparesis, ataxia (lack of voluntary muscle coordination), and loss of consciousness.

SYMPTOMS OF **PULMONARY DCS**

- Originally referred to as the "chokes" because sufferers had trouble breathing.

- It occurs within minutes of surfacing.

- It presents with substernal chest pain, cough, and dyspnea.

- It can progress to respiratory failure and shock.

SYMPTOMS OF **LABYRINTHINE OR INNER EAR DCS**

- Originally referred to as the "staggers" because of the accompanying lack of coordination.

- Symptoms include vertigo, nausea/vomiting, tinnitus (ringing in the ears), hearing loss, nystagmus (involuntary eye movement).

SYMPTOMS OF **MUSCULOSKELETAL DCS**

- Primarily characterized by general musculoskeletal pain, which can be extreme.

- Movement can exacerbate the pain, although it may be possible to reduce the pain by moving any affected joint(s) into a position of relative comfort.

SYMPTOMS OF **CUTANEOUS DCS**

- A relatively mild form of DCS characterized by skin irritation: itching, discoloration, edema, minor deformation

Injury breakdown as a percentage of calls to the Divers Alert Network (DAN) during calendar year 2007. Based on 7,872 total contacts: 5365 for information, 2,507 for actual cases.

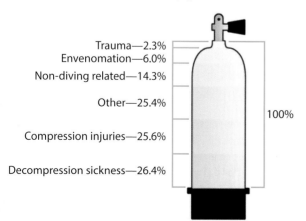

Trauma—2.3%
Envenomation—6.0%
Non-diving related—14.3%

Other—25.4%

100%

Compression injuries—25.6%

Decompression sickness—26.4%

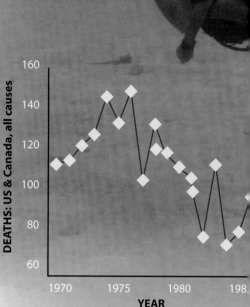

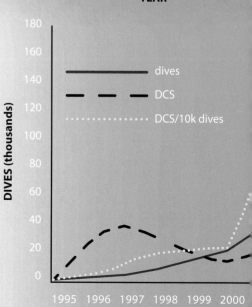

DCS type	BUBBLE LOCATION	SIGNS AND SYMPTOMS
Neurologic	Spinal cord	Ascending weakness or paralysis in the legs ● girdling abdominal or chest pain ● urinary or fecal incontinence
Neurologic	Brain	Altered sensation, tingling or numbness (paresthesia), increased sensitivity (hyperesthesia) ● confusion or memory loss • visual abnormalities ● unexplained mood or behavior changes • seizures, unconsciousness
Pulmonary	Lungs	Dry, persistent cough ● burning substernal chest pain, aggravated by breathing ● shortness of breath
Audiovestibular	Inner ear	Headache ● unexplained fatigue ● general malaise, poorly localized aches
Musculoskeletal	Mostly large joints: elbows, shoulders, hip, wrists, knees, ankles	Localized deep pain ranging from mild to excruciating; sometimes a dull ache, but rarely a sharp pain ● active and passive motion of the joint aggravates the pain ● the pain may be reduced by bending the joint to a more comfortable position
Cutaneous	Skin	Itching, usually around the ears, face, neck, arms, and upper torso ● sensation of tiny insects crawling over the skin ● mottled or marbled skin usually around the shoulders, upper chest, and abdomen, with itching ● swelling accompanied by tiny, scar-like skin depressions
Constitutional	Whole body	Headache ● unexplained fatigue ● general malaise, poorly localized aches

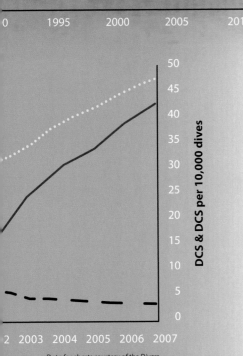

TREATMENT FOR ALL FORMS OF DECOMPRESSION SICKNESS

1. Recompression or hyperbaric therapy. This reduces the size of the nitrogen gas bubbles, promotes reabsorption of the nitrogen gas bubbles, and prevents further bubble formation.
2. Give 100% oxygen by non-rebreather to help wash out the nitrogen.
3. Use fluid IV therapy with crystalloid (aqueous solutions of mineral salts or other water-soluble molecules) to treat and prevent hemoconcentration (fluid loss in the blood resulting in a greater concentration of cells and other solids).
4. Administer diazepam or phenergan for vertigo, nausea, and vomiting.

PRECAUTIONS FOR DECOMPRESSION SICKNESS

● When the DCS patient can return to diving is dependent on several factors including the type and severity of the DCS. They should have a complete neurological exam and dive evaluation. While they may be able to dive again, they may need to wait weeks to months.

● Flying and the 24-hour rule: Because scuba diving causes the body's tissues to become saturated with nitrogen, and this nitrogen is gradually released once the diver is back on the surface, there should always be at least 24 hours between your last dive and your next airplane flight. Airlines lower the cabin pressure to an equivalent altitude of 5,000 to 8,000 feet, which promotes or hastens the release of nitrogen from the tissues, and therefore can precipitate decompression sickness while flying.

SCUBA DIVING CONTRAINDICATIONS

- Scuba diving equipment is constantly evolving, becoming more sophisticated and doing a better job of keeping divers safe; and although the sport has an excellent safety record (the risks can be well managed, despite their perceived danger), people must be aware of the medical conditions and physical limitations which may exclude them from diving completely or limit their participation.

- The following chart contains the most common medical conditions that would put a diver at risk for major diving-related injuries such as pulmonary overinflation syndrome, arterial gas embolism, and decompression sickness—each of which can be fatal by themselves or lead to unconsciousness and drowning.

- Diagnostic studies and specialty consultations should be obtained as indicated to satisfy the physician as to the diver's status.

- The list contains both relative contraindications (which may be resolved with time and/or managed with appropriate medical intervention) and absolute contraindications (which place the diver at increased risk for injury or death, so diving should be avoided completely).

- The list of conditions is **not exhaustive**; when in doubt, consult a physician who has dive-specific training.

A BRIEF HISTORY OF SUBSURFACE HUMANITY

500 BC: Escaped Greek prisoner Scyllis breathes through a reed, cuts loose Xerxe's fleet.

4th century BC: Aristotle reports the use of upended cauldrons as diving bells.

15th century: Leonardo da Vinci mentions air tanks.

1650: Otto von Guericke builds the first air pump.

1774: John Day becomes the first person known to have died in a submarine accident.

1838: Dr. Manuel Théodore Guillaumet invents a twin-hose demand regulator.

1882: Brothers Alphonse and Théodore Carmagnolle of Marseille, France, patent the first properly anthropomorphic design of ADS (atmospheric diving suit); similar at left.

1876: An English merchant seaman, Henry Fleuss, develops the first workable self-contained diving rig that uses compressed oxygen.

1915: Three US Navy divers, Frank W. Crilley, William F. Loughman, and Nielson, reached a depth at sea of 304.

1943: Jacques-Yves Cousteau & Émile Gagnan patent first modern demand regulator.

1950s: Wetsuits available, Hollywood discovers diving, YMCA starts SCUBA program.

1966: Professional Association of Diving Instructors (PADI) starts.

1988: The movie *The Abyss* shows a rat and a man breathing oxygen-rich liquid—the rat really did it, and human divers may soon do it regularly.

2006: Equipped with an ADS 2000 atmospheric suit, a US Navy diver establishes a new depth record: 2,000 feet deep (609 meters).

1914: Modern swim fins are invented by the Frenchman Louis de Corlieu.

WILDCARE™

SYSTEM	RELATIVE CONTRAINDICATIONS	ABSOLUTE CONTRAINDICATIONS
Metabolic and Endocrinological	• Hormonal excess or deficiency • Obesity • Renal insufficiency	• Diabetics on insulin therapy or oral anti-hypoglycemia medication

Pulmonary	• History of (exercise testing necessary)
	  • Prior asthma or reactive airway disease (RAD)
	  • Exercise- or cold-induced bronchospasm (EIB)
	  • Solid, cystic, or cavitating lesion
	• Pneumothorax secondary to: thoracic surgery, trauma or pleural penetration, previous over-inflation injury
	• Restrictive lung disease
		• History of spontaneous pneumothorax
		• Active RAD (asthma), EIB, chronic obstructive pulmonary disease (COPD)
		• Restrictive diseases with exercise impairment

Cardiovascular	• History of
	  • Coronary artery bypass grafting (CABG) or percutaneous transluminal coronary angioplasty (PCTA) for coronary artery disease (CAD)
	  • Myocardial infarction
	  • Dysrhythmia requiring medication for suppression
	• Hypertension
	• Asymptomatic mitral valve prolapse
	• Pacemakers (Note: Pacemakers must be depth-certified by the manufacturer to at least 130 feet/40m of sea water)
		• Congestive heart failure

Neurological	• History of
	  • Head injury with sequelae (chronic complication) other than seizure
	  • Spinal cord or brain injury without residual neurologic deficit (see absolute)
	  • Cerebral gas embolism without residual effects and with complete resolution of signs and symptoms within 24 hours; pulmonary air trapping has been excluded
	• Migraine headaches whose symptoms or severity impair motor or cognitive function
	• Peripheral neuropathy
	• Cerebral palsy in the absence of seizure activity
		• History of
		  • Seizures other than childhood febrile seizures
		  • Temporary ischemic attack (TIA) or cerebrovascular accident (CVA)
		  • Spinal cord injury, disease, or surgery with residual sequelae (see relative)
		  • Type II (serious and/or central nervous system) decompression sickness with permanent neurologic deficit
		• Intracranial tumor or aneurysm

Otolaryngological (ear and throat)	• History of
	  • Significant cold injury to pinna (auricle: external ear)
	  • Tympanic membrane (TM) perforation
	  • Tympanoplasty (reconstructed eardrum)
	  • Mastoidectomy
	  • Mid-face fracture
	  • Head and/or neck therapeutic radiation
	  • Temporomandibular joint dysfunction
	• Recurrent otitis externa (outer ear inflammation)
	• Significant obstruction of the external auditory canal
	• Eustachian tube dysfunction
	• Recurrent otitis media (middle ear inflammation) or sinusitis (sinus infection)
	• Significant conductive or sensorineural hearing impairment
	• Facial nerve paralysis not associated with barotrauma
	• Full prosthodontic devices (dental prosthetic)
	• Unhealed oral surgery sites
		• History of
		  • Middle ear surgery
		  • Inner ear surgery
		  • Round window rupture
		  • Vestibular decompression sickness
		• Open TM perforation
		• Tube myringotomy (surgical tube implant)
		• Facial nerve paralysis secondary to barotrauma
		• Inner ear disease
		• Uncorrected upper airway obstruction
		• Laryngectomy (removal of larynx) or status post partial laryngectomy
		• Tracheostomy (tracheal implant to provide airway)

Other		• Sickle cell disease (sickle cell trait is a relative contraindication) • History of panic attacks • History of unexplained syncope (fainting) • Diabetes (complex, lots of factors, consult a physician) • Pregnancy (regardless of stage—it's never safe)

THE AUGUILLE DU MIDI (needle of the south) looms far above the town of Chamonix in the French Alps and is home to the highest cable car in the world. It only takes 20 minutes to whisk tourists from the pedestrian elevation in town (1035m/3395ft) to the hypoxic air and expensive coffee at the summit restaurant (3842m/12604ft). Sure, a commercial jet would get you that high in less than half the time, but you'd stay *inside* the plane. So much elevation gain so quickly can easily bring on a whole host of altitude-related illness symptoms—at least it's easy to get back down fast. According to one tourist website, virtually everyone on the Auguille du Midi will get light-headed and "some folks feel a bit dizzy." But don't worry, the site goes on to say, once on top "it takes anywhere between 20 – 40 minutes to acclimate."

Um....NO!

THERE'S SOMETHING IN THE AIR, but there's a lot less of it the higher you go—sure, the proportion of oxygen stays exactly the same, it's just that you can't get at it. What? It's like barotrauma: it's a pounds-per-square-inch thing, but this time there's not enough pressure instead of too much, so there's less air no matter how much of it you suck in. Imagine if your arms were too short to reach your mouth—you'd have trouble eating, right? It's like that, kind of.

Huh? Pretty complicated for stuff you can't even see, isn't it? Altitude-related illness is common above 2400m (8000ft) and ranges from annoying to life threatening—let's see if we can make some substance out of this wispy stuff.

WILDCARE™

Yeah, rotate the book

OXYGEN

THE SUBSTANCE OF THINGS INHALED

OH-TWO—*the life-giving gas*

- Oxygen gas is colorless. As a liquid (-183°C/-297°F) and a solid (-219°C/-362°F), oxygen is pale blue—neither state occurs naturally.

- Oxygen is the most abundant element, by mass, in our biosphere: air, sea, and land.

- About 2/3 of the mass of the human body is oxygen.

- At the present rate of creation (by photosynthesis) and consumption (by respiration and decay) the earth's oxygen is renewed every 2000 years.

- Humans inhale more than 6 billion tons of oxygen each year.

- The bright red color of your blood is because of the oxygen attached to your red blood cells. After those blood cells have released their oxygen and picked up carbon dioxide (CO_2), it turns dark red.

- Oxygen exists in nature as dioxygen, O_2, which are two oxygen molecules bound together allowing them to share a pair of electrons that stabilize the molecule. Animals use O_2 to transport electrons between molecules, facilitating the chemical reactions that are essential to life.

MOUNT EVEREST
on a perfect May day in 1991, and American alpinist Rick Wilcox is finally on top, sucking precious life from an oxygen tank. Most climbers need supplementary O_2 to reach the highest summits on earth—and despite all the editorial license and hype, no one has ever climbed Mount Everest "without" oxygen. Since 1994, approximately 1,000 spent oxygen bottles have been removed from the high camp on Everest. Hundreds remain.

ALTITUDE . . .

WHAT'S THE BIG AIRY DEAL?

■ It's simple: air has mass and is compressible—as gravity pulls the air down, its own weight causes it to squish and become more dense. If you take a given one square-inch column of air (left), it will become more dense as you move from the outer edge of the atmosphere to the surface of the earth.

The pressure caused by this compression is measured in millimeters of mercury (in a barometer) and pounds per square inch (PSI).

■ While the proportions of oxygen to the other gases that make up the atmosphere remain the same throughout the column (known as partial pressure: 21% oxygen, 78% nitrogen, 1% other gases), because the atmospheric pressure is lower the higher we go, and the air therefore less dense, the amount of oxygen available to us decreases.

At 18,000 feet, your deep breath will have the same volume as at sea level, but there will only be half as many oxygen molecules available.

■ As we ascend, other environmental/meteorological things change: for every 1,000 feet of ascent, the air temperatures typically drops 3°F and the concentration of ultraviolet (UV) light increases by 4%; the air also gets less humid the higher we go (because it's less dense, it cannot hold as much water).

RISKS OF ALTITUDE

● **Dehydration:** we exhale 250cc of water/hour, 6 liters/day.
● **Hypothermia:** up to 6,000 calories needed to keep the core warm.
● **Frostbite:** the colder, the worse; dehydration increases the risk.
● **Snow blindness and severe sunburn** because of increasing UV.
● **Acute Mountain Sickness**—signs of lack of acclimatization.
● **High Altitude Pulmonary Edema** (HAPE), fluid in the lungs.
● **High Altitude Cerebral Edema** (HACE), fluid in the brain.

These two can be life-threatening

Mount Everest, Nepal / China border
29,035'—1/3 atmosphere (253mmHg / 4.4psi)

Only one-third of the oxygen is available—you may not be able to remember your zip code or tie your shoes quickly.

Mt. St. Elias, Alaska / Yukon border
18,000'—1/2 atmosphere (380mmHg / 7.35psi)

Only half of the oxygen is available—your head hurts and it's hard to sleep.

1" x 1" column of air

---

the Death Zone*
altitude—26,000' and up

extremely high
altitude—18,000'

very high
altitude—11,000'

high
altitude—5,000'

"The Goofyhorn," (above) is a fictional 8,000m peak just east of Cleveland, and home to such non-traditional mountaineering activities as hauling up piano players, dairy farming, and doing Sisyphus impersonations.

* The Death Zone (above 8,000m) is so-called because the human body functions so poorly at that altitude that it cannot keep up with the metabolic and physiological demands of the oxygen-starved environment—it can't even heal itself efficiently. Climbers spend as little time as possible here; even with the best physical conditioning and nutrition/hydration, survival (without supplemental oxygen) would be measured in hours to days.

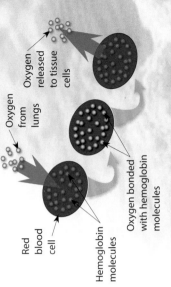

The average person will breathe over 5 million times during their lifetime.

Oxygen from lungs

Oxygen released to tissue cells

Red blood cell

Hemoglobin molecules

Oxygen bonded with hemoglobin molecules

A pulse oximeter measures the arterial blood oxygen saturation (% of O_2 bound to the red blood cells) by analyzing the color of the blood. The resulting percentage (SaO_2) is typically 95 – 100% in healthy people. Below 90% is considered low.

THE PHYSIOLOGY OF BREATHING

■ When we contract our diaphragm to inhale, the pressure in our thorax decreases, expanding the volume of our lungs, and the (higher pressure) air from the outside rushes in to equalize things. When we relax our diaphragm, the lungs also relax, due mostly to their inherent elasticity, and air rushes out—both inhalation and exhalation can be augmented by accessory muscle contraction (e.g., when exercising).

■ At the level of the alveoli, the oxygen is absorbed into the blood where it binds to a hemoglobin (Hg) molecule in the red blood cells (RBCs)—oxygen is paramagnetic, creating a magnet in the presence of a magnetic field, and is attracted to the iron (Fe) in the hemoglobin.

■ When the hemoglobin reaches a cell requiring an infusion of oxygen, the oxygen is released, then the hemoglobin heads back to the lung to get another load and the fascinating cycle repeats.

OKAY, SO THE OXYGEN IS IN THERE . . . NOW WHAT?

■ A chemical reaction fundamental to life is the production of adenosine triphosphate, (ATP)—the "molecular currency" that allow us to store and transfer intracellular energy which facilitates the chemical reactions that support and sustain life.

■ Oxygen is necessary to facilitate several chemical reactions to produce this high-energy compound

■ These chemical reactions occur within mitochondria, described as little furnaces or organelles found within each cell. Through a series of chemical reactions, called oxidative phosphorylation, oxygen is used to burn glucose, releasing its stored energy that is then used to produce ATP.

■ We do not store oxygen; instead, we accumulate the molecular currency, ATP, to be spent later.

■ But, since ATP is consumed to sustain us, it must be constantly replenished—that's why we breathe all the time, extracting precious oxygen from the air around us.

Venice, Italy*
sea level—1 atmosphere (760mmHg / 14.7psi)

All of the oxygen is available—life is great!.

At sea level, the one square-inch column of air stretching to space actually weighs 14.7 pounds. At 18,000 feet, the column of air above that point only weighs 7.35 pounds, and at 29,000 feet, only 4.4 pounds—less density, less oxygen available, harder to breathe and stay alive.

* Below: some big cities slightly higher than Venice

■ El Alto, Bolivia,13,615' (pop: 1.8m)

■ Shigatse, China, 12,585' (pop: 100k)

■ Quito, Ecuador, 9,350' (pop: >2.4m)

■ Bamyan, Afghanistan, 9,186' (pop: 137k)

■ Leadville[1], Colorado, 10,152' (pop: 2,688)

[1] Okay, maybe not so big

Climbers have reached the summit of Everest over 5,000 times since 1953. Only a small fraction of those ascents were made without supplemental oxygen.

THE
PHYSIOLOGY
OF ACCLIMATIZATION

- Acclimatization is the natural physiological process by which our body adjusts to changes in its environment so that it can maintain performance—specifically (at altitude), how it adjusts to the changes in atmospheric pressure that affect our ability to utilize oxygen.

- Humans are not designed to live permanently above 14,000 feet, but we do have the ability to adapt (acclimatize) to higher elevations, if given enough time. For example, many climbers have ascended 8,000m Himalayan peaks one step at a time without experiencing dangerous high-altitude illness (HAPE or HACE), but if one of those climbers were to fly to an 8,000m summit (1/3 atmosphere) from sea level (1 atmosphere) and step outside, they would be unconscious in 2 – 3 minutes and dead in 8 – 10 minutes (hypoxia leading to asphyxia). The physiology is remarkable (see Quito caption).

COMPENSATORY CHANGES

Hyperventilation

- Because of the low atmospheric pressure of oxygen at high altitude, each breath contains less oxygen—breathing faster increases the volume of air that we move in and out of our lungs each minute, helping to make up the difference.

- Our lungs are constantly adjusting our acid/base balance by controlling how much CO_2 is in our blood; however, hyperventilating can overwhelm the system and cause us to blow off too much CO_2.
  - The more CO_2, the lower the pH (more acidic).
  - The less CO_2, the higher the pH (more alkaline).

- Blowing off too much CO_2 causes respiratory alkalosis—which can account for some of the symptoms of acute mountain sickness (AMS).

Pulmonary Artery Pressure

- With the decrease in available oxygen, arterial pressure in the lungs increases.

- This compensatory mechanism opens up areas in the lungs where there is normally low perfusion of blood for gas exchange, which in turn increases the total alveolar surface area available, increasing oxygen absorption.

Quito, Ecuador, is the highest capital city in the world (9,350'), with an estimated population of over 2.5 million. To compensate for decreased hemoglobin saturation, a hormone secreted by the kidneys stimulates red blood cell production in the bone marrow of the people who live at these altitudes—increasing oxygen delivery. Athletes have known this for decades, and the concept of "live high, train low" has figured into the training strategy of many Olympians (contrast this with the mountaineers creed, "climb high, sleep low" in the sidebar below.)

"Sucking Ohs" … hyperventilating on Disappointment Cleaver, just below 12,000 feet on Mount Rainier—the standard route on a mountain that gives many people their first taste of high altitude mountaineering.

Hematocrit

- In response to the decreased amount of available oxygen to the cells, the kidneys will produce a hormone, erythropoietin, that stimulates the bone marrow to increase the production of red blood cells (RBC).
- The total mass of RBCs in the blood is the hematocrit. At sea level the hematocrit is about 40%, but at altitude, it can increase to about 55 – 57%, thus increasing the oxygen-carrying capacity of the blood.

2,3 – diphosphoglycerate (bisphosphoglycerate)

- This biochemical will increase in the RBCs, which aids in the release of O_2 from the hemoglobin molecules.
- This increases the quantity of O_2 that is released in the capillary beds. This is referred to as a shift in the oxyhemoglobin curve to the right.

SOB during exertion

- Even light effort will produce a feeling of shortness of breath.

Breathing patterns while sleeping

- Cheyne-Stokes Breathing—typically, during the acclimatization period, people will breathe in a pattern: short, quick breaths, followed by lengthening, deeper breaths; the pattern repeats with a short period of apnea between cycles.
- People will tend to sleep in a series of short naps interrupted with short periods of wakefulness where they stir or move around a little.

Increased urination

- Called altitude diuresis, this is a result of both peripheral vasoconstriction from the cold and the pH change in the blood caused by hyperventilation.

Long-term changes

- Increased RBC mass
- Increase in ADH (antidiuretic hormone: regulates the body's retention of water—the more ADH there is, the more water retained)

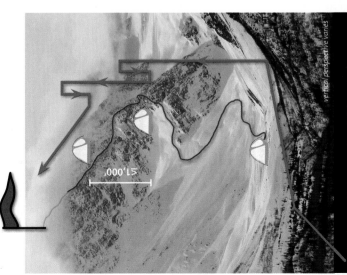

≤1,000'

vertical perspective varies

It's okay to climb more than 1000 vertical each day as long as you feel well, but drop back down each night—to help minimize altitude-related problems, your camps shouldn't be more than 1000 vertical feet apart.

THE GOLDEN RULES OF ASCENT

1. Illness at altitude is altitude illness until proven otherwise.
2. Never ascend with symptoms of Acute Mountain Sickness (AMS)—don't go up until the symptoms go down.
3. If symptoms worsen or you develop High-Altitude Pulmonary Edema (HAPE) or High-Altitude Cerebral Edema (HACE), go down, and continue going down until symptoms subside—even several hundred feet can make a difference.
4. Gain no more than 1,000 feet of sleeping altitude/day—climb high / sleep low is the rule.

GETTING HIGH WHILE STAYING WELL

Well-planned acclimatization allows most people to adapt to atmospheric pressure changes with few problems. Injury typically results from too rapid an ascent, usually above 8,000' (2,500m), and associated dehydration.

1. If possible, don't fly to high altitude: begin below 8,000 feet and then walk.
2. If you must fly to high altitude, take it really easy for the first 24 hours.
3. Overexertion and cold increases the likelihood of problems—don't exhaust yourself and stay warm.
4. For every 3,000 feet of elevation gain (over three days—see the golden rules sidebar), take a rest day.
5. Different people acclimatize at different rates—the group should only ascend as fast as the slowest person acclimatizes.
6. Avoid tobacco, alcohol, and depressant drugs (including sleeping pills).
7. Keep well-hydrated (at least 3 – 4 quarts per day) and plan a high carbohydrate diet—eat proteins and fats on rest days and avoid them at night.

At altitude, the thirst mechanism my be blunted. Cold and high altitude combine to make it easy to become profoundly dehydrated without realizing it. Keep track of fluid intake—and drink more than you want to. Monitor urine output and color (copious and clear is the goal).

ALTITUDE ILLNESS

WHAT WE COME DOWN WITH WHEN WE GO UP

Altitude illness covers a wide range of conditions from very minor and annoying to deadly. The more serious conditions are further complicated by other situational factors: the severity and remoteness of the terrain, the physiological difficulty of even healthy people functioning up high (in places like the Himalayas self-rescue may be impossible and bodies are routinely left behind), the external pressures of a team urging everyone ever upwards, the internal pressures of huge amounts of time and money expended in the pursuit of a lifelong dream, etc. Unlike more clearcut emergencies (e.g., a broken femur on a rafting trip) where the obvious thing to do is, well, obvious, altitude illness is blurred by a certain vagueness in the general atmosphere (nothing is actually broken, right?), the great allure of a summit, and the blunted mental reasoning (caused by thin air) that leads people to believe that things will work out—shoot, let's just put it in low gear and keep going—my headache and nausea will probably go away tomorrow.

SNOW BLINDNESS AND HIGH-ALTITUDE SUNBURN

These two common high-altitude problems are linked by several factors: the thin air (which doesn't filter UV rays as well as sea-level air), the typically cooler air temperatures (which make us tend to forget the sun's power), and the reflective quality of snow and ice (which means sunlight often shines *upward*.) All these things combine to fry our eyes and our skin in new ways—ever had sunburned armpits before? Seemingly innocuous, these twin sun-related problems can nevertheless cause great annoyance and be debilitating enough to interrupt a trip—prevention is the key.

Prevention

- Wear sunglasses or goggles (consider wrap-around "glacier glasses" which will help protect your eyes from reflected light.
- Keep your clothes on—If it's warm, wear lightweight garments. Wear a hat with a brim and something to protect the back of your neck.
- Use the most powerful sunscreens you can find—zinc-oxide cream on your nose, ears, and lips provides the best protection.
- Remember that the sun is not just above you—it's bouncing up off the snow underfoot—and protect areas that normally don't get exposed (e.g., the back of your legs, the undersides of your forearms).
- Keep an eye on others—warn them if they appear in danger (and remember, in bright sun and when wearing sunglasses, it is very hard to see the sizzle of sunburn).

The reflective efficiencies of different terrains.

85–90% reflection of snow and ice

10–20% reflection off soil and vegetation

15–25% reflection of water

J. Paul Robinson, May 25, 2009, two days after summitting Everest. He'd removed his mask and goggles for only 30 minutes on the triumphant day. It's not good when your face is the same color as your fluorescent red parka.

Above: traditional Inuit goggles used bone or ivory with slits for eye protection. Soot was sometimes smeared on the inside to cut down glare.

Below: it's a quarter past nine thousand feet…do you know where your head is? The scenery may be spectacular, but if you have AMS, this may be the only view you get—and it may be a little fuzzy because you're head is throbbing. Eat an energy bar, drink some Gatorade, and consider descending—don't go up.

Treatment

■ For sunburn, see the specific topic in the soft tissue injuries section.

■ For snow blindness (photokeratitis), which causes stinging pain and the sensation of sand in the eyes: apply cold, wet compresses, artificial tears eye drops, and oral pain meds. Keep the patient in the dark as much as possible. Take out contact lenses. Don't rub the eyes. The cornea and conjunctiva will usually heal in 24 to 72 hours (which may feel like an eternity on a mountaineering trip).

ACUTE MOUNTAIN SICKNESS (AMS)

AMS is a pathological effect of high altitude on humans, caused by the low atmospheric pressure at higher altitude, which makes less oxygen available. It does not typically occur below 8,000' (2,500m). It is the most common and least dangerous high altitude illness (snow blindness and sunburn excepted). It can occur in anyone, regardless of experience at altitude, underlying health, or fitness. AMS presents as a set of nonspecific symptoms that resemble the flu, caused primarily by the consequences of an increase in respiratory rate and effort. As the body acclimatizes, the symptoms will clear, and once they clear, it is safe to go higher—never go up until your symptoms go down.

Signs and symptoms—a headache accompanied by:

■ Nausea with or without vomiting
■ Fatigue or weakness
■ Loss of appetite
■ Dizziness or lightheadedness
■ Insomnia (common at altitude—not indicative of AMS if it's the only symptom)

Treatment

1. Descend immediately—500m – 1,000m is usually sufficient. Ascending with symptoms increases the risk of contracting HAPE and HACE—which can be deadly.
2. Rest.
3. Hydrate.
4. Monitor urine color (it should be copious and clear).
5. If there is no improvement over 12 – 24 hours, descend further: to the last sleeping altitude where symptoms were not present, or as far as necessary for improvement.
6. Drugs (see chart next page).

HIGH-ALTITUDE PULMONARY EDEMA (HAPE)

HAPE and HACE are killers. HAPE is non-cardiogenic pulmonary edema (fluid in the lungs) that occurs in otherwise healthy people, typically over 2,500m (8,200'), although is has been known to occur as low as 1,500m (4,900'). The pathophysiology of HAPE is not well understood; the pulmonary vasculature becomes leaky and serous fluid (the liquid part of blood remaining after clotting) in the bloodstream begins to seep into the alveoli—in effect, the person is drowning. Going too high, too fast, is a trigger. HAPE often results from ignoring the symptoms of AMS.

Signs and symptoms—signs and symptoms of AMS, accompanied by:

- Extreme fatigue
- SOB at rest, with shallow, fast breathing
- Pulmonary crackles
- Persistent cough with or without sputum
- Dyspnea not relieved by rest
- Chest tightness, pressure, or congestion
- Cyanosis of the lips and fingernail beds
- Drowsiness
- No pain—if accompanied by pain, suspect injury (e.g., ribs), acute MI, or costochondritis (inflammation of the intercostal spaces), evaluate, and treat

Treatment

1. Immediate descent: typically 500 – 1,000m, unless prohibited by unsafe conditions (e.g., weather). Never remain at altitude if it is possible to descend.
2. If descent is impossible, use a pressure bag (portable hyperbaric chamber) if available : Gamov, Certec, or PAC (see sidebar).
3. Administer oxygen, if available: 4 – 6 liters per minute by nasal cannula or with PEEP (Positive End-Expiratory Pressure).
4. Hydrate, if the patient is conscious.
5. Monitor SaO2 with a pulse oximeter.
6. Administer drugs (see chart below)

HIGH-ALTITUDE CEREBRAL EDEMA (HACE)

Fluid build-up on the brain—this is the most serious altitude-related illness. It comes on quickly and the patient (unlike the HAPE patient) may be quickly incapacitated to the point where they cannot walk. It is often caused by ascending with symptoms of AMS and can occur concurrently with HAPE. If not identified and treated immediately, the patient will deteriorate rapidly, and coma and death will follow. Like HAPE, the pathophysiology is poorly understood; in this instance, the cerebral vasculature leaks serous fluid into the parenchyma of the brain.

It's amazing that the lack of a substance that we can't even see can cause us so much trouble when we don't get enough of it—don't ignore the symptoms of high altitude illness!

Signs and symptoms—signs and symptoms of AMS, accompanied by:

- Change in mentation (the ability to think clearly and solve simple problems, e.g., the speed at which basic arithmetic can be done)
- Loss of coordination—ataxia (a voluntary lack of coordinated muscle movements, which can be subtle), patient will be unable to tandem gait walk (walk in a straight line with the toes of the back foot touching the heel of the front foot with each step)
- Possible hallucinations
- Drowsiness
- Coma
- Cheyne-Stokes breathing (see the compensatory changes section)
- Signs of increasing ICP
  - Increasing respiratory rate and depth
  - Increasing systolic BP (pounding pulse)
  - Decreasing heart rate
  - Change (deterioration) in LOC

Treatment

- The same as for HAPE: immediate and rapid descent (or pressure bag), oxygen, hydration, monitor SaO2 with pulse oximeter
- The patient may not be ambulatory—a litter (or helicopter) evacuation may be necessary—and will be greatly complicated by terrain, weather, the number and condition of rescuers, etc.)
- Drugs (see chart below)

PORTABLE PRESSURE CHAMBERS

Portable hyperbaric chambers reduce the effective altitude by raising the atmospheric pressure within a closed environment. Depending on the altitude at which they are used, they can reduce the effective altitude equal to a physical descent of up to 2,000m (6,500')—which is typically more than enough to effectively treat the symptoms of HAPE or HACE. All of the available devices work on the same principle: a person is placed inside an air-impermeable bag and then the bag

PAC chamber at Everest basecamp

is pressurized (typically via a foot pump). The pressure is typically maintained by continuous pumping, which also flushes fresh air through the bag. Typically a patient would be put in the bag for a short period of time (e.g., 1 hour), then removed and reassessed. Additionally, cycles of 'descent' and reassessment are then repeated until the patient improves enough to descend on their own or can be evacuated safely. For HAPE patients, this may take 2 – 4 hours, while the HACE patient may need 4 – 6 hours of treatment. Even after successful treatment (i.e., the patient's symptoms have disappeared), descent is still necessary to eliminate the possibility of the symptoms returning—the patient should descend 500 – 1000m (1,600' – 3,200'). There are several manufacturers, and their products are available for rental as well as purchase—a potential life-saving investment for any major high-altitude expedition.

The Gamow Bag The original, developed by Dr. Igor Gamow (pronounced Gam-Off) at the University of Colorado in the 1980s.

The Treksafe Portable Altitude Chamber (PAC) Similar to the Gamow Bag, but with a different zipper system that gives the patient access through the end.

The Certec Bag Uses a double-envelope system instead of reinforcing straps.

DRUG THERAPIES FOR HIGH ALTITUDE ILLNESS

ILLNESS	Analgesics[1]	Acetazolamide (Diamox) [2]	Dexamethasone (Decadron) [3]	Nifedipine (Adalat, Procardia) [4]
AMS	acetaminophen paracetamol aspirin ibuprofen	Prophylactic: 250mg po bid Treatment: 250mg po q12 hours until symptoms improve	4mg po q6h for severe AMS symptoms, can be given IM if patient is vomiting. Wait 12 hours after last dose. Ascend only if symptom-free.	*No usage in cases of AMS*
HAPE		Prophylactic: 250mg po bid starting 24 hours before going to altitude (sea level to 333m in one day, or ascent >600m/day over 2500m)	8mg po/IM stat, followed by 4mg po q6 hours	10mg po q6h Slow release (SR) form can also be used: SR 30mg po q8 – 12 hours, not to exceed 90 – 120mg/day
HACE				*No usage in cases of HACE*

Key: mg = milligram • po = by mouth • q = every • mg/kg = milligrams per kilogram • IM = intramuscular injection • stat = immediately • SR = slow release

[1] Analgesics: used for symptomatic treatment only

[2] Acetazolamide (Diamox): a carbonic anhydrase inhibitor that raises the blood pH, making the blood more acidic, which increases the ventilation drive—the cornerstone of acclimatization

[3] Dexamethasone (Decadron): a potent synthetic glucocorticoid steroid that reduces inflammation and swelling and thus, intracranial pressure

[4] Nifedipine (Adalat, Procardia): a dihydropyridine calcium channel blocker primarily used as an antianginal and antihypertensive drug, lowers blood pressure, and thus reduces leakage into the pulmonary vasculature

Wi nøt trei a høliday in Sweden this yër?

See the løveli lakes

The wøndërful telephøne system

And mäni interesting furry animals

Including the majestik møøse

A møøse ønce bit my sister...

Nø realli! She was karving her initials øn the møøse with the sharpened end øf an interspace tøøthbrush given tø her by Svenge—her brøther-in-law— an Øslø dentist and star øf many Nørwegian møvies

Mynd yøu, møøse bites kan be pretti nasti...

From the introductory credits to the movie *Monty Python and the Holy Grail*—edited for both brevity and good taste

Actual size...
OK, not really

Top 10 bad things
to find in your sleeping bag

1. Rattlesnake
2. Set rat trap
3. Cold JELL-O
4. Big, black scorpion
5. Poison ivy leaves
6. Live wolverine
7. Socks from last trip
8. Nest of fire ants
9. Damp sand
10. Dead wolverine

Bites, Stings, and Rashes

OF ALL THE LITTLE EMERGENCIES that may befall you, things that chomp on you, stab you, inject you, and systemically irritate you may be the most common, but

Hey! you're outside—so what do you expect?

Bites & stings

Three primary concerns

- Tissue damage
- Infection by microorganisms (e.g., viruses, bacteria)
- Envenomation

Dogs: 80%
Cats: 12%
Humans: 3%
Others* 5%

*mostly farm animals

Most bites are a result of contact with domestic animals.

Mammals

While bears, wolves, coyotes, mountain lions, and other large carnivores get the most press, the data shows something less dramatic—the everyday critters in our lives (including ourselves) do the most chomping—see graphic at right. Bites by wild animals are uncommon.

Prevention

1. Don't touch or feed wild animals.
2. Keep a clean kitchen: hang food, dispose of scraps properly.
3. Never tease or make aggressive movements toward a wild animal.
4. Back away, but don't turn your back on an animal making aggressive or predatory motions.

Rabies—description

Rabies is a viral disease that causes acute encephalitis (inflammation of the brain and spinal cord) in warm-blooded animals.

- Any mammal is susceptible.
- Raccoons are the most common carriers among wild animals (36%).
- Bats (23%) are the most likely vector (most likely to infect people).
- Skunks (24%) and canids (dogs) are also carriers/vectors.

In developing countries, canid infection is the most common rabies vector (there are many feral dogs, and inoculations are almost unheard of).

Annual rabies death worldwide: 55,000
Treatment in the US each year: 40,000 people receive rabies
prevention treatment due to potential exposure (source: CDC)

Rabies—signs and symptoms

- Depression
- Anger
- Combativeness
- Hydrophobia (fear of water)
- Intense thirst
- Seizures
- Signs and symptoms can appear in 10 – 14 days, but can be delayed for years.
- Once signs and symptoms appear, the patient generally dies in <3 weeks.

Rabies—treatment

1. Bites may cause punctures, lacerations, and avulsions.
2. Stop the bleeding (wear BSI—saliva and blood are dangerous).
3. Scrub the wound vigorously (move saliva out and away from the wound).
4. Irrigate generously with dilute (1%) iodine solution.
5. Do not close an animal bite in the wild: the risk of infection is high.
6. Evacuate to hospital for shots.
7. If abroad, contact the US embassy.

Rabies—other action to take

1. Report the bite to local authorities.
2. Bring in the animal, dead or alive, to help aid in diagnosis.
3. Handle the animal properly and safely—do not allow anyone else to be bitten or come in contact with saliva or blood.

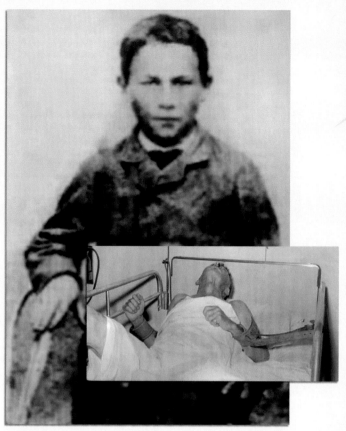

In 1885, Joseph Meister, 9 years old, (main image) became the first person inoculated against rabies. Bitten by a rabid dog, he was treated by Louis Pasteur (who was not a medical doctor and could have been prosecuted for practicing medicine without a license) using a vaccine grown in rabbits. The treatment was successful. A rabies patient in 1955 (inset) suffering through the agonies of active rabies (note the restraints).

Venomous Reptiles

While many of the topics in the bites, stings, rashes, and allergies section are merely annoying, and rarely life-threatening, reptile bites—snake bites in particular—are both common and potentially deadly. Worldwide, poisonous snake bites account for an estimated 421,000 envenomations and 20,000 deaths annually. Some, like Australia's banded krait (aka the "Two-Step Snake") and Africa's black mamba are so dangerous that untreated victims always die. (Just one more good reason to pack up and move to Newfoundland— no native snakes.)

Pygmy rattlesnake and classic snake country in the US desert southwest.

Do you see the copperhead in the leaves? Because snakes are often well camouflaged, you may feel the sting of the strike before you see the animal.

Data—kinds, types of venom, and distribution

- Venomous snakes in the US are of two types: pit vipers (rattlesnake, copperhead, cottonmouth), and coral snakes.
- Pit vipers inject a hemotoxin that is designed to both poison (kill) and digest prey by destroying red blood cells, disrupting blood clotting, and causing organ degeneration and generalized tissue damage. They can be locally common, are frequently found in the open (like along the trail on the previous page), and can be aggressive.
- In North America, pit viper distribution is widespread—they are found in all the contiguous states (although extremely rare in places like Maine). Rattlesnakes are found in virtually all states; copperheads are found in the eastern states to Texas; and cottonmouths are restricted to wetlands in the Southeast.
- Coral snakes inject a powerful neurotoxin that paralyzes the breathing muscles causing death by asphyxiation. They are found in the southern states from North Carolina west to Arizona. They are secretive, rarely seen, and non-aggressive—so bites (and deaths) are rare.
- There are two venomous lizards in North America: the Gila monster (neurotoxin) and the Beaded Lizard (hemotoxin). These are shy, reclusive animals that are rarely encountered. And, unlike the dart-like strike of venomous snakes, these lizards must gnaw on you for a while—bites are rare and envenomation even rarer. Both are found only in the deserts of the southwestern US and Mexico.
- People are typically bitten when they handle reptiles—approximately 70% of reptile bites occur on the hand.
- In habitats where venomous reptiles are known to live, wear protective clothing (boots, long pants), and be cautious where you put your hands and feet.

Snake and lizard bite—treatment

1. Keep the patient calm—a high heart rate will speed the spread of the toxin.
2. Treat the wound: clean and disinfect it.
3. Apply lymphatic compression wrap with 6" elastic bandage—wrap distal to proximal, then proximal to distal, and leave the wrap in place. This is controversial regarding pit vipers, possibly increasing the risk of localized tissue damage by concentrating the hemotoxin.
4. Monitor the pulses, especially distal to the elastic wrap.
5. Monitor for anaphylaxis.
6. Do not apply cold packs; use a tourniquet, or "cut and suck."
7. Immobilize the extremity.
8. Evacuate via carry-out or walk out, as appropriate.
9. Protect yourself: try to identify the reptile, but don't risk a bite. If possible, inform the hospital of the species so they can provide the appropriate antivenom—medication for exotic species may have to be flown in.

A coral snake is identified by the rhyme "red touching yellow kills a fellow." Similar non-venomous species are identified by "red touching black, venom lack."

The cottonmouth's name is obviously well-earned.

The chunky beaded lizard (shown) and the gila monster look very similar.

Antivenom consists of venom-neutralizing antibodies derived from a host animal, typically a horse or sheep, that has been hyperimmunized to one or more venoms. As the antivenom circulates in the patient's bloodstream, it binds to the toxin, preventing further damage. Antivenom is typically administered via IV.

The bite of a notoriously dangerous Central American pit viper, the fer-de-Lance caused this horrible tissue necrosis after just two days; the limb was subsequently amputated.

- <1,000
- 1,000 – 10,000
- 10,000 – 100,000
- > 100,000
- Not estimated
- No extant snakes

Snake envenomations per year by country. Note: distribution within each country is not even (e.g., there are no poisonous snakes in northern Canada).

A black widow spider, its abdomen sporting the classic red hourglass, watches over it's silken ball of incubating young. It is likely that insects have caused more human misery, suffering, and disease in the world than any other class of animal. They thrive in virtually every environmental niche, reproduce with rapid abandon, develop resistance to some of the very chemicals we cunningly devise to kill them, and just basically cannot be stopped. Fortunately, most are just cute (?) and harmless, and many are even beneficial. We will be concentrating our efforts on the incorrigible, the malicious, and the recalcitrant of their ilk.

INSECTS

Mammals may tear out chunks of flesh, send raging bacteria through your system, and even curse you with rabies; and venomous reptiles may digest your flesh or paralyze your breathing; but even the tiny critters behind door number three—the various members of the lineage that runs **_Animalia > Arthropoda > Hexapoda > insecta_** have the capacity to irritate, maim, debilitate, and kill. They may be small in stature, but they more than make up for it by their sheer numbers and utter nastiness.

There are over 900,000 described insect species, comprising approximately 80% of all known animal species. And at any given time (prepare yourself to be creeped out) there are some 10 quintillion (10,000,000,000,000,000,000)[1] individual insects alive. Fortunately, they are diminutive, and, although on the colonial level they can be very organized, like elementary school children, they haven't yet figured out that if they all band together they can take over the world.

Hymenoptera (bees, hornets, wasps, fire ants)—
signs and symptoms

- Pain
- Local swelling
- Redness
- Itching

Hymenoptera—treatment

1. Remove the stinger/poison sack by scraping: do not use tweezers—if there is residual poison in the sack you will just force it into the wound.
2. Assess and monitor for anaphylaxis—if a serious anaphylactic reaction develops, take appropriate steps (see Critical Care).
3. Use topical medication for comfort.
4. Give oral antihistamine for relief of swelling and itching: diphenhydramine (Benadryl) 50mg q4 x 24 hours.

The most serious complication from a hymenoptera sting is anaphylaxis, which can cause a life-threatening allergic reaction.

---

1   That's over 1 billion creepies per person—sorry, you really didn't want to know that, did you?

Arachnids (scorpions, spiders, ticks)

SCORPIONS are small, "lobster-like" creatures with an upturned stinger in their tail. Scorpions are common in the southern tier of US states and throughout the hot parts of the world. The Arizona bark scorpion, found throughout the Sonoran Desert in Arizona, California, and northern Mexico, is the only deadly scorpion found in the US. Thousands of people are stung each year in the US, but there have only been two reported human deaths since 1968. Children and those with compromised immune systems are at greatest risk.

Scorpion—signs and symptoms

- For most species, the signs and symptoms are typically minor—pain and warmth at the sting site.
- If stung by a bark spider, the symptoms will be more dramatic. In children: pain that can be intense, numbness and tingling at the sting site, little or no swelling, muscle twitching or thrashing, unusual head, neck, and eye movements, drooling, diaphoresis, restlessness or excitability and sometimes inconsolable crying. Adults are more likely to experience increased respiratory and heart rates, high blood pressure, muscle twitches, and weakness.

Scorpion—treatment

1. Immobilize the site.
2. Apply a cold pack.
3. Evacuate and monitor for anaphylaxis.

SPIDERS are eight-legged arachnids. They are extremely common—3,000 species are found in the US alone, with approximately 60 of those considered to cause medically significant bites. Only two species in the US are truly dangerous: the black widow and the brown recluse.

Black widow—Description, signs and symptoms

Black Widow spiders (previous page, upper left) are medium-sized (.5" to 1.5"), black, shiny, with long legs and a reddish hourglass mark on the underside of the abdomen. Most victims never feel the bite. Deaths are rare. Found throughout the contiguous US, more common in the south.

- Contraction of the smooth muscles of the abdomen and vasculature
- Painful abdominal cramping
- A rigid abdomen
- Elevated BP with vasoconstriction

Brown recluse—Description, signs and symptoms

A brown, fuzzy spider typically ranging from .25" to .75" with long front legs, a large mandible, and a distinct violin shape on the back of the thorax (shared by other species, so not exclusively diagnostic). They have a painful bite that injects a digestive enzyme toxin. They are found in the southern Midwest to the Gulf of Mexico.

- A coin-sized welt which becomes a necrotic growing ulcer.

Black widow/brown recluse—treatment

1. Clean the wound (and mark the margin, if a brown recluse)
2. Apply cold if the bite just occurred.
3. Monitor vital signs and watch for signs of anaphylaxis.
4. Evacuate.

The Arizona bark scorpion stings an estimated 10,000 people in Mexico each year, with 800 deaths (annual mortality due to scorpion envenomation in Mexico is ten times higher than that due to snakebite). Worldwide, scorpions kill approximately 5,000 people annually.

The venom of the brown recluse can cause extensive tissue damage: necrosis two days post-bite.

TICKS are small arachnids categorized as ectoparasites (external parasites). Functionally, they are tiny septic-tank vectors for several diseases, including Lyme Disease in humans, a potentially disabling disease first described in the 1970s. They vary in size from that of a speck of pepper up to a frozen pea, with large abdomens, small heads, and short legs. Colors range from tan to brown to almost black. They attach to their host by biting, then burying their heads in the skin to take a blood meal (which may take a day or more to accomplish).

The wood tick, also known as the American dog Tick, (above) is extremely common in the eastern two-thirds of the US. It bites animals and humans with equal abandon and is a vector for Rocky Mountain Spotted Fever. The deer tick, (upper right) also known as the black-legged tick, is a notorious carrier of Lyme disease. The two large representations are shown at their proportional sizes.

Wood tick (L) and deer Tick (R) at actual size.

Ticks—treatment

1. Remove by pulling off as close to the skin as possible, preferably with fine-tipped tweezers. Pull upward with steady, even pressure—don't twist or jerk the tick; this can cause mouth-parts to break off and remain in the skin. If this happens, remove the mouth-parts with tweezers.

2. Clean the area well.

Lyme Disease—the most widespread tick-borne disease

Named after the small town in Connecticut, Old Lyme, where a number of cases were described in 1975, it is found in temperate climates worldwide, is the most common tick-borne disease in the Northern Hemisphere, and is one of the fastest-growing infectious diseases in the US. The bacteria is carried by several species of tiny ticks including the deer tick, and causes fever, headache, depression, and a characteristic red, bull's-eye rash (right). The disease can lay dormant and symptoms may take months to appear. In its early stages, Lyme Disease can be readily treated with antibiotics. Later, after the bacteria has been widely disseminated throughout the body, treatment is more difficult and complications more serious (e.g., arthritis-like symptoms).

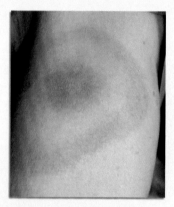

After a blood meal, the engorged wood tick reaches nearly sci-fi proportions (right, yuck).

TICKBORNE DISEASE	CAUSE PARASITE	VECTOR TICK	RESERVOIR IN NATURE	TREATMENT
Lyme Disease	*Borrelia burgdorferi*	Ixodes (hard tick)—deer or black-legged tick, *I. scapularis* (east coast), *I. pacificus* (west coast)	White-footed mouse, meadow voles, birds, domestic animals (pets)	doxycycline, amoxicillin, ceftriaxone
Human Granulocytic Anaplasmosis (HGA)	*Anaplasmo phagocytophilum*	Ixodes (hard tick)—deer or black-legged tick, *I. scapularis* (east coast), *I. pacificus* (west coast), Dog tick—*Dermacentor variabilis*	White-footed mouse, white-tailed deer, cattle	doxycycline
Human Monocytic Ehrlichiosis (HME)	*Ehrlichia chaffeensis*	Lone star tick—*Amblyomma americanum*, Dog tick—*Dermacentor variabilis* Ixodes, Hard tick—deer or blacklegged tick, *I. pacificus* (west coast)	White-tailed deer	doxycycline
Human Ewingii Ehrlichiosis (HEE)	*Ehrlichiosis ewingii*	Lone star tick—*Amblyomma americanum*	White-tailed deer	doxycycline
Babesiosis	*Babesia microti*	Ixodes (hard tick)—deer or blacklegged tick, *I. scapularis* (east coast)	White-footed mouse	clindamycin, azithromycin, atovaquone, quinine sulfate
Cat Scratch Disease	*Bartonella hensaelae*	Ticks, fleas, via a cat scratch	Cat	doxycycline, azithromycin, cipro
Rocky Mountain Spotted Fever (RMSF)	*Richettsia richettsii*	Dog tick—*Dermacentor variabilis*, Rocky Mt. wood tick—*D. andersoni*, Brown dog tick—*Rhipicephalus sanguineus*, Lone Star tick—*Amblyomma americanun*	*Dermacentor* ticks	doxycycline (regardless of age)
Colorado Tick Fever	*RNA coltivirus*	Wood tick—*Dermacentor andersoni*	Small mammals	supportive care
Southern Tick-Associated Rash Illness (STARI)	*Borrelia lonestari*	Lone star tick—*Amblyomma americanum*	White-tailed deer	doxycycline
Tickborne Relapsing Fever (TBRF)	*Borrelia* species	Lice—*edic. Humanus*, soft ticks—*ornthodoros*	Rodents	doxycycline, erythromycin
Tularemia	*Francisella tularensis*	Dog tick—*D. variablilis*, Wood tick—*D. andersoni*, Lone Star Tick—*A. americanum* , Deer flies—*Chrysops discalis*	Lagomorphs: rabbits, hares, and pikas; can be waterborne	streptomycin, doxycycline
Tickborne Encephalitis, (Deer Tick Virus, Powassan Encephalitis)	*Flavivirus*	Ixodes (hard tick)—deer or blacklegged tick, *I. scapularis* (east coast), *I. pacificus* (west coast)	Rodents	supportive care
Q Fever	*Coxiella burnetti*	inhalation of droplets, various ticks	Cattle, sheep, goats	doxycycline, ciprofloxacin
Tick Paralysis	Neurotoxin in tick saliva	Various Ticks: *Ixodes, Dermacentor, Amblyomma*	The tick itself	remove tick

The oceans of the world are full of creatures that bite and sting, like the *Portuguese Man o' War* (right), a jellyfish species of temperate and tropical waters that delivers an excruciating sting.

That *other thing* (above), is, well, we're really not sure what that is, but it sure looks like it bites.

What I didn't do on my summer vacation — I didn't touch this !!!

Marine
Bites & Stings

THINGS THAT BITE

The oceans fairly team with fish and marine mammals that may bite humans—in fact, if cornered, caught, or handled, just about any of notorious biters (sharks, barracuda, moray eels, seals, sea lions, etc.) may chomp on you, may even kill you. The best way to **treat** such encounters is to **avoid** them.

- Avoid (or be cautious) when swimming/diving in areas of known animal concentrations: power plant and waste plant outlets, organic waste areas, river mouths, etc.
- Be careful swimming/diving at night or in water of low visibility.
- Do not disturb, chase, or act threateningly to a marine creature.
- Do not reach out to touch marine animals or reach into dark places.
- Avoid wearing bright, sparkly items (e.g., jewelry).

Pat the seal? Um, no... Look at those teeth!

Treatment for bites

These wounds may be minor or severe depending on the type and size of the creature, and they will be a combination of punctures, lacerations, and occasional amputations.

1. Stop the bleeding (it can lead to frenzy activity in many species).
2. Get the patient out of the water.
3. Clean the wound aggressively—the wound is full of infectious material.
4. Do not suture or tightly close the wound because of the risk of deep infection.
5. Get the patient dry and warm.
6. In cases of shark bite, it may be better to keep the patient's wetsuit on.
7. Treat for shock as appropriate.
8. Evacuate as necessary.

THINGS THAT STAB

SEA URCHINS—These are slow-moving, lower-order sea creatures that are covered with spines which often end up in a person's body, particularly in the hands and feet. The spines are very brittle and often break off in the wound.

STINGRAYS—These are flat, diamond-shaped fish with a long tail housing a long, barbed spine. Stingrays are relatives of sharks and are relatively timid. Most stings occur when a wader steps on the ray in shallow, generally calm water. Wounds are usually in the foot, ankle, or calf; they are very dirty, and they can be very deep.

LIONFISH/SCORPION FISH—these are medium-sized, brightly colored fish with red, white, creamy, or black bands and ornate, showy pectoral fins and venomous, spiky fin rays, found in tropical waters from the Indian Ocean, through the Indonesian seas, and into the western and central Pacific Ocean; also found in the Caribbean Sea.

Treatment for stab wounds

1. Remove sea urchin spines carefully by pulling straight out—do not twist, wiggle, or bend (dark markings in the wound may be dye left over by he removed spine). Remove the stinger and/or sheath of a stingray and the stingers of a lionfish.
2. Immerse the wounds in hot (not scalding) water for 30+ minutes to relieve pain.
3. Clean the wound aggressively (scrub it) and leave it open (to help minimize the risk of infection).
4. Evacuate (the likelihood of an impaled object and the risk of infection is high).
5. If there is a long delay getting the patient to definitive care, monitor for signs of infection and give antibiotics as needed.

CONE SNAILS—this is a large genus of small to large, venomous, predatory sea snails with cone-shaped shells. They deliver their sting via a harpoon-like tooth called a radula. At least 15 human deaths have been attributed to envenomation, typically as a result of handling the shells of the living animals—they are beautiful and don't appear obviously dangerous.

Symptoms/treatment

- Sharp burning or stinging sensation, swelling, and numbness at the wound site—the patient may vomit.
- Generalized muscle paralysis may lead to respiratory failure and cardiac arrest—CPR and/or defibrillation may be necessary.
- Symptoms can start immediately or can be delayed in onset for days.
- There is no antivenom, and treatment involves providing life support until the venom is metabolized.

Top to bottom: Great white shark, urchin, stingray, lionfish, cone snail shells

this is really high on my list of "things not to be bitten by"

okay, there are places to step, and places not to step...

yeah, you're really cool, but keep your distance, please.

Um, think... "underwater porcupine"

Touch these in the gift shop, not underwater

THINGS THAT STING

These animals include **FIRE CORALS, ANEMONES,** and **JELLY FISH,** and they envenomate via a nematocyst: a capsule containing a barbed, threadlike tube that delivers a paralyzing sting when propelled into attackers and prey, and which continues to sting after the initial contact. Fire corals and jellyfish are distributed throughout tropical seas: Pacific and Indian oceans, the Red Sea, and the Caribbean; anemones are found in all the world's oceans and seas.

Symptoms

Symptoms vary by species and will depend on the specific toxin in the venom and the severity of the envenomation.

- Initial burning or stinging pain and itching in the affected area.
- In the following 5 – 30 minutes, welts develop marked by redness, warmth, and itching.
- Pain usually resolves over 60 – 90 minutes.
- If untreated, the welts will flatten over 14 – 24 hours and totally resolve over 3 – 7 days.
- Severe envenomation may result in skin necrosis, ulceration, and secondary infection.

Teatment for stings

1. Remove any tentacles (wear rubber gloves or use a towel to prevent secondary exposure). Warning: even removed tentacles and tentacles from dead jellyfish are dangerous—do not handle with bare hands.
2. Rinse liberally with sea water (**do not treat with fresh water**—this causes the nematocysts to fire).
3. Flood the area with vinegar—this **may** deactivate the nematocysts (for some species, such as the Portuguese man o' war, vinegar has been shown to renew nematocyst firing).
4. Abrade the neutralized nematocysts with sand or other mild abrasive and/or "shave" the area with a firm plastic edge (or better yet, a razor).
5. Do not use human urine, ethanol-based products, or pressure bandages—there is either no research backing up their use or research indicates they aren't effective.
6. Prolonged wound care may be needed for treatment of secondary infection.

THE DEADLIEST DATA

While all the marine animals discussed are dangerous, deaths are fortunately still very rare. While the stats are sketchy, sharks and jellyfish are likely the most deadly.

Sharks: average 100 attacks and fifteen fatalities per year; 500 +/- deaths since 1580.

Jellyfish: tens of thousands stung each year, deaths likely in the low hundreds; the most stings and deaths are reported in the south Pacific (Philippines and Australia).

Stingray case study: Although many people are stung, there are very few annual deaths. The most famous case was that of Steve Irwin, "The Crocodile Hunter", who died instantly from trauma when his chest was pierced by a stingray tail spine during a day off while filming a documentary called "Ocean's Deadliest" in September of 2006.

When triggered, the nematocyst springs out, a tiny weapon delivering repeated, stinging pain.

Nematocyst: the painful firing mechanism of many sea creatures

Don't touch, or the nematocysts will burn you

Rhymes with "an enemy"

Top to bottom: nematocyst detail, fire coral, anemone, Portuguese Man O' War, box jellyfish

Considered the most venomous sea creature

Beautiful, but really nasty!

Rashes (poisonous plants)

The common signs of *contact dermatitis* include an inflamed, rash, blisters, and often burning, incessant itchiness——and it often takes many days to go away.

Every nasty thing in this section has one common denominator—the first thing that occurs is an invasion of our epidermis, a breach of our skin. And no, plants don't have teeth or stingers and they can't chase us down and gnaw on us or prick us, but in their own vile way plants have still figured out a way to reach out and grab us. The fancy name for all this irritation is **contact dermatitis**—and we've all been contacted at some time or other.

Pathology what causes the rash?

- The sap, or juice, of the poison ivy, oak, and sumac plants causes the rash.
- Their sap contains an organic oil—urushiol, which causes the allergic reaction and resulting skin rash.
- The rash is an immune response, an allergic reaction, to the urushiol oil caused by the release of histamines from the body's mast cells.

Signs and symptoms

- Initially, the rash is red, itchy, flat, and typically presents in stripes where the plant dragged across the skin, depositing the oil as it went.
- Over time, small blisters (vesicles) may also form.
- It is a common myth that the fluid contained in the blisters can cause the rash to spread—it cannot; the urishiol oil that caused the initial allergic reaction is gone.

Treatment

Antihistamines

    Diphenhydramine: Benedryl, short-acting
    Meclizine: many trade names, short-acting
    Promethazine: many trade names, short-acting
    Chlorpheniramine: many trade names, short-acting
    Cetirzine: Zyrtec, long-acting
    Loratadine: Claritin, long-acting

Over-the-counter (OTC) steroid cream (hydrocortisone): Cortaid, Hydrocort.

- Apply sparingly to the rash three times a day.
- Not recommended for use on the face because they can cause thinning and scarring of the skin.
- With any medication, OTC or prescription, make sure you are familiar with the possible side effects

With any allergic reaction, if you begin to experience shortness of breath or wheezing, or if the rash begins to spread systemically, body-wide, seek immediate medical attention—you may need prescription-strength antihistamines or steroids

The big three

POISON IVY (*Toxicodendron rybergii*)

- **Plants** grow erect, typically 2 – 5 feet tall, but can also climb as vines (*T. radicans*) with aerial rootlets (which cling to tree bark).
- **Leaves**: trifoliate with 3 leaflets, long-stalked—the leaves exhibit a wide range of shapes and textures; they can be stiff, leathery, or thin, hairy or hairless, shiny or dull, toothed or not, and reddish when young, 4 – 14".
- **Flowers**: small, yellowish, May – July.
- **Fruits**: small, smooth, white, round, and clustered, August – November.
- **Habitat**: young woodlands, roadside, field/forest edges, thickets, path edges, sand dunes, walls.
- **Range**: northern Quebec to Florida, Nova Scotia to Texas, Arizona.

POISON OAK

- There are two varieties in North America: Atlantic (*T. pubescens*) and Pacific (*T. diversilobum*). Both varieties appear very similar—differences will be noted.
- **Plants** grow as low shrubs (when growing in direct sun) or climbing vines (when growing in shade).
- **Leaves**: trifoliate with typically 3 leaflets (sometimes 5); the Atlantic variety's leaves are shiny. Leaf shape resembles that of an oak tree, with toothed or lobbed edges. The Atlantic variety is extremely hairy and is often confused with Virginia creeper (although that plant almost always has 5 leaflets).
- **Flowers**: late spring, small, greenish-white.
- **Fruits** (Pacific): summer and fall, small clusters of ivory-white fruits with a papery exocarp (skin); Atlantic: hairy white fruit that looks like berries.
- **Habitat**: they are widespread and adapted to many habitats—typically below 5,000 feet.
- **Range** (Pacific): west coast of the US and Canada—one of California's most common woody plants; the Atlantic variety is found in all the US coastal states from New Jersey south to Florida and west to Texas, plus Arkansas, Illinois, Kansas, Missouri, Oklahoma, Tennessee, and West Virginia.

POISON SUMAC (*Toxicodendron vernix*)

- **Plants** grow as a coarse, woody, rangy shrub typically 5 – 6 feet tall, but occasionally up to 25 feet. It does not grow as a vine.
- **Leaves**: has compound leaves with 7 –13 smooth-edged leaflets.
- **Flowers**: small, yellowish-green, in loose clusters up to 12" long.
- **Fruits**: small, glossy, pale yellow, or cream-colored berries. Although the leaves can be initially be confused with three other sumacs that share the range (smooth sumac, staghorn sumac, and dwarf sumac), these three nonpoisonous species all have red berries that terminate in a distinctive terminal seed head, rather than hanging clusters.
- **Habitat**: prefers boggy areas.
- **Range**: Quebec to Florida and west to Texas; most common in the Southeastern states.

Poison ivy

Poison oak

Poison sumac

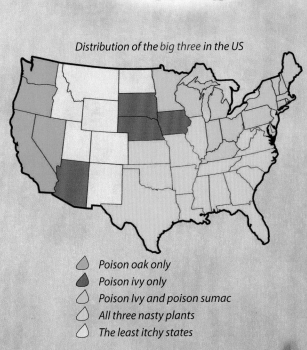

Distribution of the big three in the US

- Poison oak only
- Poison ivy only
- Poison Ivy and poison sumac
- All three nasty plants
- The least itchy states

SECTION 5

When the wilderness comes to town

The problems with "You are here" and the art of the bivouac

"Yes, you can drink the water (maybe)"

The deviousness of nasty tropical things (mostly) unseen

When the blessed event doesn't quite make the hospital

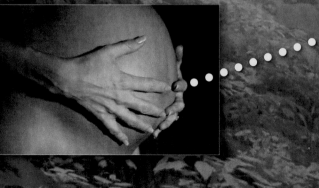

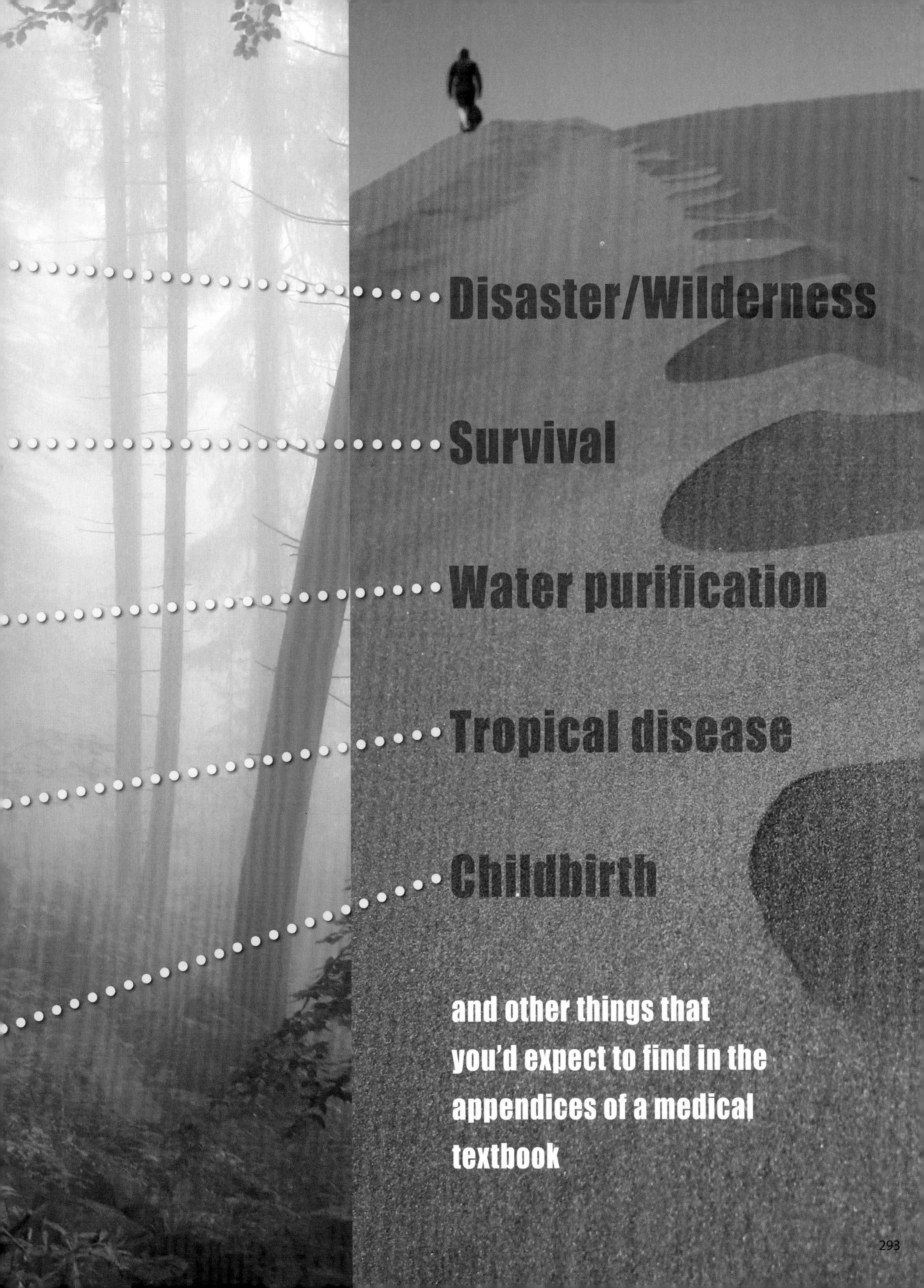

Disaster/Wilderness

Survival

Water purification

Tropical disease

Childbirth

and other things that
you'd expect to find in the
appendices of a medical
textbook

WILDERNESS

(1): a tract or region uncultivated and uninhabited by human beings (2): an area essentially undisturbed by human activity together with its naturally developed community (3): an empty or pathless area or region

---

When people think of wilderness medicine, the mental pictures that usually flash in their heads are the stereotypical scenes—a person in a litter being passed down a talus slope in the Sierras, pulling leg traction way out on the Appalachian Trail, creating a hypo-wrap in Nepal.

They think of a band of would-be rescuers cobbled together from nearby climbers, hikers, skiers, or boaters, each person tossing their medical knowledge and skills into the pot and pulling off a heroic effort for a fallen or stricken friend. It's cold, windy, and dark. It will be raining soon. Are there enough energy bars, hot Jell-O, and foam pads? Quick, someone go find a straight stick for a splint.

But what if there's asphalt instead of pine needles and the sound of blaring car horns instead of wind in the trees? What if the rescuers are wearing turnout gear or uniforms and get paychecks every other Thursday? An alternate definition of wilderness describes it as an area that "generally appears to have been affected primarily by the forces of nature, with the imprint of man's work substantially unnoticeable." Unnoticeable, or perhaps unrecognizable because

We contend that wilderness is where you find it, that the 60-minute Golden Hour is a very short time indeed, that one man's downtown can become another man's backcountry faster than you can order a tall mocha latte from Starbucks.

Blue sky day on Mt. Washington at 5,031', Tuckerman Ravine headwall in background, February 23, 2003

Remote pond, Maine, October 2009, no moose, even though we waited all morning…

Circumstances can thrust wilderness upon us quickly (sometimes in just minutes).

- Earthquakes
- Tornadoes
- Tsunamis
- Blizzards
- Floods
- Terrorist attacks

To truly understand wilderness, we need to shift our thinking. We need to tuck away those picturesque images of glaciers, deserts, and towering forests, and add images of skylines, levees, and downed power lines coated in ice. We need to understand that the comfortable, safe, well-lighted, and ordered world that we take for granted can be taken away from us in mere moments—and that help may suddenly be so far off that we are thrust into a wilderness situation that does not fit the traditional model.

Most people will agree that mountain guides, river runners, ski patrollers, hikers, and other backcountry users benefit from wilderness medicine training. When terrain, distance, weather, and other factors make help a long way off, lack of training can turn a minor injury or illness into a life-threatening situation. And a little training can go a long way. The femur must be splinted, the ankle wrapped, the bleeding stopped and bandaged. You must build a shelter, make potable water, and perhaps build a fire. You may have to administer antibiotics, create a litter with a climbing rope and tree branches, or hypo-wrap your friend. You must keep track of vital signs, make a rescue plan, and send someone for help. You've got to do it all because you're all you've got.

But what if you're at work, at home, or in your car? You spend your life within ten miles of a hospital. Professional EMS people live down the street. Well, if the world stays put and ordered, if the weather cooperates and the lights stay on, and if the Big Bad Thing doesn't happen, then you'll never find yourself in a spontaneous wilderness. But if the Big Bad Thing does happen, you may suddenly find yourself just blocks from the hospital in a wilderness of rubble.

It's easy to trust in fire trucks, ambulances, rescue squads, radios, cell phones and hospitals, electricity, running water, food, lights to see by at night, shelter from the rain—we can hardly imagine life without them. We have emergency plans, Incident Command Systems (ICS), Mass Casualty Incident (MCI) strategies, blood banks, weather satellites, early warning systems, the National Guard, and evacuation routes. When bad things happen, we simply run over, break the glass, pull the lever, and help comes with lights flashing and sirens blaring. Hurt people will be in the hospital within the hour; food, water, and blankets will be distributed immediately; the fire will be put out; and power will surge right back on to keep the steaks frozen and the DVD player spinning. Our world is civilized and ordered, right? Maybe not.

Port-au-Prince, Haiti, 2010, earthquake disaster, SOLO medical mission trip: devastation and suffering everywhere we looked.

WHEN THE WILDERNESS COMES TO TOWN

```
DISASTER: 2: a sudden
calamitous event, great
misfortune, or failure; a
state of extreme (usually
irremediable) ruin;
loss of human life, or
deterioration of health
and health services on a
scale sufficient to warrant
an extraordinary response
from outside the affected
community
```

Okay, bad things happen—what can be done? Emergency protocols, command structures, and MCI plans require one thing to work: the systems must not be overwhelmed. Can we be completely prepared for dozens of injuries? A hundred? Perhaps a few more? Yes.

Thousands? Probably not—certainly not within the Golden Hour. Part of the reason our response is limited is inherent in the nature of a disaster: they're just so big. When terrorists struck the World Trade Center, disaster arrived on the wings of airplanes at 500 mph.

Earthquake damage, Pakistan, 18 July, 2007

Flood waters entering Chennai, India, 2005

In moments, one of the most densely populated places in our country became a wilderness. EMS responded quickly, and en masse, and was nearly wiped out. Hospitals stood by—surgeons held their disinfected hands in front of them, waiting for the latex gloves and the trauma patients. Blood donors queued up in lines that were blocks long. Thousands of injuries were expected, but few patients came. There were no long, lingering, struggles for survival—the destruction was essentially complete. Even when there is advance notice and time to prepare—even when we know the bad thing is coming, where it will hit, and what it will do—disasters are often just too much to handle (remember Katrina). Red tape, poor communications, lack of medical supplies, lack of fundamental services (electricity, water, food, telecommunications), destruction of infrastructure (roads, bridges), delays in getting outside rescue teams on-site, even power struggles and egos, all have their negative influences—but the reality is that when a hurricane with 100 mph winds is aimed at a major metro area, or when a wave six meters high and hundreds of kilometers long is racing toward resort communities, or when 10,000 people all jam together and start coughing up the same microscopic bacteria, or when the mantle of the earth simply shrugs, even our best efforts can fall short.

Disasters overwhelm—so, how do you prepare for them? If a disaster is imminent (Katrina 2 will surely strike someday), you live or work in an area that is susceptible to earthquakes (southern California), or you plan to respond to a disaster somewhere else (another tsunami in Indonesia), you must prepare.

DISASTER PREPAREDNESS:

Prepare yourself—before you can help take care of others, you must be able to take care of yourself. Physically. Mentally. Educationally. Emotionally. A bivy kit contains everything you would need to survive three days—carry one.

- **WATER:** You will need at least two liters per day to survive, four liters to thrive. You will need to be able to make potable water from local sources by boiling, treating chemically, filtering, or a combination of methods.
- **FOOD:** Bring high-carb, high-glucose, high-calorie foods that are easy to digest and require little or no preparation—and bring something (e.g., Jell-O) that can be mixed with warm water. Don't rely on local food.
- **CLOTHING:** Be prepared for the environment and weather conditions. Use synthetics whenever possible and avoid cotton in cold and wet climates. Bring spares (e.g., socks, mittens). Bring a hat and rain gear.
- **SHELTER:** Be prepared to improvise. Bring a 10x10 plastic sheet, parachute cord, garbage bags, a space blanket, and a sleeping bag (if applicable). Don't count on the local Hilton to fling its doors open for you.
- **FIRE:** You should be prepared to build a fire if you have to. Bring waterproof matches, lighters, a pocket knife, and tinder (fine steel wool works great). Also, have a metal cup that you can use to heat water in.
- **NAVIGATION:** A disaster often obliterates normal navigation routes and you may need to find alternatives. Bring good, local terrain maps, a compass, and a hand-held GPS unit (and know how to use this stuff).
- **LIGHTING:** Disaster situations often wreak havoc with local utilities, and you will be working in dark places. Bring a flashlight (hand-cranked models charge themselves), a headlamp (LED headlamps don't use much juice, but neither do they throw much light), and spare batteries (lithium lasts much longer). Don't count on the ability to recharge batteries.
- **COMMUNICATIONS:** Bring a cell phone (a satellite phone is best, if expensive; can be rented). Use radios to talk to other rescuers. Bring a whistle, bright survey tape, a mirror, pad and pencil. Consider a weather radio.
- **FIRST AID:** Carry a small, personal trauma kit, and know how to use everything in it. Carry extras of items that you may not be able to replace easily (e.g., ibuprofen). Check your kit before you go—be sure it's full. If part of a rescue team, you should also have an expedition medical kit.
- **REPELLENTS:** If heading to a tropical environment, be prepared to ward off bugs, especially mosquitoes. Bring insect repellent, mosquito netting, and consider permethrin for treating your clothing.
- **OTHER STUFF:** Don't forget the little things that can make life easier.
  - A **multi-tool** of some kind (to cut, grab, and unscrew stuff).
  - Spare **prescription glasses** (don't just bring contact lenses).
  - **Sunscreen**.
  - And yes, **more socks**.

SOLO founder Dr. Frank Hubbell working in Haiti after the 2010 earthquake

Tornado: a neighborhood becomes a wilderness in seconds

What to know (and do) before you go

GET VACCINATED—your desire to help is admirable, but don't set yourself up for a world of hurt. Outside the US, Canada, and Europe, nasty diseases abound, and in a big natural disaster all bets are off. Consider your vulnerabilities and protect yourself. Here's the disaster-responder's disease punch-list.

- Cholera
- Hepatitis B
- Hepatitis A
- MMR
- Meningococcal
- Poliovirus
- Tetanus & diphtheria
- Typhoid live/oral
- Yellow fever
- Rabies pre-exposure
- Japanese encephalitis
- In addition to the applicable vaccinations, be sure to bring any other meds you take (especially prescription drugs) and bring enough to last two or three times as long as you think you'll need them.

BE PHYSICALLY FIT—If the longest emergency situation you've been involved in took just a few hours (a long litter carry, perhaps) you may be used to just running on sheer excitement—but you can't count on enthusiasm and adrenaline to carry you for days.

- Don't fool yourself into thinking that you are more fit than you are. Get in shape and stay in shape.
- Know your physical limits and stay within them.

BE MENTALLY PREPARED—Don't take it for granted that you will be able to handle the intense mental and emotional stress of a drawn-out disaster scene. You may see lots of misery, death, and destruction. You may not be able to help everyone. You may need to detach occasionally to process and catch your breath.

- Talk to other rescuers.
- Debrief frequently.
- Get enough to eat.
- Sleep whenever you can; let others take over when you're exhausted, and know when you've had enough.
- Keep a positive attitude and be satisfied with doing your very best.
- Don't become another patient.
- Prepare to step out of your medical comfort zone.

GOT IT? GOOD! YOU'RE READ TO GO, WELL ALMOST . . .

> **WE CONTEND** that wilderness is where you find it, that the 60-minute Golden Hour is a very short time indeed, that one man's downtown can become another man's backcountry faster than you can order a tall mocha latte from Starbucks.

Disasters distort time and place: the typical becomes the bizarre, things that you counted on yesterday are gone tomorrow—the hospital is *right over there*, but you can't reach it because the roads are gone.

Your cell phone doesn't work, your radio is clotted with frantic voices, and your medical protocols may not be worth the paper they're printed on.

But there they are, your patients, and you have to take care of them—not just for a golden hour, but maybe for

a golden day, or a golden week. You'll need every skill you have, and you'll have to improvise beyond that. The extended care environment requires that you think and act about medicine differently than you're used to.

Here's what we mean.

*You and the hurt person are here...
but, the hospital is over there...*

THE PATIENT ASSESSMENT SYSTEM (PAS)

When working within the Golden Hour with just one hurt or sick person, patient assessment follows a well-worn path:

- Scene safety
- ABCs
- Disability
- Environment
- Head-to-toe exam
- Vital signs
- AMPLE history
- SOAPnote
- Monitor vital signs while evacuating to definitive care.

But hold on a minute, what will you do if the nearest definitive care has vaporized because the tornado ripped right through it? Suppose there are busted-up people everywhere you look, but there's just you and one lone first responder to handle the mess? What if the *whump, whump, whump* of helicopters is many hours away? In a disaster situation or remote environment, you will have to re-think your assessment criteria and subsequent treatments.

- Definitive care isn't available in anything like the short term.
- Your personnel may be severely limited.
- You won't be off the clock in 60 minutes—in fact, you may be punched in for days (or more).
- Because of delays, the patients that you save out of the initial fray will need long-term care—not just medical, but basic life needs, too (e.g., food, shelter, bodily functions).

TRIAGE

When the Big Bad Thing happens and there are many casualties but few (comparatively) caregivers, big hard decisions need to be made immediately. At every emergency scene, you need to assess patients based on their extent of injury or illness and weigh that against the medical personnel and resources at hand, as well as the realistic expectation (and timing) of more troops (e.g., medics, ambulances, helicopters). At a disaster scene, you may find yourself dealing with more patients than you have ever seen before, and there likely will not be enough EMS people to go around. Triage is your first step.

In the standard, non-disaster triage situation, you focus on those patients who will survive if emergency lifesaving procedures are provided via on-scene care and immediate evacuation. In a disaster, as emotionally painful as it may be, you must shift your focus away from those patients (because no matter what you do to them now, you can't evacuate them to definitive care fast enough to save them) to those with the highest likelihood of surviving before you can get them to definitive care—it may be days.

Because of the time delays inherent in a disaster situation, initial triage will not be enough; patients initially needing little care (e.g., those with simple fractures), may deteriorate over time (due to infection, lack of food, water, shelter, etc.). Keep your eye on the community of patients as a whole and keep the problems from getting bigger or worse.

① Patient number on perforated corner tabs

② The time the assessment is made

③ The date the assessment is made

④ The patient's name and gender

METTAG © 1983 JOURNAL OF CIVIL DEFENSE
P.O. BOX 910, STARKE, FLORIDA 32091, U.S.A.
All Rights Reserved

⑤ The patient's home address (city, state, zip)

⑥ Injury/illness information, AMPLE history

⑦ Number colors correspond to triage tents

⑧ Color indicates the patient's condition; tear off to the appropriate triage level (if the patient's condition changes, they will get a new tag)

TRIAGE (from the French verb, *trier*): 1: a the sorting of and allocation of treatment to patients and especially battle and disaster victims according to a system of priorities designed to maximize the number of survivors

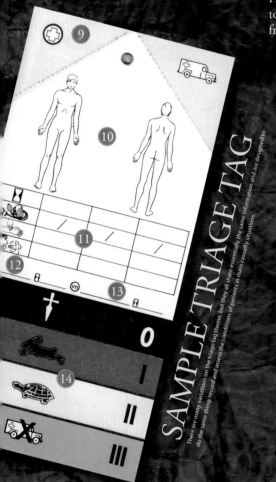

SAMPLE TRIAGE TAG

There are many variations on the triage tag theme, but they all share essentially the same information and are designed to do the same thing: record and assess the conditions of patients in mass casualty situations.

9. One tab goes to the hospital, the other goes to the ambulance

10. Graphically indicate injuries

11. Vital signs (time, BP, pulse, RR)

12. IV type (gauge), drug, and time administered

13. Intramuscular drug and time administered

14. Symbols indicate urgency:
Dagger: dead or will die
Hare: transport immediately
Turtle: transport can be delayed
No ambulance: no transport needed

Here are the triage categories as applied to disaster situations (modified slightly from the standard definitions).

- **BLACK/Expectant:** Dead or will die. Their injuries or illness are not survivable. They should be made comfortable and given painkillers if possible.

- **RED/Immediate:** Require immediate lifesaving intervention (e.g., surgery). They must be transported to definitive care without delay. In a disaster, these patients will not survive—you must move on to the yellows.

- YELLOW/Observation: Not critically injured or ill, but may deteriorate. With treatment on the scene, monitoring, and eventual transport to definitive care, they are likely to survive. Watch them closely and re-triage them frequently.

- GREEN/Walking wounded: They will require medical attention at some time in the future (hours to days) but can wait (e.g., simple fractures, soft tissue injuries). However, in a multi-day disaster situation, they must be monitored—they can deteriorate.

MONITORING

In the extended care environment, you should re-SOAP your patients every 15 minutes in order to detect underlying problems that may affect their long-term survival. Keeping detailed charts over time is one of the best ways to keep up-to-date on the entire patient community and help identify those patients whose treatments must change because of changes in their status.

- SOAPing every 15 minutes adds up to 96 observations per patient, per day! A full-time+ job.

- Careful record-keeping for the entire community of injured/sick people is imperative.
- Round-the-clock shifts will have to be set up, if possible.
- Re-triaging is vital—you must keep up-to-date on the status of individual patients as well as the entire patient community.

MANAGING THE UNCONSCIOUS PATIENT

In the non-disaster, urban environment, your responsibilities for the unconscious and unresponsive patient are straight-forward: maintain a patent airway and keep the patient stable until the hospital staff can take over long-term care. In a disaster or mass casualty situation, you may have to manage chronically unresponsive patients for hours or days. Their airway must be maintained, they must be moved regularly, their nutrition and hydration needs must be met—and don't forget, their bowel and bladder functions will continue, so you will have to attend to that, too. You will be doctor, nurse, and custodian. And these won't be the only patients who will need this type of attention; conscious patients with severe disabilities (e.g., trauma victims) will also need your tender loving care and nursing skills.

- Because so many things can influence it (for better and for worse), it is crucial to monitor LOC in all patients.
- Don't assume that chronically unconscious patients will stay that way—check for response to verbal and painful stimuli regularly.

TREATMENT

When definitive care is hours or days away, you may need to treat things that would normally be handled by hospital personnel.

- Airway management—Even in the extended care environment, the airway is your primary concern. All unconscious patients should be placed in the recovery position, and they should be monitored frequently to ensure that a patent airway is maintained. With a large number of patients and limited EMS staff, this may be extremely difficult.

- Trauma—You may need to reduce dislocations, re-align angulated fractures, deal with crush injuries, provide long-term wound care, and stabilize spinal cord injuries.

- Shock—Shock can kill. You must treat the underlying injury, protect the patient from the environment, and (if possible) give oral fluids. If a shock patient is unable to ingest oral fluids (i.e., if they are unconscious), IV fluids should be administered (you must be at least an AEMT to do this).

- Environmental emergencies—Depending on the nature of the disaster and the weather conditions, you may have to deal long-term with the issues of: hypothermia, heat exhaustion, heat stroke, frostbite, exhaustion, and dehydration.

- Medical emergencies—You may have to monitor and treat cardiac patients that present with chest pain and shortness of breath, patients whose LOC deteriorates, and those who develop abdominal pain. These problems may not come on for hours or days.

- Psychiatric emergencies. Time spent in the stress-filled environment of a disaster situation can cause many psychiatric issues to arise: from general fear and anxiety, to Post Traumatic Stress Disorder (PTSD), increase in psychosis among those vulner-

Direct pressure stops bleeding.

Hypothermic patients can be warmed by wrapping them up in a big, dry insulated/waterproof burrito...

...even a small amount of residual body heat can be remarkably effective.

The airway is everything...if that ain't working, then nothing ain't working.

Not all wilderness medicine issues are dramatic. Substance abuse (or the unavailability of certain meds) can become serious problems in the midst of chaos.

able to it, and addiction issues. In addition to meeting pure physical needs to the best of your ability, you will need to provide emotional and mental comfort as well—welcome to group therapy.

- Childbirth. In a situation where dozens (or perhaps hundreds) of disaster victims are crammed for days into one place (e.g., the New Orleans Superdome during Katrina), you may well see babies being born—labor does not stop just because the streets are flooded. You will need to be prepared not only to deliver babies, but also to provide postpartum care to the babies and their mothers—which may be complicated.

- Poisoning—From simple food poisoning to accidental ingestion of toxins to inhaled poisons (e.g., people using charcoal grills indoors for heat or food preparation and sucking in carbon dioxide), you may find that you have become your own poison control center. Learn the basics: remove, dilute, absorb, counteract.

- Substance abuse—should you

keep the drunks drunk and the dopers stoned? Maybe. Patients with alcohol or narcotic abuse issues should be handled with care. The disaster environment is not the place to detoxify them—doing so may turn them from annoying distractions to medical patients who require your care. By providing them with a maintenance-level of whatever substance they crave (or a substitute that will keep them from going into detox), and getting their cooperation, you will minimize the time and effort you will need to expend on them. Also, bear in mind that some patients may be on prescription drugs that they cannot come off of without causing serious complications—identify them and come up with contingencies for their med issues.

MOVING WAY BEYOND THE 60-MINUTE GOLD STANDARD

The Golden Hour has long been a buzz-phrase of the medical community—and it rolls off the tongue well and fits our protocols nicely. But when nature throws a monkey wrench into the works—when a disaster blows definitive care hours or days away—we need to move way beyond the 60-minute gold standard.

THE GOLDEN DAY—EXTENDED CARE

- The first 24 hours are critical in every disaster situation. The adrenalin of those first hectic hours fades, and things often shake out.
    - The first triage round is done, and most patients have lined up well under their respective color.
    - Immediate life threats have been addressed, initial treatments completed, and monitoring systems should be in place.
    - You don't have all the personnel and supplies you need, but you've done your best.
    - By the end of this first day, you should have stabilized your local environment—the immediate area where you will be treating patients and assisting others who need help with basic life needs.
    - You've done all you can to keep the big picture from getting worse: provided for basic life support—food/water/shelter, and established a chain of command and communications with the outside world.

THE GOLDEN WEEK(S)—REMOTE CARE

- If it looks like this is going to be a long haul, you need to take additional steps to organize your next few days. Prepare yourself, your team, and your patients for long-term problems.
    - Chain of command—who does what, when, and to whom will they report?
    - Basic life support—food and water supply, shelter, insect and disease control.
    - Medical supplies—get more stuff, prepare to improvise.
    - Evacuation and transportation—how are you going to move people?
    - Communication—maintain a link to the outside world.
    - Community health—help people help themselves, and help each other.
    - Personal health—your own needs for food, water, sleep, mental health.

CONGRATULATIONS, NOW, GET GOING . . .

> **WHEN I-880 PANCAKED,** the tiers of the highway were reduced to a stack just a few meters high. Inside that stack were 52 vehicles and dozens of people. As night fell amid the smoke and sirens and chaos, the lights of San Francisco General Trauma Center blinked in the darkness just across the bay—they might as well have been shining from the moon. ,,

From an account of the Loma Prieta earthquake (Oakland, CA, October 17, 1989). The temblor measured 6.9 on the Richter Scale, lasted 15 seconds, killed 63 people and injured 3,000. EMS providers were overwhelmed.

" The fire communications center was gridlocked because hundreds of emergency calls were being received, but there (were) no fire engines or trucks to send." (Excerpted from Oakland Fire Department reports and radio transcripts.)

Eighty-eight Golden Hours after the quake struck, the last victim, longshoreman Buck Helm, was pulled from the rubble beneath I-880. He died in the hospital 28 days later from the complications of his injuries. Everyone had done their best—it had just taken too long.

Bivouac: noun \'bi-və-,wak\ :
a usually temporary encampment under little or no shelter

BIVY: verb \'bi-vē\ to be forced by circumstance to bivouac (or preplanned, e.g., during a light fast alpine climb)

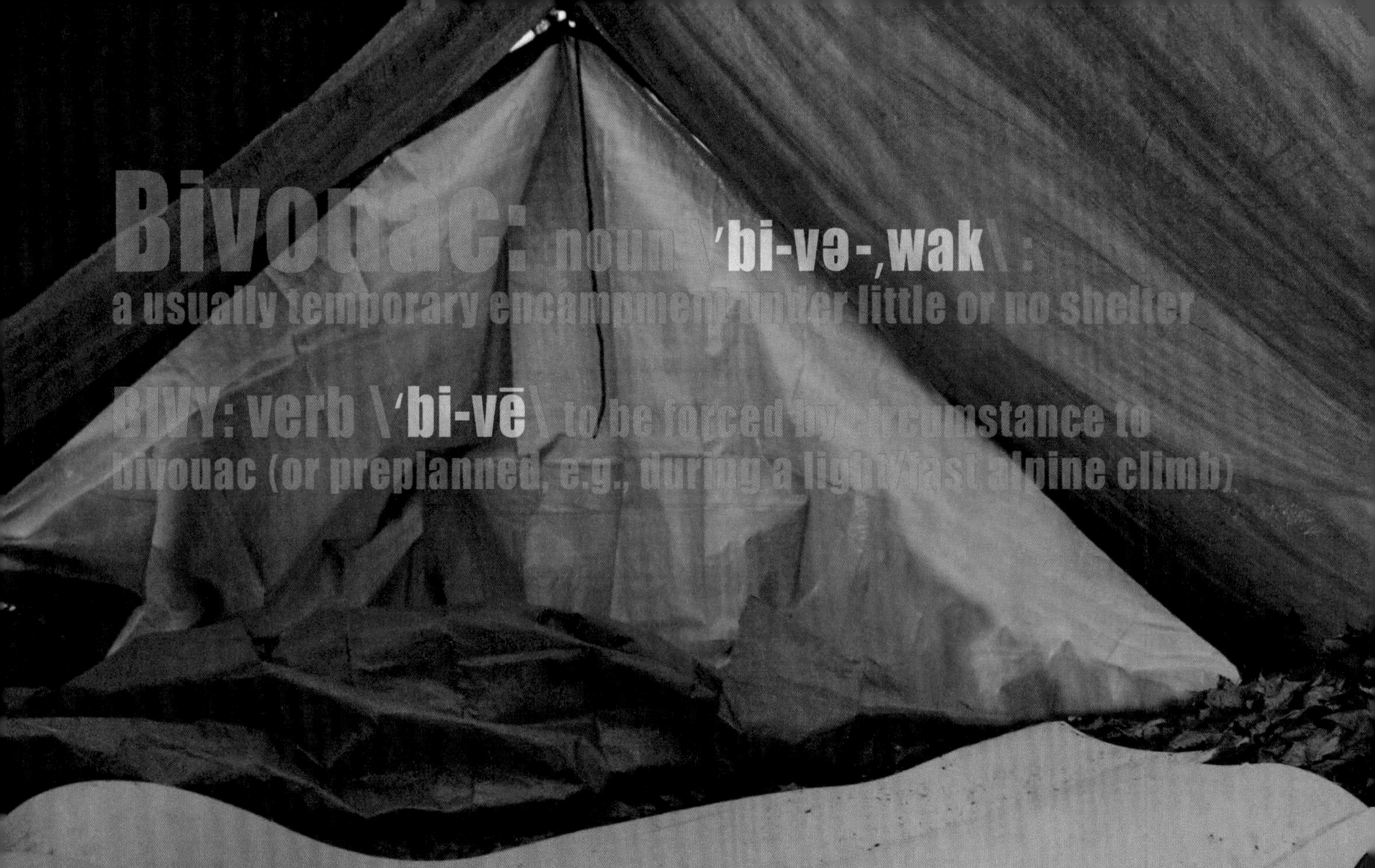

A few tarps, some cord tied to handy trees, and a floor made of foam pads:

"Hey folks, we're home!"

When faced with the need to bivouac, you must consider things beyond the care of the injured—some of which may be out of your control.

weather

- A primary concern.
- You have no control over it.
- It can have a dramatic influence on all your decision-making.
- Know the long-range forecast before you head out.
- Understand the basics of backcountry weather forecasting.

terrain

- Although you generally control the nature of the terrain across which you choose to travel, accidents or sudden illness strike unpredictably, and you may be forced by circumstances to treat a patient and consider a bivouac on terrain that may not be well-suited to that purpose.

time and distance to definitive care

- What time of day is it?
- How soon will it be dark?
- How soon will it be light?
- How far from the road are you?
- How long will it take to get out?

Components of a happy bivy:

Good weather (a warm spring night in Nevada), a natural shelter, (big ledge with walls), good pads and sleeping bags, food and water (the latter really heavy when lugged up 3,000 feet of desert sandstone), a good friend, and (at 5:00 A.M.) a sense of humor. The airplane pillows are optional (oh, so nice).

Cool, a snow cave: Cramped, damp, dark, and hard to ventilate. But they get nice and warm and are completely windproof. The flannel shirt and baseball cap are not ideal.

resources and people

- What is the size, age, experience, and skill level of your group?
- What kinds and amount of food, extra clothing, and equipment are they carrying?

the patient's needs

- It may seem as if the patient's needs should be of paramount concern; however, after their injuries/illness have been treated appropriately, the focus must turn back to the group's welfare and needs, and these must be balanced with those of the patient.
- How stable is the patient?
- Can they await evacuation?
- Considering these concerns, can the group "self-rescue" safely?
- If not, how will those same concerns affect the group if they have to bivouac?

The elements of effective bivouacs

All these elements increase the group's safety, wellbeing, and productivity.

basic considerations

- Protection from water
- Protection from wind
- The availability of fire/heat/warmth
- The availability of food and water

terrain considerations

Rocky

- Avoid high, exposed places.
- Seek natural shelter: caves, big boulders, cliff overhangs, depressions, talus fields (often provide small caves or protective overhangs—ensure stability).
- Enhance your site by building a windbreak.
- Remember, some of these places may become unsafe during a thunderstorm.

Woodlands

- Avoid marshy ground and drainage areas.
- Seek low trees—they often offer greater protection.
- Build lean-tos with tarps, trees, and tree limbs.
- Use pine trees as natural rain/snow shelters.
- Use dry leaves and duff or pine boughs for ground insulation.

Snow

- Avoid potential avalanche terrain and high snow deposition areas.
- Dig a deep trench and cover with a tarp.
- Dig a snow cave (into a slope is easier): keep the entrance low and the roof thin, and cut an air hole.
- In proper snow conditions, cut blocks for an igloo/windbreak.
- Alternately, make a quincy: make a big pile of snow (bigger than you think), compact it (the more, the better), dig into it to form a snow cave.

Water Purification

IT MAY COVER SOME THREE-QUARTERS OF THE EARTH'S SURFACE, BUT PRECIOUS LITTLE OF OUR WATER IS FIT TO DRINK

IT'S OUR MOST BASIC PHYSICAL NEED—we can survive weeks without food but only days without H_2O. The good news is that except in arid places, fresh water is usually all over the place. The bad news is that much of it is unsafe, especially in rural areas or developing countries. To help ensure that you don't get sick, assume that any water whose source you are unsure of is tainted with a host of nasties—and act accordingly.

Yeah, we know that this water blob looks like some kind of weird, bulbous-eyed creature having a bad hair day—how appropriate, since even the cleanest-looking water is full of micro-critters.

WATERBORNE DISEASES ARE SOME OF THE MOST COMMON DISEASES known to man. They are spread primarily via the oral-fecal route when a pathogen in human or animal waste contaminates the drinking water supply. The disease-causing pathogen is transmitted to people when they drink the water, consume food that was washed in the contaminated water or handled by dirty hands that prepared the food, or by washing their own hands in the contaminated water.

Most waterborne illnesses affect the gastrointestinal tract and present as an upset stomach, gas, bloating, abdominal cramping, fever, chills, and most importantly, diarrhea[1].

PRECAUTIONS

- Only consume potable water.
- Sterilize your water.
- Properly wash vegetables.
- In developing countries:
  - ☑ Avoid ice cubes—freezing won't kill all the little nasties. And no, alcohol (as in a mixed drink) will not kill the organisms in a melting ice cube.
  - ☑ Make sure that bottle water still has the factory seal—it is not uncommon for bottled water bottles to be refilled with tainted local tap water.
  - ☑ Canned drinks are always safe—they have been pasteurized.
- Wash your hands frequently—carry hand sanitizer and use it frequently.
- Swimming
  - ☑ Swimming in contaminated water is dangerous, and there is almost no way to protect yourself from bacteria and viruses.
  - ☑ If in doubt, don't take the plunge—err on the dry side.

They look so pure, like diamonds made of water. But ice cubes can, and often are, just frozen storage containers for icky stuff. Tests frequently show dangerous levels of microbial nasties, including E.coli. In 1987, 5,000 people fell ill to food poisoning after consuming beverages with contaminated ice in an outbreak in Pennsylvania and Delaware.

Fresh, raw vegetables must be vigorously rinsed with uncontaminated water—especially leafy stuff like lettuce and spinach, which are full of nooks and crannies that can harbor life you don't want to ingest. So, should you order the chef's salad in some roadside bistro in a Quatemalan village? Um, probably not.

WATER: A MOST PRECIOUS LIQUID

More than 3.4 million people die each year from water, sanitation, and hygiene-related causes. Nearly all deaths, 99%, occur in the developing world.

Lack of access to clean water and sanitation kills children at a rate equivalent to a jumbo jet crashing every four hours.

Of the 60 million people added to the world's towns and cities every year, most move to informal settlements (i.e. slums) with no sanitation facilities.

780 million people lack access to an improved water source; approximately one in nine people.

"[The water and sanitation] crisis claims more lives through disease than any war claims through guns."

An American taking a 5-minute shower uses more water than the average person in a developing country slum uses for an entire day.

More people have a mobile phone than a toilet.

Source: water.org

---

[1] Diarrheal disease is the second leading cause of death in children under five years old. It is both preventable and treatable. Diarrheal disease kills 1.5 million children every year. Globally, there are about two billion cases of diarrheal disease every year. Diarrheal disease mainly affects children under two years old.

While most
waterborne illness
is caused by
ingesting tainted
water, there are
two nasty things
that you can get by
being **in** the water.

Schistosomiasis is
the only parasitic
infection that
can invade you
through your skin
while swimming.
Once it gets on
you, the parasite
makes its way
into your body by
burrowing through
your skin—in the
process causing
a rash known as
swimmer's itch or
duck itch.

Naegleria fowleri
is an abundant,
heat-loving ameba
found in warm
water (including
hot springs) around
the world. If you
frequent these hot
springs and inhale
water containing
the ameba, it can
migrate into your
brain and cause
lethal amebic
brain infection.
Fortunately, the
risk of Naegleria
fowleri is extremely
low. There were 32
reported deaths in
the US from 2002
to 2011, despite
multiple millions
of recreational
exposures each
year. The biggest
risk to swimmers
is drowning, not
infection.

PURIFICATION METHODS

METHOD	CONSIDERATIONS	ADVANTAGES	DISADVANTAGES
BOILING	■ Rolling boil kills all disease-causing pathogens. ■ Below 8,000 feet, bringing water to a rolling boil is sufficient. ■ Above 8,000 feet, boil water for several minutes.	■ It is absolutely reliable. ■ You can see it working. ■ No precision is needed—when the water has boiled for the appropriate amount of time (see above), it's sterile.	■ It requires fuel/fire or a stove. ■ It takes time and effort. ■ You end up with hot water.
CHEMICALS (iodine and chlorine)	■ Iodine or chlorine, when added to water in appropriate quantities, are very effective disinfectants. ■ Effectiveness requires proper contact time—the chemical has to be in the water long enough to work (30 minutes minimum, 60 minutes for dirty, very cold, or very acidic water). ■ Reducing the amount of debris in the water before adding chemicals makes the chemicals more effective. ■ Dosages vary depending on chemical and water volume. ■ The cap and threads must be treated, too!	■ Both are readily available, cheap, lightweight, and safe. ■ Easy to use—just add to your water and wait. ■ Small amounts are needed (as tablets, crystals, or drops).	■ Iodine should not be used by people with thyroid disease or if they are allergic to it. ■ You must wait 30 – 60 minutes. ■ The chemicals can make the treated water taste unpleasant: drink-mix crystals can help; also, dissolving a vitamin C tablet will neutralize the bad taste—flavor the water after the sterilization time is over.
FILTRATION	■ Filtration is very effective; bacteria and protozoa are easily strained out (they are relatively big) ■ Filtration alone is not effective against viruses—they are too small. ■ Multi-stage filters will also kill viruses : 1st stage filters sediment, 2nd stage kills bacteria and protozoa, 3rd stage uses iodine to kill viruses, 4th stage (optional) uses activated charcoal to remove aftertaste.	■ Convenient and easy to use: simply pump or use a gravity feed. ■ Speed: you don't have to wait—pump and you're done. ■ No unpleasant aftertaste.	■ Can be heavy and expensive. ■ Unless multi-stage, will not filter out viruses—chemical treatment may be required after filtration. ■ Undetected defects (e.g., a cracked filter) can compromise effectiveness without your knowledge. ■ Filters can become plugged. ■ Maintenance (both at home and in the field) required. ■ Not suitable for large groups. ■ With multistage filters, it can be hard to tell when the chemical has run out.
UV LIGHT	■ Uses UVS (ultraviolet-C, short wave, or germicidal) light to kill everything. ■ Water must be clear: turbid water will not be treated effectively so must be filtered first.	■ Easy to use and effective. ■ Fast: typically less than two minutes for a liter of water.	■ Although its effectiveness against bacteria and protozoa (e.g., giardia) is high, some resistant viruses require much higher dosages (10 – 30 times). ■ Requires batteries. ■ Relatively expensive. ■ Not suitable for groups.
ELECTROLYSIS	■ Uses electricity to convert salt and water into a powerful disinfectant.	■ Destroys viruses , bacteria, and giardia in 30 minutes, cryptosporidium (protozoa) in 4 hours. ■ Compact, rugged, submersible. ■ Safety indicator shows when water is safe. ■ No health risks or unpleasant aftertaste.	■ Requires batteries. ■ Relatively expensive.

The high-tech Hiker Pro water filter from Katadyn—a world leader in personal water disinfection.

A SUN-POWERED, LOW-TECH ALTERNATIVE

Solar ultraviolet water disinfection (SODIS) uses the power of the sun and standard plastic bottles to create safe drinking water. Exposure to sunlight has been shown to deactivate diarrhea-causing organisms in polluted drinking water. There are three effects of solar radiation that are believed to contribute to the inactivation of pathogenic (disease-causing) organisms: it interferes directly with the metabolism and destroys the cell structure of bacteria; it reacts with the dissolved oxygen in the water to produce highly reactive forms of oxygen (oxygen free radicals and hydrogen peroxides that damage pathogens); and the cumulative solar radiation (including the infrared component) heats the water to levels that promote microbe death: a minimum of $30^0C/86^0F$ —above $50^0C/122^0F$ the process is three times faster.

This simple, cheap method is recommended by the World Health Organization and is used throughout the developing world.

SODIS water disinfection in Indonesia.

STEPS

1. Take clean transparent plastic water bottles (2 liters or smaller) and remove the labels.
2. Fill the bottles with water that has been strained to remove organic material and sediment.
3. Lay the bottles in strong direct sunlight (<50% cloud cover) for a minimum of 6 hours (2 days in cloudy weather). A reflective surface and turning the bottles every couple or hours is helpful.

CAUTIONS

- PVC and polycarbonate bottles should not be used—they block UV.

- Old, scratched, opaque bottles and those larger than two liters should not be used.

- The water should be used immediately and not stored—microbe re-growth can occur, especially if the bottles are stored in the dark. If stored, another round of solar sterilization should occur before consumption.

For many in the world, this is the best water they can expect.

About 75% of the earth is covered with water, but only 3% of that is non-saline water, and only 31% of that non-saline water is available as fresh water (less than 1% of the whole)—and a lot of that looks like this (yuck). ·····················➤

75%   3%   <1%

INTERNATIONAL & TRAVEL MEDICINE

TOP

Mosquito larvae hang down from the water's surface film in order to breathe. One of the most common transmitters of disease in the world's tropical regions, mosquitoes infect an estimated 700 million people a year with a host of maladies from annoying to deadly.

RIGHT

Our big home.

She was bitten by a female *Anopheles* mosquito.

She has malaria.

Is pregnant with her ninth child.

A relative helps her to breathe.

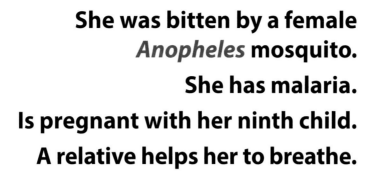

Central African Republic
(smack in the middle of the infection zone)

She'll be *dead* in seven hours.

The world's petri dish straddles the equator— incubating most of our most harmful diseases.

The world is a dangerous place. In the tropical climates that run in a band to the north and south of the equator, and especially in the developing countries, just day-to-day living means having to dodge a host of nasty things: eating, drinking, walking, bathing, working, even sleeping can be so dangerous that you might die. And when the traveler lands in a steamy hot airport far from Westernized comfort and safety—well, look out!

**malaria } dengue } river blindness } hepatitis }
Chaga's disease } dysentery } tapeworm }
amebiasis } giardiasis } diarrhea } fungus }
parasites } helminths } protozoa } bacteria } virus...**

...*you get the idea*

The areas of the world where most diseases incubate not only straddle the equator but are also closely tied to socio-economic development.

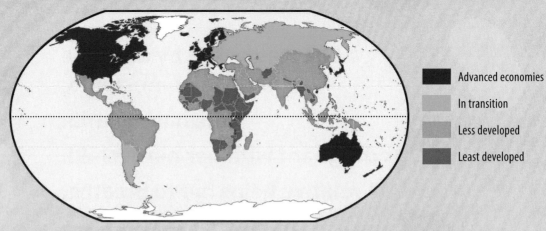

Advanced economies
In transition
Less developed
Least developed

SOCIO-EONOMICALLY advanced and transitional nations—diseases of lifestyle:

Cardiovascular disease
Cancer
Trauma
Infectious disease

Less developed and least developed nations—disease spread environmentally:

Diseases spread by insects: malaria, dengue, river blindness, Chaga's disease...

Diseases spread by food: dysentery, tapeworms, giardiasis...

Diseases spread by water: hepatitis, amebiasis, giardiasis

Double-whammy: don't drink the water and stay clear of the lemon. Consider all water (including ice) in developing countries to be bad—demand bottled water and verify the factory seal. And raw fruits, like lemon slices, are notorious for harboring nasty bacteria. Drink from cans and bottles, eat food that has been thoroughly cooked.

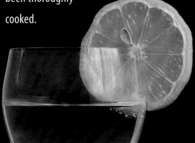

WHY TRAVELERS GET SICK:

Denial: It won't happen to me. Illnesses not commonly seen in developed countries. Illnesses not emphasized in medical school education.

Naive: Lack experience and local knowledge. Greatest risk is at the hands of another person.

Attitude: Adventurous, courageous, but will not ask for assistance.

Food and water: Commonly contaminated. The traveler is unsure what is safe to eat and drink.

Sanitation: Basic sanitation and toilet paper may not be available.

Insects: Blood suckers commonly transmit disease. The traveler does not know how to protect themselves from insects.

Sex: STDs are very common worldwide.

Accidents: Motor vehicle accidents are the #1 case of trip-related deaths.

Vaccines: I had my vaccines, so I can do whatever I want.

Antimalarial: I am taking my anti-malarial drug, so I don't need to worry about bugs.

Doctors: Bad advice: *"Don't worry, if you get malaria, we can treat it."*

TRAVEL PREPARATION

Trip itinerary: Review travel plans, urban versus rural, risk assessment

Information resources: Centers for Disease Control (www.cdc.gov/travel/); can also access the State Department for specific country warnings (www.travel.state.gov/).

Prescription medications: Carry enough of your usual prescription meds for the entire trip. Diabetics may need to plan ahead for refrigeration. Sickle cell and COPD patients may need to know altitudes.

Glasses: If you wear contact lenses, bring glasses, too (and consider prescription sunglasses).

Water purification: Boiling, filtration, UV light, or chemical disinfection with iodine or chlorine (see the water purification section)

Immunizations: What commonly happens commonly is preventable. Plan early for immunizations (some take months). Carry your International Certificate of Immunizations with your passport.

Definitive care: Know what will be available and prepare accordingly.

Flies: one of the your worst enemies—love to land on poop and then on your burrito.

Flies have dirty feet!

FOOD—PART OF THE ADVENTURE

Oral-fecal contamination: one of the most common causes of sickness, and may be the result of poor personal hygiene, local sanitation issues (e.g., open sewers, food preparation), and vector contamination (e.g., flies).

Rules to thrive by:

1. Eat from your own bowl with your own utensils.
2. Don't eat raw or undercooked veggies unless they can be peeled.
3. Don't eat undercooked meat.
4. Only eat food served hot.
5. Wash your hands (and carry hand sanitizer).
6. Beware of restaurant food: no ice, no water, no cream sauces.

Traveler's diarrhea: is the classic result of oral-fecal contamination—affecting 20% – 50% of international travelers.

1. Force fluids—drink until peeing regularly.
2. Drink commercial oral rehydration solution (ORS), **or** Gatorade, **or** make your own: 1 liter of water, 2 tablespoons sugar, 1/4 tablespoon salt, **or** use rice water (rice cooked until it is completely dissolved in the water).
3. Pepto-Bismol® (bismuth subsalicylate) **or**
4. Imodium (lopermide): 1 tab every 4 hours **or**
5. Codeine (sold in the US by prescription only)—slows peristalsis.

INSECTS—the #1 cause of disease transmission and death worldwide

Mosquitoes: *Malaria*—is the most common disease in the world and the #1 cause of death. Current prophylaxis regimen: chloroquine, mefloquine, or doxycycline. *Dengue*—aka "break bone fever" sick for 6 –12 months.

Black flies: *Onchocerus (River Blindness)*—#1 cause of blindness in the world.

Reduviid (assassin or kissing bug): *American trypanosomiasis (Chaga's Disease)*—a parasitic disease that can last months.

Ticks: these "little septic tanks" spread many diseases such as *Lyme Disease*, *Rocky Mountain Spotted Fever*, etc.

INFECTION: occurs when we become a blood meal for the insect—we become part of the food chain (yuck). Most blood suckers feed at night, injecting an anticoagulant in their saliva, which aids in blood flow and also causes a localized immune reaction (often causing an itchy rash).

PREVENTION: is the key: clothing, footwear, mosquito netting (both as head nets and canopies for sleeping), repellents for both skin and clothing.

#1 disease spreader—mosquitoes

#2 disease spreader—ticks

Insecticide-treated bed nets (ITNs) have been shown to be very effective in the prevention of malaria illness, severe disease, and death in areas where malaria is widespread. In trials in Africa, ITNs have reduced death in children under the age of 5 by about 20%.

malaria

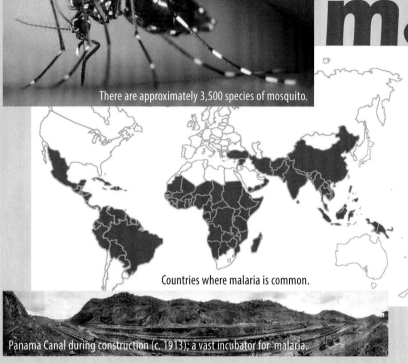

There are approximately 3,500 species of mosquito.

Countries where malaria is common.

Panama Canal during construction (c. 1913); a vast incubator for malaria.

MALARIA is one of the most significant infectious diseases in the world today. It is caused by a parasite of the genus *Plasmodium* and carried from human to human by the ubiquitous anopheles mosquito (of which over 100 species are known malaria vectors). The obligate intracellular parasite infects and destroys cells, first in the liver, and then red blood cells (RBCs). The disease effects range from minor to deadly, and some malaria strains even live dormant in their victims and can cause relapses, even many years later.

There are over 200 known species of *Plasmodium*, but only 5 species are known to cause malaria in humans: *P. falciparum* (cerebral malaria), *P. vivax* (common malaria), *P. ovale, P. malariae, and P. Knowlesis*. Of these, *P. falciparum* and *P. vivax* cause the majority of deaths. The others typically cause milder symptoms, although *P. Knowlesis*, can also cause severe disease in humans.

Malaria is widespread and common in most tropical regions of the world and has figured prominently in the history of man: influencing wars, affecting population densities, and interfering with human endeavors—for example, many members of the Lewis and Clark expedition were stricken with the disease, and an estimated 15% of the local population (mostly workers) surrounding the Panama Canal (13,000 out of 80,000) suffered malarial attacks each **week** during construction.

In the next section, prevention is discussed. Many people are confused by the difference between an insecticide like permethrin, which actually kills insects, and a repellent, like **OFF**®, which merely keeps insects at bay...but what if you missed a spot when applying the repellent?

malaria lifecycle

Plasmodium is the parasite that causes malaria. When Plasmodium enters the bloodstream via a bite from an infected mosquito (**1**), the parasites are called sporozoites. Sporozoites migrate to the liver (**2**), where they multiply, and change form, becoming merozoites. Merozoites enter red blood cells (RBCs), where they multiply (**3**). As the merozoites break out of the RBCs, symptoms appear and the person becomes ill. When a mosquito bites an infected person, they pick up the parasite and carry it to the next potential victim.

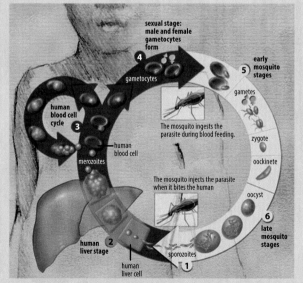

sexual stage: male and female gametocytes form

gametocytes

human blood cell cycle

human blood cell

merozoites

human liver stage

human liver cell

sporozoites

The mosquito ingests the parasite during blood feeding.

The mosquito injects the parasite when it bites the human

early mosquito stages

gametes

zygote

oockinete

oocyst

late mosquito stages

COMPARISON OF THE FOUR MOST COMMON STRAINS OF MALARIA

	P. falciparum	P. vivax	P. ovale	P. malariae
Incubation days	9 – 14	12 – 17 (up to 12 months)	6 – 18 (or longer)	28 – 40 (or longer)
Relapse possible?	No	Yes	Yes	No
Fever periodicity (hrs)	16 – 36 (or longer)	8 – 12	8 – 12	8 – 10
Severity of primary attack	Severe	Mild to severe	Mild	Mild
Drug resistance	High	Moderate	Unknown	Unknown

prevention

Prevention is two-pronged: barriers to the vector and pre-exposure medication. Barring the bugs from feeding on you will not only prevent malaria, but many other diseases spread by blood-sucking insects (e.g., dengue, Chaga's Disease): clothing, mosquito netting (the best is impregnated with an insecticide such as permethrin), window screens, repellents, and general insecticides. Protection at night is crucial—most blood-sucking insects are nocturnal.

Chemoprophylaxis (the administration of medicine to prevent disease or infection) requires that you take an anti-malarial drug prior to exposure to malarial sporozoites—which are then killed before disappearing into your liver (where your immune system cannot find them). Which drug you should take depends on your destination—consult the CDC for current information (see table, below).

signs/symptoms

FEVER: a high (>104°F) cyclic fever with associated chills, shaking rigors, and hallucinations occurs once malaria has entered the bloodstream.

FATIGUE, HEADACHE, MALAISE, ANEMIA (low RBC count), **SPLENOMEGALY** (enlarged spleen): caused by the destruction of red blood cells, which lowers O_2 carrying capacity, and releases free iron from the hemoglobin into the blood.

IN CEREBRAL MALARIA (P. falciparum) the RBCs become sticky, causing mircoemboli that can infarct small arteries in the brain, resulting in stroke-like symptoms—this makes it the most lethal form of malaria.

LIVER DAMAGE will be evident in elevated liver function tests for enzymes.

KIDNEY STRESS often occurs as the kidneys work to flush excess waste products from the RBC and liver cell destruction—urine will turn very dark.

PAIN: muscle, joint, and bone pain as a result of the damage and accumulation of waste products.

OTHER SYMPTOMS: back pain, dizziness, loss of appetite, nausea, vomiting, abdominal pain, diarrhea, dry cough, SOB.

DIAGNOSIS: from physical exam—fever, tachycardia, warm and flushed skin, enlarged spleen and/or liver, jaundice, orthostatic hypertension, mental confusion, cyanosis; examination of a peripheral blood smear will allow the observation of the infected RBCs and the identification of the malaria strain—important to determine both the choice of treatment and the risk of relapse.

treatment

When malaria is contracted, the treatment chosen is based on which form of malaria the patient has. Some forms of malaria have become resistant to several common drugs (e.g., chloroquine)—check with organizations such as the CDC and the World Health Organization (WHO) for drug updates.

malaria facts

World population: >7 billion

Population at risk: 50%[+/-] (at least 3.3 billion people in 100[+] countries)

Estimated cases in 2010: 219 million

Estimated deaths in 2010: 660,000 (1800/day, 85% children under age 5; percentage of deaths in Africa: 90%[+/-])

Malaria compared to other diseases: malaria is considered one of the six major infectious diseases (in terms of worldwide deaths). It is estimated that 90% of all infectious disease deaths are caused by, in order of deadliness: 1) pneumonia, 2) HIV/AIDS, 3) diarrhea, 4) tuberculosis, 5) *malaria*, 6) measles. (FYI: approximately 3x as many people die from AIDS each year as from malaria.)

Malaria in the US: about 1,500 cases are annually reported, even though malaria was eliminated from the US in the 1950s—three carrier-species of *Anopheles* are still present in the US, so the risk of an outbreak persists.

Malaria funding: Eradicating malaria is both a prominent and reachable goal. In 2007, $1.5 billion was spent—it is estimated that four times that rate will be required. The Bill & Melinda Gates Foundation has pledged $2 billion.

CHEMOPROPHYLAXIS DRUGS (* also used to treat active disease)

Drug	Adult dosage	Pediatric dosage
Mefloquine (Lariam)*	250mg, once a week	15 – 19kg, 1/4 tab per week
Doxycycline*	100mg, once a day	>8 years old, 2mg/kg once daily, up to the adult dose of 100mg/day
Chloroquine (Aralen)*	500mg, once a week	5mg/kg once a week up to the adult dose of 500mg
Hydroxychloroquine (Plaquenil)	400mg, once a week	5mg/kg once a week up to the adult dose of 400mg
Proquanil (Paludrine)*	200mg, once a day, in combination with weekly chloroquine	<2 years old: 50mg/day 2 – 6 years old: 100mg/day 7 – 10 years old: 150mg/day >10 years old: 200mg/day
Malarone (Atovaquone plus proguanil)*	250/100mg tab, once daily	<11 kg: not recommended 11 – 20kg: 62.5/25mg daily 21 – 30kg: 125/50mg daily 31 – 40kg: 187.5/75mg daily >40kg: 250/100mg daily

Other drugs used to treat active disease: quinine, primaquine, Lapdap (chlorproguanil plus dapsone), artemisinin

Childbirth is a natural, if dramatic, occurrence

but things can and do get complicated. Often it's just a matter of timing—the baby wants to get out, but you're not sure you can get to the hospital fast enough.

Emergency childbirth

Criteria for deciding if birth is imminent

What is the mom's due date?

The closer to the due date, the more likely it is that true labor has begun. If the due date has already passed, then you should assume that this is genuine labor and that birth is imminent.

Is this her first child?

Subsequent labors are typically shorter than the first one—so if mom has other children, expect labor to progress relatively quickly. Ask her how long her previous labors took, and where she feels she is in the process this time.

Is mom in labor?

Here are the five classic signs—if you see these (especially if you see all of them), mom is almost certainly in labor.

1. Has mom had a "bloody show" yet? Blood staining on underwear or a tissue indicates that the mucus plug has been lost.

2. Has the amniotic sac ruptured yet? Clear fluid will gush or trickle, indicating that the sac has broken—if it is colored green, brown, or gold, this may be a sign of fetal distress.

3. Is mom having contractions? If so, describe them. **Initiation**: when did contractions begin? **Frequency**: how far apart are the contractions? Is the time between contractions decreasing? If so, at what rate? **Duration**: how long does each contraction last? **Strength**: can mom talk during a contraction?

4. Does mom have lower back pain? Intense pain that radiates to the abdomen (or even to the legs), indicates labor.

5. Does mom have intestinal cramps or feel like she has to move her bowels? This clearly indicates labor.

If after going through this checklist you have determined that delivery is imminent, and you don't have time to get to the hospital—roll up your sleeves (literally) and get ready!

When you must deliver...

When you know that you're not going to be able to get mom to definitive care in time, you must prepare to deliver the baby yourself. Remember, the human body is designed for this—your job is to be there to provide knowledge, encouragement, calm reassurance and to take action if things go wrong. "Emergency" may describe how you feel rather than the situation itself.

Emergency delivery procedure

If delivery is imminent—The baby is crowning (the top of the head is emerging from the birth canal) during a contraction—prepare for delivery. Obtain an obstetrics kit (OB kit): an OB kit typically contains: latex gloves, disposable plastic apron, plastic-lined underpad, receiving blanket, disposable towels, sterile gauze bandages, OB towelettes, a disposable scalpel, a bulb syringe, umbilical cord clamps, plastic bag (for the placenta), OB pad, twist ties. If you do not have access to an OB kit, fortunately, most of these items can be improvised—but remember, improvised tools may not be sterile.

1. **Properly position mom** in the semi-Fowler's position—supine, with upper body raised at an approximately 30 degree angle.

2. **Wash your hands** thoroughly and put on sterile gloves.

3. **Place absorbent material** under mom. Drape mom's legs and abdomen with sheets or similar (for comfort, protection, and dignity). Position yourself between mom's legs with multiple layers of towels on your lap.

4. **During a contraction**, use gentle pressure on the baby's head to prevent it from coming out too quickly (which can cause tissue damage to mom). Massage the labia (the folds of skin bordering the vulva—the external genitalia) to relax and stretch them around the head. This will help prevent tissue damage.

5. **When the head is delivered**, tell mom to stop pushing, and pant instead (you can't push and pant at the same time). This helps minimize the chance of tissue damage while the baby's body is being delivered. Check if the cord is wrapped around the baby's neck; move it if necessary. Use a bulb syringe to clear the baby's airway—mouth, then nose.

6. **During the final phase of delivery**, as the baby's head rotates (face down), support it and continue to suction the baby's mouth and nose. Deliver the anterior shoulder (the shoulder pointing upward) by lowering the baby's head. Support the baby's body as it is delivered; remember, the baby will be slippery.

7. **After the baby has been delivered**, clear the baby's airway again (mouth, then nose) with the bulb syringe. The baby should start to breathe immediately (within seconds). If it does not, stimulate the baby by tapping the feet or stroking the back.

8. **Place the baby in your lap** and wrap it with a clean, dry towel to keep it warm. Tie off and cut the umbilical cord; make sure that the clamped cord from the baby does not bleed—if it does, tighten the clamp or cord. Place the bundled baby by mom's breast—nursing will stimulate the delivery of the placenta. Record the time of delivery.

9. **After the baby is delivered**, the body will automatically expel the placenta (typically within 15 – 30 minutes)—save it in a plastic bag to give to the hospital personnel. To aid the uterus while it contracts, which helps control bleeding, have mom lay flat on her back and press straight down at her belly button. If the uterus is firm, it will feel like a grapefruit or a fist—and you don't have to massage. If it does not feel firm, cup your hand and move it in circular motions over the lower abdomen, pressing firmly—this may be somewhat painful. This will stimulate the uterus to contract and become firm. Transport mom and baby to definitive care as soon as you can.

*Ohhhh....
the perfect
little result
of a good
delivery!*

Common expedition...

ALLERGIES
- Remove the problem, or remove the patient from the problem.
- Use specific allergy medications if patient has them.
- Know how to identify and treat anaphylaxis.

BLISTERS
- Prevent first with correct sock/boot combination.
- It's best if blisters can heal by themselves, but they are difficult to hike on.
- To prevent surface skin from tearing, draining is recommended.
- Make a small pinhole at the base.
- Cover the area with a moleskin doughnut, lubricating the layer inside the hole; cover entire area with moleskin, tape, etc.
- Use tincture of benzoin to help adhere the bandage to the skin; it's very sticky and it toughens skin.

BURNS
- Remove the source; cool for 15 – 20 minutes.
- You may need to remove charred clothing or other burnt material from wound.
- Cover 1st and 2nd degree burns with moist, sterile dressing.
- Cover 3rd degree burns with a dry, sterile dressing.
- Keep the patient hydrated.
- Monitor for shock, dehydration, and infection.

COLDS/COUGH
- Probably related to allergies or adjusting to different environment.
- Treat with allergy medication and rest.
- Keep hydrated.

CONTACT DERMATITIS
- Poison ivy/oak/sumac skin allergies.
- Wash area with cool water and soft, mild soap.
- Sores are not contagious once the oil has been washed from the area.
- Severe reactions may need additional drugs.
- May need to evacuate.

DEHYDRATION
- Prevent.
- Rehydrate.
- Drink a lot.
- Drink often.

DIARRHEA
- The body is trying to flush out whatever the cause of the problem—help it.
- Keep the patient well-hydrated.
- Watch for nausea, fever, vomiting, etc.
- Patient can be given rice water or an over-the-counter medication such as Pepto-Bismol® or Imodium.
- Electrolytes will be lost and must be replaced (ORS, etc.).

FROSTBITE
- Prevention is best.
- Skin-to-skin rewarming for 1st and 2nd degree frostbite.
- Leave third degree frostbite frozen.
- Do not field rewarm.
- Insulate to prevent further freezing.
- Evacuate.

HEADACHE
- Probably associated with dehydration.
- Try rehydration before drugs.
- Follow local protocols.

INSECT BITES
- Protect with clothing and insecticides/repellents.
- Use topical itch cream on bites.
- Know how to recognize and treat anaphylaxis.

HEAT EXHAUSTION
- Prevention is easy.
- Don't overexert yourself, especially in hot/humid weather.
- Rest before you get overheated.
- Eat and drink enough (both quantity and frequency).
- Supplement plain water with beverages such as Gatorade, which help replenish electrolytes.
- Mild cases are relatively common.
- Can progress to heat stroke (which is life-threatening—please refer to the heat stroke section).

...problems

MINOR FRACTURES
- Splint and evacuate.

MINOR HYPOTHERMIA
- Remove the patient from environment.
- Get wet stuff off and put dry stuff on.
- Stoke the fire with warm, sweet liquids.
- Encourage light exercise if the patient feels up to it and the weather allows.
- Apply heat packs to the core and specific chilled areas.

MINOR MUSCULOSKELETAL INJURIES: STRAINS AND SPRAINS
- RICE.
- Remove boot if it's an ankle sprain.
- Apply cold for 20 – 30 minutes.
- Rewarm to normal body temperature.
- Test it—have the patient try to use it.
- Splint it if necessary.

MINOR SOFT TISSUE INJURIES
- Stop the bleeding.
- Prevent infection.
- Promote healing.

OBJECTS IN THE EYE
- Flush the eye thoroughly with clean water.
- Check for eye injuries.
- If a bandage is necessary, bandage both eyes to avoid sympathetic movement in the uninjured eye.
- Leave a pinhole in the uninjured eye so the patient can walk on their own.
- Do not remove objects impaled in the eye.
- Immobilize the object with a doughnut bandage.
- Evacuate.

RASHES: ATHLETE'S FOOT, JOCK ITCH
- Wash the area.
- Keep the area clean and dry.
- Use powder if available.

SMALL IMPALED OBJECTS
- Remove them.
- Wash area thoroughly with soap and water.
- Monitor for infection.

SUNBURN
- Prevention is best.
- Wear clothing that protects the arms, legs, neck, and head.
- Limit sun exposure, especially in the middle of the day.
- Use sunscreen with a minimum SPF of 15 (>30 is overkill).

URINARY TRACT INFECTIONS
- More prevalent in women.
- Potentially severe if the infection travels to the kidneys.
- Painful, burning, frequent urination.
- There may be blood in urine.
- Keep well-hydrated.
- Drink cranberry juice to offset pH in bladder.
- Evacuate the patient, as antibiotics will most likely be required.

VAGINITIS
- Itchy, painful inflammation with possible discharge.
- Caused by bacteria, yeast or parasite.
- Treat with prescription medications, including oral (Flagyl, Diflucan, Tindamax), gel (MetroGel), or cream (Cleocin, Monistat, Vagistat): which med(s) depends on proper diagnosis.

Adventure is almost always fun and rewarding. And fortunately, most emergencies are annoying rather than life-threatening—so get ready, and then get out there!

Summit of Bridge Mountain (6,955')
Spring Mountains, Nevada

Acronyms

(S)AMPLE	Signs/Symptoms, Allergies, Medications, Past Pertinent History, Last Oral Intake, Events
a&O	Alert and Oriented
a&O x 1	Alert and Oriented times one (person)
a&O x 2	Alert and Oriented times two (person, place)
a&O x 3	Alert and Oriented times three (person, place, time)
a&O x 4	Alert and Oriented times four (person, place, time, events)
AAA	Abdominal Aortic Aneurysm
ABCDE	Airway, Breathing, Circulation, Disability, Environment/ Exposure
ADL	Activities of Daily Living
AED	Automated External Defibrillator
AEIOU TIPS	Acidosis (or alcohol), Epilepsy, Infection, Overdose, Uremia, Trauma, Insulin, Psychosis, Stroke
AEMT	Advanced Emergency Medical Technician
AGE	Arterial Gas Embolism
AHA	American Heart Association
ALOC	Altered Level of Consciousness
ALS	Advanced Life Support
AMI	Acute Myocardial Infarction
AMS	Acute Mountain Sickness
APGAR	Appearance, Pulse, Grimace, Activity, Respiration
ART	Attitude, Resources, Techniques
ASAP	As Soon As Possible
ASTM	American Society for the Testing of Materials
AV	Atrioventricular Node
AVPU	Alert, Verbal, Pain, Unresponsive
BEAM	Body, Elevation, And Movement
BID	Twice a Day
BLS	Basic Life Support
BP	Blood Pressure
BSA	Body Surface Area
BSI	Body Substance Isolation
BUFF	Big, Ugly, Fat, Fluffy
BVM	Bag Valve Mask
C/C	Chief Complaint
CDC	Centers for Disease Control and Prevention
CHF	Congestive Heart Failure
CISD	Critical Incident Stress Debriefing
CNS	Central Nervous System
C/O	Complaining Of
COPD	Chronic Obstructive Pulmonary Disease
CP	Command Post
CPR	Cardiopulmonary Resuscitation

CSF	Cerebral Spinal Fluid
CSM	Circulation, Sensation, and Motion
CVA	Cerebrovascular Accident
CVD	Cardiovascular Disease
CVS	Cardiovascular System
DEET	Diethyltoluamide
DNR	Do Not Resuscitate
DO	Doctor of Osteopathy
DOA	Dead On Arrival
DOT	Department of Transportation
DRT	Dead Right There
DT	Diphtheria & Tetanus Booster
DTs	Delirium Tremens
ECG	Electrocardiogram
ED	Emergency Department
EGTA	Esophageal Gastric Tube Airway
EKG	Electro-cardiogram (also ECG)
EMR	Emergency Medical Responder (the street term for FR)
EMS	Emergency Medical Services
EMT	Emergency Medical Technician
EOA	Esophageal Obturator Airway
ER	Emergency Room
ETA	Estimated Time of Arrival
ET	Endotracheal Tube
ETOH	Alcohol
FAST	Face, arms/legs, speech, time
FBLP	Full Bore Linear Panic
FBAO	Foreign Body Airway Obstruction
FEMA	Federal Emergency Management Agency
FOAM	Free of Any Movement
FR	First Responder (see EMR)
FUS	Fat Ugly Splint
Fx	Fracture
GI	Gastrointestinal
H7	Hypothermia, Hyperthermia, Hypoglycemia, Hyperglycemia, Hypoxia, Hypovolemia, Head Injury
HAC	High-Altitude Cachexia (extreme weight loss)
HACE	High-Altitude Cerebral Edema
HAFE	High-Altitude Flatulent Expulsion
HAPE	High-Altitude Pulmonary Edema
HARH	High-Altitude Retinal Hemorrhage
HAV	Hepatitis A Virus
HAZMAT	Hazardous Materials
HBV	Hepatitis B Virus
HIV	Human Immunodeficiency Virus
HMO	Health Maintenance Organization
HPI	History of Present Illness
HR	Heart Rate

HTN	Hypertension
Hx	History
IC	Incident Commander
ICP	Intracranial Pressure
ICS	Incident Command System
ICU	Intensive Care Unit
IM	Immediate Treatment
IV	Intravenous
JVD	Jugular Vein Distention
KED	Kendrick Extrication Device
KTD	Kendrick Traction Device
LAF	Look, Ask, Feel
LLQ	Left Lower Quadrant
LOC	Level of Consciousness
LPM	Liters per Minute
LT RX	Long-Term Treatment
LUQ	Left Upper Quadrant
MAST	Medical Anti-shock Trousers
MCI	Mass (Multiple) Casualty Incident
MD	Medical Doctor
MDI	Metered Dose Inhaler
MI	Myocardial Infarction
mmHg	Millimeters of Mercury
MMI	Marine Medicine Institute
MMR	Measles, Mumps, and Rubella
MOI	Mechanism of Injury
MVA	Motor Vehicle Accident
NAEMT	National Association of Emergency Medical Technicians
NOI	Nature of Illness
NPA	Nasopharyngeal Airway
NRB	Non-rebreather (oxygen mask)
NREMT	National Registry of Emergency Medical Technicians
NSAID	Non-steroidal Anti-inflammatory Drugs (e.g., ibuprofen)
N/V	Nausea and/or Vomiting
OBGYN	Obstetrics and Gynecology
OPA	Oropharyngeal Airway
OPV	Oral Polio Vaccine
OPQRST	(re: pain) Onset, Palliates/ Provokes, Quality, Radiates, Severity, Time
OR	Operating Room
OSS	Oregon Spine Splint
OTC	Over-the-Counter
PAS	Patient Assessment System
PASG	Pneumatic Anti-shock Garment
PCR	Patient Care Report
PERRL	Pupils Equal, Round, Reactive to Light
PNS	Peripheral Nervous System
PO	By Mouth (for administering medications)
PR	By Rectum (for administering medications)
POC	Position of Comfort

POF	Position of Function
PT	Patient
QD	One a Day
QID	Four Times a Day
RBC	Red Blood Cell
RICE	Rest, Ice, Compression, Elevation
RLQ	Right Lower Quadrant
RMSF	Rocky Mountain Spotted Fever
ROM	Range of Motion
RR	Respiratory Rate
RRQ	Rate, Rhythm, Quality
RUQ	Right Upper Quadrant
Rx	Prescription (Treatment)
S/S	Signs and Symptoms
SA Node	Sinoatrial Node
SAR	Search and Rescue
SCTM	Skin, Color, Temperature, Moisture
SHARP	Swollen, Hot, Achy, Red, Pus (signs of infection)
SOAP	Subjective, Objective, Assessment, Plan
SOB	Shortness of Breath
SOLO	Stonehearth Open Learning Opportunities
STI	Soft Tissue Injury
TBO	"The Big One" (Heart Attack)
TBSA	Total Body Surface Area (pertaining to burns)
TIA	Transient Ischemic Attack
TID	Three Times a Day
TIL	Traction-In-Line
Tx	Traction
UTI	Urinary Tract Infection
VF	(V-Fib) Ventricular Fibrillation
VS	Vital Signs
VT	(V-Tach) Ventricular Tachycardia
WBC	White Blood Cell
WEMT	Wilderness Emergency Medical Technician
WFR	Wilderness First Responder
WHO	World Health Organization
WMS	Wilderness Medical Society

Prefixes (with examples)

a/an—without; absence of (asystole)

brady—slow (bradycardia)

cardio—having to do with the heart (cardiovascular)

cerebro—having to do with the brain (cerebrospinal)

contra—opposed to (contraindicated)

cyan—blue (cyanosis)

dys—difficult (dyspnea)

epi—above, upon (epidermis)

gastro—having to do with the stomach (gastroenteritis)

glyco—sugar (glycogen)

hepato—having to do with the liver (hepatitis)

hemi—half (hemiplegia)

hemo or hema—having to do with the blood (hemoglobin)

hyper—too much (hypertension)

hypo—too little (hypothermia)

intra—inside (intracranial)

myo—muscle (myocardium)

neo—new (neonate)

peri—around (periosteum)

pneumo—air (pneumothorax)

pulmo—lungs (pulmonary)

poly—many, much (polyuria: too much urine)

retro—behind (retroperitoneal)

sub—below, under (subdural)

tachy—rapid (tachycardia)

vaso—having to do with the vessels (vasogenic)

Suffixes (with examples)

algia—pain, painful condition (neuralgia)

ectomy—to remove surgically (appendectomy)

emia—blood (hypoglycemia)

esthesia—sensation (paresthesia)

genic—originating from (neurogenic)

gram—record (electrocardiogram)

ia—state or condition (pneumonia)

ion—process (extraction)

itis—inflammation (arthritis)

ology—science of (osteology)

opia—vision (myopia)

(o) stomy—to make an opening (tracheostomy)

(o) tomy—cutting into (lobotomy)

pathy—disease of (osteopathy)

plegia—paralysis (hemiplegia)

paresis—weakness (hemiparesis)

pnea—breathe, breathing (dyspnea)

Glossary

Abolition — Elimination or stopping of

Abscess — Localized collection of pus

Abrasion — An area of the epidermis and dermis that is scraped

Accessory muscles — Secondary muscles used to assist breathing during respiratory distress—many accessory muscles are located in the neck

Acidosis — An abnormal increase of hydrogen ion concentration in the body that causes the blood pH to fall below normal levels, as in diabetic ketoacidosis

Acute — Characterized by rapid onset, severe symptoms, and a short course

Adrenaline — A hormone released by the body in response to stress—it has many effects on the body including increased heart rate, respiratory rate, and blood pressure (Synonym epinephrine)

Agonal — Very painful—associated with the pain of dying

Alkalosis — Excess of alkali or reductions of acid in the body; common causes include hyperventilation, excessive vomiting/diarrhea

Allergen — A substance that produces a hypersensitive reaction in the body; there are many different kinds of allergens (pollen, various foods, etc.), and the reactions they cause range from insignificant to life-threatening; related terms anaphylaxis, histamine

Alveoli — Extremely small air sacs in the lungs where gas exchange occurs

Ambient — Surrounding—in the context of wilderness emergencies it typically refers to the pure temperature of the environment without taking into account other factors, such as wind

Amniotic sac — (aka "bag of waters") sac of fluid containing the developing fetus

Anaerobic — Living without oxygen—relating to microorganisms that can live and grow without the presence of oxygen

Ana-kit — A kit consisting of epinephrine and antihistamines used to treat someone in anaphylactic shock (aka, "bee-sting kit")

Anaphylaxis — An exaggerated, life-threatening allergic reaction that causes bronchoconstriction and vasodilation

Aneurysm — A ballooned-out area of a blood vessel caused by the weakening of the vessel wall

Angina — A condition marked by intense, suffocating pain; one who suffers angina pectoris usually has severe substernal pain that can radiate to the jaw, arms and abdomen

Anoxia — A deficiency of oxygen

Anterior — Toward the front; on the belly side

Antibody — A specific, protective protein made in response to an antigen; antibodies fight antigens

Antigen — A foreign protein or substance that stimulates the formation of antibodies

Antivenom — An antitoxin specific to an animal or insect venom

Aphasia — Difficulty in speaking and/or understanding speech caused by an injury or disease that affects the speech centers in the brain

Apnea — An absence of breathing

Arrhythmia — Abnormality in the rhythm of the heart

Arteriole — A small artery

Artery — A muscular, thick-walled blood vessel that carries blood away from the heart

Asphyxia — Suffocation

Aspiration — The accidental inhalation of fluid and/or particles into the lungs

Asystole — Absent ventricular contractions resulting in a loss of a detectable balance

Ataxia — Lack of coordination—the inability to coordinate muscles correctly

Atherosclerosis — The thickening and hardening of arteries

Atria — The upper chambers of the heart—the right atrium receives blood from the body; the left atrium receives blood from the lungs

Atrophy — The deterioration or decrease in size of tissue due to lack of use

Aura — A peculiar sensation or warning of an impending attack (e.g., seizure)

Auscultate — To listen through a stethoscope

Avulsion — A soft tissue injury that leaves a flap of skin partially attached to the body

Axillary — Region of the body commonly called the armpit

Bandage — Any material used to hold a dressing in place

Baroreceptor	A sensing mechanism located in the aortic arch and carotid sinus that detects changes in blood pressure	**Cerebral**	Pertaining to the brain	**Contusion**	A bruise—an injury that causes hemorrhaging in or beneath the skin without breaking the skin
		Cervical	Pertaining to the neck, as in the cervical vertebrae		
Barotrauma	Physical damage to body tissues caused by a difference in pressure between an air space inside or beside the body and the surrounding fluid—scuba divers sometimes suffer barotrauma as a result of the combination of extreme water pressure and insufficient time spent decompressing	**Cervix**	The neck, or lower part, of the uterus; also, any neck-like structure	**Convection**	The transfer of heat in gas or liquid caused by the circulation of currents; a person standing in the wind loses heat via convection
		Cheyne-Stokes breathing	An abnormal breathing pattern characterized by a series of quick breaths followed by no breaths at all	**Coronary**	Pertaining to the blood vessels that supply blood to the heart itself
		Chronic	Long, drawn out—used to describe a disease that is not acute, e.g., chronic bronchitis	**Costal**	Pertaining to the ribs
				Crackles	Fine or coarse bubbling sounds produced by fluids in the lower airway
		Coccyx	Pertaining to the lowest part of the spine—the coccyx vertebrae	**Cranial**	Pertaining to the skull
Bifurcate	To divide into two branches	**Colostomy**	Establishment of an artificial cutaneous opening into the colon	**Cravat**	A piece of material used for bandaging and/or making slings
Bleb	Blister				
Bounding	Leaping—often used to describe a patient who has an abnormally strong, throbbing pulse	**Compensatory**	Stabilizing; serving as a substitute or counterbalance; used to describe the first stage of shock in which the body tries to compensate	**Crepitus**	Grating and crunching of fractured bone ends—crepitus can be felt and heard
Brachial	Pertaining to the arm—A brachial pulse can be taken between the biceps and triceps muscles of the upper arm	**Compliance**	The act of following another's will; in medical terms, it describes the stiffness of the lungs; as compliance decreases, the lungs become more difficult to artificially ventilate	**Crowning**	The stage during childbirth when the presenting part of the baby can be seen at the opening of the vagina
Bradycardia	Slow heart rate, less than 60 beats per minute				
Bronchi	The two tubes that the trachea splits into at its lower end			**Cyanosis**	Bluish coloration of the skin due to lack of oxygen and excess carbon dioxide in the blood
Bronchospasm	A sudden constriction of the bronchial tubes due to involuntary plain muscle in their walls	**Concussion**	An injury to an organ, especially the brain, caused by violent jarring and followed by a temporary or prolonged loss of function	**Cardiothoracic**	Pertaining to the heart and chest cavity
				Carina	Where the trachea splits into the two main bronchi
Bronchus	One of the main branches of the lungs	**Conduction**	The transfer of heat through one object to another—A person lying directly on cold ground loses heat via conduction	**Cosmesis**	Appearance and shape
Cardiac	Pertaining to the heart			**Dead space**	That portion of inhaled air that does not reach the alveoli and so is not involved in gas exchange
Carotid	Either of two main arteries, one on either side of the neck, that supply blood to the head				
		Congenital	Any condition that exists or was acquired before birth	**Death, biological**	Irreversible brain damage
Cartilage	Tough, relatively elastic tissue that works like bone to support the body; among other places, cartilage is found in the nose, ears, and joints	**Contraindication**	A situation that prohibits the use of a drug or treatment	**Death, clinical**	The moment that the heart stops
				Debridement	Excision of devitalized tissue and foreign matter from a wound
Cephalic	Pertaining to the head				

Decompensatory	Characterized by the inability of the heart to maintain adequate blood circulation—describes the second stage of shock in which all body functions fail rapidly	**Ecchymosis**	Discoloration or bluing of the skin	**Fibrillation**	Disorganized movements of the heart muscle resulting in ineffectual contractions of the heart chambers
		Eclampsia	A condition that occurs during pregnancy and is characterized by high blood pressure and seizures—also called toxemia	**Flaccid**	Soft, limp
Defibrillate	Use of electric shock to stop ventricular fibrillation			**Flail**	To wave or swing vigorously as in a flail chest that moves erratically because it is unstable
Dementia	General mental deterioration due to organic or psychologic factors	**Ectopic**	Located away from normal position as in an ectopic pregnancy where the embryo develops in a space other than the uterus		
Dependent lividity	A bruising or darkened discoloration on the bottom side of the body, caused by blood leaking from the vasculature after death			**Flexion**	The act of flexing or bending; bending of a joint so as to approximate the parts it connects—opposite of extension
		Edema	Swelling		
		Embolism	A solid, liquid, or gaseous mass that circulates in the blood and can potentially block blood vessels	**Gastric**	Pertaining to the stomach
Dermis	The inner or middle layer of skin that contains hair follicle roots, sweat glands, nerves, and blood vessels			**Glucose**	Simple sugar used by the cell for energy
		Endotracheal	Within or through the trachea	**Halogenation**	Using one of the chlorine group of elements (iodine or chlorine, specifically) to disinfect water
Diagnosis	Identification of a disease or condition	**Epidermis**	The outermost layer of skin		
Diaphoretic (sweating)	Often used to describe patients who are pale, cool and clammy	**Epinephrine**	See adrenaline		
		EpiPen	An auto-injectable means of delivering epinephrine, used to treat someone in anaphylactic shock	**Hematoma**	Swelling filled with blood
Diastole	The period of ventricular relaxation when the ventricles rest and refill with blood			**Hematopoiesis**	The formation of blood
		Epistaxis	A nosebleed	**Hyperbaric**	A condition of increased pressure
Differential diagnosis	A systematic method used to identify unknowns, typically through a process of elimination—used by medical professionals to help make a diagnosis	**Evaporation**	The changing of a liquid into a gas—sweating works as a cooling mechanism because of the heat transfer that occurs as the moisture on the skin evaporates	**Hemiparesis**	Weakness on one side of the body
				Hemiplegia	Paralysis of one half of the body
				Hemoglobin	A protein that carries oxygen in the blood
		Evisceration	An injury that causes organs in the abdomen to protrude from the body	**Hemorrhage**	Bleeding, especially severe bleeding
Dilate	To get wider or larger, to expand			**Hemothorax**	Bleeding into the pleural cavity of the lungs
Diplopia	Double vision, seeing two objects when only one is present	**Exacerbate**	To make worse, to aggravate		
		Extension	To stretch out, the act of bringing the distal portion of a joint in continuity with the long axis of the proximal portion—opposite of flexion	**Hernia**	Protrusion of any organ into a space where it does not belong
Distal	Farther from the heart as a point of reference—the ankle is distal to the knee			**Histamine**	A protein released by the body in response to an antigen—histamine can cause inflammation, vasodilation, and bronchoconstriction
Dorsal	Toward the back, posterior	**Febrile**	Characterized by fever		
		Femoral	Pertaining to the femur or the thigh—the femoral artery delivers blood to the leg		
Dressing	Sterile material that is placed directly on a wound			**Hitch**	A fastening loop or knot, often which can be released by pulling against the strain that holds it
Dyspnea	Difficulty breathing, shortness of breath				

Homeostasis	A tendency to constancy and stability in the body, equilibrium	**Infarction**	Death of tissue caused by cutting off the blood supply to that tissue	**Larynx**	Voice box, a structure made of cartilage and muscles that is located between the pharynx and the trachea
Hydration	The taking in of water	**Inhaler**	An apparatus for administering pharmacologically active agents by inhalation	**Lateral**	Of or towards the side, away from the midline of the body
Hydrophobia	Literally, a fear of water, one of the signs/symptoms of rabies (rabies is sometimes referred to as hydrophobia)	**Irrigation**	The washing out of a cavity or wound with fluid	**Lethargic**	Extreme sleepiness combined with apathy and sluggish behavior
Hyperglycemia	Abnormally high concentration of sugar in the blood	**Insulin**	A hormone that helps the body utilize sugar	**Ligament**	Fibrous tissue that connects bones to other bones
Hypoglycemia	Abnormally low concentration of sugar in the blood	**Integument**	Skin	**Lumbar**	Pertaining to the lower back as in the lumbar vertebrae
Hypokalemia	Abnormally low concentrations of potassium in the blood	**Intravenous**	Within or into a vein		
		Intubation	The placement of a tube into the trachea or esophagus	**Lymph**	Colorless fluid that circulates in the lymphatic system and helps remove bacteria and certain proteins from cells
Hyponatremia	Abnormally low concentration of sodium in the blood	**Ischemia**	Lack of oxygen in a tissue as a result of lack of blood-flow to that tissue		
Hypoperfusion	Lack of supply of oxygenated blood to cells (shock)	**Jugular**	Pertaining to the throat or neck as in the jugular veins that carry blood away from the head	**Lysis**	Disintegration of membrane of cells or bacteria
Hypotension	Low blood pressure systolic <110, diastolic <70			**Mania**	An emotional disorder characterized by euphoria, increased psychomotor activity, rapid speech, flight of ideas, decreased need for sleep, distractibility, grandiosity, and poor judgment—usually occurs in bipolar disorder
Hypothalamus	A region of the brain that regulates many fundamental body functions, including temperature	**Ketoacidosis**	A condition in which the body metabolizes fat and produces too many ketones and acids in the blood causing thirst, urination, nausea, vomiting, and sometimes coma		
Hypovolemia	Abnormally decreased amount of blood and fluids in the body				
		Kussmaul's breathing	Deep, heavy breathing that attempts to blow off body wastes—Kussmaul's breathing is characteristic of a diabetic in ketoacidosis	**Meconium**	Fetal intestinal contents that stain the amniotic fluid green or black
Hypoxic	Used to describe someone who has a deficiency of oxygen at the cellular level—someone who is hypoxic may be restless, short of breath, confused, and/or lethargic			**Medial**	Toward the midline of the body
		Labored	Requiring a lot of effort, strained	**Mediastinum**	The space between the lungs
Ileostomy	Establishment of a passage through which the ileum discharges directly to the outside of the body	**Laceration**	A cut or tear in the skin—lacerations vary in dimension and severity depending upon their location and whether they have gone through any major blood vessels	**Meninges**	Highly vascular membranes that separate the brain from the skull
				Metabolism	The sum of the chemical changes occurring in tissue
Incontinence	The inability to control the elimination of urine or feces			**Midline**	Imaginary line running vertically from the nose through the belly button thus splitting the body in half
Indications	The circumstances under which a drug or treatment is suited for use	**Laryngospasm**	Convulsive involuntary muscular contraction of the larynx, usually accompanied by spasmodic closure of the glottis		
Inebriated	Intoxication, especially from alcohol			**Myocardial**	Pertaining to the musculature of the heart (myo = muscle)

Narcosis	Unconscious state caused by narcotics or other toxic substances in the body	**Pathogen**	An agent that causes a disease	**Prognosis**	Probable outlook for recovery
Necrosis	Death of tissue, usually caused by lack of blood supply	**Pedal**	Pertaining to the foot	**Prone**	Lying flat with the face downward
Nematocyst	A stinging cell of coelenterates consisting of a poison sac and a coiled barbed stinger capable of being ejected and penetrating the skin of an animal on contact—of considerable consequence in large jellyfish and Portuguese man-of-war, whose large numbers of these stinging cells can cause great pain and even death	**Perfusion**	The flow of blood through tissue such that the tissue has an adequate supply of oxygen and nutrients	**Prophylactic**	Preventative—e.g., taking one aspirin a day as a prophylactic measure
		Pericardium	The thin sac surrounding the heart	**Proteinuria**	The presence of urinary protein
		Peripheral	Pertaining to an outside boundary or outer edge—the peripheral nervous system consists of all the nerves that extend from the brain and spinal cord	**Proximal**	Closer to the heart as a point of reference—the knee is proximal to the ankle
				Psychogenic	Arising from the mind, as opposed to the body
		Pertinent	Relevant, having logical, precise relevance to the matter at hand	**Pulmonary**	Pertaining to the lungs
				Purulence	The condition of containing or forming pus
Neurogenic	Originating in or pertaining to the nervous system	**Pharynx**	The portion of the airway between the nasal cavity and the larynx—The pharynx includes the nasopharynx, oropharynx and laryngopharynx	**Radial**	Pertaining to the wrist—a radial pulse can be taken at the wrist
Obligate	Characterized by the ability to survive only in a particular set of environmental conditions			**Radiation**	Emission of energy in rays or waves—a campfire radiates heat
Occlusion	Obstruction, blockage—a blood clot can cause the occlusion of a vessel	**Pituitary**	A gland located in the brain and responsible for regulating all other glands	**Rales**	Fine breath sounds that represent the opening of collapsed alveoli—the sound can be simulated by rubbing hair between the fingers
Palliate	To make less severe or intense, to mitigate, to relieve	**Pleura**	Membranes that line the outer surface of the lungs, the inner surface of the chest wall, and the thoracic surface of the diaphragm	
Pallor	Extreme or unnatural paleness			**Renal**	Pertaining to the kidneys
Palpate	To examine or explore by touching			**Rigor**	A shaking chill
Palpitate	To move with a tremulous motion, to tremble, shake, or quiver	**Pneumothorax**	Air trapped in the pleural space that can cause the underlying lung to collapse	**Rigor mortis**	The stiffening of the body after death
				Sacrum	Pertaining to the lower spine as in the sacral vertebrae
Paradoxical	Contradictory, when used to describe respirations, paradoxical refers to the collapse of the chest upon inhalation (as opposed to the expected chest rise)	**Polydipsia**	Excessive thirst that is relatively chronic	**Sepsis**	Infection, contamination
		Polyphagia	Excessive eating	**Septum**	A dividing wall that usually separates two cavities
		Polyuria	Excessive excretion of urine	
		Posterior	On the back or dorsal side	**Shock**	Inadequate tissue perfusion caused by a number of conditions including but not limited to heart failure, nerve failure, and loss of blood volume
Paresis	Slight paralysis or weakness	**Postictal**	Pertaining to the period after the convulsive state of a seizure	
Paresthesia	A numbness or pins-and-needles sensation that indicates some disturbance in nerve function	**Priapism**	Sustained erection of the penis, sometimes associated with spinal cord injury	**Sign**	An indication of injury or illness that the examiner observes
Parietal	Pertaining to a wall			
Patent	Not blocked, open; expanded	**Primigravida**	A woman in her first pregnancy	

Sling	A securing device that runs around the arm and the back of the neck such that it immobilizes the arm	**Tidal volume**	The volume of one breath
Splint	A device that supplies stabilization and immobilization to an unstable body part	**Tonic-clonic**	Tonic—state of continuous muscular contraction; Clonic—series of intermittent muscular contraction and relaxation
Sprain	An injury in which a ligament is stretched or torn	**Tracheal shift**	Movement of the trachea away from midline
Sputum	Expectorated (coughed-up) matter, especially mucous associated with lung diseases	**Traction**	The act of drawing or pulling, a pulling or dragging force exerted on a limb in a distal direction
Strain	The over-stretching of a muscle or the injury of a muscle, often from overuse	**Urticaria**	Hives
		Vasoconstriction	The narrowing of blood vessels
Stridor	A harsh, high-pitched sound associated with severe upper airway obstruction	**Vasodilation**	The widening of blood vessels
		Vector	A carrier, often an invertebrate animal (tick, mite, mosquito, fly, etc.) capable of transmitting an infectious agent among vertebrates, transmitting a pathogen from a reservoir to a host
Subcutaneous	Underneath the skin		
Sublingual	Beneath the tongue		
Superficial	On the surface		
Supine	Lying flat with the face upwards	**Vein**	A blood vessel that carries blood toward the heart
Swath	Something tied around the body to enhance the immobilization of a part	**Ventral**	Toward the front, anterior
		Ventricle	A thick-walled lower chamber of the heart that receives blood from the atrium and pumps it out to the lungs and body
Symptom	An indication of illness or injury that is not observable and must be related by the patient		
Syncope	A brief lapse in consciousness	**Vertigo**	A sensation of irregular or whirling motion, either of oneself or of external objects, imprecisely used as a general term to describe dizziness
Systemic	Throughout the entire body		
Systole	Period during which the ventricles contract and are active		
Tachycardia	Rapid heart rate, over 100 beats per minute	**Visceral**	Pertaining to the organs of the chest or abdomen
Tachypnea	Increased rate of respirations		
Tendon	A tough band of fibrous connective tissue that attaches to muscle to bone		
Thoracic	Pertaining to the thorax, as in the thoracic vertebrae		
Thready	Weak and shallow, as in a thready pulse		
Thrombolysis	The process of dissolving blood clots		

IMAGE CREDITS (all images used by permission in accordance with copyright laws)

Page	Credit/source
cover	Martin M303, Shutterstock.com (Isle of Skye, Scotland)
2	S. Peter Lewis for SOLO
4	S. Peter Lewis for SOLO (Frank Hubbell, selfie, Lee Frizzell, T.B.R Walsh for SOLO (selfie), Liam Quinn, Flickr (penguins)
5	S. Peter Lewis for SOLO (Jill MacMillan, Josh MacMillan, Paul MacMillan (selfie) Frank Hubbell (Frank and Lee)
6	John Nyberg, stock.xchng.com (ocean)
8	SOLO (classroom, campus)
9	Frank Hubbell for SOLO (Haiti, earthquake), S. Peter Lewis (Mt. Washington)
10	Mister Falcon (ambulance), Chuck Abbe (rollover accident), Edith Wolfson Medical Center and Deror avi (operating room), public domain (helicopter), T.B.R. Walsh for SOLO (dislocation drawing), S. Peter Lewis for SOLO (traction splint, bivouac, litter carry)
11	Steffen Zelzer, stock.xchng.com (highway), Flávio Mendonça, stock.xchng.com (ocean), Me Me, stock.xchng.com (mountain), Shlomi Kastoryano, stock.xchng.com (moon)
12	S. Peter Lewis for SOLO (head)
13	S. Peter Lewis for SOLO (hand)
17	S. Peter Lewis for SOLO (virus caricature)
18	T.B.R. Walsh for SOLO (blood splatter, airborne, doorknob, mosquito, dog and toilet)
19	S. Peter Lewis for SOLO (gloved hands), T.B.R. Walsh for SOLO (mask, goggles), Martin Sach, stock.xchng.com (mosquito)
20	S. Peter Lewis for SOLO (syringe), public domain (polio stamp)
21	T.B.R. Walsh for SOLO (body systems)
22	Eric Jensen (mountain bike), Dalibor Ogrizovic (stopwatch)
24	T.B.R. Walsh for SOLO (stop/go), OCAL, Clker.com (falling man silhouette)
25	S. Peter Lewis for SOLO (hand on head), T.B.R. Walsh for SOLO (look, listen, feel)
26	S. Peter Lewis for SOLO (airway, chin lift, rescue breath), T.B.R. Walsh for SOLO (recovery position)
27	S. Peter Lewis for SOLO (chest rise, log roll, mouth-to-mask, BVM), Tony Meiklejohn (alone sidebar)
28	S. Peter Lewis for SOLO (carotid, CPR, bleeding), Tony Meiklejohn (stop CPR)
29	S. Peter Lewis for SOLO (deformity, traction splint, assessing spine, c-collar)
30	S. Peter Lewis for SOLO (scene safe, moving onto pad, film strip)
31	Tony Meiklejohn (others in group), Wikipedia.org (tent)
33	S. Peter Lewis for SOLO (hand), T. B. R. Walsh for SOLO (AVPU), Steve Ford Elliott, Flickr.com (bubbles)
34	S. Peter Lewis for SOLO (radial pulse, blood pressure)
35	S. Peter Lewis for SOLO (skin, capillary refill, pupils)
36	S. Peter Lewis for SOLO (cutting jeans, scanning for deformity, listening, palpating abdomen)
37	S. Peter Lewis for SOLO (palpation, head, neck, shoulder, chest)
38	S. Peter Lewis for SOLO (abdomen, pelvis, legs, arms, back)
39	S. Peter Lewis for SOLO (patient interview)
40	S. Peter Lewis for SOLO (SOAPnote)
42	Ernie Mills (rescue, image modified)
43	S. Peter Lewis for SOLO (improvised map)
44	S. Peter Lewis for SOLO (lifting, crane graphic)
45	S. Peter Lewis for SOLO (patient assessment checklist)
46	Ernie Mills (water rescue)
48	S. Peter Lewis for SOLO (level of consciousness)
50	Geo Okretic (airway), stock.xchng.com (meatball)
51	iStockphoto.com (clouds), S. Peter Lewis for SOLO (woman)
52	B S K, stock.xchng. com (blood), Ivan Prole, stock.xchng.com (bottles—modified)
53	S. Peter Lewis for SOLO (direct pressure, tourniquet)
54	S. Peter Lewis for SOLO (chest pain), Esra Su (aspirin), stock.xchng.com (wasp)
55	Michael Lorenzo, stock.xchng.com (header electricity)
56	Wikimedia Commons (Matterhorn disaster)
58	S. Peter Lewis for SOLO (ice climber)
60	Wikimedia Commons (X-ray), T.B.R. Walsh for SOLO (injury montage drawing)
61	S. Peter Lewis for SOLO (skin), Paul Englefield, Flickr.com (pig)
62	S. Peter Lewis for SOLO (skin), T.B.R. Walsh for SOLO (skin diagram), stock.xchng.com (girl)
63	Leroy Skalstad (man), Tom Terwilliger, Wikimedia Commons (bodybuilder)
64	Wikimedia Commons (ankle)
65	T.B.R. Walsh for SOLO (circulatory system), S. Peter Lewis for SOLO (direct pressure, pressure dressing)
66	Wikimedia Commons (commercial tourniquet), S. Peter Lewis for SOLO (improvised tourniquet)
67	T.B.R. Walsh (cleaning wound)
68	S. Peter Lewis for SOLO (abscess, laceration, avulsion, impaled object, burn, hand), Berkely Robinson, stock.xchng.com (blister), James Heilman, MD, Wikimedia Commons (puncture), Berteun, Wikimedia Commons (abrasion), Neeta Lind, Wikimedia Commons (amputation)
69	S. Peter Lewis for SOLO (ACE bandage, gauze), T.B.R. Walsh for SOLO (raccoons), Wikimedia Commons (abrasion)
70	S. Peter Lewis for SOLO (bandages, laceration, avulsion)
71	Neeta Lind, Wikimedia Commons (amputation), S. Peter Lewis for SOLO (finger on ice, foot with banana), James Heilman, MD, Wikimedia Commons (puncture)
72	S. Peter Lewis for SOLO (puncture in foot, ice axe in abdomen)
73	S. Peter Lewis for SOLO (fishhook)
74	S. Peter Lewis for SOLO (pressure bandage)
75	S. Peter Lewis for SOLO (all bandage materials and bandaging images)
76 – 78	T. B. R. Walsh for SOLO (all bandaging sequence drawings), S. Peter Lewis for SOLO (jacket sling, pg., 77)
79	William Warby (flames)
80	Jon Sullivan (flames in header), B. Cleary (flame), Snack Admiral, stock.xchng.com (match), stock.xchng.com (power lines, nuclear plants), Mathieu Boise, Wikimedia Commons (batteries)
81	Iker, stock.xchng.com (smoke), Wikimedia Commons (burn),T.B.R. Walsh for SOLO (burn diagrams)
82	T.B.R. Walsh for SOLO (burn coverage diagrams), Wikimedia Commons (matches)
83	Tony Meiklejohn (facial burn)
84	Public domain (background fire)
85	S. Peter Lewis for SOLO (all burn images), Raphael Pinto, stock.xchng.com (quarter)
86	David Duncan, stock.xchng.com (coals)
87	Stock.xchng.com (smoke), Brent Pin (sunrise), Marek Brzezinski, iStockphoto.com (skin)
88	Nadya Peek, Wikimedia Commons (toe), Richard Dudley, stock.xchng.com (canoe), T.B.R. Walsh for SOLO (blister treatment)
89	Grzegorz Rejniak, stock.xcnhg.com (boot), T.B.R. Walsh for SOLO (blister diagrams), stockxxchng.com (bubble wrap)
90	James Heilman, MD, Wikimedia Commons (cellulitis)
91	S. Peter Lewis for SOLO (diagrams)
92	T.B.R. Walsh for SOLO (lymphatic diagram), Wikimedia Commons (abscess), S. Peter Lewis for SOLO (abscess illustration)
93	Wikimedia Commons (dental abscess), T.B.R. Walsh for SOLO (abscess incising)
95	S. Peter Lewis for SOLO (foot)
96	Mihai Tamisila, stock.xchng.com (eye), S. Peter Lewis for SOLO (eye injury illustration)
97	Patrick J. Lynch, Wikimedia Commons (eye vision illustration), Flickr.com (brain), T.B.R. Walsh for SOLO (eye anatomy illustration), Constantin Jurcut, stock.xchng.com (eye background)
98	S. Peter Lewis for SOLO (all illustrations), stock.xchng.com (eye)
99	S. Peter Lewis for SOLO (visual fields, extraocular movement)
100	Wikimedia Commons (eye background), S. Peter Lewis for SOLO (checking pupils), T.B.R. Walsh for SOLO (hyphema, inverting eyelid)
101	Wikimedia Commons (speck in eye), S. Peter Lewis for SOLO (Kleenex)
102	Free.extras.com (eye background), Dion Gillard, Flickr.com (blunt trauma), S. Peter Lewis for SOLO (glasses with pinhole)
103	Wikimedia Commons (eye background), T.B.R. Walsh for SOLO (impaled object treatment)
104	Wikimedia Commons (eye background), S. Peter Lewis for SOLO (eye icon, rinsing eye), T.B.R. Walsh for SOLO (detached retina)
105	Wikimedia Commons (welding), Alex Shröder, Flickr.com (glacier glasses)
106	Gökç Özaslan, stock.xchng.com (smile), T.B.R. Walsh for SOLO (tooth anatomy illustration)
107	T.B.R. Walsh for SOLO (teeth diagram)
108	S. Peter Lewis for SOLO (palate eval, Cavit), Wikimedia Commons (broken tooth), Amanda Slater (cloves)
109	S. Peter Lewis for SOLO (luxation), Wikimedia Commons (avulsion)
110	Wikimedia Commons (X-ray, dental caries)
111	Wikimedia Commons (oral abscess), Flickr.com (statue)
112	T.B.R. Walsh for SOLO (musculoskeletal illustration)
113	deafstar, stock.xchng.com (gears)
114	T.B.R. Walsh (all illustrations)
115	Nick Lobek, stockx.chng.com (bone), T.B.R. Walsh for SOLO (skeleton illustration), Julien Tromeur (torso background)
116	T.B.R. Walsh for SOLO (injury drawings)
117	S. Peter Lewis for SOLO (evaluating injury)
118	Wikimedia Commons (foot), Quinn Dambrowski, Flickr.com (bag of ice), S. Peter Lewis for SOLO (ankle in stream, ankle range of motion)
119	S. Peter Lewis for SOLO (runner, ankle wrap)
120	J. P. Davidson, Flickr (background), Miguel Saavedra, stock.xchng.com (arm in cast), Dimashoo, Flickr.com (bike crash)
121	T.B.R. Walsh for SOLO (fracture drawings)
122	Wikimedia Commons (bone matrix background), Zach Dishner (skier), S. Peter Lewis for SOLO (arm eval)
123	S. Peter Lewis for SOLO (traction in line), Tony Meiklejohn (litter carry)
124	S. Peter Lewis for SOLO (background traction splint, splinted arm), Just some dust, Flicker.com (broken arm X-ray)
125	S. Peter Lewis for SOLO (all evaluation pics)
126	Thomas Mueller, Flickr.com (boy with cast), S. Peter Lewis for SOLO (pulling traction), Wikimedia Commons (compound fracture)
127	S. Peter Lewis for SOLO (all images)
128	T.B.R Walsh for SOLO (all splinting drawings)
129	T.B.R. Walsh for SOLO (all splinting drawings)
130	Eric Schmuttenmaer, Flickr.com (fractured femur—image modified)
131	T.B.R. Walsh for SOLO (femur illustration)
132	Tony Meiklejohn (femur fracture), S. Peter Lewis for SOLO (traction splint)
133	T.B.R. Walsh for SOLO (all traction splint drawings)
134	S. Peter Lewis for SOLO (wrist splint)
135	T.B.R. Walsh for SOLO (all drawings), S. Peter Lewis for SOLO (runner, knee splint)
136	Wikimedia Comons (dislocation X-ray)
137	Naparazzi, Flickr.com (rugby)
138	Anthony DeLorenzo, Flickr.com (bike crash)
139	S. Peter Lewis for SOLO (all dislocation pics), YouTube (YouTube icon)
140	S. Peter Lewis for SOLO (all dislocation pics)
141	S. Peter Lewis for SOLO (all dislocation pics)
142	T.B.R. Walsh for SOLO (spine drawing, spine detail), S. Peter Lewis for SOLO (falling man)
143	T.B.R. Walsh for SOLO (skull, spine detail)

Page	Credit/source
144	Benjamin Pop, stock.xchng.com (falling man), S. Peter Lewis for SOLO (holding head), Sigurd Decross, stock.xchng.com (question mark, sign—image modified), Tony Meiklejohn (C-spine immobilization), Ilker, stock.xchng.com (flag)
145	S. Peter Lewis for SOLO (feet, range of motion pics)
146	T.B.R. Walsh for SOLO (skeleton)
147	Wikimedia Commons (skull), T.B.R. Walsh for SOLO (skull detail)
148	T.B.R. Walsh for SOLO (brain, brain detail)
149	Malehmann, Flickr.com (scalp hematoma), Wikimedia Commons (skull)
150	Sharlene Jackson, stock.xchng.com (clamp), Flickr.com (brain), S. Peter Lewis for SOLO (CSF circulation)
151	Josh MacMillan (head injury), S. Peter Lewis for SOLO (breathing patterns)
152	S. Peter Lewis for SOLO (smiley face)
153	Ladida, iStockphoto.com (bandaged face), S. Peter Lewis for SOLO (airways)
154	S. Peter Lewis for SOLO (all pics)
155	T.B.R. Walsh for SOLO (skull), S. Peter Lewis (toothache bandage)
156	T.B.R. Walsh for SOLO (all skull drawings)
157	T.B.R. Walsh for SOLO (eye anatomy), S. Peter Lewis for SOLO (eye bandage missing), Wikimedia Commons (concussion illustration)
158	T.B.R. Walsh for SOLO (nasal anatomy, skull)
159	T.B.R. Walsh for SOLO (all ear illustrations)
160	S. Peter Lewis for SOLO (all photos)
161	S. Peter Lewis for SOLO (all photos)
162	Comotion Design, iStockphoto.com (chest illustration)
163	T.B.R. Walsh for SOLO (chest anatomy illustrations)
164	T.B.R. Walsh for SOLO (circulation illustration)
165	Wikimedia Commons (heart, top), T.B.R. Walsh and S. Peter Lewis for SOLO (heart diagram)
166	Wikimedia Commons (ECG background, heart painting)
167	Stock.xchng.com (artery painting), Andrew Mason, Flickr.com (blood painting)
168	Wikimedia Commons (background torso photo), T.B.R. Walsh for SOLO (chest drawing overlay)
169	S. Peter Lewis for SOLO (positioning diagram)
170	T.B.R. Walsh for SOLO (cardiothoracic trauma drawing—spread)
172	Wikipedia.com (avalanche)
173	Wikimedia Commons (AED), Wikimedia Commons (AED inset photo)
176	Svilen Milev, sxc.hu (open book), T.B.R. Walsh for SOLO (pelvis)
177	S. Peter Lewis for SOLO (pelvis treatment)
178	Thom W., stock.xchng.com (statue background)
179	Tony Meiklejohn (palpation), T.B.R. Walsh for SOLO (abdominal anatomy)
180	S. Peter Lewis for SOLO (crush injury)
181	Wikimedia Commons (compartment syndrome)
182	United States Navy, Flickr.com (medical emergency—spread)
183	Sigurd Decroos, stock.xchng.com (question mark)
185	Public domain (penguin), Wikimedia Commons (thermometer), S. Peter Lewis for SOLO (taking notes)
186	S. Peter Lewis for SOLO (LOC sequence)
189	S. Peter Lewis for SOLO (poison gas graphic)
190	Wikimedia Commons (brain circulation)
191	Wikipedia Commons (poison symbol, bee), H. Berends, stock.xchng.com (ingested poison), Kriss Szkurlatowski, stock.xchng.com (inhaled poison), Peter Organisciak, Flickr.com (absorbed poison)
192	Ján Messaros, stock.xchng.com (sugar cubes)
193	Wikimedia Commons (sugar molecule)
194	Public domain (bracelet), Tony Alter, Flickr.com (obese person)
195	Geraint Rowland, Flickr.com (man on park bench), Michaela Kobyakov, stock/xchng.com (blood glucose meter)
197	Stock.xchng.com (orange), Ján Messaros, stock.xchng.com (sugar cubes)
198	S. Peter Lewis for SOLO (seizure pics)
199	alh1, Flickr.com (statue), S. Peter Lewis for SOLO (brain drawings)
200	S. Peter Lewis for SOLO (behavior background)
202	Reid Parham, stock.xchng.com (man), Wikimedia Commons (thermometer), Julien Harneis, Flickr.com (measles)
203	Wikimedia Commons (virus, bacteria), S. Peter Lewis for SOLO (germ illustration)
204	Wikimedia Commons (runners, frostbite), William Heinrich (overdose), sportstock, iStockphoto.com (hiker)
205	S. Peter Lewis (drugs)
206	James Vaughan, Flickr.com (lung expander), T.B.R. Walsh for SOLO (lung anatomy), Wikimedia Commons (alveoli detail)
207	T.B.R. Walsh for SOLO (asthma/airway anatomy)
208	Wikipedia.org (airway anatomy)
209	Cristiano Giacomelli, stock.xchng.com (cigarettes)
210	Wikimedia Commons (both illustrations)
211	Wikimedia Commons (background image) T.B.R.Walsh for SOLO (alveoli detail), Quinn Comendant, Flickr (lung X-ray)
212	Wikimedia Commons (man with bag over head)
214	Michal Zacharzewski (pump), Stephen Stacey (pipes), Marek Bernat (blood cells)
215	S. Peter Lewis for SOLO (rocks on chest)
216	Sigurd Decroos (heart graphic)
217	Julien Tromeur, stock.xchng.com (abdomen side view)
218	Roy Blumenthal, Flickr.com (nausea drawing)
219	Tony Meiklejohn (palpating abdomen)

Page	Credit/source
220	Guenter M. Kircgweger, stock.xchng.com (mountain scene)
221	Adventurejay.com (climbers), S. Peter Lewis for SOLO (fern, tarp)
222	S. Peter Lewis for SOLO (boy with antler)
223	S. Peter Lewis for SOLO (thermometer graphic)
224	T.B.R. Walsh for SOLO (all illustrations)
225	T.B.R. Walsh for SOLO (evaporation, hydrated man drawing), Matt Marshall, stock.xchng.com (waterfall)
226	Matt Marshall, stock.xchng.com (waterfall), Allesandro Paiva, stock.xchng.com (plate), John Nyberg, stock.xchng.com (pasta), S. Peter Lewis for SOLO (napkin, lettuce)
227	sportstock, iStockphoto.com (hiker)
228	S. Peter Lewis for SOLO (state graphic)
229	Reid Parham, stock.xchng.com (man)
230	Stephan Hoerold, iStockphoto.com (women), S. Peter Lewis for SOLO (sweaty hand)
232	Kati Neudert, iStockphoto.com (man drinking)
233	S. Peter Lewis for SOLO (desert montage), Google Earth (screen shot of map detail)
234	Piotr Menducki, stock.xchng.com (mountains)
235	S. Peter Lewis for SOLO (paper scrap)
236	S. Peter Lewis for SOLO (thermometer)
237	S. Peter Lewis for SOLO (shivering)
238	S. Peter Lewis for SOLO (climber), Ben C., stock.xchng.com (tent), Gregory Runyen, stock.xchng.com (moutains behind tent), Ali. A, stock.xchng.com (kayaker)
239	S. Peter Lewis for SOLO (hypowrap sequence)
240	Colin Higgins, stock.xchng.com (ice cave—image modified), stock.xchng.com (toes—image modified)
242	stock.xchng.com (background), Brad Harriso (icicles—-modified), T.B.R. Walsh for SOLO (frotsbitten fingers illustration), Lidija Macej, stock.xchng.com (dog foot), stock.xchng.com (human foot)
243	S. Peter Lewis for SOLO (crampon with bare foot)
244	Bill Alexander, stock.xchng.com (background), Wikimedia Commons (trench foot), S. Peter Lewis for SOLO (Raynaud's)
245	S. Peter Lewis for SOLO (chilblains, hand with snowball)
246	Bill Alexander, stock.xchng.com (background), T.B.R. Walsh for SOLO (Raynaud's treatment sequence)
247	Wikimedia Commons (chilblains), Christine Zenino, Flickr.com (Greenland village)
248	Bill Alexander, stock.xchng.com (background), Wikimedia Commons (trenchfoot poster, men in trench, foot—modified)
250	Clint Spencer, iStockphoto.com (lightning background)
251	Gregory Runyan, stock.xchng.com (thunderhead), S. Peter Lewis for SOLO (US map)
252	Mykola Swarnyk, Creative Commons (thunderstorm background, Volker Muehlenbruch, stock.xchng.com (field)
253	Brian Delaney, Creative Commons (cloud-to-cloud lightning), stock.xchng.com (cloud-to-ground lightning)
254	Barun Patro, stock.xchng.com (background), Krzysztof Falkowski, stock.xchng.com (lake), Miguel Saavedra, stock.xchng.com (ocean)
255	Shiella VooDoo, stock.xchng.com (life-saving ring)
256	Tolga Ilginer, stock.xchng.com (diver with bubbles), Christ West, stock.xchng.com (diver in background), Oktaviani Marvikasari, stock.xchng.com (school of fish in background), Olga Zielinska, stock.xchng.com (bubbles in headline)
257	j-bary, Creative Commons (bridge), Rick Hawkins, stock.xchng.com (scuba diver)
258	Jan KratÃ¿½na (<as it appeared in attribution), Davide Guglielmo, stock.xchng.com (earth), T.B.R. Walsh for SOLO (pressure chart illustration)
259	Maxime Perron Caissy, stock.xchng.com (hand silhouette—modified)
260	Flickr.com (scuba diver)
261	Wikimedia Commons (dive chamber), T.B.R. Walsh for SOLO (ear diagram)
262	S. Peter Lewis for SOLO (pinching nose), Octoviani Mavikasary, stock.xchng.com (scuba diver)
263	S. Peter Lewis for SOLO (plastic bottles)
264	Juan Velasquez, stock.xchng.com (scuba diver), Meral Akbulut, stock.xchng.com (free diver)
266	Tolga ILGINER, stock.xchng.com (diver), Public domain (scuba tank)
268	Marcus Ranum, deviant art (old dive suit), Yarik Mishin, stock.xchng.com (water), public domain (flippers)
270	stock.xchng.com (mountain background)
271	stock.xchng.com (snow foreground), Rick Wilcox (himself on Everest)
272	T.B.R. Walsh for SOLO (altitude and air pressure graphics)
273	Adrielle Joy Parlee, stock.xchng.com (snow background), Adeh DeSandies, stock.xchng.com (mountain), S. Peter Lewis for SOLO (pulse oximeter, blood cell graphic)
274	Crissie Hardy, stock.xchng.com (Quito, Ecuador), Clay Junell, Flickr.com (climber—modified)
275	Gregory Runyan, stock.xchng.com (mountain for climb-low-sleep-high- graphic), Valentin Santarosa, stock.xchng.com (mountain background), S. Peter Lewis for SOLO (water bottle)
276	Nik Thaele, stock.xchng.com (mountain background), stock.xchng.com (mountain reflection), J. Paul Robinson (sunburned climber),
277	adventurejay.com (climber), S. Peter Lewis for SOLO (wooden goggles)
278	Sarah Brucker, stock.xchng.com (mountain background), Dave Hamster, Flickr.com (helicopter), adventurejay.com (rescuers)
279	Treksafe (PAC pressure chamber)
280	Wikimedia Commons (biting moose, scorpion)
281	Wikimedia Commons (dog outline, goat outline, cat outline), public domain (human outline), Jeff Jones, stock.xchng.com (raccoon), Lies Meirlaen, stock.xchng.com (bat), Tori Roberts, stock.xchng.com (skunk), Vairaatea, Creative Commons (dog)
282	Wikimedia Commons (boy with rabies, man with rabies), John Boyer, stock.xchng.com (rattlesnake), stock.xchng.com (desert)
283	Public domain (copperhead), Wikimedia Commons (coral snake, snake envenomation map), Greg Schechter, Flickr.com (cottonmouth), Wikipedia (beaded lizard, necrosis, tagged for commercial use), Adam Ciesielski, stock.xchng.com (IV bottle)
284	Wikimedia Commons (black widow), Tommi Nikkla, stock.xchng.com (bee)

Page	Credit/source
285	Wikimedia Commons (scorpion, brown recluse, bite)
286	T.B.R. Walsh for SOLO (wood tick, deer tick), Wikimedia Commons (engorged tick, bullseye rash)
287	deadpoolrus, deviantart.com (weird sea creature), Wikimedia Commons (jellyfish), Billy Alexander, stock.xchng.com (photo frame), Nick Holdstock, stock.xchng.com (seal)
288	Wikimedia Commons (shark, stingray, lion fish, cone snail—the latter modified), Toni Petrovic, stock.xchng.com (urchin)
289	T.B.R. Walsh for SOLO (nematocyst) Wikimedia Commons (coral), pfly, Flickr.com (anenome), Olaf Gradin, Flickr.com (man-o-war), L.C. Nøttaasen, Flickr.com (box jellyfish)
290	Wikimedia Commons(poison ivy, foot, rash in background)
291	T.B.R. Walsh for SOLO (ivy, oak, sumac), S. Peter Lewis for SOLO (map)
292	Krzysztof Górecki, stock.xchng.com (background), Dr. Frank Hubbell (Haiti), Andi O., stock.xchng.com (mountains), S. Peter Lewis for SOLO (hand in water, bacteria), Johan Cloete, stock.xchng.com (pregnancy)
293	Volker Schumann, stock.xchng.com (dunes)
294	S. Peter Lewis for SOLO (all images)
295	Dr. Frank Hubbell (Haiti)
296	S. Peter Lewis for SOLO (background), Guru Thilak (India, flood), M. Mani (Pakistan, earthquake)
297	Dr. Frank Hubbell, (treating child), S. Peter Lewis for SOLO (vaccination), Carolyn Fox, iStockphoto.com (tornado damage)
298	S. Peter Lewis for SOLO (traige card, background), Jocelyn Augustino/FEMA (flooding)
299	S. Peter Lewis for SOLO (triage card)
300	S. Peter Lewis for SOLO (all images)
301	S. Peter Lewis for SOLO (all images)
302	S. Peter Lewis for SOLO (bivuoac, background)
303	S. Peter Lewis for SOLO (snow cave, camping)
304	Claudio Jule, stock.xchng.com (water)
305	Wikimedia Commons (ice cubes), S. Peter Lewis for SOLO (lettuce)
307	Vivek Chugh, stock.xchng.com (hand silhouette), Jan Kratĺ¿½na, stock.xchng.com (earth—attribution not a typo), Wikimedia Commons (water pump, water bottles in the sun, pond with women and cow), Clker.com (water drop)
308	Jan Kratĺ¿½na, stock.xchng.com (earth, attribution not a typo), Wikimedia Commons (mosquito larva)
309	hdptcar, Flickr.com (woman with malaria), Jean-Raphaël Guillaumin, Flickr.com (mosquito), Wikimedia Commons (tick)
310	Wikimedia Commons (malaria map), Graham Briggs, stock.xchng.com (lemon slice in glass)
311	Thomas Picard, stock.xchng.com (fly), T.B.R. Walsh for SOLO (mosquito, tick), Wikimedia Commons (mosquito netting)
312	Wikimedia Commons (mosquito, Panama Canal, malaria lifecycle), S. Peter Lewis for SOLO (malaria map)
314	Ben Earwicker, stock.xchng.com (pregnant woman)
315	Jess Jolin (infant feet)
316	Volker Schumann, stock.xchng.com (desert banner)
317	S. Peter Lewis for SOLO (hiker)
326	Piotr Menducki, stock.xchng.com (dune background)
328	John Nyberg, stock.xchng.com (ocean background)

We just couldn't resist one more beautiful image—and we hope
this place is about as far from definitive care as you can get!

WARNING

READER   BEWARE

MANY OF THESE SKILLS

Are to be used specifically in the extended-care setting
- Wilderness
- Disaster
- Remote
- Military
- Extreme / austere environments
- Beyond the Golden Hour

SOME OF THESE SKILLS

Require specific training, practice, and certifications

Are not commonly taught or practiced by pre-hospital personnel in the United States

Are beyond the normal scope of practice for EMS providers

Need the approval of your State Bureau of EMS